LEGAL SPEECHES *of* DEMOCRATIC ATHENS

Sources for Athenian History

LEGAL SPEECHES *of* DEMOCRATIC ATHENS

Sources for Athenian History

Edited and Translated by
Andrew Wolpert
and
Konstantinos Kapparis

Hackett Publishing Company, Inc.
Indianapolis/Cambridge

Copyright © 2011 by Hackett Publishing Company, Inc.
All rights reserved
Printed in the United States of America
14 13 12 11   1 2 3 4 5 6 7

For further information, please address
  Hackett Publishing Company, Inc.
  P.O. Box 44937
  Indianapolis, Indiana 46244-0937
  www.hackettpublishing.com

Cover design by Abigail Coyle
Interior design by Elizabeth L. Wilson
Composition by Innodata-Isogen, Inc.
Printed at Sheridan Books, Inc.

Library of Congress Cataloging-in-Publication Data

Wolpert, Andrew, 1965–
  Legal speeches of democratic Athens : sources for Athenian history / edited and
translated by Andrew Wolpert and Konstantinos Kapparis.
    p. cm.
  Includes bibliographical references and index.
  ISBN 978-0-87220-927-5 (pbk.) — ISBN 978-0-87220-928-2 (cloth)
   1. Law, Greek. 2. Forensic orations—Greece—Athens—History—To 1500.
3. Athens (Greece)—History—Sources.
I. Kapparis, K. A. II. Title. KL4115.A75W65 2011
    340.5'38—dc22

                        2010044763

The paper used in this publication meets the minimum requirements of American
National Standard for Information Sciences—Permanence of Paper for Printed
Library Materials, ANSI Z39.48–1984.

Contents

Preface

Within the last generation, there have been significant advances in our understanding of Athenian history, in part because of a new appreciation for and new approaches to the study of Attic oratory. There have also been published important new critical editions, commentaries, and translations of many Greek orators. Since these works have made Athenian law and Attic oratory more accessible to students and have provided a variety of ways that classical rhetoric can be incorporated into a syllabus for the study of Athenian history, one may not expect that there is need for yet another translation of Attic speeches. Only a small sample of the speeches that were delivered in classical Athens survives, but still there are some one hundred fifty speeches, and no one collection can do justice to all the questions that they raise. We have found for our own courses on Athenian history that we cannot provide our students with a collection that provides most of the texts that we require them to read. So we offer this new collection primarily as a service to them, and we hope that others may also find it useful.

When possible we have offered speeches that are not in other collections, so that our volume can be used in conjunction with other textbooks for courses on Athenian law, but speeches have also been chosen that are, in our opinion, essential for understanding classical Athens so that the volume can be used alone for those courses that may devote only a portion of the semester to Attic oratory. Aeschines 1, "Against Timarchus," Demosthenes 21, "Against Meidias," and [Demosthenes] 59, "Against Neaera," have arguably received the most attention in contemporary scholarship, and we provide them now for the first time in one volume. So too we have included Lysias 1, "On the Murder of Eratosthenes," and Demosthenes 54, "Against Conon," which are equally important for understanding Athenian social history. Together these five speeches have become central to discussions on Athenian attitudes about sexuality, civic identity and citizenship, the family and the household, violence and cooperation, democratic values and beliefs, the dispute process, and the social dynamics of the courts.

Lysias 24, "On the Suspension of the Benefit of the Disabled Man," provides an excellent opportunity to explore the difficulties in interpreting a speech and determining its authenticity. If authentic, it is perhaps one of the few speeches in the corpus that was intended for a poor Athenian to deliver. Lysias 23, "Against Pancleon," shows the problems that a litigant may encounter as he tries to build his case against his opponent, and [Demosthenes] 53, "Against Nicostratus," includes a remarkable story about the plight of an individual captured at sea and shows the kinds of conflicts that can arise between neighbors and the different ways loans were secured. Demosthenes 32, "Against Zenothemis," and Demosthenes 41, "Against Spudias," also provide a window into the Athenian economy. While "Against Zenothemis" concerns long-distance trade, large-scale loans, and insurance fraud, "Against Spudias" is an important source for the household economy. It shows that women were more actively involved in lending than has often been assumed, and it reveals some of the difficulties that an Athenian father might face when trying to marry his daughters and secure an heir to his estate.

Isaeus 12, "On Behalf of Euphiletus," concerns the disputed citizenship of Euphiletus, who appealed the decision of his deme to remove him from the registry, and shows how private animosities played out in politics at the deme level. Antiphon 6, "On the Chorister," as a case of unintentional homicide, reveals some of the differences between the dicastic and homicide courts and shows how legal procedures can be manipulated, whether to pursue grievances or block disputes from appearing in court. To round off the collection, we include two speeches that show, in high relief, politics of Athens after the overthrow of the Thirty, as the Athenians were trying to recover from a civil war that tore apart the fabric of their society: Lysias 12, "Against Eratosthenes," and Lysias 16, "For Mantitheus." These two speeches shed light on how the courts provided a venue for the Athenians to come to terms with their past. They help us learn how political unrest affected families and how the courts had to balance the personal desire for retribution with the social need for reconciliation.

As a whole, the collection has been designed to allow for the study of a wide range of questions concerning the public and private lives of the various people that inhabited democratic Athens and to encourage discussion on the relationship between Athenian politics and society. Speeches have been arranged chronologically by author for the sake of simplicity since so many of the speeches have overlapping themes and can be taught in many different arrangements. Each speech is accompanied by an introduction that briefly explains the disagreement between the parties of the dispute, the history of their animosities, the laws that apply to their argument, and the historical significance of the case. Following the introduction, key details about the dispute are provided in outline format to help the reader keep track of the various intricacies of the trial (e.g., the parties of the dispute, their relationship to each other, the legal action that the court is hearing, the penalties for the offense, and the date of the trial). Since women's names were rarely mentioned in Athenian courts and speakers often did not mention their own names, these details can become confusing quite quickly. So we hope this equivalent to a scorecard will make it easier for the reader to follow the speeches.

The translations are based on the Budé editions by Gernet for Antiphon and Roussel for Isaeus; the Oxford Classical Texts by Carey for Lysias and Rennie for Demosthenes 32, 41, 54, and [Demosthenes] 53; the Teubner edition by Dilts for Aeschines; MacDowell's edition of Demosthenes 21 published by Oxford; and Kapparis' edition of [Demosthenes] 59, published by de Gruyter. In addition, the following commentaries have been consulted: Gagarin's commentary on Antiphon, the commentaries by Todd and Carey for Lysias, Wyse for Isaeus, MacDowell for Demosthenes 21, Isager and Hansen as well as Pearson for Demosthenes 32, Carey and Reid for Demosthenes 54, Kapparis for [Demosthenes] 59, and Fisher for Aeschines 1. We have also benefited greatly from the translations of the Attic orators in the Loeb Classical Library, the University of Texas Press series on the Oratory of Classical Greece, Carey's *Trials from Classical Greece,* and Phillip's *Athenian Political Oratory.* As much as possible, we have tried to remain true to the Greek while making the speeches accessible to an English-speaking reader, a balancing act that must always be at best imperfect. Inevitably something is always lost in translation, but it is also true that something is learned from the incongruity between the original and the translation.

Names of people and places have been Latinized. When possible, legal procedures and technical terms are either translated or Anglicized (e.g. "public suit" for *graphe* and "metic" for *metikos*). When an Anglicized version is used, it is not italicized (e.g., "trierarch"). Typically the transliterated Greek is provided in parentheses the first time a translated term is used in a speech, to assist those readers who may be familiar with the Greek. For some technical terms, such as *thesmothetes* and *basileus,* the transliterated form appears in the text and an explanation of the term is provided either in parentheses or in a footnote the first time the term is used in the speech, since a translation would be too cumbersome or confusing and an Anglicized form is unavailable. A glossary is appended, with definitions for most terms that are mentioned in multiple speeches. Internal citations to speeches in the collections are in bold font to distinguish them from external citations.

We thank de Gruyter for permitting Kapparis to base his new translation of [Demosthenes] 59 on his 1999 version that it published, Kristen Kalilich, James Kinch, Father Andreas Kramarz, Samantha Marsh Adamczyk, Jillian Moscowitz, Victoria Pagán, and the anonymous readers for their comments and suggestions, Rick Todhunter for his care and attention in the preparation of the book, and our colleagues at the University of Florida, with whom it has been our pleasure and honor to work. This book is dedicated to our students who have encouraged us to publish it, and we hope that they will benefit from it as much as we have enjoyed writing it.

Introduction

Athenian Law and Oratory

1. The History of Athenian Law

The Athenian legal system evolved over a long period of time as significant social, economic, constitutional, and ideological changes laid the path for the democracy. Law was an important part of this process. It was both a product of the democracy and a force for promoting and generating democratic practices. The first law code attested in the sources, the notorious Draconian legislation, was introduced around 620 BCE.[1] It appears to have focused on the most serious offenses, homicide, theft, and assault, with such severe penalties that Draco's laws were famously said to have been written in blood. His legislation was probably intended to curb the worst excesses plaguing Athens under the restrictive rule of a few aristocratic families and perhaps prevent social revolution, as was occurring elsewhere in the Greek world where individuals known as "tyrants"[2] seized power. The code succeeded in one critical aspect: it established law as an answer for social problems and paved the way for future law reforms. While the Athenians changed their laws as they developed their democracy, that part of Draco's code that dealt with homicide continued to be used throughout the classical period (i.e., the fifth and fourth centuries). Murder was thought to create a form of religious pollution (*miasma*) that threatened to contaminate the community unless the *miasma* was contained, and the homicide laws of Draco addressed this problem (see **Ant. 6**).

The Draconian legislation was incapable of resolving the growing social tensions that archaic Athens continued to face as the aristocratic families remained intractable. So in 594 Solon introduced a much more ambitious legislative program intended to regulate all aspects of life, from the public sphere to the private, from the specific entitlements and rights of each property class in public life to inheritance and family law, and from the regulation of prostitution around the city to the orderly conduct of legal minors. By ending debt slavery, Solon essentially established citizenship. Athenians were guaranteed the right of freedom, at least within their own

---

1. Hereafter all dates are before the Common Era unless specified otherwise.

2. This title came to be identified with cruelty and oppressive authoritarianism, but originally it was used simply to identify an individual who obtained power through unconstitutional means.

homeland, thus making them a distinct class separate from those foreigners living in Attica, whether as slaves or as free persons who did not receive such protection. This guarantee of freedom was the first step in bridging the gulf that separated wealthy Athenians from the poor since the poor could no longer be forced into slavery because of economic hardship. But in others ways Solon reinforced social and economic distinctions. Wealthy Athenians of common birth were now no longer excluded from political office and could compete with men from aristocratic families in elections, but the poor still had few if any opportunities to voice their political views. In later centuries, speakers in Athenian courts attributed practically every existing law to Solon even though some were clearly introduced much later. This makes it very difficult for us to recognize true Solonian laws except in a number of cases where archaic language or outdated constitutional and cultural concepts betray a date as early as the beginning of the sixth century. The most systematic attempt to identify the laws of Solon is that of Ruschenbusch (1966), but still much uncertainty prevails. Regardless of these difficulties, the Solonian reforms were undoubtedly an important step in the development of the Athenian legal system, and the Athenians themselves fully recognized them as such.

Paradoxically, Pisistratus, the popular tyrant who ruled Athens in the middle of the sixth century, contributed further to the development of the Athenian legal system with the introduction of locally traveling judges.[3] While he maintained many of the existing political arrangements and sought to curry the favor of competing families by allowing them to hold political offices, he also attempted to weaken potential rivals by diminishing the importance of regional affiliations and the villages (demes) spread throughout Attica. Through his reorganization of Athenian festivals and rebuilding and repairing of temples, he drew more attention to the city of Athens and promoted a greater sense of Athenian identity at the expense of local associations, which provided the necessary political conditions for more comprehensive reforms.

---

3. Pisistratus seized control of Athens in 560 and was expelled twice before he finally secured his rule in 546, remaining in power until his death in 527. His sons, Hippias and Hipparchus, succeeded him, but their rule was relatively short lived. In 514 a plot to overthrow the tyrants failed, but Harmodius and Aristogeiton were able to kill Hipparchus before they were arrested. Then in 510 Hippias was expelled, thanks in part to the efforts of the Alcmaeonids, an aristocratic family that first held political offices under the tyranny but was eventually exiled by the tyrants. The Athenians could not, however, simply turn back the clock and return to politics as usual. The Pisistratids had ruled for many years and permanently changed Athens in the process.

In 508/7,[4] Cleisthenes proposed revolutionary reforms that fundamentally changed the dynamics of Athenian politics but were only implemented after the Athenians rallied together to expel Spartan troops sent in to stop the reforms. The Athenians kept the original four tribes, phratries (brotherhoods), and *gene* (clans), which continued to meet primarily for religious purposes. However, now the deme served as the base political unit, with its own assembly for discussions on local matters, and citizenship now depended upon enrollment and membership in one of the 139 demes, and not the ancestral phratries as probably was the case before Cleisthenes.[5] The demes were distributed into ten new tribes, named after the heroes of Attica so that each tribe had demes from all over Attica and was a microcosm of the entire community, and each tribe contributed fifty members to the Council of Five Hundred (often referred to in the sources as "the Council"). There is also some indication that the Assembly (*ekklesia*) gained importance as a result of the Cleisthenic reforms.

As the Athenians turned increasingly to lottery rather than election to fill political offices, the Areopagus, consisting of ex-archons who served for life, was the last brake on the democracy. Then in 462, Ephialtes stripped the Areopagus of its political powers and transferred them to the Assembly, the Council of Five Hundred, and the courts. The democracy continued to develop and remained relatively stable throughout the classical period except for two brief interruptions when oligarchs seized control of the city in 411 and 404 (see **Lys. 12, 16**). At the height of the Athenian empire, one of the first laws to limit citizenship was enacted when in 451 Pericles proposed that citizenship be restricted to those of Athenian descent on both sides of their family.[6] The law was simple in its premise, but the precise motives and the extent of its influence upon the Athenian legal system are highly controversial issues.[7] Nonetheless, it is certain that its implications were far reaching and affected many areas of family, property, and inheritance law. During the Peloponnesian War (431–404), as Athenian families were devastated by heavy losses, the Periclean law was suspended, but it was restored when the war was over and enforced throughout the fourth century. Following the restoration of the democracy in 403, the

---

4. The Athenian year was named after the eponymous archon. Since the archons held office for one year, starting in the summer, the Athenian year spans two years in the modern calendar. Inclusive years separated by a forward slash are used to indicate an Athenian year.

5. For the importance of the deme in classical Athens, see **Isaeus 12** and **Lysias 23**.

6. See **[Demosthenes] 59** for some of the consequences of this law.

7. Arist. *Ath. Pol.* 26.4, *Pol.* 1275b31, 1278a34; Plu. *Per.* 37; see Rhodes 1981: 331–35; Patterson 1981; Walters 1983: 314–36.

Athenians reviewed the existing laws they wished to retain, introduced new procedures for the adoption of laws, and created formal distinctions between laws that were enacted by *nomothetai* (panels of jurors) and decrees passed by the Assembly. Since the Athenians regarded the democracy as their ancestral constitution, these new regulations were introduced not as a check on democracy but as a safeguard against those who opposed it. By making it difficult to repeal long-standing laws, the Athenians prevented oligarchic conspirators from using the legislative process to overthrow the democracy, as they had done in the fifth century.

2. Athenian Politics and Society

The most distinctive feature of the Athenian democracy is the active and extensive involvement of ordinary citizens in the political affairs of the city. All men whose parents were Athenian had the right to attend, speak, and vote at the meetings of the Assembly, which were held forty times per year. Since the quorum was six thousand and the citizen population for the fourth century was approximately thirty thousand, at least 20 percent of the citizens would have attended any given meeting of the Assembly. The Council drafted and set the agenda. It consisted of five hundred members, fifty from each of the ten tribes, with each of the 139 demes contributing members on a proportional basis. The councilors were selected annually by lot for terms lasting only one year. Since no Athenian was able to serve more than twice on the Council, this duty extended quite widely. In fact, Socrates, who says that he avoided political life, served on the Council. Like every other councilor, he was a member on its steering committee for one-tenth of the year, when it was the turn for the councilors of his tribe to be presiding officers (*prytaneis*). And as it so happens, when Socrates was a presiding officer he was selected by lot to chair the meeting of the Assembly at which the Athenians tried the generals who failed to recover the shipwrecked sailors at the Battle of Arginusae.[8] So even Athenians who did not seek to be involved in politics would have been much more active than most citizens of modern representative democracies.

In addition to the five hundred councilors, there were approximately six hundred other officials. With the exception of the generals and treasurers, most of these positions were selected by lot for terms that lasted only one year. Officials tended to serve on boards rather than hold solitary offices. This applied to the highest political officials, the nine archons, who consisted of the six *thesmothetai,* the polemarch (war archon), the *basileus* (king archon), and the archon (also known as the eponymous archon because

---

8. See **Lys. 12.36**; Pl. *Ap.* 32b1–c3.

the year was named after him). The *thesmothetai* convened the popular law courts (*dikasteria*) and presided over most public suits, while the polemarch presided over private suits that involved metics (resident aliens) and the *basileus* presided over the Areopagus for homicide trials. The fact that the archons had judicial responsibilities highlights the political importance of the law courts.

The economic disparity between the very rich and the rest of the citizen population was less than what commonly occurs in modern industrial societies. Even some Athenians considered wealthy had fairly modest means by our own standards. Approximately twelve hundred citizens were members of the liturgical class, required to perform public services, known as liturgies, such as the *choregia,* which entailed paying for the performance of a lyric or dramatic choral production, and the trierarchy, which required the liturgist to pay for the upkeep and maintenance of an Athenian warship (trireme). The very wealthy also paid the special tax (*eisphora*), first levied in times of war but later whenever the city was in financial need. The liturgical class was certainly more actively involved in politics than the rest of the population, especially in positions of leadership. But based on the numbers of citizens required to attend the Assembly, serve on the Council, sit on juries, and hold political offices, the Athenian political system required extensive participation from a fairly broad segment of the citizen population in order to accomplish the business of the city.

It is sometimes said that the Athenians were able to promote this level of participation because of slavery. While it is certainly true that the democracy depended upon slavery, it is not for the reasons generally believed. Much uncertainty remains about the percentage of the population that had slaves and the percentage of the workforce that consisted of slaves. Certainly some poorer citizens possessed slaves, but they would have had at most only one or two, and many would have had none (e.g., **Lys. 24.4**). Most of the poorer citizens were subsistence farmers, who were able to participate in politics primarily because there were certain times of the year in which there was less agricultural activity. Slavery was in many ways more important to them because it provided the wealthy with a workforce so that poor peasant farmers worked for themselves. With economic autonomy, they could assert their independence when they appeared in the political forum. They were both literally and metaphorically free to disagree with those who had more economic resources and social capital since they did not depend on the rich for their economic livelihood and even outnumbered them demographically. Slavery, like masculinity, also provided the poor with important ideological grounds to claim a stake in politics and declare that they held more in common with the rich than what distinguished them and therefore they deserved an equal share in the privileges of citizenship. The Athenian democracy depended upon the conceit that the citizens were equal because they shared in common the one necessary political good: their birth as free men of Athenian ancestry. So the justification for the inclusion of poor Athenian men in politics simultaneously served to justify those restrictions imposed upon women, slaves, and metics. The political equality that Athenian citizens possessed did not cause them to extend rights to others. It caused them to perpetuate the inequalities to which others were subjected.[9]

Political power tended to concentrate in the Assembly, the Council, and the courts, since officials had short terms and worked on boards. Therefore, those seeking to gain political importance and influence had to be effective public speakers, capable of persuading mass audiences that consisted of hundreds and thousands of people. To be a politician was, in effect, synonymous with being an orator (*rhetor*). When we think of politicians, we think of men and women who hold various political offices, and we consider them politicians only for as long as they are serving in an office. They are generally only accountable to the voter when an election takes place, whether it be every two, four, or six years. Political leaders in Athens, by contrast, did not have to hold political offices, and their positions were more precarious, with their prestige waxing and waning depending on their success in convincing mass audiences to vote as they recommended. Every time an Assembly met, approximately every nine days or so, they were directly accountable. They would, of course, also seek offices that might help them maintain their prominence and influence policy, such as embassies for important negotiations with allies or enemies. In 346, for example, both Aeschines and Demosthenes, two rivals who advocated very different policies, served on the same embassy that negotiated an agreement with Philip II of Macedon to end the Third Sacred War. The Athenians considered it a failure, and so the two leaders attempted to protect themselves from the political fallout by launching a series of prosecutions against each other that touched upon their involvement in the negotiations (see **Aesch. 1**).

3. The Athenian Courts

This brings us to another important aspect of Athenian politics. To be successful, a political leader needed to go to court, whether to appear as a prosecutor in order to prevent the ascendancy of his rivals, as a defendant forced

---

9. **Demosthenes 41**, however, shows that Athenian women exerted more power and influence in the private sphere than such blanket statements about Athenian political institutions and the rhetoric of the courts would suggest.

to respond to the legal challenges of his opponents, or as a supporting speaker (*synegoros*) to protect and assist his political allies. Since Athenian law depended primarily on voluntary prosecution by private individuals, the litigant was able to decide how best to pursue a legal grievance against a rival. For any decree or law that an Athenian proposed, the legality of the motion could be challenged in court. There were also occasions when officials could be sanctioned. Before holding an office, each candidate first had to undergo a scrutiny (*dokimasia*), at which any individual could lodge objections in order to prevent the candidate from assuming the office (see **Lys. 16**), while in office an impeachment proceeding (*eisangelia*) could be initiated, and at the end of the official's term an audit (*euthyna*) took place. So the legal dangers for those who sought political power were quite real. Aristophon even boasted that he had been acquitted seventy-five times for proposing illegal motions (Aesch. 3.194). In the case where his rival neither held a political office nor proposed a motion, the political leader needed to rely on less direct means of attack. So too an Athenian might avoid lodging an action against a rival in order to avoid possible legal consequences if he was unsuccessful. Apollodorus, for example, served as a supporting speaker in the prosecution of Stephanus' mistress, while his brother-in-law, Theomnestus, formally charged Neaera with illegally usurping the right of citizenship (see **[Dem.] 59**). A conviction would, of course, have had direct impact on her, but it also would have damaged Stephanus' reputation.

Equally noteworthy is how the Athenians arranged their legal institutions and procedures so that each citizen needed to be active in protecting himself, pursuing his own grievances, and promoting his own interests. Without a regular police force, professional lawyers, or state attorneys, private individuals generally had to take action on their own behalf when a law was violated.[10] While only the victim could initiate a private suit (*dike*), any Athenian was permitted to lodge a public suit (*graphe*). However, as the extant speeches show, it was usually the victim who initiated public suits. False testimony, battery, and murder are, for example, charges lodged by private suit, while impiety, outrage (*hybris*), and misconduct on an embassy were actionable by public suit. For private suits, penalties were paid to the victims, while for most public suits, which had monetary penalties, they were paid to the treasury. The other main difference between private and public suits was that the prosecutor of a private suit could drop his charge or settle out of court. The prosecutor of a public suit was fined one thousand drachmas and was prohibited from lodging a similar suit if he dropped his

---

10. In certain instances, Athenian officials could fine individuals for minor offenses that concerned or interfered with their official duties.

charge or failed to receive at least one-fifth of the jurors' votes.[11] Although Athens did not have lawyers, litigants could either pay a logographer to write a speech, which the litigant delivered on his own behalf, or share his allotted time in court with a supporting speaker as mentioned above.

In some ways, such legal arrangements may seem to have placed the poor at a disadvantage since they had limited time and resources to pursue a legal action. We are unable to gauge with any certainty how they would have fared in court because, with the possible exception of **Lysias 24**, the speeches that have survived and make up the corpus of Attic orators were either delivered by politicians and orators or written by logographers for clients who were quite wealthy. When litigants spoke before large juries, of which the majority of jurors had modest means, the litigants were sometimes defensive about their wealth and went to great length to show that they had performed the required liturgies and had used their resources for the benefit of the community. To be sure, litigants sometimes presented their opponents as believing that their wealth both granted them special privileges and required the jury to show them deference for their services. In such instances, however, these litigants were clearly trying to outrage the jury so that it would not be receptive to the arguments of their opponents (e.g., **Dem. 21.151–53**).

So, too, it is important to recognize that the autonomy and independence, which the democratic institutions promoted for all Athenian citizens, came with certain responsibilities and obligations. To be treated on equal terms, the poor had to have the wherewithal to actively look after their own interests rather than passively depend on others to protect them and serve as their guardians. Just as the Athenian democracy could not function without a broad range of the citizenry actively participating in political discussions, law required citizens to turn to each other in their capacity as private individuals so that the law became interwoven in the fabric of their daily lives rather than a profession of a certain segment of the population. In the absence of a regular police force, Athenians needed to help themselves and seek out assistance from friends, neighbors, and bystanders. When Euphiletus learned that his wife was sleeping with another man, before he burst into the bedroom and killed the adulterer, he first rounded up his neighbors so that he had witnesses who could provide testimony in court to prove that it was justifiable homicide (**Lys. 1.23–24**). When Conon and his sons beat up Ariston, those who were passing by

---

11. Six obols equaled one drachma, one hundred drachmas equaled one mina, and sixty minas equaled one talent. Members of the liturgical class had property worth at least three or four talents. This fine of one thousand drachmas was therefore a significant penalty.

brought the injured man back to his house, and later Ariston relied upon them for their testimony when his case came to court (**Dem. 54.9, 32**). These individuals were under no formal obligation to become involved, but Athenian law could not function properly unless they chose to do so.

After a legal violation occurred, usually the aggrieved party had to decide how best to proceed with his legal complaint. Ariston states that he consulted with friends about the offense and sought their advice before lodging a formal complaint. Although they said that Conon was guilty of outrage (*hybris*) because of the shameful and abusive manner in which he attacked Ariston, they recommended instead that he initiate a private suit given his age and his legal inexperience (**Dem. 54.1**). Demosthenes tells the jurors that he could have brought a private suit against Meidias instead of a public action, and therefore he deserves their thanks since he gave up the financial reward that he would have received and preferred instead for the city to benefit solely from Medias' conviction (**Dem. 21.28**). Besides financial and social considerations, the prosecutor might also base his decision on the penalty prescribed for the action. Public suits generally had more severe penalties, but then, of course, the prosecutor had greater risks since he was fined if he did not receive at least one-fifth of the jury's votes. The action that the prosecutor chose to pursue significantly influenced how he presented his case. Although prosecutors in private suits sometimes state the impact that the outcome of the case would have on the community, prosecutors tend to make such claims more often in public suits. In fact, public prosecutors address the jury as "men of Athens" more often than other litigants. Since this was the way speakers generally addressed the Assembly, public prosecutors used this address to impress upon the jury the public significance of the trial and the impact that the verdict would have on the entire community.

Typically, once the injured party had decided on the appropriate charge, he selected two individuals to witness his summoning of the defendant to appear before the appropriate official at a specific day and time.[12] When that day arrived, the prosecutor delivered to the official the charge in writing. The official might either accept the charge or reject it if it was not within his purview or if no law applied for the alleged offense. Court fees, if due, were paid then, and the date of the preliminary hearing (*anakrisis*) was set for cases other than homicide, which had instead three pre-trial hearings (*prodikasiai*). The official then posted a notice of the charge in front of the statues of the Eponymous Heroes of the ten

---

12. For some offenses, the alleged perpetrator was summarily arrested and could be executed without a trial if he admitted his guilt. A denouncement (*eisangelia*) could be heard first before the Council or the Assembly.

tribes, in the agora. In homicide cases, the *basileus* also made a proclamation banning the alleged murderer from appearing in places prohibited by law, which included the agora, temples, and public meetings. At the preliminary hearing, each side swore an oath either affirming or denying the accuracy of the charge. It appears that the hearing also provided the parties and the presiding official the opportunity to ask questions about the dispute and to present evidence. The defendant could charge the prosecutor with bringing an illegal accusation (*paragraphe*), which stopped the original suit and required a court to hear the defendant's complaint (see **Dem. 32**; **Lys. 23**). For public suits, the date of the trial was set at the preliminary hearing. For most private suits other than homicide, a public arbitration was scheduled next.

The two parties of a private suit then prepared their cases and collected all the evidence (testimony of witnesses, laws, challenges, and oaths) that they intended to present before the public arbitrator. Some of this entailed duties that police and attorneys now perform. The prosecutor of Pancleon describes how he had to go around Athens to gather information about the defendant's true identity (see **Lys. 23**). Litigants also had to have their witnesses ready and to furnish the text of any law that they wished to have cited. Typically this required them to find the inscription of the law, which was usually placed in front of the court to which the law applied, and often they were required to go to many different courts for the relevant laws. Evidence from a slave was only admissible if submitted under torture (*basanos*), and both sides had to agree on the terms for the examination of the slave. While the extant speeches provide many examples of litigants challenging their opponent to have slaves give evidence under torture, none of these challenges were accepted (see below). Once each side provided all its information and finished questioning the other side, the arbitrator proposed a settlement. If either party rejected the settlement, the arbitrator collected and sealed all the evidence and a date for the trial was arranged. The arbitration provided litigants with an important opportunity to learn how the opposing party intended to argue at the trial, and we find that they often responded to the other side's arguments based on information that they obtained from the pre-trial stages of the dispute.

In an elaborate and complicated sorting process that took place on the day of the trial in order to prevent bribery, jurors, cases, and presiding officials were assigned to the various courts. Private suits typically had juries of two hundred to four hundred jurors. Public suits had juries of five hundred and sometimes one thousand and even more jurors. It has been estimated that the total number of jurors needed on any given court day was probably around fifteen hundred to two thousand. Only those six thousand Athenians over thirty who had volunteered for and were selected by lot at the annual sortition were able to serve during that year.[13] After the annual sortition, those chosen were required to swear an oath stating that they would adhere to the laws of Athens, but unlike public officials jurors did not undergo a scrutiny or an audit. Since they were not assigned specific court days but simply showed up when they wanted to serve, the courts could not function unless hundreds of eligible Athenians regularly showed up for jury duty on their own volition. The city provided the eligible jurors with bronze tokens (*pinakia*) used to assign them to courts, and some of these tokens have been discovered in graves, presumably because of their symbolic value and as statements about the political identity of the deceased. Jury duty was clearly regarded much more highly than it is today.

Private suits could last perhaps less than one hour if the sum in question was under one thousand drachmas, and maybe more than two hours if over five thousand drachmas. Public suits generally went all day, for approximately nine hours. Water clocks (*klepsydrai*) measured the time for each side, and they were stopped (i.e., plugged) in private suits when laws, witness testimony, and other sealed evidence were read out by the court's clerk. Witnesses had to appear to affirm the accuracy of the testimony that the litigant had read out, but they were neither questioned nor cross-examined. If a witness was ill and unable to attend, then a proxy affirmed on his behalf that the testimony was accurate. The trial began with the reading of the charge and the reply of the defendant. The prosecution gave its speech first and then the defense. For private suits, next followed the reply of the prosecutor and then the counter-reply of the defense. The jury then voted, without deliberation. In cases with fixed penalties, the verdict was read out and the trial ended. For cases without a fixed penalty, the verdict was read out and, if the defendant was found guilty, the prosecutor then proposed a penalty and the defendant an alternative penalty; in Socrates' trial, he famously first suggested that he dine at public expense in the Prytaneum, but after the prompting of his friends he proposed a fine of thirty minas (Pl. *Ap.* 35e1–38b9). The jury then voted on the penalty,

---

13. Hansen 1991: 186–88. Some suggest that the juries would have consisted primarily of retired men. When one takes into consideration the number of jurors needed per court day, the percentage of the population that was over sixty, and the fact that this segment of the population would have been less mobile, it is unlikely that elder citizens could have regularly dominated the juries as depicted in Aristophanes' *Wasps*. It is certainly likely that they were overrepresented, but a substantial number of citizens younger than sixty would still have been needed for the juries to reach the requisite number.

again without deliberation. At the end of the day each juror received three obols, which was a rather modest stipend since skilled laborers made two to two and a half drachmas per day in the fourth century (i.e., four to five times the amount that a juror received).

The jury's verdict was final and could not be appealed. However, there were various ways a litigant could directly or indirectly dispute the outcome. First, he could accuse a witness of giving false testimony, and if he won such a suit it sometimes resulted in either a direct or indirect reversal of the original suit. If the defendant was required to pay a financial penalty to the prosecutor, it was the prosecutor's responsibility to obtain the sum. If the defendant refused to pay him, the prosecutor could then lodge a suit of ejectment against the original defendant. If the prosecutor won, the defendant then had to pay a fine to the city, and the prosecutor was now granted the right to use force to obtain the original sum owed to him so that he was not liable for battery or damages. A litigant might also seek revenge against the opposing party by initiating suits on other matters. Meidias first came into contact with Demosthenes when he assisted his guardians in blocking Demosthenes' suit against them. Meidias and Demosthenes then pursued a quarrel against each other that lasted some fifteen years and involved a complicated array of legal suits and procedures, as described in **Demosthenes 21**.

Forensic oratory has become a particularly valuable source of information for Greek historians, in part because the speeches were delivered before an audience that consisted of the entire spectrum of the citizen population. The speakers therefore tended to express values and beliefs that most of their fellow citizens also endorsed. Their lives and property were at stake, and they did not want to risk offending their audience. Since the litigants had no idea who would be on the jury for their trial, their remarks had to appeal as widely as possible. So when criticizing the rich or poor, they generally did not make blanket statements of condemnation but qualified their remarks so that they only criticized those whose wealth or lack of wealth caused them to shirk their responsibilities or engage in decadent or lawless activities. They often presented the dispute as creating a crisis that threatened Athens, but they always offered a solution. As long as the jury sided with them and voted against their opponents, the order that the dispute in question had disrupted could be restored and the jury could show everyone the consequences of violating the law and not adhering to Athenian values. Just as funeral orations give a highly idealized representation of Athens, so too does forensic oratory. The difference is that the forensic speaker depicts the dispute between the two parties as creating a fissure that either is harming or can harm Athens, but the verdict can repair the damage. Forensic oratory, while focusing on a momentary crisis, always offers the jury a solution, so that the Athenians can then believe in the image of their city that is found in funeral oratory.

Since the disputes often focus on disagreements between friends and family, neighbors and business partners, and political opponents and bitter rivals, they give us the opportunity to learn more about the daily lives of Athenians than we can from other sources. The historians, for example, tend to focus instead on foreign policy and military strategy rather than domestic affairs. Of course, we also have to take into consideration that the corpus of Attic orators is very selective and rather exceptional. These speeches survive because of the high regard for the orators and logographers who wrote (or were thought to have written) them, and not because of an interest in Athenian legal or social history. For that reason, the sections of the speech that included witness testimony and citation of laws were usually omitted (see below). One must also bear in mind that a litigant's description of a dispute was always shaped by his need to persuade the jurors. He retroactively framed his actions to conform to the jurors' legal expectations. The actual reasons for the litigant's actions may have been quite different from what he told the jury. Forensic oratory may provide us a window into Athenian disputes, but always from the vantage point of the courtroom. The disputes might have appeared quite different when the parties discussed and described them in the privacy of their own homes, talking only in front of friends and relatives. Even those private disputes heard in court had a public and even political dimension, since at least one of the parties refused to accept the arbitrator's decision and chose instead to have a jury render its verdict. For many disputes settled out of court, the legal and social dynamics may have been quite different.

4. The Attic Orators

The corpus of Attic orators consists of some one hundred fifty speeches written by orators, rhetoricians, and logographers from 420–320. They survive first and foremost because they were regarded as some of the finest examples of rhetoric from classical Athens and were attributed to the ten of its most renowned practitioners: Aeschines, Andocides, Antiphon, Demosthenes, Dinarchus, Hyperides, Isaeus, Isocrates, Lycurgus, and Lysias. When one examines the legal speeches in the corpus, it immediately becomes clear that they were also selected because of either their historical significance or their sensational content. They discuss murder, adultery, prostitution, insurance fraud, piracy, and long-standing feuds between famous and even notorious politicians. Spectators apparently came to hear the speeches when they were delivered in court, and they have proven to be popular long after the juries delivered their verdicts.

Antiphon (c.480–411), an Athenian from an aristocratic family, is the first logographer known to us and the first of the ten Attic orators. Commenting on his skill as an advocate, Thucydides (8.68.1) says, "He was regarded with suspicion by the crowds because they thought of him as too clever, but among those involved in a dispute in the courts or the Assembly, more than any other man, he was capable of benefiting with his advice anyone who consulted him." Three forensic speeches and three sets of model speeches (*technai*) suitable for homicide cases survive under his name, and all reveal his skill as a litigator. His tight, robust, eloquent, and often sly argumentation can easily be the envy of any modern litigator, while his prose, when compared, for example, with his contemporary Thucydides, demonstrates a level of development that matches the mature prose of the fourth century. His involvement with the Four Hundred, who carried out a short-lived coup in 411, led to a very public trial resulting in his execution. Although the speech that he delivered in his defense was his finest, it was to no avail (Thuc. 8.68.2).

Lysias (c.445–c.380) was a metic whose father was invited to Athens by Pericles. The family had quite a successful business until the Thirty came to power (404), executed Lysias' brother Polemarchus, and seized their assets. When the democracy was restored, Lysias was forced by financial necessity to start a career as a logographer. He even appeared in court on his own behalf to deliver what was perhaps his most famous speech, when he spoke against Eratosthenes, a member of the Thirty (**Lys. 12**). He wrote speeches for some thirty years, amassing a fortune large enough to be able to afford one of the most exclusive Corinthian courtesans (**[Dem.] 59.21**) and securing for himself a place of honor in Greek rhetoric for his mastery of a style marked by simplicity, clarity, and a truly outstanding portrayal of character (*ethopoeia*). Later in antiquity his speeches were used as models for the virtues of the simple style in contrast with the more ornate style of Demosthenes. By the time of Cicero, Lysias had become the quintessential symbol of Attic oratory, and "to Atticize" meant to speak with simplicity and elegance like Lysias, without flowery excesses or pointless elaboration.

Isaeus (c.420–c.345), a near contemporary of Lysias, is said (perhaps incorrectly) to have been a student of Isocrates. He stands between the two great masters in terms of his artistry and style. He has some Lysianic simplicity and elegance, and also some Isocratean richness and texture, blended into an effective mix of convincing, powerful oratory (cf. D. H. *Isae.* 3). In addition, Isaeus was one of the most successful litigators of the early fourth century. Rich Athenians in disputes over inheritance and wills concerning large estates sought his legal advice and his talent as a speechwriter, without a doubt for a very handsome fee. With the exception of **Isaeus 12**, which survives only because Dionysius of Halicarnassus quoted a large section of it, the rest of Isaeus' extant speeches all concern inheritance disputes. This suggests that such cases were his specialty, making him unique among the Attic orators. Dionysius of Halicarnassus (*Isae.* 16), half in admiration and half in disdain, summarizes his skill as an advocate as follows: "He outsmarts the opponent, his stratagems defeat the jurors, and he would do anything that best serves the case in question." In some ways, Isaeus is the Attic orator who comes closest to resembling the modern lawyer in terms of his methods and objectives.

A story circulated in antiquity describing how Demosthenes (384–322) decided, when he was a young man, to become an orator after he had heard Isaeus speak. Another story, certainly apocryphal, recounts how Isaeus helped him prepare his speeches in his dispute against his guardians over his inheritance (D. H. *Isae.* 1). These stories are, however, correct in the motives that they ascribe to Demosthenes for his study of rhetoric. His father died when he was a child, leaving him a sizeable estate that his guardians were to manage until he reached adulthood. It quickly became clear that they were seizing his assets for their own use and that his estate would be used up long before he was an adult and could pursue a grievance against them. So Demosthenes prepared for the day when he could lodge a suit against his guardians, and as soon as he was an adult, he took action. But his guardians were also well prepared, and Demosthenes was only partially successful after his guardians forced him into a web of prolonged and protracted lawsuits. These early experiences probably helped shape the man whom Cicero considered the premier Attic orator, a view that many scholars have shared through the centuries. As a logographer, he was brilliant and very successful. Commanding a high price for his speeches, he amassed a large fortune and was feared and respected by anyone who dared to stand against him in court.

He is better known for his actions as a statesman and *rhetor*. He attempted to restore Athens to its former greatness, prevent Philip II of Macedon from conquering the Greek mainland, and preserve the political autonomy of Athens. This contest was romanticized in later centuries as a struggle over the freedom of the Greek polis with Demosthenes, who tragically stood up against unstoppable forces, as the last great leader of the classical period. Unable to withstand Macedonian domination, he witnessed Philip and Alexander build their empire and usher in the Hellenistic period, and he made himself a marked man, dying for a cause that could not be won.

In style, Demosthenes is quite different from the other Attic orators. Bold and ornate, his sentences often are loaded with a complex array of dependant and independent clauses, neatly balanced, serving to punctuate his points and convey to the listener the urgency of his appeal. For the modern reader more accustomed to a simple style where less is more, such meaty sentences may be difficult to appreciate fully. This is one of the reasons why he is sometimes accused of being bombastic, but this criticism misses the mark and fails to recognize his genius. Such fullness of expression helped Demosthenes capture his audience's attention, draw them away from questions or concerns that did not support his argument, and focus instead on matters that made his case compelling.

Among Demosthenes' works, seven speeches have been preserved, written in a style that is very different from that of Demosthenes, yet powerful and effective in its own right. Scholars from antiquity knew that these speeches were not written by Demosthenes, but it was not until the modern period that they were identified as the works of Apollodorus the son of Pasion (394–c.340).[14] In recent years the Apollodoran authorship of these speeches has been universally accepted, and in the words of Pearson, Apollodorus has been added to the canon as "the Eleventh Attic Orator."[15] He was the son of the banker Pasion, a former slave, who gained his freedom and eventually Athenian citizenship because of the immense wealth that he had accumulated from his successful business as a banker. Apollodorus had a good education and was politically ambitious, but only his forensic speeches are extant. Like Demosthenes, he became embroiled in an inheritance dispute. When he came of age, he engaged in extensive litigation against his stepfather, Phormio, and his younger brother, Pasicles, over the fortune of Pasion. One speech (Dem. 47) undoubtedly bears all the marks of Apollodoran oratory, but it is not related to any of his cases. Unless it is a speech that he wrote for a friend, it might bear witness to an attempt of Apollodorus to follow the path of Demosthenes and become a logographer. For some reason, however, it seems that he did not take this path, and most of his speeches are related to his own lawsuits.

The main strength of Apollodoran oratory lies in its extensive and rich narrative. Ancient rhetoricians believed that this style was more suitable for historiography and thus a flaw. Modern scholars have come to recognize this style as a strength. A good story can often enchant and persuade an audience—especially in the case of a large and diverse one, like an Athenian jury—much better than sophisticated legal arguments. Apollodorus has a style that is for the most part simple, but he sometimes sacrifices brevity in favor of emotional outbursts that interrupt the natural flow of his sentences and contain moralizing sentiments serving to curry the jury's favor. The fact that a man as wealthy as Apollodorus wrote speeches regularly over a span of thirty years suggests that he was a relatively successful litigator.

---

14. Schaefer 1885: 3.2.130–99.

15. Pearson 1983: 211. The most systematic study of Apollodorus as a historical person and an author is that of Trevett 1992.

In contrast to Demosthenes, his main rival, Aeschines (c.389–c.314) came from humble origins. Entering political life when the Athenians were locked in a struggle against Philip II, he sought to accommodate the king of Macedon. For a period of fifteen years after his first visit to Phillip, he opposed the policies of Demosthenes and the anti-Macedonian faction. Several times he became enmeshed in litigation with his illustrious rival and won. These speeches have survived, showing us why he was such a successful orator and how he was able to outmaneuver a politician as adept as Demosthenes. But in his last and most famous lawsuit, he staked his political future on his prosecution of Ctesiphon. Charging him with proposing an illegal motion (*graphe paranomon*) to award Demosthenes a crown, Aeschines attempted to discredit his rival and his failed military strategies, but he failed to receive one-fifth of the jury's votes and was fined one thousand drachmas. Since he could not pay the fine, he was disfranchised and voluntarily left Athens and went to Samos, where he taught rhetoric.

5. Technique and Style of the Attic Orators

Once the Assembly and the courts gained considerable political power, politicians needed to be persuasive speakers in order to be successful, and *technai,* illustrating how to compose and deliver speeches, began to circulate. The *technai* did not provide step-by-step instructions, like modern manuals; rather they were model speeches, serving to demonstrate by example how to present an effective argument and illustrate the different parts of a speech. Orators and logographers certainly benefited from *technai,* but they probably also learned much from each other. Even if Demosthenes did not decide to focus his attention on oratory after hearing Isaeus speak, this ambitious young man probably paid close attention to the techniques and strategies of one of the best logographers. These two factors probably explain the presence of the vast amount of common topics (*topoi*) that regularly appear in the extant speeches. Each speechwriter took note of tropes, appeals, and arguments that were successful in the past, as well as the tone and tenor, mannerisms and gestures, and phrasing and wording of effective speakers. So, by trial and error, speechwriters discovered which methods, strategies, and approaches to their art were most successful, and they regularly borrowed from each other and recycled any device that seemed effective until they had a common arsenal at their disposal.

For example, it is typical in the introduction of a speech for the litigant to express his trust in the fair-mindedness of the jurors, remind them of his past services to the city and spotless record, or reassure them that he was pursuing his grievance not because he was meddlesome or vindictive but because his opponent had harmed him and committed offenses for which he deserved to pay the consequences. Sometimes the main body of the speech, especially in those of Lysias and Demosthenes, has two parts. The first part contains the narrative of the events that landed the litigants in court, sometimes stretching back many years to the beginning of their feud. The second part is argumentative, containing proofs in order to establish the probability that the version of the dispute that the litigant presents is likely to be true. There are, however, other equally effective ways to arrange the body of a speech. Isaeus usually chooses to discuss one aspect of the dispute and then offers his explanation, providing arguments and evidence to support his conclusion before he moves on to his next point. Aeschines and Apollodorus place more emphasis on narrative and less on argument. Apollodorus sometimes even devotes three-fourths of his speech to narrative. While Aeschines' and Apollodorus' approaches differ substantially from those of Lysias and Demosthenes, they clearly have their reasons. And as it turns out, three of Aeschines' court cases against Demosthenes survive, and he won two of them.

The closing sections in Attic forensic speeches are usually quite predictable. The orators appeal to the jurors' inherent sense of justice or piety by reminding them that the gods are watching. They often acknowledge that the case is now in the jurors' hands and ask them to do what is right and fair, as their oaths require. Prosecutors request that they impose a punishment that fits the crime. Defendants ask them not to cause more harm by punishing them when they are innocent, and they plead with the jurors to pity if not them then at least their families and their relatives. Frequently there is an element of *amplificatio*, an attempt to expand the scope of the particular case and present it as a matter that concerns everyone, with the verdict having an impact on not only the litigants, but the entire community and even beyond.

The preferences of the orators when it comes to documents, witnesses, readings from Greek literature, and other supporting evidence are quite diverse. Aeschines is particularly fond of quoting poetry. He devotes nearly a third of his speech against Timarchus to passages from Homer, Euripides, and other poets, and he digresses with stories and anecdotes relating only loosely to his case. Certainly these stories and readings served to keep the jurors entertained so that they would continue to hear him favorably, but Aeschines also needed to prove that his views on sexuality conformed to those of his fellow citizens and respond to the accusations of Timarchus that he was a hypocrite. In his speech against Neaera, Apollodorus has a lengthy digression on the Plataeans and selectively quotes Thucydides to fit the needs of his argument. Apollodorus also frequently calls on witnesses, asking them to verify even minor facts that will not determine the outcome of the case and are sometimes quite tangential. Nineteenth-century scholars were quite critical of this use of witnesses, perceiving Apollodorus as being incapable of judging what was important to his case. Yet, he clearly brought forth so many witnesses for a dramatic effect, in order to leave the jury with the impression that his argument was unassailable.

In contrast to the modern trial, which routinely has expert witnesses, such as health or forensic professionals, this practice was fairly uncommon in Athens. Since ancient doctors and scientists did not have conclusive proof for the assertions that they might make, their evidence was of limited value. So from time to time they were summoned to verify that an individual had been ill or to describe the severity of the person's medical condition (e.g., **Dem. 54.10, 12**), but such instances were not common, and their testimony was not more compelling than that of any other citizen. Equally surprising to the modern reader is the limited use of written documents. Documents could be easily falsified, and even when they existed, the testimony of witnesses was necessary to confirm their authenticity. An ancient trial was primarily an oral process, and the statements of free persons were the primary form of evidence. As noted above, the testimony of slaves could be formally introduced in court only if submitted under torture, but such testimony is not provided in any of the extant speeches. It appears that the litigant regularly worded the challenge in such a way that he insured that his opponent would refuse. Then the litigant presented the opponent's refusal as proof that the slave would have corroborated the contents of the challenge. So, too, when litigants offered to swear an oath or challenged their opponent to do so, they knew that their challenge would be rejected. But here again the rejected challenge provided litigants an opportunity to call into question the motives of their opponents and to suggest to the jury that their opponents refused the challenge because they were hiding something.

Witness testimony is frequently missing from the surviving speeches. In some cases, however, a number of documents have been inserted in the text. How this happened is easy to understand. Documents, such as laws, testimonies, or other supporting evidence, were not read by the litigant. The clock was stopped, and the clerk of the court read them aloud at the invitation of the litigant; then the witnesses were asked to confirm the documents. For that reason, they would not have been a part of the speech that the litigant read but were on a separate scroll or dossier handed over to the clerk of the court at the beginning of the trial. It is conceivable that some of these documents were still around when the speeches were published, but a scribe wanting to incorporate them had to search in the city archives or other possible sources. Laws, decrees, and perhaps archived testimonies of public officials might be easy to find, but testimonies of private citizens would have been long discarded, and so any such insertions tend to be forgeries. Sometimes the wrong law might be retrieved, as in the speech against Meidias where, instead of inserting the law on public arbitration, the scribe inserted the law on private arbitration (**Dem. 21.94**). It is often difficult to decide whether a document is authentic or a forgery. For that reason, unless there is corroborative evidence supporting the authenticity of a certain document, it is necessary to view an inserted text with skepticism.

The outcome of only a few cases is known (e.g., **Aesch. 1**), and even for those cases, it is difficult, if not impossible, to determine how the jury reached its verdict. It is, however, quite likely that the jurors viewed the evidence differently and had different reasons for the verdict that they delivered. Litigants, therefore, attempted to cast their net as wide as possible, presented arguments that touched on all aspects of the dispute, and when possible, avoided making assertions that might have offended any segment of the jurors. As Aristotle observes, litigants sought to persuade the jurors not simply by discussing the facts of the case, but also by establishing their own character and by eliciting a particular emotional response in the jury (*Rhet.* 1356a1–4). Without forensic evidence to verify the claims of the parties, arguments based on probability helped the jury decide whether a defendant was likely to have committed the offense for which he was charged. For that reason, arguments of character were an integral part of the litigant's speech. But this does not mean that social and political considerations were the primary concern of the jury; rather law was never viewed as separate from society or politics. And while litigants often cite their public service, it is clear that they do so to establish their character and not because they expect the jury to favor them out of a sense of obligation. Similarly, the jurors are asked to pity a defendant who is innocent and has been unfairly charged with a crime, not one who is knowingly guilty of a crime. So, in theory, arguments based on character and emotion helped the jury make the right decision. Of course, there is always the possibility in any trial—whether ancient or modern—that a jury might make a mistake. We seek to prevent such a miscarriage of justice through a legal system that has a professional class of lawyers to act as intermediaries between the parties of the dispute, trained judges to monitor how lawyers present their cases, and juries to decide the outcome. The Athenians, by contrast, placed their faith in the collective wisdom of a mass audience. They had hundreds of citizens serve on each jury because they believed that such an audience was likely to represent the communal sense of justice and was more likely to do what was fair. Although they were willing to acknowledge the temperamental nature of their juries and the unpredictability of legal dispute, Athenians still trusted their legal system as a whole and believed in its ability to dispense justice.

Recommended Reading

Anderson, Greg. 2003. *The Athenian Experiment: Building an Imagined Political Community in Ancient Attica, 508–490 B.C.* Ann Arbor: University of Michigan Press.

Blundell, Sue. 1995. *Women in Ancient Greece.* Cambridge, MA: Harvard University Press.

Carawan, Edwin, ed. 2007. *Oxford Readings in the Attic Orators.* Oxford: Oxford University Press.

Finley, Moses I. 1980. *Ancient Slavery and Modern Ideology.* London: Chatoo and Windus.

———. 1985. *The Ancient Economy.* 2nd ed. Berkeley: University of California Press.

———. 1988. *Democracy Ancient and Modern.* Revised ed. New Brunswick: Rutgers University Press.

Gagarin, Michael, and David Cohen, eds. 2005. *The Cambridge Companion to Ancient Greek Law.* Cambridge: Cambridge University Press.

Hansen, Mogens Herman. 1991. *The Athenian Democracy in the Age of Demosthenes.* Oxford: Blackwell.

Johnstone, Steven. 1999. *Disputes and Democracy: The Consequences of Litigation in Ancient Athens.* Austin: University of Texas Press.

Kennedy, George. 1974. *The Art of Persuasion in Greece.* Princeton: Princeton University Press.

MacDowell, Douglas M. 1978. *The Law in Classical Athens.* Ithaca: Cornell University Press.

Ober, Josiah. 1989. *Mass and Elite in Democratic Athens: Rhetoric, Ideology, and the Power of the People.* Princeton: Princeton University Press.

Raaflaub, Kurt A., Josiah Ober, and Robert W. Wallace, eds. 2007. *Origins of Democracy in Ancient Greece.* Berkeley: University of California Press.

Todd, Stephen C. 1993. *The Shape of Athenian Law.* Oxford: Oxford University Press.

Worthington, Ian, ed. 2007. *A Companion to Greek Rhetoric.* Oxford: Blackwell.

Abbreviations

Ancient Authors and Works

Aes.	Aeschylus
Eum.	*Eumenides*
Aesch.	Aeschines
And.	Andocides
Ant.	Antiphon
Ap.	Apollodorus
Ar.	Aristophanes
Pl.	*Wealth*
Arist.	Aristotle
Ath. Pol.	The Aristotelian *Athenaion Politeia* (also known as *the Constitution of Athens*)
Pol.	*Politics*
Rhet.	*The Rhetoric*
Athen.	Athenaeus
Dem.	Demosthenes
[Dem.]	Speech by Apollodorus wrongly ascribed to Demosthenes
D. H.	Dionysius of Halicarnassus
Isae.	*Isaeus*
Din.	Dinarchus
D. S.	Diodorus Siculus
Eur.	Euripides
Andr.	*Andromache*
Hec.	*Hecuba*
Med.	*Medea*
Harp.	Harpocration
Hes.	Hesiod
Op.	*Works and Days*
Hom.	Homer
Il.	*Iliad*

Isae.	Isaeus
Isoc.	Isocrates
Lyc.	Lycurgus
Lys.	Lysias
Pl.	Plato
Ap.	*Apology*
Plu.	Plutarch
Caes.	*Caesar*
Cim.	*Cimon*
Per.	*Pericles*
Phoc.	*Phocion*
Soph.	Sophocles
Ant.	*Antigone*
Elect.	*Electra*
OT	*Oedipus Tyrannos*
Thuc.	Thucydides
Xen.	Xenophon
Hell.	*Hellenica*
Oec.	*Oeconomicus*

Brackets

{. . .}	Braces are for spurious insertions by scribes.
<. . .>	Chevrons indicate words erroneously dropped from the manuscript.
[. . .]	Square brackets indicate a text attributed in antiquity to the wrong author, such as "**[Dem.] 59**," which Apollodorus is now believed to have written.

ANTIPHON 6

ON THE CHORISTER

Introduction

This is one of the oldest speeches to survive that was intended to be delivered in an Athenian law court (419/8).[1] It was prepared for a defendant, whose name is not provided, charged by Philocrates with the unintentional homicide of his brother Diodotus.[2] The victim had been a member of the boys' chorus that the defendant was producing as a *choregos* for the Thargelia, a festival in honor of Apollo held in late spring. The case was heard in the Palladium before a panel of fifty-one *ephetai*, probably selected from members of the Areopagus.[3] If convicted, the defendant would have been exiled. The facts of the case are not in question, but the parties offer very different interpretations of the events that transpired. So the narrative is mixed with the argumentation to allow the speaker to offer a point-by-point account of the disagreement (see Gagarin 2002: 139–46). Both sides agreed that Diodotus died as a result of a potion given to the boy while he was training for the chorus in the house of the speaker. Philocrates argued that the chorus producer was responsible for Diodotus' death, while the defendant denied any part in the unfortunate accident.

The speaker insists that he did not administer the potion in person, did not order anyone else from his staff to do so, and was not even present when the boy consumed it (**15**). He argues that even Diodotus' family knew that he was not legally responsible for the death; otherwise Philocrates would not have allowed so much time to elapse between the death of his brother and the eventual trial, and he would not have agreed to a reconciliation with the chorus producer. He only began legal proceedings for murder

---

Translated by Konstantinos Kapparis.

1. Dover 1950; Gagarin 1997: 244–55.

2. Although the defendant indicates that he was charged with planning unintentional homicide (see **16**), the "planner" was as liable as the "agent," and it appears to be the case that the same legal action was used for both (Gagarin 1990, 1997: 223–24; contra MacDowell 1963: 60–69). For Athenian law on homicide, see MacDowell 1963; Gagarin 1979, 1981; Tulin 1996; Carawan 1998; Phillips 2008.

3. Alternatively, some scholars believe that dicastic jurors, who swore the Heliastic oath and heard cases in the popular law courts, replaced the *ephetai* sometime after 403. For the composition of the ephetic courts, see MacDowell 1963: 51–57; Wallace 1985: 102–5; Carawan 1991; Todd 1993: 81–82.

after reaching an agreement with some men charged by the defendant with embezzlement of public funds. According to our speaker, Diodotus' death provided them with the perfect opportunity to block his case and prevent him from prosecuting them. As soon as an individual was charged with homicide, the accused could not enter the temples, the agora, or other public places, including all court buildings.[4] Their plot, however, backfired: the *basileus* (king archon), who was in charge of accepting homicide cases, refused their case because there was not enough time remaining in his term of office for it to be heard. Philocrates could not continue with his suit until the next *basileus* entered office, which was a month or two away. In the meantime, the speaker's case against his opponents went to trial, and he was able to secure their conviction for embezzlement. The homicide proceedings, however, continued as an act of revenge by the convicted embezzlers and their friends, and the trial took place several months later. As the defendant maintains, his trial had less to do with the death of Diodotus and more with the charges that he had lodged against these men (**34–46**).

Significant details are neglected in the defendant's speech. We do not know who administered the potion, what it consisted of, or its purpose. We also do not know whether Diodotus was the only member of the chorus who took it or whether our speaker participated at all in the decision to give the boy this particular potion.[5] It is possible that it was meant to enhance the boy's performance in the chorus or serve as a remedy for a cold or some other ailment that may have affected his singing. The defendant denies all involvement, but should we believe him? Both his refusal to name or blame any member of his team for the administration of the lethal potion and his reluctance to provide significant details could be plausibly explained as an attempt to protect someone else. If, for example, the person who gave the boy the potion was Phanostratus, his son-in-law, and our speaker was shielding him, we would not expect the defendant to give specific details that could incriminate him. If, indeed, Phanostratus or another member of the team had given the boy the potion, then that person should have been prosecuted. But one must also bear in mind that the prosecution of the chorus producer, whether successful or unsuccessful,[6] did not prevent Philocrates

---

4. Homicide courts always tried cases in the open air to avoid the risk of contamination from a killer.

5. The possibility that all boys took the same potion but only Diodotus reacted badly to a normally innocuous substance remains open. If, for example, the mix given to the boys contained crushed nuts, and Diodotus was allergic, he could have died by the same potion which was harmless, even if not beneficial, to the other chorus members.

6. As is the case for most extant legal speeches, the outcome of **Antiphon 6** is not indicated in the manuscripts and remains unknown.

from charging anyone else who may also have been involved, including the individual who handed the potion to Diodotus. So the defendant had good reason to avoid discussing any pertinent details about the boy's death.

Beyond these questions, the speech is an important source for understanding not only homicide law and Athenian perception of the homicide courts, but also the religious sanctions imposed on those accused of murder as well as Athenian anxiety over the pollution that threatens the community if a murderer is allowed to come in contact with others. In addition, the speech shows how disputes, as they are played out, frequently draw more people into the conflict. They often have many unforeseen consequences, and the parties involved regularly interpret Athenian law and legal procedures quite creatively and even in self-serving ways in order to triumph over their enemies. The speech also shows how important the choral competitions were for the Athenians who performed and produced them. The religious festivals provided the chorus producers and the chorus members an opportunity to stand out for their performances and be recognized by their fellow citizens. The competitions could become quite fierce (see also **Dem. 21**). Philocrates never would have brought his charge to trial unless it seemed believable to his fellow citizens that the defendant would have risked the life of his brother for the sake of winning. As the chorus producer, he was responsible for the boy who was training in his house for the festival, and even if he did not deliver the potion or ask anyone else to do so, the question still remains what responsibility he had for the boy that was serving in his chorus and was under his care.

Key Information

Speaker	The unnamed defendant was accused of being responsible for the unintentional death of Diodotus, who was a chorister (member of the chorus produced by the speaker).
Prosecutor	As the brother of Diodotus, Philocrates prosecuted the speaker.
Victim	Diodotus died after drinking a potion while he was training to be a chorister for the speaker and under his care.
Other individuals	Phanostratus, son-in-law of the speaker, took care of the needs of the chorus so that the speaker could turn his attention to a lawsuit that he had lodged.
	Aristion, Philinus, and Ampelinus were prosecuted and convicted for embezzlement by the speaker,

	who lodged a denunciation (*eisangelia*) against them.
Action	Unintentional homicide.
Court	The Palladium.
Penalty	Exile.
Date	419/8.

On the Chorister

[1] It would be truly wonderful, men of the jury,[7] if a man did not have to risk his life, and one might pray for this in his prayers; if, however, someone should be forced to be in harm's way, then he might pray for it at least to be the case, which I think is best in such a situation, that he know in his heart that he has done nothing wrong, and if some misfortune should occur, it happened without malice or shame, and because of bad luck rather than wrongdoing.[8] [2] All should praise the laws that are established for such matters as the best and most sacred. They happen to be the oldest in this land, and they have remained the same for the same offenses, which is the clearest sign that they are good, because time and experience teach people what is bad.[9] So you should not determine from the words of the prosecutor whether the laws are good or not, but the laws should be the measure of their words, whether they are saying to you what is right and fair or not. [3] This trial is a very serious matter for me who is the defendant and at risk. However, I think that it is also of

---

7. Litigants typically reserved such an address for the jurors of the popular law courts and normally addressed the jurors in the homicide courts as "men" and in the Areopagus either as "council" or "men" (see **Lys. 1.1** n.).

8. In the opening section, the defendant sets the tone by speaking about a tragic accident rather than malicious intent. The phrase "for his life" (*tou somatos*), which would normally refer to the death penalty for intentional homicide, is undoubtedly an exaggeration in this case. In section **4**, the speaker describes the likely penalty which he would receive if convicted, and this is exile. Thus this trial was, curiously, a prosecution for unintentional homicide, even though the prosecution alleges intent in the administration of the potion, probably because both sides agreed that Diodotus' death was an accident (see Gagarin 2002: 139–46; MacDowell 1978: 116).

9. It is a frequent commonplace (*topos*) in Athenian literature that stable laws are bound to be good, such as those of Lycurgus for Sparta or Draco's homicide laws for Athens. In reality, Draco's laws were never repealed for religious reasons.

much importance for you the jurors to judge homicide cases correctly, first for the sake of the gods and for piety, and then for yourselves. There is only one judgment in such a case, and if it is incorrect, it prevails over what is just and true. [4] It is necessary for the defendant, if you condemn him, even if he is not the murderer or guilty of the crime, to adhere to your verdict and by law stay away from the city, sacred places, the games, and sacrifices, which are the greatest and oldest among men. This law creates such an imperative that, even if someone kills one of his own slaves and there is no one to seek retribution, out of fear of human custom and divine law, he purifies himself and will abstain from places mentioned in the law, hoping that by doing so he will prosper.[10] [5] Most matters in human life are marked by hope; however, one who commits impiety and breaks the laws of the gods deprives himself of hope, which is the greatest human good. No man would dare to disobey the verdict of a trial out of conviction that he is innocent of the crime or, if he knows in his heart that he has committed this crime, to violate this law. It is necessary to obey the verdict, even if it is contrary to the truth, and submit to the truth, even if there is no one to seek retribution. [6] This is the reason why the laws and the oaths and the sacrifices and the proclamations and all these procedures that constitute a homicide trial are very different from other trials, because it is extremely important for the facts to be assessed correctly in light of the risks. If the verdict is right, the injured party is avenged, but if an innocent person is declared by the vote to be a murderer, it is an error and a transgression against the gods and the laws.[11] And it is not the same for the prosecutor to make improper accusations as it is for you to misjudge the case. His accusations are not final, but they come before you and the court; if, however, you do not deliver the correct verdict, there is no place where one might convey the blame so as to be absolved from it.

[7] I do not have, men, the same attitude about my defense that the prosecutors have about their prosecution. They claim that they have brought their lawsuit for the sake of piety and justice. However, the entire prosecution is based upon malice and deception, which is the most unjust crime among humans. They do not want to exact a fair punishment from me after

---

10. Because of the religious implications of homicide, which was regarded as a form of pollution (*miasma*), even the murder of a slave was regarded as abominable and required purification. A killer, who failed to do so and dared to pollute temples and rituals with his unclean presence, could be punished for this additional offense. For the concept of *miasma* in homicide cases, see Parker 1983; Arnaoutoglou 1993; Hirayama 1998.

11. Since the punishment was execution, the conviction of an innocent defendant was tantamount to murder and therefore as offensive to the gods as the acquittal of a murderer.

they prove that I have committed some crime, but they are slandering me and want to have me punished and banished from this land, even if I have committed no crime at all. [8] First, I believe that I ought to respond about the matter itself and explain to you everything that happened. Then, if it pleases you, I would like to defend myself against the other accusations that they are making. I believe that this will bring me honor and benefit while it will bring shame upon the prosecutors and those who have influenced them. [9] It is terrible, men; they had the opportunity to expose and convict and punish a man who was their personal enemy and at the same time benefit the city, if I had committed some wrong against the city either as a chorus producer (*choregos*) or in some other capacity, but no one could prove that I had done anything wrong, small or great, against the people. However, in this trial, when they are prosecuting me for homicide and the law is such that the prosecutor is required to keep to the facts of the case, they are scheming against me, fabricating lies, and saying slanderous remarks about my public record. For the city, if it has in fact been wronged, they offer accusations instead of redress; and yet they expect to exact private punishment for actions that, they claim, have injured the city.[12] [10] But such accusations warrant neither thanks nor trust. He does not lodge a prosecution, for which the city would obtain satisfaction if it had been wronged, so as to deserve the city's thanks. And when he makes accusations other than those for which he pursues such an action, he deserves not so much your trust as your disbelief. I am pretty certain of your opinion and how you would not cast a ballot of conviction or acquittal on any other grounds except the facts themselves; for this is consistent with divine and human law. So here I will begin.

[11] When I was appointed chorus producer for the Thargelia, and Pantacles was appointed by lot to be the chorus trainer, and my tribe {the Erechtheid}[13] was paired with Cecropis, I started performing my duties as a chorus producer as best as possible and as fairly as I could.[14] First, I furnished

---

12. The speaker is referring to the distinction in Athenian law between public suits, for which a convicted defendant had to pay a penalty to the city, and private suits, for which the prosecutor received financial compensation from the defendant (see the Introduction). As a private action, the charge of murder could only be lodged by the family of the victim and could not be used to address other offenses against the city. For religious reasons, the procedures for homicide cases were stricter, and the litigants took an oath to adhere to the point (cf. **6**). Lanni (2006: 75–114) suggests that litigants strayed less from the matter at hand when appearing before the homicide courts as a result of these rules.

13. These words were probably added by a later scholiast.

14. The chorus producer was a rich Athenian who financed the training of a chorus for a religious festival. In this case, it was for the festival of the Thargelia, celebrated in late spring as a purification ceremony before the harvest. Boys from the ten

the most suitable part of my house where I had also taught the chorus when I served as chorus producer for the Dionysia. Next I assembled the best chorus that I could, without imposing fines on anyone, demanding securities, or making any enemies, but in a manner that was most pleasing and most suitable for both parties, I made my requests and appeals, and they sent their sons willingly and voluntarily.[15] [12] When the boys arrived, at first I did not have the time to stay behind and look after them. I was busy with the lawsuit against Aristion and Philinus, and I considered it to be a matter of great importance, since my denunciation was before the Council and the people, to be able to support it in an appropriate and fair manner.[16] While my attention was turned to these matters, I put Phanostratus in charge of the needs of the chorus. He is from the same deme as my accusers and is related to me by marriage (he married my daughter). I asked him to look after it as best as possible. [13] In addition to him, I appointed two more men. One was Ameinias from the Erechtheid tribe, which had elected him to recruit and supervise its choruses in the various festivals, and I considered him be a decent man. The other was from the Cecropid tribe and always assembles the choruses from this tribe.[17] A fourth man was added, Philip, whose task was to shop and spend for the needs of the trainer or one of the others so that the boys were instructed as best as possible and

---

tribes were paired for the chorus competitions of the Thargelia and trained by an instructor selected by lot from a group of qualified instructors. The speaker mentions Pantacles by name because he was a well known chorus instructor and some of the *ephetai* would have recognized his name. For the Thargelia, see Parke 1977: 146–55; Parker 1996: 95–96.

15. Since some fathers apparently did not wish to send their sons to be part of a chorus, the chorus producer had the authority to fine those fathers who refused to permit their sons to participate, or to demand a security in the case of a father who had an excuse, which was forfeited if proven to be invalid (Gagarin 1997: 229). Our chorus producer insists that his chorus consisted only of boys whose families had no objection.

16. In section **35**, the speaker explains that he lodged a denunciation (*eisangelia*) for embezzlement of public funds against Aristion, Philinus, Ampelinus, and the undersecretary of the *thesmothetai*.

17. Scholars suspect that the name of the second man, the representative of the Cecropid tribe, has been accidentally omitted by the scribes, but this is not necessarily the case. Nothing seems to be missing from the text. The speaker may have chosen to omit the name of the second supervisor of the boys either because he did not remember his name or because he was less illustrious than the notoriously proper Ameinias of the Erechtheid tribe, and he did not believe that the *ephetai* would have known his name.

were not deprived of anything because I was too busy.[18] [14] The training of the chorus was thus arranged. If I am lying about any of these matters in order to excuse myself, the prosecutor will have the opportunity to respond to any point he wishes in his second speech.[19] The case is as follows, men: many of the spectators know precisely what happened, and they heard the officer who administered the oaths, and now they are paying close attention to my response.[20] To them I wish to appear as a man who keeps his oath and who persuades you to acquit me by speaking the truth.

[15] First, I will prove to you that I did not ask the boy to drink the potion,[21] nor forced him, nor gave it to him, nor was I present when he drank it. And I do not insist on this in order to exonerate myself and put the blame on someone else. No, I do not blame anyone except fate, which is the cause of death of many other people too. Neither I nor anyone else would be in the position to prevent our fate from becoming what it is meant to be for each of us.

WITNESSES[22]

[16] The witnesses have been heard about the matter, men, as I promised you. On this basis you need to consider the statement that my accusers gave under oath and the one that I gave, and decide which of the two is more truthful and faithful to his oath. They stated under oath that I killed

---

18. Even if the defendant did not provide Diodotus with the potion, the jury might still have concluded that he was responsible for his death because of negligence. As a result, he discusses at length the steps he took and the people he entrusted to care for the boys in his absence so that Diodotus' death might seem more like an accident rather than the result of neglect.

19. While in a public lawsuit each litigant had one long speech to make his case, each litigant in private suits had two shorter speeches and could use his second speech to respond to his opponent's argument.

20. Athenian trials apparently attracted an audience, probably as a form of entertainment and because some would have been interested in hearing the arguments if they knew the parties involved or had witnessed some of the events that would be discussed (see Lanni 1997). The size of the audience probably varied depending on the importance of the dispute and the accusations that were to be heard, with more sensational cases attracting greater interest.

21. The Greek, *pharmakon,* can refer to a substance that has medical or magical powers intended either to help or harm the individual who receives it.

22. Although there is not an announcement for the witnesses to come forward, it is unlikely that they appeared unannounced. The part of the text where they were summoned has probably been omitted accidentally from the manuscripts.

Diodotus and that I orchestrated his death while I stated that I did not kill him, neither with my own hand nor by design.[23] [17] They allege that the person who made the boy drink the potion, either by force or by persuasion, is guilty. I will prove that I am not guilty of the accusations that they are making against me. I did not ask, force, or give it to him to drink, and I will add that I was not even present when he drank it. If they maintain that whoever gave the order is guilty, I am not, because I did not order him. If they maintain that whoever forced him is guilty, I am not, because I did not force him. If they consider the person responsible who gave him the potion, I am not responsible, because I did not give it to him. [18] Anyone who wants can make accusations and tell lies as he has the capacity to do so. I, however, believe that their words do not determine whether what did not happen happened or the person who did nothing wrong is guilty; rather this is determined by justice and the truth. In the case of a murder, premeditated and carried out in secret with no witnesses, it is necessary to reach a verdict from the accounts of the prosecutor and the defendant, by keeping track of what is said with skepticism for the slightest reason, and to vote on the basis of probability rather than firm knowledge. [19] In this instance, however, the prosecutors themselves admit that the death of the boy was not from forethought or preparation. Moreover, the incident itself happened in the open and in the presence of many witnesses, men and boys, free and slave, and for that reason if anyone had done something wrong, he would be immediately revealed, and if someone made accusations against an innocent man, he would be easily refuted.

[20] It is worth recalling, men, both the attitude of my opponents and how they approach the case. From the beginning they have treated me very differently from the way I have treated them. [21] Philocrates here came before the court of the *thesmothetai* on the day when the boy was buried and said that I killed his brother when he was a chorus member, by forcing him to drink the potion.[24] When he said this, I went to the court

---

23. At the beginning of homicide trials, each party was required to swear an oath, invoking destruction upon himself and his household if he lied.

24. Homicide proceedings formally began once the *basileus* accepted the case and proceeded with a proclamation that barred the accused from appearing in public places (see **36**; Arist. *Ath. Pol.* 57.2). When the *basileus* refused to accept the case because there was insufficient time remaining in his term, Philocrates could not block the chorus producer's suit against Aristion and his associates, since he had to wait until the new *basileus* entered office to charge him with murder. Before that he allegedly came before the court of the *thesmothetai* in order to sidestep the *basileus* and interfere with the chorus producer's upcoming suit. Since the *thesmothetai* were the six junior archons who oversaw many public suits (see MacDowell 1978: 35–36),

and said to the same jurors that Philocrates was unjustly invoking the law, accusing and slandering me to the court, when my trials against Aristion and Philinus were going to take place the next day and the day after, and that this was the reason behind such a claim. [22] His accusations and slanderous remarks would easily be exposed as lies, because a lot of people knew about it, free and slave, young and old, a total number of over fifty people. They knew what was said about the drinking of the potion and everything that happened {and was said}.

[23] I said all this before the court, and I challenged him right away, and again, the next day before the same jurors, I asked him to take as many witnesses as he wanted and go to those who had been present. I mentioned everyone by name and asked him to question and cross-examine them, the free men in a manner suitable for free persons, who would tell the truth of what happened on their own behalf and for the sake of justice, and the slaves, if they appeared to him to be answering truthfully to his questions.[25] If they did not appear to be telling the truth, I was prepared to hand over all my slaves to him to interrogate under torture (*basanos*), and if he asked for any slaves who belonged to other men, I agreed to persuade their owners to hand them over to him to torture however he wanted. [24] Although I presented this challenge and said all this in court, where the jurors themselves and many private citizens were present as witnesses, they did not want to agree to this just course of action, either then right away or afterwards, because they knew well that this proof would not turn against me but very much against them, since they were not making any fair or truthful accusation. [25] You know, men, that this kind of compulsion is the strongest and greatest among people, and in matters of law it provides the clearest and most reliable forms of proof when there are many people who know the facts, whether they be free men or slaves. It is possible to exert pressure

---

including the case of embezzlement that the chorus producer had lodged before the Council (**35**), Philocrates made his statement before their court.

25. A decree was passed in the archonship of Scamandrius (510/9) prohibiting the torture of free persons during judicial inquiries. The testimony of slaves, by contrast, could only be introduced if submitted under torture (*basanos*). Litigants frequently mention how they challenged their opponents to permit *basanos* to take place so that evidence from a slave could be introduced into court, but in none of the extant speeches are such challenges accepted. Clearly litigants often made such challenges, knowing that their opponents would reject them, so that they could then use the rejected challenge as evidence that the other party was attempting to conceal information that was damaging to its case. It remains disputed among scholars whether we should further conclude that by the late fifth century *basanos* was no longer actually carried out and had become, in effect, a legal fiction used primary for rhetorical advantage; see Thür 1977; Gagarin 1996; Mirhady 1996.

upon free men through oaths and pledges, which hold the greatest weight and the highest value for free men, and it is possible to compel slaves by other forms of necessity by which, even if they will die should they make their denunciations, still they are compelled to tell the truth since the current compulsion for each person is stronger than the one which is going to come.[26] [26] So I made my challenge to them for all of this, and they had the option to learn what is truthful and just by whatever means a mortal man has, and no excuse remained. I, the accused and the criminal, as they allege, was ready to allow them to prove the allegations against me in the fairest way. They, however, the accusers and supposedly the injured party, did not want to prove whether they suffered some kind of injustice.

[27] If they had made the challenge, requested the names of those who were present, and I did not want to reveal them, or if they asked me to hand over some slaves and I refused, or if I avoided some other challenge, they would have used this against me as the greatest proof that their accusations were truthful. But when I have made the challenge and they avoided the proof, it is only fair that I can use the same as evidence against them that their accusation against me is not true. [28] I am certain about this too, men, that if the witnesses who were present had testified against me, they would have treated this as very powerful evidence and they would have declared it very clear proof. Now when the same witnesses confirm what I say is true and what they say is not, they advise you to disbelieve the witnesses testifying for me and claim that you should believe their words, which (if I had said without witnesses) they would have denounced as lies. [29] It is terrible indeed if the same witnesses would be reliable were they to testify for them and will be unreliable when they testify for me. If no witnesses at all had been present and I still provided witnesses, or if witnesses had been present and I did not provide them, but some others, then it would be reasonable to trust their words rather than my witnesses. But when they agree that witnesses were present, and I provide those who were present, and from the very first day it will be clear that I and all the witnesses were saying what we are saying right now in front of you, what other evidence than this, men, can make what is true believable and what is not unbelievable? [30] When someone explains what had happened, but fails to provide witnesses, one would say that his words need the support of witnesses; and when one provides witnesses, but not arguments that corroborate the witnesses, one can criticize accordingly, if

---

26. The perverse logic of this argument is as follows: if the slaves testify to the truth, they may later die at the hands of their angry master, but if they keep lying, they will continue to suffer at the hands of their merciless tormentor. So the slaves would prefer to tell the truth in the present in order to put an end to the torture even though they may as a result be killed by their master.

he wishes. [31] And yet I make a convincing case, with witnesses to confirm my case and facts that agree with the witnesses, and arguments based upon the facts themselves, and, in addition to this, two of the greatest and most compelling proofs: the fact that they have been proven wrong by themselves and me and that I have been proven innocent by them and myself. [32] When I was willing to be tested about the accusations that they were making against me and they did not want to prove whether I had done something wrong, they effectively absolved me and became witnesses against themselves that their accusations were not at all just or true. So if, in addition to my own witnesses, I present my opponents themselves as witnesses, where else do I need to turn or what other evidence do I need to provide to absolve myself of blame?

[33] I believe that on the basis of what has been said and what has been proven, men, you would be justified to acquit me, and all of you know that this accusation does not in any way concern me. In order to be better informed, I will tell you more, and I will demonstrate that my accusers are the worst perjurers and the most unholy men, who deserve to be hated not only by me, but also by all of you and the rest of the citizens because of this suit. [34] On the first day, when the boy died, and the next day, when the body was laid out, they did not even think to accuse me of having done something wrong in this case, but they were perfectly social and on speaking terms with me.[27] However, on the third day, when the boy was buried, they had already been persuaded by my enemies and were prepared to make accusations and a proclamation that I was barred from places that the law prescribed.[28] Who persuaded them and why were they susceptible to persuasion? I need to tell you this, too. [35] I was about to prosecute Aristion, Philinus, Ampelinus, and the undersecretary of the *thesmothetai* who took part in their embezzlement, which was the grounds of my denunciation (*eisangelia*) before the Council. They had no hope of acquittal on the merits of the case itself; their crimes were so great. However, they persuaded the family of Diodotus to proceed with a prosecution and a

---

27. If the boy's relatives had believed that the defendant was the murderer, they would have avoided contact with him out of fear that he would contaminate them from the pollution that he carried as a killer.

28. Since the killer was thought to be polluted and capable of contaminating those who came in touch with him, the family made a series of proclamations, first at the burial and then in the agora, ordering the murderer to stay away from places specified by law, which included the temples, the agora, and other public areas and buildings. Until the family came before the *basileus* to lodge the charge and he registered the case and made his own proclamation, the ban from public places was not legally enforceable (see **36**, **38**; MacDowell 1963: 24–26).

proclamation that I was barred from places the law prescribed because they thought that this was their only salvation and escape from all troubles. [36] The law states that once someone is registered as charged with homicide, he is barred from the places the law prescribes. I could not prosecute if I was barred from places prescribed by law, and if the person who denounced them and knew well the facts could not prosecute them, they would easily be acquitted and escape punishment for their crimes. And I was not the first victim of the machinations of Philinus and the rest; they tried this before with Lysistratus, as you have already heard.[29] [37] They were willing to register me right away, on the day after the boy was buried, before they had even purified the house and performed the appropriate rites, carefully choosing the day when the first of them was to go on trial, so that I could not prosecute even one of them and expose their crimes in court.

[38] When the *basileus* read them the laws, and explained that there was not enough time to register the charge and complete the necessary number of summonses, I brought to court those involved in these machinations, and I secured the conviction of all of them, and they suffered the punishment which you already know.[30] Thus, these people here were unable to offer the assistance that they had been paid to provide. At that point they approached me and some common friends, begging for a reconciliation,

---

29. The unique requirements of homicide cases certainly afforded litigants the opportunity to exploit the legal system, whether as a way of blocking litigation in unrelated matters, as the speaker alleges here, or as weapon against political rivals. In the speech, "Against Neaera," Theomnestus suggests that the homicide proceedings were unjustly used to temporarily remove his father-in-law, Apollodorus, from the political stage of Athens ([Dem.] 59.9–10). One can imagine, however, that few people would have been willing to swear destruction upon themselves and their family and then proceed to lie unless they were in grave danger or the stakes were high.

30. Each magistrate had to undergo an audit (*euthyna*) at the end of his term and give an account of his year in office, and according to the speaker, the *basileus* could not leave any of his work unfinished for his successor to complete. Since murder cases normally included three preliminary hearings (*prodikasiai*), which had to be held in three successive months before the actual trial took place, new murder cases could not begin in the last two months of the year and had to be postponed until the new *basileus* took office. The chorus producer was, as a result, able to continue with his original prosecution of his opponents before the popular courts and secure their conviction before he could be prosecuted for murder. Gagarin (1997: 243) suggests that this interpretation of the law is not entirely correct. While the *basileus* had the discretion to refuse a case that could not be completed during his term, he was not legally required to do so. This explains why the prosecutor claims that the *basileus* had acted unfairly, but did not speak up against him at his audit (see 43).

and they were even prepared to make restitution for their previous wrong-doings. [39] I was persuaded by my friends and agreed to a reconciliation during the festival of the Diipoleia³¹ in the presence of witnesses, who reconciled us in the temple of Athena. Afterwards, we met and talked in the temples, in the agora, in my house, in theirs, and everywhere else. [40] Finally, by Zeus and all the gods, Philocrates here stood with me on the podium in the Council House in front of the entire Council; he was touching me and having a conversation, calling me by name, and I was calling him by name too. As a result, the Council thought that it was incredible when it found out that the very people they saw the day before talking and associating with me had made a proclamation that I should stay away from places prescribed by law.

[41] Consider this and remember my words, men. Not only will I prove to you with witnesses, but you will also easily realize that I am telling the truth from their very own actions. First, their accusation that the *basileus* was unwilling to accept the prosecution because of pressure from me will serve as proof that they are not telling the truth. [42] Once he accepted the prosecution, he had to make three preliminary hearings in three months and bring the case to trial on the fourth month, as has happened with these proceedings.³² He, however, had only two months left in his term of office, the Thargelion and the Skirophorion.³³ He could not, of course, bring the case to trial himself, nor is it possible to hand over a homicide trial; no *basileus* has ever handed over a homicide trial to his successor in this land. Since he could not introduce it to court nor hand it over, he did not venture to register the case against your laws. [43] This is the greatest proof that he has not done them any wrong: Philocrates here hounded other magistrates when they were being audited with malicious accusations (sykophancy), but he did not come forward to prosecute that very same *basileus* at his audit who he claims has done terrible and awful things.³⁴ What would be greater proof for you that he was not injured either by me or by him?

---

31. Based on a note of Harpocration, Scheibe suggests that the text refers to the festival of Diipoleia, celebrated on the Acropolis in early summer.

32. The magistrate who received the charge also typically presided over the court that heard the case, but he had no authority to decide either the verdict or the penalty. In the homicide courts, this decision belonged to the Areopagus or the fifty-one *ephetai*. In the popular law courts, the decision belonged to a large jury of citizens (see the Introduction).

33. These are the last two months of the Attic calendar (i.e., May/June and June/July). The Athenian year began in the summer on the new moon following the summer solstice.

34. For sykophancy, see **Lys. 12.5** n.

[44] When the current *basileus* took office, starting with the first day of Hecatombaeon, there were thirty consecutive days, on whichever of them they wanted, they could have registered their charge, and yet they did not do so. And then starting from the first day of Metageitnion, they could have registered their charge on any day they wanted, and still they did not do so, but another twenty days of this month passed by. So the total number of days was more than fifty, during the term of this *basileus,* on which they could have registered their charge but did not. [45] Everyone else who does not have sufficient time to complete the process under the same *basileus* . . .[35] However, despite the fact that they knew all the laws, they saw me serving as a member of the Council and entering the Council House— and in the Council House itself there is a shrine of Zeus the Councilor and Athena the Councilor, and the members of the Council pray as they enter, and I was one of them and did the same. I entered into all the other temples with the Council, and I sacrificed and said prayers on behalf of this city, and moreover, I served as one of the *prytaneis*[36] through the entire first prytany except for two days, performing religious duties and sacrifices on behalf of our democracy. I was openly supervising the voting and making proposals on the most important and worthy matters in the city. [46] They were present in town, and although they could have registered the case and barred me from all of this, they did not think that they ought to do so. If they had been wronged, they had sufficient reasons to remember and be angry for their own sake and that of the city. So why did they not register the case? This is because they were socializing with me and talking to me, and they were socializing with me because they did not believe that I killed the boy, was guilty of the murder, or had anything to do with these charges.

[47] How could men be more wretched or criminal than those who try to convince you, when they are not convinced themselves, and ask you to find guilty whom they have acquitted by their own actions? While others prove words with facts, they seek to make facts unbelievable with words. [48] Even if I had not said or proven anything else, and even if I had not presented any witnesses but I demonstrated only this, that when they were bribed to come after me, they made accusations and proclamations,

---

35. Undoubtedly a phrase or two have been accidentally omitted in our copies, probably saying that everyone else who could not complete the process in the end of the year would rush to begin the prosecution as soon as there was a new *basileus* in place.

36. For one-tenth of the year called a prytany, a councilor served as one of the *prytaneis* together with the other councilors from his tribe, and they presided over the Council. This service was rotated so that each tribe had a prytany.

but when no one was around to bribe them, they met and spoke with me, this alone should have been sufficient proof to acquit me and consider them the worst perjurers and the most unholy men. [49] What charge would these men not bring to court, which jury would they not mislead, what oath would they not dare to break, when they even recently accepted a bribe of thirty minas from the public fundraisers, the sellers, the fine collectors, and the undersecretaries who assist them?[37] They expelled me from the Council House, and took such solemn oaths, simply because when I was one of the presidents I found out that they were committing terrible and appalling crimes, denounced them before the Council, and proposed that the Council should investigate and prosecute the matter. [50] Now they, and those with whom the money was deposited, have paid the penalty for the wrongs they have committed, and their actions have been exposed so that they will not easily be able to deny them even if they want to. This is how things have turned out for them. [51] Which court would they not try to deceive, which oath would they not dare to break—these impious men, who know that you are the most pious and fairest jurors among the Greeks, and still they come to you with the intent to deceive you, if they can, with such solemn oaths?

---

37. The fundraisers (*poristai*) were public officials who prepared reports on how the state could raise needed funds, the sellers (*poletai*) sold property confiscated by the state, and the fine-collectors (*practores*) collected fines imposed by magistrates or courts. All these public officials, as well as the secretaries who assisted them, managed public money and, according to the speaker, were corrupt. For that reason, they paid thirty minas to have their accuser disqualified and at least temporarily removed from public life.

LYSIAS 1

ON THE MURDER OF ERATOSTHENES

Introduction

This speech was written for Euphiletus, who was charged with the murder of Eratosthenes. Euphiletus admits that he killed Eratosthenes, but he argues that he did so when he caught Eratosthenes having sex with his wife, and therefore he is protected by the law on justifiable homicide. Such cases were heard in the Delphinium before a board of *ephetai* (see the introduction to **Antiphon 6**). The law on justifiable homicide granted immunity for a contestant who unintentionally killed a competitor in an athletic competition, a soldier who mistakenly killed one of his comrades in battle, and a doctor whose patient died while under his care. An individual who protected himself or his property during an attack was also covered if he killed, in self defense, an individual who attacked him first, a thief who used force or committed the theft at night, or a highway robber at anytime. One was also permitted to kill an individual exiled for murder, if he illegally returned to Athens, and anyone caught trying to overthrow the democracy (MacDowell 1963: 70–84).

The application of the law on justifiable homicide in cases concerning sexual misconduct is difficult for the modern observer to understand for three reasons. First, the law on seduction (*moicheia*) rendered it illegal for a man to have a sexual relationship with a respectable Athenian woman without the consent of her guardian (*kyrios*).[1] Unlike wives, Athenian husbands were not legally required to remain faithful and could have sexual relationships that a modern reader would now classify as adulterous.[2] Second, the law applied to any Athenian woman who was not a prostitute. It covered not only married women but also unmarried daughters and sisters and in theory even widows, in which case the offense was against the male guardian of the house (i.e., the father, brother, or son). Thus, certain sexual

---

Translated by Andrew Wolpert.

1. See Paterson 1998: 107–25; Omitowoju 2002: 72–115; Todd 2007: 46–49; contra Cohen (1991: 98–132), who argues from comparative evidence that *moicheia* only applied to married women. There is much uncertainty over the extent to which the law on *moicheia* applied to non-Athenian women.

2. There are, however, instances when men sometimes chose to refrain from such extramarital relationships or at least from participating in such relationships openly, out of respect for their wives (e.g., **[Dem.] 59.21–22, 29–30**).

relationships that a modern reader would not classify as adulterous were considered unlawful in Athens. This is why *moicheia* is translated in our text as "seduction," as it is commonly elsewhere, although the English word "seduction" might not connote as serious an offense as the Greek *moicheia* did for the Athenians. The sexual activity of free women was regulated in Athens not primarily for religious or moral reasons but because the right of an Athenian man to hold citizenship, inherit his father's estate, and own landed property stemmed from the legitimacy of his birth.[3] Finally, Lysias 1 concerns an individual caught in the act of seduction, and Euphiletus claims that seduction was a more serious offense than rape. However, the law on justifiable homicide did not specifically address the question of consent. It applied to any man caught engaging in sexual intercourse with a respectable Athenian woman without the consent of the guardian. The law, therefore, applied equally to cases of rape (see **32** n.).

Euphiletus does not depict the murder of Eratosthenes as a crime of passion, caused by a fit of anger as he saw Eratosthenes in bed with his wife. Rather he insists that he was merely doing as the law mandated (**26**). Despite his assertions, he was under no such obligation. The law only granted him immunity if the seducer was caught in the act. Euphiletus was not prohibited from accepting Eratosthenes' monetary offer (**25**), and he could have chosen instead to subject him to physical abuse (see Kapparis 1996). But by declaring that he had no choice, he simplified his defense and did not have to explain why he chose a punishment that some might have considered extreme and why he did not show mercy to Eratosthenes when he was pleading for his life. Moreover, it would have been difficult for Euphiletus to present the murder as a crime of passion, when two slaves had told him about the affair. Could he really claim that he caught his wife in bed with another man when he already knew about the affair and even arranged to kill Eratosthenes when he found him next with his wife? Euphiletus, however, undercuts the force of such questions by explaining how he was only filled with suspicion when he heard about the affair from the jilted lover's slave (**17**), and then, even after his own slave confirmed it, he was still not convinced but needed proof (**21**). The status of the two slave women gave him the grounds for arguing that evidence of the affair was lacking until he saw it with his own two eyes. So too Euphiletus carefully portrays himself as naïve and too trusting, both to explain how it was possible for his wife to have an affair with another man without him noticing and to dispel any suspicion that he was capable of entrapping Eratosthenes.[4]

---

3. Metics could only own landed property by special grants.

4. For characterization in Lysias 1, see Usher 1965: 102–4; Carey 1989: 75–76; Todd 2007: 50–52.

At first glance, the case of the defense appears quite compelling. Euphiletus even had witnesses testify that they were present to see him come upon Eratosthenes lying naked in bed with Euphiletus' wife, in the throes of passion. The prosecution, we are told, intended to accuse him of having his slave bring Eratosthenes to his home in the night in question (**37**) and of dragging Eratosthenes from the streets and killing him as he sought refuge at Euphiletus' hearth (**27**). While Euphiletus may be distorting the prosecution's case so as to make the accusations appear unconvincing, we can reconstruct some elements of its case that are quite plausible. The prosecution probably argued that Euphiletus could not use justifiable homicide as a defense, since he trapped Eratosthenes and did not kill him on the spot and in the act. But did the prosecution have evidence to show that Euphiletus tricked Eratosthenes into believing his wife was preparing a rendezvous so that he could then catch Eratosthenes in the act? Would he have really dragged Eratosthenes into his house and killed him so that he could use justifiable homicide as a defense? These scenarios seem far-fetched, to say the least, but Euphiletus raises such suspicions by admitting that he told his slave that he wanted to wait to do anything until he found Eratosthenes in bed with his wife. So, too, it seems strange how he could have been in the house while his wife was sleeping with another man and not have heard any noise except that made by doors of the house (**14**). Lysias, however, keeps the jury's attention away from this question by having Euphiletus first discuss how his wife locked him in the upstairs bedroom so that she could then rendezvous with Eratosthenes (**11–13**). This encounter is even more puzzling and makes what happens next in the narrative seem quite plausible, given the preceding actions of Euphiletus and his wife. The defendant's case depends not only on the artful characterization of the parties involved in the dispute but also on the skillful arrangement of the narrative, which carefully paves the way so that the jury is prepared to accept the story as it unfolds.

The speech is especially useful to us for the information that it provides about the lives of Athenian women. On the one hand, it vividly reveals the views of Athenian men. Euphiletus mentions the men involved in the dispute but not the women, since it would have been shameful to have their names uttered in a public setting, especially when the circumstances were so embarrassing (see Schaps 1977). Even though his wife had brought him shame by committing adultery, and as a result he was required to divorce her, he still attempts to protect her from some of the humiliation for her actions. So too he does not blame her for the affair; he blames Eratosthenes. His wife was merely a victim, and for that matter, just one of Eratosthenes' victims, since he made it a habit of going around town seducing Athenian women (**16**). On the other hand, the speech shows us how we must be careful to distinguish ideology from practice. Although women are often depicted in our sources as living lives of seclusion, they clearly were involved in economic and religious activities that took them out of the home, as even Euphiletus acknowledges. We must, therefore, recognize that Athenian women spent most of their lives not in seclusion, but separated from men.[5] The speech also reveals that women were not merely the passive objects of men's desires, but they actively pursued their own interests, which sometimes brought them into conflict not only with their husbands and guardians but even with other women.[6]

Some have suggested that Eratosthenes, who is the subject of **Lysias 1**, was the same man Lysias prosecuted for his involvement in the rule of the Thirty (see the introduction to **Lysias 12**).[7] This is quite unlikely, since the oligarch was so famous that it would have been difficult for Euphiletus to claim he did not know him, and it is hard to imagine how he could have spoken against Eratosthenes without some reference to his involvement in the rule of the Thirty. Finally, there is some doubt whether the speech was delivered in court (see Porter 1997). The names of the two men involved are too coincidental: the etymology of Euphiletus is "beloved" while Eratosthenes' is "vigorous in love." Moreover, the description of the affair fits the pattern that is typical in Greek novels (see also Kapparis 2000). But as the saying goes, art imitates life. For that matter, there are many modern detective novels and dramas that not only are based upon actual crimes and trials but even advertise this fact to their audiences. So many legal cases are sensational that it is easy to doubt that the reported crimes took place unless one was a party of the dispute.

Key Information

Speaker	Euphiletus admitted that he killed Eratosthenes, but he claimed that the murder was not a punishable offense, since it happened when he caught Eratosthenes in the act with his wife.
Victim	Eratosthenes, who allegedly had an affair with Euphiletus' wife, was killed by him.
Other Individuals	Sostratus, a friend of Euphiletus, was in the house on the night of the murder.

---

5. Cohen 1989; 1991: 133–70; Katz 1995.

6. Johnstone 1998; Wolpert 2001.

7. See for example Avery 1991. Todd (2007: 60) suggests that Eratosthenes may have been a relative of the oligarch.

	The names of Euphiletus' wife and their slave and Eratosthenes' former lover are not provided.
Action	Justifiable homicide.
Court	The Delphinium.
Punishment	Execution and confiscation of property.
Date	Early fourth century.

On the Murder of Eratosthenes

[1] I would greatly appreciate it, men,[8] for you to judge me in this trial as you would judge yourselves if you had suffered what I have. I know well that if you should hold the same judgment about others as you do about yourselves, none of you would be upset at the things that have happened, but you would all consider the punishment minor for those who engage in such practices. [2] This view would be shared by not only you but all of Greece. This is the only offense for which democracy and oligarchy both grant the same compensation to the weakest against the strongest so that the lowliest enjoys the same rights as the highest. Hence, men, all consider this outrage[9] to be most terrible. [3] As for the severity of the punishment, I think that you all hold the same opinion, and no one is so remiss as to believe that those responsible for such acts ought to receive forgiveness or deserve a lesser punishment. [4] But I think, men, that I ought to prove that Eratosthenes seduced[10] my wife, corrupted her, brought shame on my children, and committed an outrage against me by going into my home. There existed no enmity between him and me other than this, and I did not act

---

8. Because this case was heard by a homicide court, Euphiletus does not address the members as "men of the jury" (*o andres dikastai*); see Todd 2007: 88. *O andres* is often translated into English as "sirs" or "gentlemen," which now are terms used generally to refer to men of any social class. We prefer instead the translation "men," since the Greek does not contain even a latent reference to class but does draw attention to the importance of masculinity in Athenian ideology; see Halperin 1990: 88–112; Winkler 1990: 45–70; Cohen 2002.

9. English does not have a word equivalent to the Greek *hybris,* but "outrage" is fairly close since *hybris* is an act that is intended to bring dishonor on another and is the result of an individual who excessively values his own worth, seeking to harm another for sheer pleasure. For more on the meaning of *hybris,* see the introduction to **Demosthenes 21**.

10. For *moicheia,* see the introduction to this speech.

for the sake of money in order that I might rise out of poverty to become rich, nor for any other gain except compensation in accordance with the laws. [5] I will, therefore, reveal to you all of my troubles from the beginning, leaving nothing out, but speaking the truth, since I believe that this is my only protection, if I can tell you all that happened.

[6] When I decided to marry, men of Athens, and I led my wife home, I first felt that I ought neither to bother her nor indulge her in whatever she wanted, but I watched her as much as I could and paid attention to her as was fitting. But when my child was born, then I trusted her and entrusted her with all of my possessions, since I thought that this was the best marriage. [7] At first, men of Athens, she was the best of all wives. She was a skillful and thrifty housekeeper, carefully looking after everything.[11] But when my mother died, her death was the cause of all my troubles. [8] My wife followed in her funeral procession and was seen by this man, who in time corrupted her.[12] By watching for the slave girl, who went to the agora,[13] and handing her messages, he caused her[14] downfall.

[9] First of all, men, I must tell you, my house is two stories, with the women's quarters on the second floor equal in size to the men's quarters below. But when our child was born, its mother nursed it. So that she wouldn't risk an accident every time she went downstairs to wash the child, I spent my time on the second floor while the women were on the first floor. [10] And we soon became so used to living like this that my wife often went downstairs to sleep with the child in order that she might nurse it and it wouldn't cry. For a long time this was our routine, and I never suspected anything but was so foolish as to believe that my wife was the most faithful of all the women in the city. [11] But when some time had passed, men, I came home unexpectedly from the country, and after dinner the child was crying and acting fussy. The slave girl was intentionally riling it up so that it would behave this way, since the man was inside: I later learned everything. [12] I told my wife to go downstairs and nurse the

---

11. Since much of the business of a farm and even a workshop was carried out inside the home by women, the wife had important responsibilities that extended well beyond what is sometimes supposed about the modern housekeeper.

12. With the death of his mother, Euphiletus lost an important ally who could tell him about what was going on in the house while he was away. It is unclear what Eratosthenes was doing at the funeral. Was he a relative or was he just passing by? The former seems unlikely since Euphiletus claims that he had never seen Eratosthenes before the affair.

13. I.e., go to the market and run errands.

14. The ambiguity of the Greek is retained, but it seems more likely that Euphiletus is referring here to his wife and not the slave; see Todd: 2007: 97.

child to make it stop crying. She first refused, pretending that she was glad to see me home after so long. But when I began to get angry and I told her to go, she said, "You want to go after the slave girl here. You grabbed her before when you were drunk." [13] I laughed, and she stood up and closed the door on her way out, pretending to be playing around, and she locked it. I thought nothing of this and did not suspect her, but I was glad to sleep, since I had come from the country. [14] When it was almost morning she came and opened the door. I asked her why the doors made noises during the night, and she said that the lamp beside the child had gone out and she got a light from the neighbors. I didn't say anything, and I believed that this is what happened. But it occurred to me, men, that she had put makeup on even though it had not yet been thirty days since her brother had passed away. Nevertheless, I did not say anything about it but left in silence.

[15] After this, men, some time passed and I was completely unaware of my troubles, when an old slave woman approached me. She had been sent by a woman who had been seduced by Eratosthenes, as I later learned. Since she was upset and considered herself slighted because he no longer visited her, she kept a watch until she found out what the reason was. [16] The slave approached me near my house, where she was waiting, and she said, "Euphiletus, don't think that I am meddling by approaching you. The man committing this outrage against you and your wife happens to be our enemy. If you take the slave girl, who goes to the agora and serves you, and you torture her, you will learn everything. It is," she said, "Eratosthenes of the deme Oe, who does this. He has corrupted not only your wife but also many others. He makes this his trade." [17] After she said these things, men, she left, and I was immediately at a loss. Everything came back to my mind, and I was full of suspicion as I thought about how I had been locked up in the bedroom, and I remembered how the inner and outer doors[15] made noises during that night, which had never happened before, and it had occurred to me that my wife was wearing makeup. All these things came back to my mind, and I was full of suspicion. [18] After I came home, I ordered the slave girl to follow me to the agora, but I led her to the house of one of my friends, where I told her that I had learned all that had happened in our house. "You," I said, "have two choices, either to be whipped and then thrown into the mill and never stop suffering such torment, or to reveal the whole truth and not suffer any harm but win my forgiveness for your misbehavior. Don't lie, but speak the whole truth." [19] She first denied it and told me to do as I pleased since she didn't know anything.

---

15. A house typically had two sets of doors, one leading from the house to the courtyard and the other from the courtyard to the street (cf. **Lys. 12.15**). For the Greek house, see Nevett 1999.

But when I mentioned Eratosthenes to her and said that I knew that he was visiting my wife, she was shocked, thinking that I knew every last detail. So she then flung herself before my knees, and I promised her that she would not suffer any harm. [20] She first disclosed how he approached her after the funeral procession; then how she finally passed messages and how my wife was persuaded, in time; the different ways he gained entrance,[16] and how at the Thesmophoria[17] she went—when I was in the country—to the temple with Eratosthenes' mother. She reported precisely everything that had happened. [21] And when she had told me everything, I said, "See to it that no one will learn about this; otherwise, none of my promises to you will hold. I expect you to show it to me in the act. I don't need words but the deed to be revealed, if it is indeed true." She agreed to do this.

[22] Afterwards four or five days passed, as I will show you by compelling evidence.[18] But I first wish to explain what happened on the last day. I have a close friend named Sostratus. I met him at sunset as he was coming from the country. Since I knew that he was returning at a time when he would have nothing at home to eat, I invited him to dine with me. When we came to my house, we went to the second floor, where we ate. [23] When he was full, he left, and I went to sleep. Eratosthenes, men, entered, and the slave girl immediately woke me up and said that he was inside. I told her to watch the door, and I went downstairs and out of the house in silence. I came to the house of this man and that man. I found some at home, and I discovered that some were not in town. [24] Assembling as many as I could from those who were home, I walked back. We took torches from the closest tavern and entered the house. The door was open, thanks to the slave, who had it ready. We forced the door to the bedroom open, and those of us who entered first saw him still lying beside my wife while those entering later saw him standing naked on the bed. [25] I struck him, men, and threw him down. Pulling his hands behind his back and tying them, I asked why he was committing this outrage by invading my home. He admitted that he was guilty, but he begged and beseeched me not to kill him but to accept money. [26] And I said, "I will not kill you, but the law of the city will, which you violated and considered of less importance than your own pleasures. You preferred to commit such harm to my wife and my children than to obey the laws and to be a decent man."

---

16. Alternatively, "the different ways *she* provided him entry."

17. This religious festival, in honor of Demeter and in which only women participated, was celebrated in the fall; see Burkert 1985: 242–46.

18. Since Euphiletus does not elaborate, some suggest that there is a gap in the text; see Todd 2007: 115–16.

[27] So, men, that one received what the laws demand from those who commit such offenses. He was not seized from the road nor did he flee to the hearth as they allege.[19] For how could he, when he was struck in the bedroom and immediately fell down, and I tied his hands behind his back, and there were so many men inside that he could not flee since he did not have a knife or a club or any other weapon with which he could have warded off those approaching? [28] But, men, I believe that you also know that those who act unjustly do not admit that their enemies speak the truth, but through their lies and machinations they instill anger in their audience against those who act justly. So, first read the law.

LAW[20]

[29] He did not dispute, men, but admitted that he was guilty. He begged and pleaded that he not be killed, and he was ready to pay recompense. I did not agree to his assessment because I considered the law of the city to be of greater authority and exacted that punishment that you established for those who engage in such acts because you believe it to be most just. May the witnesses to this please come forward.

WITNESSES

[30] Please also read the law that is in front of the Areopagus.[21]

LAW

You hear, men, that the Areopagus, which has the ancestral right and continues to our day to judge homicide cases, expressly states that he is not guilty of murder who exacts this punishment when he seizes a seducer with his wife. [31] The lawgiver considered this to be so just in the case of wedded women that he imposed the same penalty in the case of concubines even though they are of lesser status.[22] And yet, it is clear that if he had a

---

19. The hearth was the religious focal point of the house, where a suppliant could try and seek sanctuary (see Carey and Reid 1985: 76; Todd: 2007: 122–23).

20. Typically the content of the laws and the statements of the witnesses, which the litigant asked to have read, are not included in the manuscripts.

21. The council of the Areopagus, consisting of ex-archons, functioned primarily as a homicide court.

22. Demosthenes (23.55) explains that the law applied in the case of concubines kept "for the purpose of free children."

greater penalty than this one in the case of wives, he would have assigned it. But as it is, since he was unable to find a greater penalty than this in the case of wives, he thought it right to apply the same penalty also in the case of concubines. Please also read this law.

LAW

[32] You hear, men, how the law orders, if someone rapes[23] a free man or boy, to pay double damages, and if he rapes one of those women, in whose case it is permitted to kill the seducer,[24] to apply the same penalty.[25] Hence, men, the lawgiver believed that those who use force deserve a lesser penalty than those who persuade.[26] He assigned death as a punishment for the latter and double damages for the former [33] because he recognized that those who accomplish their ends with force are hated by those whom they have violated and those who use persuasion so corrupt the women's minds that they make other men's wives more devoted to themselves than their husbands and all of the house comes under their control, and it becomes uncertain who are the children's fathers, the husbands or the seducers. The lawgiver, therefore, established the death penalty for them.

[34] Furthermore, men, the laws not only find me innocent but they even instruct me to exact this penalty. It is in your power to decide whether the laws must be enforced or are to be of no value. [35] I believe that all cities establish laws in order that we might go to them, whenever we are uncertain about something, and can decide what we must do. They instruct those who are the victims in such situations to exact this penalty.

---

23. Literally, "forcefully shames."

24. Here, Euphiletus is referring to that category of women for whom the law on seduction applies: wives, mothers, sisters, daughters, and free mistresses (and not prostitutes); see Carey 1989: 79.

25. That is to say, the damages in the case of rape of a free man, boy, or woman who has not engaged in prostitution were twice that of the damages in the case of rape of a slave.

26. This claim is misleading, since it was certainly the case that the law on justifiable homicide applied equally to cases of rape and seduction. Moreover, it is possible that a rapist was punishable for his offense by the law on *hybris*. On the other hand, there were certain penalties in cases of seduction that were not available for rape because of the social disgrace that the family suffered and the doubts that would have been raised about the parentage of the children once the extramarital relationship was exposed. A seducer could be kept against his will until he paid the ransom that the injured party demanded, or he could be subjected to physical abuse. See Harris 1990; Carey 1995a.

[36] I think that you ought to deliver the same judgment as the laws. Otherwise you will grant such immunity to seducers that you will even encourage thieves to say that they are seducers since they will know that if they claim this excuse for themselves and say that they enter others' houses for this reason, no one will touch them. As a result, all will know that they must say goodbye to the laws on seduction and fear your vote since it has the greatest authority over all in the city.

[37] Consider, men, as follows: they accuse me of ordering the slave girl to fetch the young man on that day. I, men, would regard my actions to be just if I tried in any way to seize the man who corrupted my wife. [38] If I ordered her to fetch him when words had been spoken but the deed had not been done, I would have been guilty. But if I seized him, however I could, after everything had already been done and he had entered my house on many occasions, I would think that I was acting with self-restraint. [39] But consider how they lie in this regard as well; you will easily learn this from what follows. As I was saying before, men, my close friend Sostratus met me as he was coming from the country at sunset, and he dined with me. When he was finished, he left. [40] First of all, men, consider the following: if I was plotting against Eratosthenes on that night, was it better for me to dine elsewhere or to bring Sostratus to my house to dine with me? The latter would have made Eratosthenes less likely to enter my house. In addition, does it seem likely to you that I would have dismissed my dinner companion and left myself alone and by myself, or would I have bid him to stay in order that he might help me avenge the seducer? [41] Furthermore, men, doesn't it seem likely to you that I would have sent messages to my friends during the day and bid them to assemble at the nearest of their houses rather than run around during the night, as soon as I was aware of Eratosthenes' presence, when I did not know whom I would find at home or who would be away? I came to the house of Harmodius and someone else's, even though they were not in town (since I did not know). I discovered that others were not in, and so I went, taking as many as I could find. [42] Yet surely if I had known beforehand, doesn't it seem likely that I would have readied my slaves and sent messages to my friends in order that I might enter as safely as possible (for how did I know whether he had some knife?), and would have sought revenge with as many witnesses as possible? As it turns out, I did not know what was going to happen on that night, and so I took whom I could find. May the witnesses to this please come forward.

WITNESSES

[43] You have heard the witnesses, men. Consider among yourselves about this matter accordingly, and examine whether there was ever any enmity between Eratosthenes and me other than this. You will find none.

[44] He did not maliciously lodge public suits against me,[27] nor try to have me expelled from the city, nor lodge private suits, nor was he aware of some wrong, which I feared that someone might learn about, and therefore wanted to kill him, nor did I expect to receive money from somewhere if I had carried out this deed. There are those who plot the death of one another for these reasons. [45] We were so far from being involved in some verbal or drunken altercation or any other dispute that I had never seen the man except for on that night. Why would I have been willing to take such a risk unless I had suffered the greatest injury at his hands? [46] Furthermore, did I summon witnesses to my impiety, although it was possible for no one to have knowledge of my acts if I desired to kill him unjustly?

[47] Therefore, men, I do not consider this to be my own private vengeance; it was on behalf of the entire city. Since those who commit such acts see the kind of prizes that await offenses of this sort, they will be less likely to harm others if they see that you hold the same opinion. [48] Otherwise it is much better to erase the established laws and create new ones that will punish those who keep a watch over their own wives and give full immunity to those who injure other men's wives. [49] That would be much more just than for citizens to be ensnared by the laws that order the person who catches a seducer to treat him however he wishes, while trials are rendered more terrifying to the victims than those who shame other men's wives in violation of the laws. [50] For now I am risking my life, my property, and everything else because I obeyed the laws of the city.[28]

---

27. I.e., engage in sykophancy; see **Lys. 12.5** n.

28. From this closing sentence, MacDowell (1963: 116–17) concludes that confiscation of property was an additional penalty imposed on a defendant for intentional homicide, whether he was found guilty and sentenced to death or fled Athens before delivering his second speech.

LYSIAS 12

AGAINST ERATOSTHENES

Introduction

This is the only extant speech in the corpus of Lysias that was intended for him to deliver on his own behalf in an Athenian court. It is also extraordinary because the defendant is Eratosthenes, a member of the Thirty, whom Lysias accused of being responsible for the murder of his brother, Polemarchus. It gives a unique autobiographical account of the life of Lysias during some of the most turbulent years in Athenian history and an overview of the rule of the Thirty from the perspective of one of their victims (cf. Lys. 13). There are some doubts—although not very compelling—about the likelihood that it was delivered in court, and some suggest instead that it was circulated as a political pamphlet. Still, it provides enormously useful information on the politics of reconciliation after the Thirty and the social divisions the Athenians faced as they attempted to come to terms with their past after a violent civil war.

In 404, the Athenians were forced to surrender to Sparta and accept the conditions that Theramenes had negotiated following the destruction of the Athenian fleet at the Battle of Aegospotami (405). Shortly after the surrender, conspirators with Spartan backing overthrew the democracy and installed an oligarchy, known as the Thirty, which was headed by Critias and included Theramenes and Eratosthenes, among others. The Thirty then proceeded to terrorize the population through a series of confiscations, banishments, and executions. They even rounded up the inhabitants of Eleusis and Salamis and executed some three hundred of them after they were tried in one mass group (**52**). By the time the democracy was restored in 403, only thirteen months after its overthrow, some fifteen hundred individuals were said to have been killed by the oligarchs. Clearly, much of their violence was directed against opposition and potential opposition, but it is also the case that terror was a means for the Thirty to repoliticize the community. Athens had been a participatory democracy that could not function unless thousands of citizens were actively involved in politics throughout the year by serving as officials and jurors and attending the meetings of the Assembly and their individual demes. This made it particularly difficult for the Thirty to establish a restrictive form of government and maintain their control after they had been responsible for disfranchising such a politically active citizen population and when

---

Translated by Andrew Wolpert.

only three thousand citizens were allowed some form of participation in the oligarchy. Violence became a way for the Thirty to recondition the population, force the disfranchised to accept their new role as political subjects, and isolate them so that they could not form effective resistance (see Wolpert 2006).

Such authoritarian regimes are, however, inherently unstable, and it was only a matter of time before the Thirty were ousted. In the winter of 403, Thrasybulus set out from Thebes with a band of seventy exiles and successfully seized the Athenian fort at Phyle, located in the rugged terrain bordering Boeotia. After the Thirty suffered additional reversals, they tried and executed Theramenes, accusing him of attempting to save himself by plotting against the oligarchy, just as he had done during the rule of the Four Hundred in 411. Thrasybulus then defeated the oligarchs in a battle in which Critias was killed, and he seized the Piraeus, the principal port of Athens, making it his base of operation for the rest of the civil war. Other exiles joined Thrasybulus and his supporters in the Piraeus and provided them with additional aid. For this reason, the democratic exiles were later referred to often as "the men of Piraeus." In contrast to the title, "the men of Phyle," which sometimes was also used and served to remind the audience of the origins of the democratic resistance, the "men of the Piraeus" was a title that was more inclusive and called to mind the eventual success of the democratic rebels. Meanwhile, the men in the city deposed the Thirty, who fled to Eleusis, and elected a board of ten, ostensibly for the purpose of settling their differences with Thrasybulus and his supporters, but the Ten continued the war against the democrats until Sparta negotiated a peace that restored the democracy (**53–60**).

Under the terms of the peace agreement, the men who had remained in the city during the civil war had two choices. They could live in Athens under the restored democracy, where there would be an amnesty for all offenses except for murder "by one's own hands," which was extended without other conditions to most Athenians and to the leaders of the oligarchy, including the Thirty and the Ten, if they submitted to an audit (*euthyna*). Those who did not want to live with the democrats were permitted to settle in Eleusis, which the Thirty had already taken, and live there as a separate and autonomous community by their own laws. The community at Eleusis, however, only lasted until 401, when the democrats attacked it because they had learned that the residents were planning to retake Athens. The amnesty was then extended to the survivors, and Eleusis was reincorporated.[1]

---

1. Arist. *Ath. Pol.* 39–40; Xen. *Hell.* 2.4.39–43. See Krentz 1982: 102–24, 31–52; Wolpert 2002: 15–35. For an alternate chronology of the amnesty, see Carawan 2006.

There is ample praise in the ancient testimony for the restraint that the Athenians exhibited following the restoration of the democracy, and indeed the absence of insurgency after 401 suggests that it was a success. But as the legal cases from this time period reveal, it was much more complicated to end the hostilities that surfaced during the civil war than such blanket statements suggest. Even if victims could not prosecute perpetrators for crimes committed during the civil war, they sometimes called to mind the atrocities of the Thirty in trials concerning unrelated offenses. They also had more routine occasions when they could recall events that had happened during the civil war, such as when their opponents had to undergo a scrutiny before holding a political office (e.g., **Lys. 16**). Many were upset over their losses and their suffering, and many were complicit in the atrocities of the Thirty. This anger and resentment did not simply vanish overnight, nor was it easy for the Athenians to explain how they could have treated each other in such a fashion. Those in the city often attempted to present themselves as though they had been biding their time until they could actively oppose the Thirty, and some (as Lysias' speech against Eratosthenes reveals) even presented themselves as part of a group working with Theramenes to overthrow the oligarchs from within. Even those who supported the exiles were not without suspicion. Doubts were easy to raise about their actions prior to joining the exiles. In the end, there were so many divisions in Athens after the civil war that it was difficult to pursue a campaign of recrimination against any particular group, and it was easier to heap most of the blame on those in the upper echelon of the oligarchy, who were formally excluded from the amnesty.

For that reason, Eratosthenes' task was particularly onerous. He even admitted that he was responsible for the arrest of Polemarchus, which resulted in his summary execution, and this was the main grounds for Lysias' prosecution. At the same time, Eratosthenes also insisted that he spoke out against the arrests of the metics when the Thirty were considering the plan and that he participated in the order only because he feared reprisals from his colleagues if he refused (**25**). Moreover, based on Lysias' speech, it appears that Eratosthenes attempted to present himself as consistently in opposition to the brutal policies of the Thirty. He supported the cause of Theramenes (**62–68**), who allegedly favored a more moderate government, and the men of the city even allowed Eratosthenes to remain in Athens after they deposed the Thirty (**53–54**). Lysias, in response, spends a significant portion of his own speech trying to debunk this positive portrayal of Theramenes and the Ten and proving that the oligarchs were not at odds with each other over policy, but leadership roles (**38–78**).

The content of the speech suggests that it was intended for either a murder trial or Eratosthenes' audit, since he had been a member of the Thirty and could only have participated in the amnesty after undergoing an audit. The former, however, is unlikely. Eratosthenes could only have been tried for murder if he had passed his audit. Then the terms of the amnesty would have provided him with legal protection, and Lysias would have needed to prove that Eratosthenes' actions constituted murder "by his own hands" (cf. Lys. 13.85–87). But unlike in his speech against Agoratus, Lysias does not explicitly make such an accusation against Eratosthenes. Therefore, if the speech was delivered in court, it was heard shortly after the reconciliation at Eratosthenes' audit (Todd 2000: 13–14). There has been some doubt about whether Eratosthenes would have taken his chances with an audit and whether Lysias would have been permitted to bring an action against him if he did so. Some suggest that Lysias may have circulated the speech as a political pamphlet to show how he would have challenged Eratosthenes if he had been willing to submit to an audit. Since Lysias spent the rest of his life as a metic exempt from paying the resident alien tax (*isoteles*), he could only have brought the case to an Athenian court if such metics generally had this privilege, if he was subsequently granted this right for his assistance to the democratic exiles, or if the reconciliation agreement allowed metics to bring forth accusations against the oligarchs on their own behalf (see Todd 2007: 13–16).

It is possible that too much doubt has been raised concerning the delivery of the speech simply because Lysias was a metic. We have little reason to assume that only citizens were allowed to speak at an audit. Unfortunately, evidence is lacking to prove this. One might be tempted to try and resolve the question of delivery by considering instead the status of the defendant. It is hard to imagine that Eratosthenes, as a former member of the Thirty, would have been willing to take his chances and undergo an audit rather than join the oligarchs living in Eleusis. But we must remember that Eratosthenes stayed in Athens after the Thirty were deposed (**54**), and Rhinon, who was a member of the Ten, not only passed his audit but was even elected to be a general under the restored democracy (Arist. *Ath. Pol.* 38.4). The corpus of the Attic orators is, in so many ways, a collection of exceptional and extraordinary cases that we cannot rule out the possibility that the speech was heard in court simply because it was so unusual. That, after all, is one of the main reasons why it has survived.[2]

---

2. For further discussion on the Athenian civil war and reconciliation, see Krentz 1982; Loraux 2002; Wolpert 2002.

Key Information

Speaker	Lysias, a metic (resident alien), lodged an objection against Eratosthenes when Eratosthenes sought to live in Athens under the restored democracy and enjoy the rights and privileges of the amnesty.
Defendant	Eratosthenes had served as a member of the Thirty that ruled Athens from 404–403.
Other Individuals	Polemarchus, Lysias' brother, was arrested by Eratosthenes and executed during the rule of the Thirty.
	Theognis, Peison, Melobius, and Mnesitheides were members of the Thirty who participated in the arrest of the metics.
	Damnippus, Lysias' friend, agreed to help Lysias escape when he was seized by the Thirty and brought to Damnippus' house.
	Theramenes was a member of the Thirty who was executed when he opposed Critias, the leader of the oligarchs.
	Thrasybulus led the democratic resistance that overthrew the Thirty.
Action	Audit (*euthyna*) before a law court to determine whether Eratosthenes would be granted civic rights under the restored democracy and be protected by the terms of the amnesty, or whether he could be held liable for offenses that he committed during the civil war.
Date	Shortly after the restoration of the Athenian democracy in 403.

Against Eratosthenes

[1] Beginning my accusation does not seem to me to pose a problem, men of the jury; how to stop speaking does. They have carried out against the people offenses that are so many and so great that one could not even by lying accuse them of crimes worse than what they have done, nor could

one who wants to tell the truth say everything, but either the prosecutor must fall into exhaustion or his time run out. [2] I think that my situation will be the opposite of what prosecutors have encountered in the past when they had to explain their hostility for the defendants. Now it is necessary to ask the defendants why they are hostile to the city and what caused them to dare to commit such offenses against it. I do not, however, make these statements because of a lack of private enmity or misfortune but because all have a great abundance of animosity either for personal reasons or on behalf of the public.[3] [3] Although I have never, men of the jury, brought an action on behalf of myself or another, I am now compelled to prosecute this man because of what he did. So I have often fallen into despair out of fear that my inexperience will cause my prosecution to be less than what it should and can be for my brother and myself.[4] Still, I will attempt to explain my case to you from the beginning, as briefly as I can.

[4] Pericles[5] persuaded my father, Cephalus, to immigrate to this land, where he lived for thirty years, and never did he or any of us appear in a lawsuit as a prosecutor or a defendant, but we lived under the democracy so as to neither injure nor be injured by another. [5] But when the Thirty came to power, behaving as wicked sykophants,[6] but saying that they had to purge the city of criminals and make the rest of the citizens good and law abiding, they dared no such thing in spite of what they said, as I will try to remind you, speaking first about my own troubles and then about yours. [6] Theognis and Peison spoke among the Thirty about the

---

3. Here Lysias seeks to balance both his need to explain his own personal reasons for his appearance in court and his recognition of the impact Eratosthenes' offenses have had on the entire community of Athens.

4. Litigants regularly attempted to gain the trust of the jury by remarking on their inexperience in litigation; cf. **Dem. 32.3**; **41.3**; **[Dem.] 53.13, 59.14**; see Ober 1989: 165–77.

5. This is a reference to the famous Athenian leader who introduced pay for jury duty, promoted military policies that led to the expansion of the Athenian empire and war with Sparta, and is perhaps most known for the funeral speech that he delivered after the first year of the Peloponnesian War as recorded by Thucydides.

6. Sykophants were individuals who intentionally lodged or threatened to lodge malicious accusations, often for financial gain, as is the case here, since Lysias accuses the Thirty of arresting metics in order to take their property. Because sykophants were regularly viewed as harassing rich and prominent Athenians and as part of the excesses of democracy, this co-opting of the term by Lysias to describe the Thirty is ironic and has the effect of throwing elite criticism back onto itself. For further discussion on sykophancy, see Harvey 1990; Osborne 1990; Christ 1998.

metics,[7] how there were some who were hostile to the government, and by appearing to punish them, they had a perfect pretense for actually making money, since the city was broke and the regime needed revenue. [7] They persuaded their listeners without any difficulty, since they thought nothing of killing people and everything of getting hold of money. So they decided to seize ten men, two of whom were poor, in order that they could offer the excuse to others that their actions were not for the sake of their own gain but in the interest of the city, as if they had reasonable explanations for any of their other actions! [8] After dividing up the houses, they headed for them. They seized me while I was entertaining some guests,[8] and they drove them out and handed me over to Peison. The others went to my workshop and took an inventory[9] of my slaves. I asked Peison if he would be willing to save me if I gave him money. He said that he would, but it would have to be a lot. [9] So I said that I was ready to pay him a talent of silver, and he agreed to this.[10] Although I did not believe that they had any regard for gods or men, nevertheless I thought that it was particularly necessary in the present situation to make him promise me. [10] After he swore an oath that he would save me if he received a talent, invoking destruction upon himself and his children, I went into the bedroom and opened up the chest. Peison noticed and entered. He called out to two of his attendants when he saw the contents and told them to seize what was in the chest. [11] Since he had not

---

7. Theognis and Peison were members of the Thirty. As resident aliens, metics were easy targets of the new regime because they did not have citizen rights. Metics often had long-standing ties to Athens, since the Athenians rarely granted citizenship to resident aliens and quite a few came from families that had lived in Athens for many generations. They served in Athenian armies, paid taxes, and showed their loyalty to the Athenian people through other acts of public generosity, such as those described by Lysias (**20**). So even though they may not have been citizens, the Thirty had good reason to believe metics opposed them and wanted to help the democratic opposition, and as it turns out, many did.

8. The Athenians regarded such invasions into peoples' private homes as particularly heinous and typical of the lawlessness that characterizes tyrannical and oligarchic regimes (cf. **30**). Democracies, by contrast, were viewed as respecting the sanctity of the private sphere because they promote and adhere to the rule of law (Cohen 1991: 228–31).

9. The purpose of this inventory (*apographe*) was to keep track of the number of slaves to be confiscated.

10. This is a considerable sum of money. For an Athenian to be a member of the liturgical class and thus required to perform public services for the city, such as the trierarchy, he had to own property worth three or four talents. It would take an ordinary Athenian more than ten years to earn one talent; see Hansen 1991: 115.

what we agreed to, men of the jury, but three talents of silver, four hundred Cyzicene staters, one hundred Persian darics, and four silver cups,[11] I asked him to give me travel money, and he said that I should be glad to be alive. [12] Melobius and Mnesitheides,[12] who were coming from the workshop, happened upon us as we were leaving, and finding us at the door they asked us where we were going. Peison said to my brother's house in order to examine its contents as well. They told him to go and ordered me to follow them to Damnippus' house. [13] Peison went up to me and told me to keep quiet and not to worry, since he would be going there. At Damnippus' house, we found Theognis guarding some others. They handed me over to him and left again. I decided to take my chances at this moment, since death was now awaiting me. [14] Calling out to Damnippus, I said to him, "You are my friend, and I come to your house. I have done no wrong, and yet I am to die because of money. Since I am in this predicament, see to it that you work zealously for my safety." He promised to do so, but he thought that it would be better for him to speak with Theognis, since he thought that Theognis would do anything for money. [15] While he was speaking with Theognis (I happened to be familiar with the house and knew that it had two entrances),[13] I therefore decided to try to save myself. I thought that either I would be saved if I went undetected or, if I were caught and Damnippus had persuaded Theognis to accept the money, I would be released nonetheless, and if he didn't, I would die all the same. [16] With this resolve, I fled while they were guarding the outer door. All three doors I had to go through happened to be open. After I arrived at the house of Archeneus, the shipowner, I had him go to the city[14] to find out about my brother. When he returned he reported that Eratosthenes seized him on the road and led him away to prison. Upon hearing the news, I sailed the following night

---

11. In the ancient world, wealthy individuals often kept a sizeable amount of cash at home, since banks were not insured and there was always the danger that the depositor would lose all of his money if the bank failed.

12. Two other members of the Thirty.

13. I.e., it had two separate entranceways from the street. Houses normally had an outer door leading from the street to the courtyard and an inner door leading from the courtyard into the house (cf. **Lys. 1.17**). Damnippus' house apparently had a second outer door that opened onto the street and presumably was not being guarded because such a configuration was not typical.

14. Archeneus' house was located in the Piraeus, the port of Athens. Information on the fate of Lysias' brother was most likely to come from Athens, where the Thirty were conducting their affairs, but Lysias was a wanted man and could not return to the city without jeopardizing his own safety. So he sent Archeneus.

to Megara. [17] The Thirty gave their customary order to Polemarchus to drink hemlock without explaining why he was to be executed. So far was he from having a trial and the opportunity to defend himself! [18] When his dead body was carried out of the prison, they[15] were not allowed to conduct his funeral from any of our three houses but had to rent a hut where they laid him out. Although we had many cloaks, they were not given one for the burial in spite of their requests, but one of our friends gave a cloak for the funeral, another a pillow, and everyone else whatever they had. [19] They had seven hundred of our shields; so much silver and gold; bronze, ornaments, furniture, and women's clothing, more than they expected to get; and one hundred twenty slaves, of which they kept the most fit and handed the remaining over to the treasury. Yet they were so insatiable and shameless in their greed as to reveal their real character: the gold earrings that the wife of Polemarchus happened to be wearing Melobius snatched from her ears as soon as he entered the house. [20] They were not moved to show us pity for even the tiniest piece of our property. They committed the kind of offenses against us for money that others would do out of anger over serious infractions. We did not deserve this from the city after we had produced choruses, often paid the war taxes, lived in a decent manner, followed every order, made no one into an adversary, and ransomed many Athenians from the enemy.[16] Yet they thought that such was what we deserved despite the fact that we conducted ourselves so much better as metics than they did as citizens! [21] They drove many citizens to the enemy, they illegally killed many men and denied them burial, they disfranchised many full citizens, and they prevented the daughters of many from marrying.[17] [22] They have now reached such a height of audacity as to come here and defend themselves, and they say that they have not done anything terrible or shameful. I would wish that they were telling the truth, since my share in the gain would not be the smallest. [23] But as it turns out, their conduct neither toward the city nor toward me was as they describe. My brother, as I said before, was killed by Eratosthenes, not because he suffered a private

---

15. This use of the third person serves in an understated way to indicate to the jury that Lysias could not participate in his brother's funeral because he was in exile, and it adds to the pathos of the narrative.

16. Even wealthy metics were required to perform some liturgies, such as the *choregia,* which entailed serving as the producer of a chorus and paying for its production, and had to pay the war tax (*eisphora*); see **Dem. 21.1** n.

17. By confiscating the property of their opponents, the Thirty deprived them of the means of providing dowries for their daughters, who as a result could not get married.

wrong or saw Polemarchus committing an offense against the city but because he was eagerly satisfying his lawless appetite. [24] I would like to bring him to the podium and question him, men of the jury.[18] As far as I am concerned, I think that it is impious even to discuss this man with another, should it benefit him, but it is right and holy to speak with him should it be to his detriment.[19] Therefore, please come to the podium and answer what I ask you.

[25] Lysias: Did you or did you not arrest Polemarchus?

Eratosthenes: I did what the rulers commanded, out of fear.

Lysias: Were you in the Council when there was a discussion about us?

Eratosthenes: I was.

Lysias: Did you speak in favor or against those calling for us to be killed?

Eratosthenes: I spoke against, in order that you not be killed.

Lysias: Do you believe that we were harmed unjustly?

Eratosthenes: Yes.

[26] Are you saying, most cruel of all men, that you spoke out in opposition in order to save us and you took part in the arrests in order to kill us? When the power rested in the majority of you to save us, you say that you spoke in opposition to those who recommended that we die, but when the power was with you alone either to save Polemarchus or not, you led him away to prison? So then, do you think that you deserve to be considered a good man because, as you say, you spoke out in opposition even though you provided no help, and although you arrested him and had him killed, you don't believe that you should pay the penalty to me and these men here?

[27] Besides, even if he is telling the truth when he says that he spoke out against the decision, one should not believe that he was following their orders.[20] They certainly did not use metics to test his loyalty. Who was less likely to receive the order than the man who made his opinion known by speaking out against it? And who was less likely to obey than the man who spoke out against what they wanted done? [28] Yet I think that it is a reasonable excuse for the rest of the Athenians to blame the Thirty for what happened. But if the Thirty blame themselves, how is it reasonable for you to accept this excuse? [29] If there was some more powerful authority in the city that illegally ordered him to kill men, it would perhaps

---

18. Although witnesses could not be questioned and could only have their statements read in court, litigants were allowed to cross-examine the opposing side; cf. Lys. 22.5; Pl. *Ap.* 24d1–26d7.

19. A murderer was considered polluted, and therefore had to be avoided; cf. **Ant. 6.34, 40**; **Dem. 21.118–20**.

20. I.e., his actions imply consent.

be reasonable for you to forgive him. But whom then will you ever punish if the Thirty will be permitted to say that they were doing what the Thirty ordered? [30] Furthermore, it was not in his house, but on the street, where he arrested Polemarchus and led him away, although he could have saved him and obeyed the orders of the Thirty.[21] You are angry with all who entered your houses in order to search for either you or one of your family members.[22] [31] Yet, if you must forgive those who caused the death of others in order to save themselves, it would be more just for you to do so in the case of those men. It was dangerous for them not to go where they were sent or to deny finding their victim. Eratosthenes, however, could have said that he did not come upon Polemarchus or see him, since there was no proof or test that, even if his enemies wanted to, could disprove him. [32] If you really were a good man, Eratosthenes, you ought all the more to have informed those going to die unjustly rather than to arrest them. But as it turns out, your actions have shown that you were not upset with what was taking place but delighted in it. [33] The jurors must therefore base their verdict on your actions rather than your words and must consider what they know that you have done as evidence for what you said at that time, since witnesses to your statements cannot be furnished. We were barred not only from their meetings but even from our own homes; this is why, in spite of all of the harm that they have done to the city, they can speak of all their good. [34] I, however, do not dispute this claim but concede to you, if you want, that you spoke out against the arrests. Yet I wonder what on earth you would have done if you had spoken in favor of the proposal when you had Polemarchus killed after allegedly speaking out in opposition.

Suppose you were the brothers or sons of this man, what would you have done? Would you have acquitted him? But, men of the jury, Eratosthenes must show either that he did not arrest Polemarchus or that he did so justly. Yet, he has admitted that he arrested him unjustly so that he has made it easy for you to render your verdict about him. [35] Many citizens and foreigners have come here to learn what your decision will be in these matters.[23] Your fellow citizens will leave having learned that

---

21. I.e., Eratosthenes could have used the excuse that he had gone to Polemarchus' house to arrest him as ordered but he was not home, and no one would have known that he had seen him on the street.

22. See **8** n.

23. Litigants regularly warned the jurors of the consequence of their verdict (Lanni 2004). That is to say, the jury can either deter crime by showing through its verdict that the guilty will pay the penalty for breaking the law or encourage others to break the law if they see that the guilty go unpunished. After the restoration of the

either they will pay the penalty for their crimes or, if they accomplish their goal, they will become tyrants of the city, and if they are unsuccessful, they will remain on equal terms with you. Those foreigners who are here will learn whether it is wrong or right for them to ban the Thirty from their cities. If those who suffered terribly will let the Thirty go when they have them, they will certainly believe that it is needless trouble for them to keep a watch for you. [36] Wouldn't it be outrageous that you[24] sentenced to death those generals who won the naval battle[25] although they said that a storm prevented them from rescuing sailors from the sea, since you thought that they owed the dead compensation for their bravery? The Thirty, by contrast, did whatever they could as private citizens to make us lose the naval battle,[26] and when they came to power, as they admit, they intentionally executed many citizens without a trial. And yet should neither they nor their children receive from you the most severe punishment?

[37] Well, men of the jury, I think that my accusations suffice. I believe that the prosecutor need only speak until the defendant is shown to warrant death because of his actions. This, after all, is the most severe punishment that we can impose on them. I do not know why I need to speak at length against such men who, even if they died twice for each of their crimes, could not pay a sufficient penalty. [38] Moreover, he cannot do

---

democracy in 403, litigants sometimes used the consequence of the verdict to elicit the jurors' fear of renewed civil unrest. The jurors were told that either they had to adhere to the terms of the amnesty in order to prevent civil war (*stasis*) or the guilty had to be punished in order to discourage disloyal citizens from overthrowing the democracy (e.g., And. 1.105; Isoc. 18.42–44; **Lys. 12.85, 88**; 25.24; 26.16; see Wolpert 2002: 86).

24. Litigants regularly addressed the jury when referring to meetings of the Assembly (e.g., **Dem. 21.18, 36, 120, 171, 176**); see Hansen 1990: 216–22; Ober 1996: 116–22; Wolpert 2003). Until 355, the Assembly had the power to hear cases of treason.

25. The Battle of Arginusae was in 406. The Athenians executed six of the generals for failing to save the shipwrecked sailors. Five were illegally tried together in a meeting of the Assembly, despite the objections of Socrates, who was serving as one of the presiding officials of the meeting (Pl. *Ap.* 32b–c). Erasinides was convicted on charges of misconduct and imprisoned before the trial of the other five generals (Xen. *Hell.* 1.7.2).

26. Practically the entire Athenian fleet was destroyed at the Battle of Aegospotami in 405, forcing Athens to surrender the following year. After the restoration of the democracy, the Athenians engaged in this kind of revisionist history on the causes of their surrender to Sparta in order to deflect blame from themselves by accusing the oligarchs of conspiring against the democracy even before Aegospotami; see Wolpert 2002: 119–36.

what has become the custom in the city, whereby defendants say nothing in response to the accusations but, speaking about themselves concerning other matters, they sometimes deceive you when they show how they are brave soldiers, captured many ships of the enemy when they served as trierarchs,[27] or ended hostilities with enemy cities. [39] Demand that they show where they killed as many of the enemy as they have citizens, or where they captured as many ships as they surrendered, or what city they conquered that is as great as our city, which they enslaved. [40] But surely they stripped the enemy of as many weapons as they took from you, and they captured walls like those of their fatherland that they tore down, when they were the ones who destroyed the forts throughout Attica and showed you that they did not reduce the Piraeus because the Spartans ordered them but because they believed that this made their rule more secure!

[41] I have often marveled at the audacity of those who speak on his behalf, except when I consider how those who are the kind to commit every evil act also praise men like themselves. [42] This was not the first time that he opposed the multitude of you. At the time of the Four Hundred,[28] he tried to establish an oligarchy in the army, and he abandoned the ship he commanded and fled from the Hellespont along with Iatrocles and some other men whose names I do not need to say. When he arrived in Athens, he opposed those who wanted the democracy. I will provide you with witnesses to this.

WITNESSES

[43] I will skip over the intervening period of his life. But after the naval battle and the disaster that befell the city and when there was still a democracy, then they began civil unrest. Five ephors[29] were appointed by the so-called companions[30] to rally the citizens, lead the conspirators, and act in opposition to the multitude of you, and they included Eratosthenes and

---

27. A trierarch was responsible for maintaining and commanding an Athenian warship.

28. I.e., in 411.

29. The conspirators chose the number and borrowed the title to assign to their leaders from Sparta, which had a board of five ephors who were the highest political officials, elected annually to serve as a check on the power of the hereditary kings. The conspirators may have intended to model their government after the Spartans; see Krentz 1982: 67–68.

30. These were wealthy and aristocratic Athenians who privately socialized together as a "group of companions" (*hetaireia*), especially at drinking parties (*symposia*), and supported each other in their political careers (cf. **55**).

Critias. [44] They appointed a leader for each tribe, they dictated which motions to vote for and who was to hold office, and they had the power to do whatever else they wanted. Not only the enemy but even these citizens were plotting against you so that you could not pass any useful measure and would be short of many necessities. [45] They knew very well that they would not otherwise succeed, but if you were having difficulties, then they would be successful. They recognized that in your desire to put an end to your ongoing troubles you were not going to think about the future. [46] That he was one of the ephors, I will present to you witnesses, not the ones who were then in collusion with them (since I couldn't), but those who heard about it from Eratosthenes. [47] And yet if his accomplices had any sense, they would testify against them and inflict a severe punishment on the teachers of their crimes. If they had any sense, they would not consider oaths binding should they be harmful to their fellow citizens, but would readily break them for the benefit of their city. Such I say about them; please call the witnesses. Come forward.

WITNESSES

[48] You have heard the witnesses. Finally, when he held office, he accomplished nothing that was good but much that wasn't. If he were a good man, it was incumbent upon him first to avoid holding power in violation of the law and then to notify the Council that all the impeachments (*eisangeliai*) were false and that Batrachus[31] and Aeschylides did not disclose true information, but they brought forth impeachments fabricated by the Thirty and concocted to harm citizens. [49] Moreover, men of the jury, all who were hostile to the multitude of you had nothing to lose if they kept silent, since there were others whose words and actions caused the greatest possible harm for the city. As for those who say that they were loyal, how is it that they did not show it then by saying what was most helpful and by deterring those who were committing crimes?

[50] Perhaps he could say that he was afraid, and this will be a sufficient explanation for some of you so long as he is not shown to have expressed an opinion in opposition to the Thirty. Otherwise it will be clear from this that he was pleased with their actions, and he was so powerful that he did not suffer any harm at their hands even though he opposed them. [51] He ought to have shown his eagerness for your safety and not for Theramenes,

---

31. Batrachus was notorious for his service to the Thirty as an informer who was responsible for the death of many of the oligarchs' opponents. For this reason, he did not return to Athens after the restoration of the democracy even though he was protected from prosecution by the terms of the amnesty (see Lys. 6.45). Aeschylides is not mentioned elsewhere.

who carried out many crimes against you.[32] He considered the city his enemy and your enemies his friends, and I will furnish much evidence to prove these two points, and that those disagreements they had with each other were not for your sake but concerned themselves, to determine which faction would manage affairs and rule the city. [52] If they were, in fact, divided over the treatment of their victims, when was it better for one of the rulers to show his loyalty to you than when Thrasybulus[33] seized Phyle? Instead of offering or providing some aid for those at Phyle, he went with his colleagues to Eleusis and Salamis, led away to prison three hundred citizens, and sentenced them all to death with one vote.[34]

[53] When we took the Piraeus and there was much commotion and talk about a reconciliation, both sides had high expectations of reaching an agreement with each other, as we both showed.[35] Although the men of the Piraeus had the upper hand, they allowed the other side to retreat. [54] The latter returned to the city[36] and expelled the Thirty except for Pheidon and Eratosthenes, and they elected men who were the bitterest enemies of the former Thirty to rule, since they thought that those who hated the Thirty were likely to welcome the men of the Piraeus.[37] [55] They included Pheidon, Hippocles, Epichares of Lamptrae, and some

---

32. After the civil war, some Athenians sought to rehabilitate Theramenes in order to defend their own involvement in the oligarchy. They claimed that they sided with that faction of the Thirty, headed by Theramenes, which was allegedly opposed to the more brutal measures of the oligarchs and was seeking to reform the government from within; see Wolpert 2006.

33. Setting out from Boeotia with seventy exiles, Thrasybulus began his campaign to overthrow the Thirty by establishing a base of operations at Phyle, a fort on the outskirts of Attica. From Phyle they proceeded to march out against the oligarchs and seized the Piraeus, the main port of Athens.

34. These were some of the worst atrocities that the Thirty committed. For further discussion on the rounding up of the residents of Eleusis and Salamis, see Lys. 13.44; Xen. *Hell.* 2.4.8–10.

35. Throughout the rest of the speech, Lysias refers to the two sides as "the men of Piraeus" (i.e., the democratic exiles led by Thrasybulus) and "the men of the city" (i.e., those Athenians who stayed in Athens after the Thirty seized power and who eventually reached a reconciliation with the democratic exiles after the Thirty retreated to Eleusis).

36. The oligarchs returned to Athens following the Battle of Munychia in the Piraeus, where Critias was killed.

37. This is a reference to the Ten, who replaced the Thirty. While it may be coincidental, Sparta installed decarchies (i.e., boards of ten rulers) in cities that had been members of the Delian League at the end of Peloponnesian War. Except for Pheidon and Eratosthenes, who were allowed to remain in Athens, the rest of the Thirty withdrew to Eleusis.

other men who seemed to be most at odds with Charicles and Critias and their political association.[38] But when they came to power, they greatly exacerbated the civil war between the men of Piraeus and the men of the city. [56] They thus openly showed that they stirred up strife neither for the sake of the men of Piraeus nor for those who died unjustly. They were not bothered by the fact that men had died or were going to die, but by those who were becoming too powerful or growing too rich. [57] So once they were in office and had control of the city, they made war on both sides: the Thirty, who committed all sorts of evils, and you, who suffered all of them. Yet all clearly know that if the exile of the Thirty was fair, yours was unfair, and if yours was fair, then the Thirty's was unfair, since this and nothing else is the reason why they were expelled from the city.[39] [58] So you should be very angry at Pheidon. Although he was elected to arrange a reconciliation and restore you, he joined in the same endeavors as Eratosthenes, and with the same resolve he was ready to use you to harm those of his own party, who were more powerful, but he did not wish to return the city to you, who had been unjustly exiled. Instead he went to Sparta and tried to persuade them to send an army, by falsely claiming that the city was going to fall under the control of the Boeotians and saying whatever else he thought would be especially persuasive.[40] [59] When he was unsuccessful, because either religious omens were unfavorable or the Spartans were unwilling, he borrowed one hundred talents in order to hire mercenaries, and he asked Lysander[41] to command them, since he was the biggest supporter of the oligarchy, had a keen animosity for the city, and especially loathed the men of Piraeus. [60] Hiring all kinds of men for the destruction of Athens and receiving aid from other cities and finally from the Spartans and as many of their allies as they could persuade, they were preparing not to bring about a reconciliation but to destroy the city. And they would have done it had it not been for some good men, whom you must show that you will return the favor by punishing their enemies.

---

38. Pheidon was the only member of the Thirty who, as far as we know, also served on the Ten. For the meaning of "political association" (*hetaireia*), see **43** n.

39. In trials after the civil war, litigants regularly addressed the jurors as if they all had opposed the Thirty; see Wolpert 2002: 91–95.

40. Relations between Sparta and Thebes were strained because Sparta granted Athens generous terms of surrender in spite of the objections of its allies, and the Thebans suspected that Sparta wanted the city of Athens to remain intact so that it could serve as a buffer against Thebes.

41. Lysander's political influence rivaled that of the Spartan kings because his victory against the Athenian fleet at Aegospotami forced Athens to surrender. He installed the Thirty and provided the oligarchs with most of their assistance.

[61] Although you yourselves know about these matters and I know that it is unnecessary for me to provide witnesses, nevertheless I will, since I need to pause, and some of you will prefer to hear the same account from as many people as possible.

WITNESSES

[62] Well then, I will discuss Theramenes as briefly as I can, and I ask you to listen for my sake and for the sake of the city. Let no one think that I am accusing Theramenes when Eratosthenes is the one on trial. Rather, I have learned that he will defend himself by saying that he was a supporter of Theramenes and he joined in the same endeavors. [63] If he had participated in politics with Themistocles, I am quite certain that he would have claimed responsibility for building the walls when now he claims to have destroyed them along with Theramenes.[42] I do not think that the two should be considered alike. Themistocles built the walls against Spartan wishes while Theramenes destroyed them by deceiving his fellow citizens. [64] So the opposite of what was expected has happened to the city.[43] The supporters of Theramenes ought therefore to perish along with him unless there happened to be one who opposed him. But as it turns out, I see that they rely on him for their defense, attempting to win honor from their association with him, as though he were responsible for many benefits and not terrible evils. [65] First of all, most of the blame for the previous oligarchy[44] goes to him for persuading you to hand over the government to the Four Hundred. His father, who was a member of the special commission,[45] had the same objective as he, and he was appointed by them

---

42. Archon of Athens in 493/2, Themistocles was responsible for increasing the size of the Athenian navy and the naval strategy that led to the Greek victory at Salamis in 480. After the Persian Wars, he arranged for the rebuilding of walls on the Acropolis in spite of Spartan opposition. In 404, Theramenes negotiated the surrender to Sparta, which required the Athenians to tear down sections of the Long Walls that ran between Athens and the Piraeus (see **68–70**).

43. I.e., Theramenes promised his fellow citizens that he would negotiate terms of surrender that would not require Athenians to tear down the walls, but he did just the opposite. Whereas Themistocles tricked Sparta so Athens could rebuild its walls, Theramenes tricked his fellow citizens so that the Spartans could destroy them.

44. Cf. **42**.

45. Because of the destruction of the fleet in Sicily, the Athenians passed an emergency measure in 413 to deal with the crisis and appointed a special commission, which was granted extraordinary powers, including the right to initiate deliberations, prepare measures to be submitted to the Assembly, and convene the

to be a general because he seemed to be especially loyal to their cause. [66] As long as Theramenes was held in honor, he remained loyal. But when he saw Peisander, Callaeschrus, and some other men advancing ahead of him, and the multitude of you were no longer willing to heed them, he joined in Aristocrates' efforts out of jealously of them and fear of you.[46] [67] Since he wanted to appear loyal to the multitude of you, he accused Antiphon and Archeptolemus, although they were his closest supporters, and he had them executed. He went so far in his depravity that he enslaved you to gain their trust and killed his friends to gain yours. [68] Although he was honored and received the highest distinctions, he was the very one who destroyed the city that he himself had promised to save, alleging that he had found a great solution that was particularly worthwhile.[47] He promised to arrange a peace without giving hostages, tearing down the walls, or surrendering our ships. But he was unwilling to tell anyone how but bid you to trust him. [69] When the council of the Areopagus was planning for your safety and many men were speaking in opposition to Theramenes, you, men of Athens, knew that other men keep secrets because of the enemy, while he was unwilling to tell his fellow citizens what he was going to say to the enemy. Nevertheless you entrusted to him your fatherland, your children, your wives, and yourselves. [70] He did none of the things that he had promised. Instead, he was so convinced that the city had to become weak and powerless in order to persuade you to do neither what the enemy ever proposed or any citizen expected nor what he was compelled by the Spartans to suggest but what he himself promised to them—to tear down the walls of the Piraeus and dissolve the established constitution—because he knew very well that unless you were robbed of all hope you would be quick to punish him. [71] Finally, men of the jury, he did not permit the Assembly to convene until that moment stated by the enemy, which he was carefully watching for. He sent for Lysander's ships from Samos, and the enemy was stationed on our land. [72] Then, under these conditions, and with Lysander, Philochares, and Miltiades present, the Assembly convened concerning the constitution so that no speaker could oppose or threaten them and you could not choose what was useful

---

Council and Assembly (Arist. *Ath. Pol.* 29.2; Thuc. 8.1; see Ostwald 1986: 338–41; Munn 2000: 134).

46. Theramenes helped remove the Four Hundred and transfer power to the Five Thousand, who ruled until the full democracy was restored in 410. Peisander and Antiphon (who is mentioned in the next sentence) were among the most intractable of the Four Hundred, advocating a very restrictive form of government.

47. Lysias now returns to his discussion on Theramenes' involvement in the negotiations for surrender, which he started in **64**.

for the city but had to vote what they planned.[48] [73] Theramenes stood up and ordered you to entrust the city to thirty men and implement the constitution Dracontides proposed. Although you were in such a predicament, nevertheless you shouted that you would not do so since you knew that you were deciding between freedom and slavery at the meeting of the Assembly on that day. [74] Theramenes, men of the jury (and I will call on you to be my witnesses to this), said that he was not at all concerned about your commotion, since he knew that many Athenians had the same objective as he, and he said that Lysander and the Spartans agreed. Next Lysander stood up and said, in addition to many other things, that he held you to be in violation of the truce and that it is not your constitution that will be in jeopardy, but your lives, should you not do as Theramenes ordered. [75] Those in the Assembly who were good men saw through the plot and the coercion. Some of them stayed there but kept silent, while others left, comforting themselves in the fact that they did not vote for anything harmful to the city. A few wicked men with ill intentions voted what was ordered. [76] They were commanded to vote for ten whom Theramenes selected, ten whom the recently appointed ephors instructed[49] and ten from those who were present. They saw that you were so weak and they were so powerful that they knew beforehand what would happen in the Assembly. [77] You need not take my word for it when you have his. When he was defending himself before the Council,[50] he said everything that I have. He reproached the exiles[51] because they owed their return to him when the Spartans did not care at all about them. He criticized those participating in the government because he received such treatment, in spite of all of his services that he performed in the manner as I have described and although he had provided them much proof of his loyalty through his actions and had received oaths from them. [78] Although he is responsible for these and so many other terrible offenses, both long ago and more recently, some minor and others very serious, nevertheless these men will dare to present themselves as his supporters. Theramenes did not, however, die for your sake but because of his own villainy. He paid the penalty that he deserved under the oligarchy (since he had already caused its destruction),

---

48. Philochares and Miltiades are not otherwise known. Adams (1905: 113) speculates that they may have been Athenians who supported the coup, since their names are Attic.

49. See **43** n.

50. I.e., Council of the Thirty, which put him on trial and sentenced him to death for plotting against their regime.

51. I.e., those Athenians banished under the democracy who returned to Athens once the Thirty seized power.

and it would also be right for him to die under the democracy. Twice
he enslaved you because of his contempt for the constitution that was in
place and his desire for what was not, and he adopted the fairest-sounding
euphemism when he became the teacher for the most atrocious acts.[52]
[79] My accusations against Theramenes are sufficient. The time now
comes for you not to show either forgiveness or pity in your opinion
but to exact punishment from Eratosthenes and his colleagues. Do not be
stronger than the enemy in waging war and weaker than your adversaries
in voting. [80] Do not show more gratitude to them for what they say that
they will do than anger for what they did. Do not make plans against the
Thirty in their absence only to let go of them when you have them.[53] And
do not protect yourselves less zealously than does Fortune, who has surrendered these men to the city.

[81] Such are the charges against Eratosthenes and his supporters, on
whom he will rely on for his defense and with whom he had carried out
these acts. The contest between the city and Eratosthenes is, however, not
on an equal basis. He was the prosecutor and judge of those being tried,
and we now present the case of the prosecution and the defense. [82] They
executed those who were innocent without a trial, while you think that
those who ruined the city deserve a trial in accordance with the law, and
even if you wanted to punish them in violation of the law, you could not
exact from them a punishment that is fitting for their crimes against the
city. What would they have to suffer for them to pay the penalty that their
actions warrant? [83] If you executed them and their children, would we
receive sufficient compensation for the murder of our fathers, sons, and
brothers, whom they executed without a trial? If you confiscated their
visible[54] property, would this be enough either for the city, from which
they have taken much wealth, or for private individuals, whose houses
they plundered? [84] Since you could not inflict a sufficient punishment
on them even if you did all this, how is it not shameful for you to forego
whatever punishment someone would want to inflict on them?

I think that the man would have to be very bold who comes here to
defend himself before the very witnesses to his villainy when the jurors are
none other than his victims. Either he thinks so little of you or has so much

---

52. Cf. 5.

53. By the terms of the reconciliation agreement of 403, the former members of
the Thirty lived as a separate community in Eleusis until 401, when the Athenians
destroyed their stronghold and reincorporated Eleusis after learning that they were
preparing to attack Athens.

54. I.e., land and houses, in contrast to money, jewelry, precious metals, and
furniture, which are regarded as "invisible" because they can be hidden or moved.

trust in others. [85] You must watch out for both possibilities and recognize that they would not have been able to achieve their ends without others assisting nor would they now have attempted to come here unless they believed that they would be rescued by those same men.[55] Their supporters come here not to help them but because they believe that they will have much impunity for their own actions and can do whatever they want in the future if you will let men who are guilty of the worst crimes go after you have caught them. [86] It is right to marvel at the supporting speakers. Will they plead as good and noble men (*kaloi kagathoi*)[56] and present their own outstanding qualities as exceeding the wickedness of these men—I would have wished that they had been as eager to save the city as these men were to destroy it—or, as clever speakers, will they make a case for the defense and declare the actions of these men to be outstanding? Yet none of them ever attempted to do what is just on your behalf.

[87] You ought to gaze at the witnesses who accuse themselves by testifying for these men. They consider you very forgetful and gullible if they think that the multitude of you will help them save the Thirty with impunity, when Eratosthenes and his colleagues made it dangerous even to attend funerals for the dead. [88] And yet if these men are saved, they could again destroy the city, and those men whom they destroyed have lost their lives and cannot exact vengeance on their enemies. Isn't it terrible if the friends of those who died unjustly were in danger of perishing with them while many, I think, will attend the funerals of the men who destroyed the city, since there are so many who are ready to help them? [89] Furthermore I think that it would be much easier to speak out against your injuries than in defense of their actions. And yet they say that Eratosthenes committed the fewest crimes of the Thirty, and for this reason they believe that he should be saved. And when he has harmed you more than all the other Greeks, don't they think for this reason he ought to perish? [90] Show what your opinion is in these matters. If you convict him, you will show that you are angry at what has been done. If you acquit, you will appear to desire the same objectives as they, and you will not be able to say that you did what the Thirty ordered.[57] [91] No one now compels you to vote against your will. I therefore advise you not to acquit them and

---

55. See **35** n.

56. Using this term here has the effect of calling into question the claims to special privilege that these Athenian aristocrats maintained they deserved because of their birth (cf. **5**, **94**). If they were upstanding citizens, as they maintained, deserving the trust and confidence of their fellow citizens, they would have avoided involving themselves with men like Eratosthenes.

57. Cf. **27–29**.

convict yourselves. Do not think that your verdict is secret, since you will be revealing your opinion to the city.

[92] Before I soon step down, I would like to remind both of you, the men of the city and the men of Piraeus,[58] to regard the misfortunes that you suffered because of these men as a lesson when you render your verdict. To begin with those of you who were from the city, you must recognize that these men were so oppressive in their rule over you that you were compelled to fight against your brothers, sons, and fellow citizens in a war in which your defeat brings you the same rights as the victors, but if you had won, you would have been enslaved to these men. [93] They enlarged their private estates from their political activities, and yours have been diminished as a result of the war you waged against each other. They did not think that you deserved to share in the gain, but they forced you to share in the blame. They had such disdain for you that they did not earn your trust by making you partners of their profit, but they believed that you would be loyal by giving you a share of their infamy. [94] In return, now be as confident as you can and punish them on behalf of yourselves and the men of Piraeus. Recognize that you were ruled by the most wicked men; realize that you live as citizens with men who are now the best,[59] you are waging a war against the enemy, and you are deliberating about the city; and remember the mercenary troops that these men installed on the Acropolis to secure their own regime and enslave you.

[95] Such I say to you, although I could say much more. For those of you from the Piraeus, remember first your weapons, with which you fought many battles on foreign land and of which you were deprived not by the enemy but by these men in a time of peace. Then remember that you were banished from the city that your fathers had bestowed to you, and when you were living in exile, they demanded your surrender from the cities harboring you. [96] In return, exhibit the same anger that you felt when you were in exile and remember all the other injuries that you suffered from them. They seized some by force from the agora and some from the temples, and they killed them. Others they dragged from their children, their parents, and their wives, and they forced them to kill themselves, and they did not allow them to have the customary burial, thinking

---

58. This is an unusual instance when a litigant acknowledges that some members of the jury had remained in the city during the civil war; see **53** n., **57** n.

59. Here again Lysias challenges elite pretensions and co-opts aristocratic language to suggest that the supporters of the democracy have shown by their actions that they possess what was traditionally viewed as aristocratic virtues and hence could be called the best (*aristoi*). For further discussion, see Wolpert 2002: 129–33.

that their regime was mightier than vengeance of the gods.[60] [97] Whoever escaped death endured dangers in many places, wandered to many cities, and were banished from all of them. Lacking necessities, some left their children in a fatherland now hostile, others in a foreign land, and in spite of the many opponents, you came to the Piraeus. In these great dangers you were valiant men. You freed some and restored others to their fatherland. [98] If you had been unfortunate and failed in your objective, you would have gone into exile out of fear that you might suffer the same harm as before. Because of the character of these men, neither temples nor altars, which are a sanctuary even for criminals, would have helped you, though you were the victims. Those of your children who were in Athens would have been subjected to outrage (*hybris*)[61] at the hands of these men, and those in a foreign land would have fallen into slavery from their debts, because they would not have had people to help them.

[99] I do not, however, want to discuss what would have happened, when I cannot say what these men have done. This is a job not for one prosecutor or two, but many. Still, my concern is not lacking for the temples that they either sold or polluted by entering, the city that they reduced, the dockyards that they demolished, and the deceased, whom you were unable to rescue when they were alive but can help now that they are dead. [100] I believe that they are listening to us and will know who you are by the verdict you deliver. They will conclude that those of you who acquit these men will have sentenced them to death and those who punish these men will have avenged them.

I will stop my prosecution here. You have heard, you have seen, you have suffered, you have them: give your verdict.

---

60. Cf. **17–18**.

61. For the meaning of *hybris,* see the introduction to **Demosthenes 21**.

LYSIAS 16

FOR MANTITHEUS

Introduction

Before holding a political office, an Athenian first had to undergo a scrutiny (*dokimasia*). For most offices, the scrutiny took place before a jury. For those selected by lot to be archons and members of the Council, as is the case for Mantitheus, the scrutiny first took place before the outgoing Council. Candidates for the archonship were required to have a second scrutiny before a jury regardless of the outcome of the first scrutiny. A candidate for the Council only had a second scrutiny before a jury if he was rejected by the outgoing Council and appealed its decision. Candidates were asked a series of preliminary questions to determine whether they were Athenian citizens with full civic rights, thereby establishing whether they were legally permitted to hold a political office. Afterwards, individuals were permitted to come forward with objections against the candidate.[1] If an individual challenged a candidate's right to hold office, the hearing was apparently suspended to allow the candidate the opportunity to prepare a response that was to be heard at a subsequent meeting of the Council; otherwise Mantitheus could not have had Lysias write a speech for him to deliver in response (Adams 1905: 134).

In addition to the scrutiny of candidates for the Council and the archonship, the Council also conducted scrutinies for (1) new citizens (ephebes), to verify that they had reached the required minimum age; (2) invalids, to establish that they met the requirements for disability pay (see introduction to **Lysias 24**); and (3) knights, to determine the condition of their horses and their preparation for fighting.[2] Other powers of the Council included the right to imprison individuals suspected of treason and tax collectors in debt to the city and to impose fines of no more than five hundred drachmas, subject to appeal to the court. It could also investigate any official, and any citizen could lodge a denunciation (*eisangelia*) against an official before the Council, but its vote was preliminary, and any fine of more than five hundred drachmas had to go to court (Hansen 1991: 257–59).

Translated by Andrew Wolpert.

1. Arist. *Ath. Pol.* 45.3, 55.1–4; Din. 2.17–18; for further discussion on the *dokimasia*, see MacDowell 1978: 167–69; Todd 1993: 285–89.

2. For the scrutiny of public speakers, see the introduction to **Aeschines 1**.

It seems likely that in most instances the scrutiny for political office would have been perfunctory, but it is impossible for us to know. First, *dokimasia* speeches only survive for those occasions when the candidate was formally challenged. Second, these speeches are entirely from the corpus of Lysias (**16**, 25, 26, 31, fr. 9 Todd), and in each case the candidate is forced to respond to accusations concerning his conduct during the civil war and the rule of the Thirty. We cannot determine how regularly the scrutiny was used for such purposes, but it clearly provided enemies the opportunity to air their grievances against the candidates. It seems also to have provided victims of the Thirty with a way to circumvent the terms of the amnesty and seek retribution against collaborators (see the introduction to **Lysias 12**). Even if the jury did not reject a candidate because of his conduct during the civil war, victims of the Thirty were able to publicly humiliate collaborators and receive some form of satisfaction by outing them. For our purposes, these speeches are useful because they show that the Athenians did not simply forget the past and let bygones be bygones as stated in the ancient testimony. The civil war remained quite troubling for some years after the restoration of the democracy, and the Athenians had difficulty coming to terms with their past.

The speech of Mantitheus is particularly valuable for the information that it provides on Athenian attitudes towards the cavalry. The Thirty received important military assistance from the cavalry, which had been effective at harassing the exiles stationed at Phyle and preventing them from more effectively following up their victory. After the reconciliation, various measures were passed, such as the recall of the equipment allowance that they had received under the Thirty (**6**), which did not formally violate the amnesty, but was clearly punitive.[3] Mantitheus maintains that service in the cavalry of the Thirty did not prohibit him from holding an office. Yet at the same time he goes to some trouble to prove that he had not served in the cavalry of Thirty, and he reveals how he avoided involvement in the cavalry after the restoration of the democracy. When he was called up for military duty, he asked to be placed in the infantry rather than the cavalry. He claims that he made the request because the infantry would be facing greater dangers than the cavalry (**13**).

It is possible that he was more involved in the rule of the Thirty than he admitted, and this is why he later attempted to distance himself from the cavalry. Although he was away from Athens at the start of the civil war, he returned when the Thirty were still in power, and he does not explain why he and his family chose to return to Athens under the oligarchy rather than remain in exile or why the oligarchs permitted their return (**5**). While

---

3. For the cavalry under the Thirty and subsequent measures, see Bugh 1988: 121–53.

Mantitheus argues that the register of the cavalry under the Thirty, on which he was recorded, is inaccurate, he asks the Council to trust another list that does not include him as one of the knights required to return the equipment allowance that they had received under the Thirty (6). But perhaps he returned to Athens only after the Thirty stopped providing this equipment allowance since they were short of money (Todd 2000: 179). Finally, Mantitheus tries to convince the Council that his opponents are challenging his candidacy because they resent him for his ambition. Although he is a young man, he has already begun to have an active political profile and has even spoken before the Assembly (20). Since the oligarchs too were actively involved in Athenian politics before they overthrew the democracy, his opponents may have put a very different spin on such activities (see 18).

In the speech, internal references to the Corinthian War (395–387) allow an approximate dating of Mantitheus' *dokimasia*. The battles of 395 and 394 are given greatest attention (13–17), and the biting remark about Thrasybulus (15) would seem inappropriate if Mantitheus had delivered the speech after his death. So in all likelihood it was probably delivered sometime after 394 and no later than 389.[4]

Key Information

Speaker	Mantitheus was required to respond to objections about his eligibility to serve on the Council of Five Hundred.
Challenger	Not known.
Action	Scrutiny (*dokimasia*) for public office to determine whether Mantitheus would be allowed to be a member of the Council of Five Hundred.
Audience	The Council of Five Hundred.
Date	c.394–389.

For Mantitheus

[1] If I did not know, members of the Council, that my accusers were planning to harm me in every possible manner, I would have been very thankful to them for their accusation. I believe that such men provide the

---

4. Adams 1905: 136; Todd 2000: 179.

greatest service to those unfairly slandered, by compelling them to undergo a review of their life.⁵ [2] I am so very confident in myself that I even expect anyone who dislikes me to change his opinion and think much more highly of me in the future once he has heard me describe my conduct. [3] I do not believe that I deserve any special privilege, members of the Council, if I will only show to you that I am loyal to the established government and that I have been compelled to experience the same dangers as you.⁶ If, however, I will also show that I have lived my life with self restraint in other regards contrary to the opinion and the claims of my enemies, I ask you to vote in favor of my holding political office and to think worse of them. First, I will show that I did not serve in the cavalry, and I neither was in Athens during the rule of the Thirty nor participated in their government.

[4] Before the disaster in the Hellespont,⁷ my father sent us to live at the court of Satyrus⁸ in the Pontus. We were not in Athens either when the walls were torn down or when they were changing the constitution, but we came back five days before those from Phyle returned to the Piraeus.⁹ [5] Since we arrived at such a crucial moment, it was not likely that we would have wanted to share in the dangers of others, nor is it the case that they would have agreed to share their government with men who had been away and had not committed any offenses, when they were in the habit of disfranchising even those who had helped them dissolve the democracy. [6] Furthermore, it is foolish to determine who served in the cavalry from the register.¹⁰ Many who admit that they were in the cavalry are not on the register, while some are listed who were not in Athens. But here is the greatest proof: when you¹¹ returned, you voted to have

---

5. The invalid begins his *dokimasia* speech with a similar conceit (**Lys. 24.1**).

6. After the civil war, speakers regularly attempted to establish their loyalty by comparing their suffering during the period of social unrest to that of the democratic exiles and regularly addressed their audience as though all listening had remained loyal to the democracy; see Wolpert 2002: 100–18.

7. I.e., the Battle of Aegospotami in 405, where the Spartans under Lysander's command destroyed nearly the entire Athenian fleet without a battle and forced the Athenians to surrender in the following year.

8. A king of what is now Crimea.

9. The speaker does not explain why he chose to return to Athens when it was still under oligarchic rule or why he did not join the exiles. For the events of the civil war, see the introduction to **Lysias 12**.

10. A wooden tablet intended only for temporary display.

11. Cf. **Lys. 12.57**.

the tribal officers[12] hand over a list of those who had served in the cavalry in order to recover the equipment allowance from them. [7] No one could, however, show that I have been placed on the list by the tribal officers, have been summoned to the revenue commissioners, or returned the equipment allowance. Yet it would have been easy for anyone to know, since the tribal officers were required to pay a fine if they did not disclose those who had the equipment allowance. You should therefore place more trust in this list than the register. Whereas anyone who so wished could easily erase their name from the latter, the tribal officers were required to place the names of those who had served in the cavalry on the former. [8] Moreover, if I had served in the cavalry, members of the Council, I would not deny it as if I had done something terrible. Instead I would think it right, after I had shown that I had not harmed any citizen, to pass my scrutiny for political office. And I see that you hold the same opinion, since many who had served in the cavalry at that time are now members of the Council and many others have been elected generals and cavalry commanders.[13] Therefore, do not think that I defend myself for any reason other than because they openly dared to accuse me falsely. Please come forward and furnish your testimony.

WITNESS

[9] I do not know what more I need to say about this accusation. I think, members of the Council, that it is enough for the defendant to respond only to the actual accusations at other trials, but when one undergoes a scrutiny for public office, it is right to give an account of one's entire life. I therefore ask you to listen favorably to me, and I will make my defense as brief as I can.

[10] Because of the misfortunes that befell my father and the city, I did not inherit much property. Nevertheless I gave a dowry of thirty minas to each of my two sisters, I divided up the inheritance so that my brother acknowledged that he received more than I, and I have so conducted myself in all of my relationships with other people that I have not yet had a legal dispute with anyone. [11] Thus I have managed my private affairs. As for public matters, the greatest proof of my propriety is the fact that all those young men who spend their time gambling or drinking or

---

12. Each of the ten tribes annually elected an officer, called the phylarch, to command the tribe's unit of cavalry. The entire cavalry were commanded by two hipparchs.

13. At the *dokimasia* of Euandrus, the challenger claims that service in the cavalry of the Thirty is grounds for rejecting candidates for the Council; see Lys. 26.10.

in other such decadent activities are, as you will see, at odds with me, and they spread many false stories about me. And yet if we were engaged in the same pursuits, they would certainly not have such an opinion of me. [12] Still, members of the Council, no one could show that I have been a party to a shameful private case, or a public suit, or an impeachment, even though you see that others are often involved in such legal actions. As for military campaigns and hazards of war, consider how I rendered myself to the city. [13] First of all, when we made an alliance with the Boeotians and support was needed at Haliartus, I was called up by Orthobulus to serve in the cavalry.[14] I saw that all believed that the cavalry would be safe, while the infantry would be in harm's way. Some that were not registered illegally mounted horses, but I approached Orthobulus and asked him to remove my name from the list, since I believed that it was shameful, when the multitude was going to face danger, for me to see to my own safety on the expedition. Please come forward, Orthobulus.

WITNESS

[14] When the members of my deme assembled before we set out, I was aware that some of them were brave and loyal citizens but lacked provisions, and I said that those who were well off should provide what was necessary to those in need. I not only offered this advice to everyone else, but I even gave two men each thirty drachmas, not because I was wealthy, but to make an example to everyone else. Please come forward.

WITNESSES

[15] Afterwards, members of the Council, when we marched out to Corinth and all knew the dangers that we would be facing, others were drawing back while I sought to fight against the enemy in the first rank.[15] Although my tribe suffered the worst losses and had the most men die, I held out longer than that proud man from Steiria[16] who had rebuked everyone for cowardice. [16] A few days after this, strongholds were taken in Corinth to prevent the passage of the enemy, and Agesilaus set out to Boeotia. The commanders decided to dispatch some contingents for assistance. When everyone was afraid (as was to be expected, members of the

---

14. This mobilization occurred in 395 (see Xen. *Hell.* 3.5).

15. The battle took place in 394 (see Xen. *Hell.* 4.2).

16. This is most likely a reference to Thrasybulus of Steiria who led the resistance against the Thirty; see the introduction to **Lysias 12**.

Council, since it was terrifying to go again into harm's way after we had just barely survived), I approached the taxiarch and asked him to send our contingent without drawing lots. [17] So if any of you are angry at those who seek to be involved in the political affairs of the city but avoid its dangers, it would not be right for you to bear such resentment against me. Not only did I courageously obey my orders but I even volunteered for hazardous duty. I did so not because I thought so little of fighting the Spartans but so that, if I should ever be unjustly embroiled in a legal action, I would, for this reason, be held in higher regard by you and would enjoy all my rights. May the witnesses of this please come forward.

WITNESSES

[18] I never fell short of my duty in any other military campaign or garrison, but throughout my entire life I have marched out in the first ranks and retreated in the last. You ought to make up your mind about those who are ambitious and behave as good citizens from such actions, and not hate someone because he wears his hair long.[17] Such practices do not harm private individuals or the public good, but all of you benefit from those willing to risk facing the enemy. [19] You ought not, members of the Council, either like or dislike someone because of his appearance, but rather you ought to consider his actions. There are many who, speaking little and dressing modestly, have caused the greatest harm while others, paying no heed to such matters, have performed many services for you.

[20] I recently noticed, members of the Council, that there are some who hate me because I dared to address the Assembly when I am so young. First, I had to speak before the Assembly on matters that concerned me. Second, I think that I am more ambitious than is necessary because I am aware of my ancestors and how they never stopped performing services for the city, [21] and I see that you (for I must tell the truth) consider only such men to be worthy of anything. When one sees that you have such an opinion, who would not be eager to act and speak on behalf of the city? Why would you be upset with such men? No others are judges of them but you.

---

17. This was a Spartan style. Since Athens was at war with Sparta and the Thirty had relied on Sparta to maintain their rule, some Athenians would have considered such an appearance as evidence that the individual was hostile to the restored democracy; cf. **Dem. 54.34.**

LYSIAS 23

AGAINST PANCLEON

Introduction

At the height of the Peloponnesian War, the decree of Hippocrates awarded Athenian citizenship to the survivors of the destruction of Plataea who had found refuge in Athens (427). Henceforth, the Plataeans would be citizens with the same legal rights as any other citizen except for a few religious restrictions (see Kapparis 1995: 359–78). "Against Pancleon" concerns this privilege. Our speaker, otherwise unknown, explains that he had been at odds with Pancleon for some time until he eventually sought legal action against him. He approached Pancleon at the shop where he worked and summoned him to appear before the polemarch (war archon). Pancleon objected, arguing that he was a Plataean and thus an Athenian citizen (**2**). This meant that the lawsuit should have been submitted to one of the tribal judges, since they oversaw private suits involving citizens while the polemarch handled cases involving metics. So Pancleon blocked the speaker's suit by lodging a countersuit (*paragraphe*), which was a new procedure, introduced in 400, not long before Pancleon's trial was to take place.[1] The *paragraphe* provided defendants with greater flexibility than the *diamartyria*, an older procedure that could only be used if one of the parties had evidence from a witness that had bearing on the legality of the suit. As it turns out, Pancleon had raised a similar objection in a previous case that Aristodicus had brought before the polemarch, and Aristodicus used the *diamartyria* to verify Pancleon's status as a metic so that he could proceed with his original suit without interruption (**13–14**). In his dispute with our speaker, Pancleon could have followed the same course of action as in his dispute with Aristodicus and forced a *diamartyria*, but for whatever reason he chose instead to block the speaker's suit with a *paragraphe*.

Translated by Konstantinos Kapparis.

1. See Isoc. 18.1–3; Wolff 1966; Isager and Hansen 1975; Todd 1993: 136–39; Wolpert 2002: 34–35. The speaker refers to Pancleon's suit as an *antigraphe* (**5, 10**); some scholars suggest that *antigraphe* was a variant of the *paragraphe* (see for example Todd 1993: 168). Such a procedure is not, however, mentioned in any other speech, and Pancleon's countersuit occurred shortly after the *paragraphe* was instituted. So, the speech, as MacDowell (1978: 216) has suggested, probably only shows that the Athenians had not yet reached a consensus on the name of this new procedure.

Once the countersuit was lodged, the roles of the prosecutor and defendant were reversed, making Pancleon the prosecutor and our speaker the defendant. If successful, the speaker would have had to bring his case again before the polemarch in order to proceed further with his charge against Pancleon. If unsuccessful, he was still able to lodge a suit against Pancleon, but it would have appeared before one of the tribal judges instead of the polemarch. Unlike other countersuits that have survived (e.g., **Dem. 32**), the speaker here does not discuss any of the details of his original suit. This speech, therefore, does not provides us with any clues to explain why the speaker did not simply resubmit the case before one of the tribal judges and avoid the delay of having the countersuit heard first. It is, however, possible that Pancleon's status had some bearing on the original suit. Such is typically the case for inheritance disputes, for obvious reasons. The lateral relatives of Phile, for example, attempted to prove that she was illegitimate and thus not entitled to her father's inheritance (Isae. 3). Aeschines alleges that a man by the name of Leuconides paid Timarchus to erase his brother-in-law, Philotades, from the deme register of Cydathenaeum. If Philotades were disfranchised, his sister, who was married to Leuconides, would have become the sole heiress of the family estate and Leuconides would have been able to gain control of the property (see **Aesch. 1.115** n.). Euxitheus accuses Eubulides of seeking to strip him of his citizenship because they were political opponents (Dem. 57). The fact that Pancleon was the son of a poor manual laborer might have made it easier to dispute his citizenship. Demosthenes made similar allegations against Aeschines (18.130–31), and Euxitheus was compelled to explain how his mother was a citizen even though she had worked as a wet nurse to earn some desperately needed income for the family (Dem. 57.40–42). So it may be the case that Pancleon, as a descendant of Plataean immigrants with weak ties to his own community and working the lowly job of a fuller, could easily be taken for a poor metic, freedman, or even a runaway slave.

Although this short speech provides so few details about the dispute between these two men, it is enormously valuable because of the information that it reveals about the steps the speaker took to build his case against Pancleon. We learn that he relied on the suggestions of the people he met during his investigations on how best to proceed with his suit. Active participation was apparently fostered in Athens not only in politics at the deme or city level but also informally in private matters. The speech shows us that a litigant's case may take unexpected turns and its success may depend upon accidental or unexpected discoveries along the way (see **9–10**). We also gain a glimpse into the social networking of classical Athens: the Deceleans usually gathered at a particular barbershop (**3**) while the Plataeans would meet at the fresh cheese market at the beginning of every month (**6**). Long before the Internet, individuals could only stay informed about the lives of their friends and neighbors by meeting face to face with them at mutually convenient locations. The speech is generally believed to have been written by Lysias; the exception is Usher (1966), who has called into question its authenticity for stylistic reasons.

Key Information

Speaker	The unnamed speaker lodged a charge against Pancleon before the polemarch since he thought Pancleon was a metic.
Prosecutor	Pancleon blocked the original suit on the grounds that it should have appeared before the tribal judges since he was an Athenian citizen.
Other Individuals	Nicomedes seized Pancleon as a runaway slave.
	Aristodicus won a suit he had lodged against Pancleon before the polemarch.
Action	Countersuit to determine whether the speaker could continue with his original suit against Pancleon before the polemarch or must instead go before the tribal judges.
Date	400/399(?).

Against Pancleon

[1] I could not say much about this case, men of the jury, nor do I think that it is necessary to do so. I will only try to prove to you that I brought my lawsuit against Pancleon, who is not a Plataean, in accordance with the correct procedures.

[2] Since he was causing me harm over a long period of time, I went to the fuller's shop where he was working and summoned him to follow me to the polemarch because I believed that he was a metic.[2] When he said that he was Plataean, I asked him which was his deme after one of the bystanders advised me to summon him also to the court of the tribe that

---

2. A private lawsuit against a citizen was submitted to the tribal judges, known as the "Forty" because there were four for each of the ten tribes. Suits against metics were submitted to the polemarch.

he claimed was his.[3] When he said that he was from Decelea, I summoned him to appear before the tribal court of Hippothontis.[4] [3] Then I went to the barber shop near the Herms,[5] which is frequented by Deceleans, and I asked every Decelean that I could find whether he knew a man called Pancleon who was a member of the deme of Decelea.[6] Since no one said that he knew him, and in the meantime I learned that he was a defendant in other lawsuits before the polemarch, and some of them he lost, I lodged my suit accordingly.

[4] First I will present as witnesses those of the Deceleans I questioned, then the other men who happened to be present and have successfully prosecuted and convicted him before the polemarch. Please stop the water clock.[7]

WITNESSES

[5] Persuaded by them, I brought the lawsuit before the polemarch, but when Pancleon blocked it with a countersuit, alleging that the procedure had been incorrectly initiated, I was very mindful not to appear arrogant towards anyone rather than seek justice for the injuries that I had suffered. First I asked Euthycritus, one of the oldest Plataeans around, whom I thought was most likely to know, whether he knew a Plataean called Pancleon, son of Hipparmodorus. [6] Then when he replied that he knew

---

3. Athenian citizenship was based upon membership in the deme of one's father. The speaker needed to know Pancleon's deme in order to verify his citizenship and determine his tribe so that he could lodge the suit before the appropriate tribal judge.

4. Decelea belonged to the Hippothontis tribe.

5. A well-known and very central location in the agora with numerous pillar statues of Hermes, extending from the Painted Stoa to the Basileios Stoa (see Hutton 2005: 262 n. 63).

6. It is interesting to note that the speaker did not consult the deme register, which was the most obvious place to begin, since it would have indicated whether Pancleon was enrolled in Decelea. Registries can, however, be disputed (e.g., **Lys. 16.6**) or destroyed (e.g., Dem. 57.26), and litigants typically provided the testimony of witnesses to verify written documents. Decelea was a medium-sized deme; so it was not unreasonable for the speaker to assume that some Deceleans would have known Pancleon at least by name. On the other hand, the speaker could have consulted the register or the demarch (chief official of the deme) in order to confirm what the Deceleans had told him informally and thereby strengthen his case. This suggests that the speaker either was an inexperienced litigator or perhaps had reason to believe that the register might not support his assertions.

7. Each party had a time limit to present its case. In private suits, the water clock was stopped when witness testimony, laws, and oaths were read.

Hipparmodorus but did not know that he had a son, either named Pancleon or by any other name, I started asking everyone else I knew who was Plataean. Since they did not know his name, they told me that I could learn for certain by going to the fresh cheese market on the first day of the month, because the Plataeans gather there every month on that day. [7] When I came to the cheese market on that day, I went around asking them whether they knew a citizen of theirs called Pancleon. All of them said they did not know him, except one man, who said he did not know any citizen with that name but had a runaway slave named Pancleon, and he said the slave was the same age and practiced the same trade as that man.

[8] That I am telling you the truth, I will present as witnesses Euthycritus whom I first asked those I approached from the rest of the Plataeans, and the man who said he is the master of this one here. Please stop the water clock.

WITNESSES

[9] A few days later I saw Pancleon here being seized by Nicomedes, who testified he was his master; I approached because I wanted to know what was going to be done about him. When they stopped fighting, some of the supporters of this man said that he had a brother who would secure his release as a free man.[8] After providing guarantees that they would present him on the next day, they left. [10] The next day, on account of the countersuit and the trial itself, I thought I should be present with witnesses in order to find out who would secure his release as a free man and what he would say as he did so. With regard to the terms of the guarantee, neither his brother nor any other man came forward; however, a woman appeared, claiming that he was her slave, disputing ownership rights with Nicomedes, and asserting that she was not going to allow Nicomedes to take him away. [11] What was said there would take a long time to report, but he and his supporters became so violent that although Nicomedes wanted to let him go, and so did the woman, if someone should either secure his release as a free man or seize him, claiming that he was his slave, they did neither, but taking him away, they left. That sureties were provided on his behalf on these terms the day before, and then they went away taking him by force, I will present witnesses for you. Please stop the water clock.

---

8. Literally, "remove him to freedom" (cf. **[Dem.] 59.45; Aesch. 1.62**) refers to the legal procedure *aphairesis eis eleutherian,* whereby a third party could secure the release of an individual wrongly seized as a runaway slave. He had to provide sureties to insure that the alleged slave would not flee Athens if the man claiming to be the owner demanded a hearing (see Kapparis 1999: 248–50).

WITNESSES

[12] Thus it is easy to know that not even Pancleon considers himself to be a Plataean, much less a free man. This man chose to make his friends guilty of assault, as he was forcibly carried away by them, rather than be released according to the laws and obtain justice against those who seized him. It is not difficult to understand why he was afraid to provide sureties and stand trial for his freedom, since he knew well that he was a slave.

[13] On the basis of this evidence, I believe that you know pretty well that he is far from being Plataean. But you will learn from his actions that even he, who knows best his own affairs, did not expect you to believe that he is a Plataean. In the affidavit for the lawsuit that Aristodicus brought against him, he disputed that the polemarch was the appropriate magistrate to receive the lawsuit and made his opponent present a witness asserting under oath that Pancleon was not a Plataean. [14] Although Pancleon denounced this witness, he did not prosecute him but allowed Aristodicus to win the case against him.[9] When he did not pay the penalty by the deadline, he had to pay the full amount of the disputed sum, making whatever arrangements he could. I will present witnesses confirming that this is true. Please stop the water clock.

WITNESSES

[15] Before coming to an arrangement with him, he left and went to live as a metic in Thebes because he was afraid of Aristodicus. And I believe you know that if he were a Plataean, he would rather move anywhere else other than Thebes.[10] I will present witnesses that he lived there for a long time. Please stop the water clock.

WITNESSES

[16] I think what I said is enough, men of the jury. If you keep it in mind, I know that you will vote for what is right and true, as I am asking you to do.

---

9. When Aristodicus furnished a witness who gave testimony (*diamartyria*) that Pancleon was not a Plataean, Pancleon made a denunciation (*episkepsis*) against the witness for lying. However, he did not take the next step and block the suit by formally charging the witness with false testimony (*dike pseudomartyrion*). So the suit went to court and Aristodicus won; see Gernet 1955: 83–102; MacDowell 1978: 212–14; Todd 1993: 127, 169.

10. Sparta captured Plataea in 427, killed all the men still remaining, sold the women into slavery, and razed the city in order to placate Thebes (see Thuc. 3.68).

LYSIAS 24

ON THE SUSPENSION OF THE BENEFIT OF

THE DISABLED MAN

Introduction

If authentic, this may be one of the few extant speeches intended to be delivered by a poor Athenian. It is also extraordinary for the speaker's use of humor to make his case. As a recipient of the disability benefit of one obol per day (**13**, **26**), he was required to undergo a scrutiny (*dokimasia*) before the Council periodically to verify his eligibility.[1] By the end of the fourth century, recipients had to be unable to perform any work and had to own less than three minas to qualify for the benefit (Arist. *Ath. Pol.* 49.4). Since the speaker of Lysias 24 mentions that he had a trade, which earned him a modest income, it is possible that the eligibility requirements were less stringent in the early fourth century (see **6** n.). In most cases, the scrutiny was probably a formality, especially for a disabled Athenian seeking to renew an existing benefit. If, however, a citizen was prepared to come forward and challenge the recipient, then a separate hearing followed before the Council, where the challenger explained why the claim should be denied and, as in the present speech, the recipient responded. The arrangement of Lysias 24 has been criticized by Usher, but well explained by Carey as a point-by-point response to the objections of his opponent.[2] The challenger claims that the benefit should be denied because the claimant lacks the qualifications for receiving it: he was not disabled, since he could ride horses, and he was not poor, since he owned a workshop and practiced a craft that brought him substantial income. As further proof of the claimant's wealth, his opponent cites that he socializes with rich men (**5**). To top these accusations, his opponent alleges that the claimant's character is questionable: he is violent, arrogant, and immoral, and the people who frequent his shop are of similar questionable character (**15**, **19**).

Translated by Konstantinos Kapparis.

1. Aeschines' speech against Timarchus (**1.104**) indicates that disabled persons received the benefit once per prytany (i.e., ten times per year). For disability benefits in Athens, see Dillon 1995: 27–57; for disability in the ancient world, see Haj 1970; Garland 1995.

2. Edwards and Usher 1985: 263; Carey 1990: 44–51.

Our speaker does not dispute many of his opponent's allegations; rather he objects to the inferences drawn from them, using humor and pathos to make questions about his eligibility for the disability benefit appear ridiculous and cruel (see Carey 1990: 49). He admits that he rides horses but explains that he does so because he cannot walk long distances. Since horses were quite expensive and ownership would imply wealth, he is careful to point out that he had to borrow horses from friends because he was too poor to own even a mule (**10–12**). He also admits that he owns a workshop and practices a craft but claims that his income is minimal and certainly not enough to secure his sustenance. As proof he cites the fact that he does not have an apprentice because he cannot afford to pay for one (**6**). In response to the accusations concerning his character, he notes how the wealthy and the young are prone to violence, not the old and weak (**16–19**). He then proceeds with counteraccusations. His opponent is so arrogant and insolent that he has the nerve to argue that a man in need of two walking sticks is able bodied, and he seeks to take away an invalid's benefit as if it were the fortune of an heiress (**12–14**).

The authenticity of the speech was called into question by Harpocration and has been debated by a number of scholars throughout the nineteenth and twentieth centuries.[3] Some infer from the weaknesses of the case that Lysias could not have written it, since he would have provided the claimant with a better response, and they suggest that it may have been a rhetorical exercise by some other author. However, the discrepancies between the speech and the *Athenian Constitution*, a text well known to the rhetoricians of later antiquity, speak for the speech's authenticity, since a later rhetorician would have probably used the *Athenian Constitution* as a source of information. Others point out that the invalid, if he was as poor as he maintains, would not have been able to hire a logographer. However, he apparently had rich friends; so perhaps they assisted him, or perhaps Lysias reduced his fees. In the words of Jebb (1893: 250–51), the speech is "a composition excellent of its kind, and excellent in a way suggestive of Lysias." Only this master of *ethopoeia* could have created such a nuanced and skillfully crafted character (see Usher 1965), and this was one of the main arguments Albini used to support its authenticity. Lysias created a character, somewhat eccentric, sly, and witty, but also likeable and trustworthy, hoping that such a character would carry the jury. The *ethopoeia* in this speech is

---

3. Harp., s. v. *adynaton*. Against its authenticity: Darkow 1917: 73–77; Roussel 1966. In support of its authenticity: Jebb 1893: 251–52; Adams 1905: 234–35; Albini 1952: 28–38; Dillon 1995: 38–39. Todd (1990b: 166–67; 2000: 253–54) offers compelling arguments in favor of its authenticity.

truly masterful, carries most of the case, and is probably responsible for the popularity of the speech through the centuries.

Key Information

Speaker	A poor invalid verifying his eligibility to receive the disability benefit of one obol per day.
Challenger	Unknown.
Action	Scrutiny (*dokimasia*).
Audience	The Council of Five Hundred.
Date	Early fourth century.

Lysias 24: On the Suspension of the Benefit of the Disabled Man

[1] I almost owe the prosecutor my thanks, members of the Council, for getting me involved in this trial. In the past I did not have an excuse to give an account of my life, but now I have, because of him.[4] I will try in my speech to prove that he is lying and I have lived my life up to the present day in a manner that deserves praise rather than envy; for it seems to me that he did not involve me in this litigation for any other reason except envy. [2] And yet when someone envies those whom others pity, from what kind of wrongdoing do you think that this kind of man would abstain? He is not slandering me for money, and if he claims that he is punishing me as his enemy, he is lying.[5] Because of his unworthiness I never had any dealings with this man either as a friend or as an enemy. [3] It is obvious, members of the Council, that he is envious of me because, despite my misfortune, I am a better citizen than he. I think, members of the Council, that one should

---

4. Our speaker acts as if he were an important Athenian excited by this opportunity to talk about himself and to set the record straight; cf. **Lys. 16.1**. He is intentionally using a *topos* employed by wealthy defendants to disarm his opposition and make light of the dispute so that the jury might find the case amusing and the speaker instantly likeable.

5. The text of the manuscripts is unsatisfactory at this point. Most scholars believe that something is missing. Carey retains the transmitted text. We have accepted an emendation of Sauppe, which (although far from certain) provides the text with some logical flow.

heal illnesses of the body with the accomplishments of the soul;[6] for if my mindset follows closely my misfortune and I live the rest of my life in this manner, how am I going to be any different from him?

[4] What I have said about these matters ought to be sufficient; as for what I need to talk about, I will speak to you as briefly as I can. The prosecutor claims that it is not right for me to receive money from the city, because I am able bodied, and not disabled, and I possess a craft that would allow me to live even without the benefit.[7] [5] As proof of my bodily strength, he uses the fact that I ride horses, and as proof of the wealth from my craft, he uses the fact that that I can associate with men who can afford to spend. I believe that all of you are well aware of my financial circumstances and my lifestyle, whatever that is. Nonetheless, I will tell you briefly. [6] My father left me nothing, and I only stopped supporting my mother three years ago, when she died. I still do not have any children to look after me, but I have a craft that can bring in a small income.[8] I already have difficulty practicing it myself, and I cannot get someone to take it on.[9] I do not have any other income except this, and if you take it away from me, I would be in danger of finding myself in the most dire circumstances. [7] Do not, members of the Council, destroy me unjustly when you can do justice and save me. Do not deprive me of the same benefit, which you granted me when I was younger and stronger, now that I am getting older and weaker. Before, you seemed to show the greatest pity for people who had nothing wrong with them; so now do not, because of him, treat savagely those who are pitied even by their enemies. And do not upset others who are in the same situation as I, by having the heart to wrong me. [8] It would certainly be strange, members of the Council, if I appeared to receive this benefit when my misfortune was uncompounded and then be deprived of

---

6. This psychosomatic concept of health and disease is prevalent in ancient medicine.

7. Aeschines confirms that these benefits were granted on the basis of financial need, and thus well-off citizens with disabilities were ineligible (see **Aesch. 1.102–4**).

8. By the time of Aristotle, the recipient had to be incapable of doing any work. Since our invalid would have been disqualified by his own admission if this were the case for the early fourth century, Carey (1990: 44) suggests that the law was not interpreted literally and was intended to provide only supplemental assistance. An obol was, after all, only one-third of the daily wage of an unskilled worker. Alternatively, restrictions may have been added later in the fourth century, which disqualified invalids capable of doing some work. In fact, the Athenians apparently passed a law that increased the benefit from one obol per day to two (see **13, 26**; Arist. *Ath. Pol.* 49.4); so it is quite possible that they added stricter eligibility requirements when they increased the amount of the benefit (cf. Dillon 1995: 38).

9. I.e., his trade does not provide him with enough income to purchase a slave to do the work for him.

it now, when old age and illness and all the evils that come with them have befallen me. [9] It seems to me that the prosecutor himself could explain the level of my poverty better than anyone else. If I had been appointed a chorus producer (*choregos*) for a tragedy and challenged him to an exchange of property (*antidosis*), he would have preferred ten times to serve as a chorus producer than exchange his property with mine just once.[10] How is it not terrible if now he accuses me of associating with the richest men on an equal footing because of my affluence, but if something were to happen such as I have just mentioned, then he would say that I am in my current condition or even worse?[11]

[10] As for my equestrian skills, which he dared to mention to you, neither fearing fate nor having any shame, I will not say much. It is natural, members of the Council, for all persons who have had a misfortune of this kind to seek and study how to cope with their condition with as little distress as possible. As one of those who have suffered such misfortune, I found this relief for myself for the longer journeys that I must make. [11] It is easy to grasp, members of the Council, the greatest proof that I ride horses because of my misfortune and not because of arrogance (*hybris*), as he claims.[12] If I had money, I would be carried on a saddled mule, and I would not ride other people's horses. But as it is, because I cannot afford to buy one, I am frequently forced to borrow the horses of others. [12] Yet, how is it not strange, members of the Council, that he would have said nothing if he saw me carried on a mule (what could he say?), but now that I ride borrowed horses, he attempts to convince you that I am able bodied? When I use two walking sticks, while others use only one, he does not take this to be a sign that I am able bodied; however, he argues from my riding horses that I am able bodied. But I need the assistance of both for the same reason.

[13] He has surpassed everyone in shamelessness to such a degree that he tries to convince you, although you are so many and he is only one

---

10. Wealthy citizens were required to perform public services, known as liturgies (see the introduction to **Demosthenes 21**). A person chosen to perform a liturgy could challenge another Athenian of the liturgical class, who had not recently performed a liturgy and was not exempt, either to perform the liturgy in question or to exchange property (see **Dem. 21.78** n.).

11. The ellipsis in the Greek has puzzled many previous editors, and while there is some uncertainty in the text, the speaker's main point is reasonably clear. He uses the hypothetical challenge to suggest that his opponent actually believes that he is poor since his opponent would never be willing to exchange property with him.

12. Here we have retained the transmitted text. For the meaning of *hybris*, see the introduction to **Demosthenes 21**.

man, that I am not disabled. If he convinces some of you, members of the
Council, what stops me from drawing lots to be one of the nine archons
and you from depriving me the obol for being healthy and voting it to him
for being disabled?[13] Surely you will not take away the benefit from a man,
because he is able bodied, whom the *thesmothetai* will prevent from entering the lottery for the nine archons because he is disabled? [14] You do not
think like him, and he does not think like you—fortunately. He comes here
to lay a claim on my misfortune as if it were an heiress, and he is attempting
to persuade you that I am not what you all can see. You, on the other hand,
(and this is the task of sensible men) should rather trust your own eyes than
his words.

[15] He says that I am arrogant and violent, with a vile temperament,
as though he would be telling the truth if he used terrifying words and
he would not if he spoke calmly. But I think, members of the Council,
you must clearly distinguish those who have the opportunity to commit
outrage (*hybris*) from those who do not have what it takes. [16] It is not
likely for poor and destitute men to commit outrage, but it rather suits
those who possess much more than the necessities; nor those with disabled bodies, but those who have great confidence in their own bodily
strength; nor those who are advanced in years, but rather the young with
a youthful way of thinking. [17] Rich men buy their way out of danger
with their money, but poor men in their need are forced to show self-
control. Young men obtain forgiveness from their elders, but when the
elderly cross the line, they are met with disapproval by both age groups.
[18] Powerful men are in the position to subject whomever they wish
to outrage and nothing happens to them, while weak men cannot even
defend themselves against their aggressors when they are the victims of
outrage, and if they want to commit outrage, they cannot prevail over
their victims. So, I think the prosecutor was not serious when he spoke
about my arrogance, but he was joking, and his objective was not so much
to convince you that I am this kind of man but rather to ridicule me, as
though that was a worthwhile thing.

---

13. The nine archons, appointed by lot, were the highest officials of Athens. Any
citizen could be selected, except from two clearly defined groups: those whose
health and physical condition prevented them from performing the numerous
religious and sacrificial duties of the archons and those whose improper conduct
made them unsuitable for such duties, such as male prostitutes and individuals
who mistreated their parents (see the introduction to **Aeschines** 1). Although
technically *thetes* (laborers who were part of the lowest economic class of Athens)
were still in the fourth century prohibited from holding the archonship, candidates
were not asked whether they met the economic requirement.

[19] He also claims that many wicked men gather at my shop, who have squandered their own fortune, and they scheme against those who prefer to keep their property. You should keep in mind that when he says such things he is not accusing me any more than all those people who practice a trade, or my clientele any more than that of other tradesmen. [20] Each of you is accustomed to frequent either a perfumery or a barber shop or a shoe shop or some other place, and most people visit more often the businesses near the agora while few people visit those very far away from it. So, if someone accuses my own clientele of wickedness, clearly they should be accusing the clientele of everyone else, and if they do that, they are accusing all Athenians, because all of you are accustomed to frequent some place and spend some time there.[14]

[21] I do not see why I should go through every single point in great detail and trouble you for much longer. If I have touched upon the most important matters, why should I fuss about minor matters, as he does? All I am asking you to do, members of the Council, is to have the same opinion about me that you had in the past. [22] Do not, because of him, take away from me that one thing in the city that fortune has allowed me to share. Do not let this one man persuade you to take away from me what all of you in common have given me. Since fate, members of the Council, has deprived us of the greatest offices, the city voted to grant us this stipend, believing that fortune, whether good or bad, comes to everyone. [23] How would I not be the most wretched man, if I were deprived of the greatest and nicest things because of my misfortune and at the same time I lost what the city has provided for individuals in such a situation, because of my accuser? Do not, members of the Council, cast such a vote. And what reason would there be to treat me like this? [24] Because someone was brought to trial and lost his property on account of me? But not a single person could prove such a thing. Would it be because I am meddlesome and bold and argumentative? But I do not use the livelihood that I happen to have, for such purposes. [25] Would it be because I am very abusive and aggressive? Not even my accuser would make such claims, unless he were to lie about this in the same manner as he has lied about everything else. Would it be because under the Thirty I acquired power and mistreated many of the citizens? But I fled with the multitude of you to Chalcis, and although I had the opportunity to live under the oligarchic regime without fear, I still chose to share

---

14. He argues that his shop has the same diverse crowd that any other shop in the agora would have and therefore represents the diversity of the Athenian people. So by accusing his clientele of wickedness, his opponent is essentially criticizing the members of the Council, since men like them would also frequent his shop.

your dangers and flee with you.[15] [26] May I not, members of the Council, receive from you the same fate as those who have committed grave crimes, but may you vote the same way for me as the previous Councils, keeping in mind that I am not being audited for managing public funds or for an office that I held; I am making a case for only one obol. [27] Thus all of you will make the right decision, I will be grateful to you for receiving fair treatment, and my accuser will learn for the future not to plot against weaker men but to triumph over those who are his equals.

---

15. Following the civil war of 404–403, speakers regularly addressed their audience as though they had all fled the Thirty and supported the democratic opposition (see Wolpert 2002: 91–95).

ISAEUS 12

ON BEHALF OF EUPHILETUS

Introduction

This is probably the last among the surviving speeches of Isaeus, written in or shortly after 346. The aging logographer, who had written speeches for some of the wealthiest Athenian families involved in inheritance disputes over large estates, was called in to build the case in defense of Euphiletus, son of Hegisippus, whose citizenship had been questioned by his deme. When a young man of Athenian birth reached the age of eighteen, he became a full citizen after registering in his father's deme. The candidate was presented by his father or another close male relative, and the members of the deme voted whether to admit him. If the demesmen voted against his admission, he could appeal their decision to a court but would be sold into slavery if he lost. However, if he won, the members of the deme were compelled to accept him, and he enjoyed the full rights of an Athenian citizen. Euphiletus was initially rejected by the deme, but when the matter went to protracted arbitration, the deme lost and was compelled to admit him into the deme (**11–12**).

Despite their setback with the arbitration, the demesmen of Erchia were determined to expel Euphiletus, and when another opportunity presented itself, they seized it. Around the middle of the fourth century, Athenians were apparently concerned that non-citizens had fraudulently entered into the citizen-registers of the demes. In 346 the decree of Demophilus ordered a scrutiny of all registers in order to remove from the demes those who should not have been granted citizenship. All demes had to take a vote on each of their members (*diapsephisis*); those who were removed from the demes' register could appeal to the courts with considerable risk.[1] While personal or political animosities cannot be excluded from the present case, the deme of Erchia, as it seems, argued that Euphiletus was not the biological son of Hegisippus but was illicitly adopted as an infant. The vote of the deme went against Euphiletus during the *diapsephisis*. The deme's decision was met with firm and determined opposition by a united family, who

---

Translated by Konstantinos Kapparis.

1. Demosthenes' speech against Eubulides (Dem. 57) was delivered for such a case and reveals how local politics and personal quarrels offered fertile grounds for the abuse of this procedure (see Kapparis 2005).

rallied around Euphiletus, initiated an appeal (*ephesis*), and took the deme to court.

Only part of Euphiletus' defense has been preserved, as a lengthy quotation by Dionysius of Halicarnassus (*Isae.* 16). He dates the speech to the citizen scrutinies (*diapsephiseis*) of 346 and informs us that Euphiletus appealed the decision of the deme of Erchia to remove him from the register.[2] The quotation is not from Euphiletus, but his older half brother, son of Hegisippus from a previous marriage, acting as a supporting speaker (*synegoros*) for the defense. His help was especially valuable, since he was the one person who would have directly benefitted if Euphiletus were to be disfranchised and he did not have to share his patrimony (**4**). Euphiletus had, in addition, the support of his stepsisters and their husbands, and with a whole array of other relatives prepared to back his claim, including his mother and father (**1, 5–6, 9**), one cannot help but wonder what evidence the deme could use against such weighty testimony.

Dionysius introduces the quote as follows: "These facts have been explained in detail, and confirmed with witnesses, while the technique he uses to consolidate the testimonies, in my judgment, is crafted to perfection." One has to agree that this is an exceptional sample of Attic oratory. The barrage of key witnesses to support the citizenship of Euphiletus, the firm and tightly knitted argumentation, and the relentless pounding of the jury with compelling evidence make it difficult to imagine how one could convincingly argue against the citizenship of Euphiletus or how the deme could ever hope to win its case against such odds. The fact that we do not have the main narrative deprives us of important details, but if we were to judge from the supporting speech, it would seem unlikely that the jury could have delivered any verdict other than one in favor of Euphiletus.

Key Information

Speaker	The half brother of Euphiletus served as a supporting speaker (*synegoros*) for the defense.
Defendant	Euphiletus, son of Hegisippus.
Action	An appeal (*ephesis*) of the decision by the deme of Erchia to remove Euphiletus from the deme's register of enrolled citizens.

---

2. Wyse (1904: 715–16) would prefer that the speech concern an earlier scrutiny of citizens (*diapsephisis*), but no other scrutiny is attested except that of 346.

Penalty   Enslavement.

Date   c.346.

On Behalf of Euphiletus

[1] You have heard, men of the jury, not only us but all of our relatives testify that Euphiletus here is our brother.[3] Consider first why our father would lie and acknowledge him as his son if he was not his.[4] [2] You will find that all men who take such actions are forced to bring strangers into their family either because they have no legitimate children of their own or are compelled by poverty so that they can make some profit from them if they make them Athenian.[5] Our father had neither of these concerns; we are both his legitimate sons, so that he would not need to do this because of

---

3. It was not unusual for a litigant to invite a family member or friend to stand up and serve as a supporting speaker (*synegoros*) for some or even most of the time that he had at his disposal (e.g., **[Dem.] 59**). It was essential for the credibility of the litigant to establish that this support was offered freely by a concerned friend or family member and not by someone paid to represent him. Athenian juries would have distrusted someone who served as a paid advocate, and this is why the professional advocate is absent from the courts of the Athenian democracy. For *synegoria* in the Athenian legal system, see Rubinstein 2000.

4. Since the jury would already have heard the main arguments of the defense when Euphiletus spoke, his brother's speech does not contain a narrative and only refers indirectly to the points already made. Thus we are left with the difficult task of trying to reconstruct the case of the defense, and to make matters more complicated, as Wyse (1904: 714) puts it, "it is not Isaeus' way to state candidly and honestly the position of an adversary."

5. The speaker refers to two different types of adoption. The first was the legal and appropriate way of securing an heir. A man who did not have legitimate sons could adopt an Athenian of any age to be his heir. The second form of adoption was illegal and surreptitious. An Athenian could claim a child born to a foreigner or resident alien as his own, but since the adoption of non-Athenians was not permitted by law, he had to lie that the child was his biological offspring. The reason why one would do so, according to the speaker, apart from childlessness, was bribery by an alien seeking to secure the future of his child in Athens as a citizen. We have no hard evidence of such incidents, but this is hardly surprising under the circumstances. For adoption in Athens, see Rubinstein 1993.

childlessness.[6] [3] He does not need to secure either food or a comfortable life from him since he possesses a sufficient livelihood. Moreover, witnesses have testified that my father raised my brother from childhood and educated him and introduced him to his phratry, and these are no small expenses. So, it would not make sense, men of the jury, if my father attempted such an illicit undertaking without any benefit. [4] Then, no one should believe that I would be so foolish as to bear false witness in his favor only to end up sharing my patrimony with more heirs. I would never be able in the future to enter into a property dispute with him, alleging that he is not my brother, because none of you would hear a word, if now, while I am liable for perjury, I testify that he is my brother, but later I would appear to contradict this. [5] You can reasonably conclude, men of the jury, that not only we but also the other relatives have told the truth. First bear in mind that the husbands of our sisters would never give false testimony. His mother was a stepmother to our sisters, and frequently stepmothers and stepdaughters are very much at odds with each other. If he were the son of their stepmother from another man and not our father, my sisters would never have permitted or entrusted their husbands to testify. [6] Nor would our uncle from our mother's side, who is completely unrelated to his mother, give false testimony, which is obviously harmful to our interests, if we had brought a complete stranger into our midst as our brother. Besides them, how could one accuse of bearing false witness Demaratus here and Hegemon and Nicostratus, who first of all will never be shown to have done anything shameful, and second, as our relatives who know us, each one of them has given evidence on his own relationship to Euphiletus? [7] I would love to hear from the most pious of my opponents whether he could prove that he is an Athenian by any means other than the ones that we are using to prove that Euphiletus is Athenian. I do not think that he would have anything else to add except that his mother is Athenian and the lawful wife of his father, who is also a citizen, and he would present his relatives as witnesses that he is telling the truth. [8] So, if they were on trial, men of the jury, they would expect you to believe the testimonies of their relatives and not the prosecutors. But when we are providing all the necessary evidence, they expect you to believe their words and not the father of Euphiletus, me and my brother,

---

6. The deme seems to believe that Euphiletus was not the biological son of Hegisippus but was brought into the family as an infant. They probably argued that he was the child of Hegisippus' second wife by another man, whom Hegisippus accepted and presented as his own son. We find similar accusations in other speeches. The prosecutors of Neaera, for example, accused Stephanus of presenting her children as his own (see **[Dem.] 59**), and Euctemon allegedly introduced as his own the child of the former prostitute Alce (Isae. 6.21–24).

our phratry members, and all our relatives. And while they are doing this risk free, motivated by private enmities, all of us have to give evidence with the risk of a prosecution for false testimony.[7] [9] In addition to the testimonies, the mother of Euphiletus, who is accepted as a citizen by our opponents, wanted to take an oath before the arbitrator at the Delphinium that Euphiletus here is her and our father's son. Who could know this better than she? Then our father, men of the jury, who should also know his own son better than anyone else except his mother, then and now is willing to swear that Euphiletus is his own son from a citizen woman who is his lawfully wedded wife. [10] In addition, men of the jury, I was thirteen years old, as I mentioned to you before, when he was born, and I am ready to swear that Euphiletus here is my brother from the same father. So you would be right, men of the jury, to believe that our oaths are more trustworthy than their claims. We know exactly and are willing to swear an oath on his behalf while they are repeating rumors they heard from his opponents or invented themselves. [11] In addition, men of the jury, we summoned our relatives as witnesses before the arbitrators, as we are doing before you, and they deserve your trust. While Euphiletus brought the previous lawsuit against the deme and against the demarch of the time, who is dead now, the arbitrator kept the case open for two years, and still they could not produce a single witness confirming that he is the son of someone else and not of our father. This was very clear proof for the arbitrators that our adversaries were lying, and they both found against them.[8] Take the testimony about the previous arbitration.

---

7. Since this was an appeal initiated by Euphiletus against the decision of his deme, there was no risk to his opponents if they failed to receive one-fifth of the jury's votes, as was typically the case for public lawsuits in order to discourage frivolous prosecutions. For both public and private lawsuits, there was always an element of risk for witnesses, because they could be sued for false testimony by the opposing side.

8. It appears that the present case was not the first time that the members of the deme attempted to expel Euphiletus. The speaker mentions how an arbitration from a previous suit dragged on for two whole years (**9–11**). Since public arbitrators served only for one year, and each arbitrator had to close all his cases before the end of his term, it is not entirely clear how the arbitration could last for so long (see **Ant. 6.38**). Perhaps the death of the demarch (**11**) forced the suspension of all proceedings and their renewal in the next year under a new arbitrator. An alternative possibility is that both parties agreed to entrust the case to private arbitration, for which normally more than one person would be asked to serve and there was no deadline for the arbitrator to reach his decision. In this case, the arbitration could have taken two years. The complex details of this arbitration have been discussed by a number of scholars (see Kapparis 2005: 86–87). Whatever the case, the arbitration

TESTIMONY

[12] You have heard how they lost that arbitration. Men of the jury, just as they would have said that it was compelling proof that he was not the son of Hegisippus if the arbitrators had found for them, so now I ask for the same to be treated as proof in our favor that we speak the truth when the arbitrators found that the demesmen were wrong to remove him from the register after they had properly accepted him as an Athenian citizen in the first place. That Euphiletus here is our brother and your fellow citizen, and that he was unlawfully treated with insolence (*hybris*) by a clique in his deme, I believe has been sufficiently demonstrated to you, men of the jury.

---

went against the demesmen, probably due to the lack of witnesses in support of their claim.

DEMSOTHENES 21

AGAINST MEIDIAS

Introduction

In 348 Demosthenes volunteered to produce the men's chorus for his tribe at the City Dionysia (13–14), the annual festival in honor of Dionysus, which was celebrated at the end of March and included tragic and comic performances as well as choral songs.[1] His long-standing enemy, Meidias, allegedly set out to stop his chorus from winning the competition through various means. First, Meidias tried to prevent the chorus from receiving the typical exemption from military duty (15), and then he attempted to destroy their wardrobe but was unsuccessful (16). He conspired with the director to undermine the chorus's training, and on the day of the performance he bribed the judges of the contest, hindered the chorus from entering the stage, and hit Demosthenes as he appeared in the theater (5–6, 17–18). Immediately following the Dionysia, the Assembly convened in the theater to hear any complaints of "misconduct concerning the festival," which were lodged by the procedure of *probole*. Demosthenes used this opportunity to take action. The Assembly found in his favor and passed a vote of condemnation against Meidias, but it only had the power to censure him. Demosthenes still had to present his complaint to a dicastic court for legal sanctions to be imposed, but he waited until 347/6 to proceed further with his complaint, and the speech that we have is from this trial.[2] Some suggest that the prosecutor had to use a different procedure in court from the one used in the Assembly.[3] Demosthenes does in fact devote much of his time to arguing that Meidias was guilty of impiety and outrage (*hybris*). Yet, he also states that Meidias will object to his use of the *probole,* and he claims that if he had charged Meidias with impiety or outrage Meidias would then have argued that Demosthenes should instead have accused him of committing a wrong at the festival by *probole* (25–28). So, clearly

---

Translated by Andrew Wolpert.

1. The first speech in the collection, **Antiphon 6**, also concerns an offense arising from a choral production. In that dispute, the defendant was a chorus producer (*choregos*) accused of unintentional homicide for providing a potion to a chorus member that resulted in his death.

2. See Harris 1985; MacDowell 1990: 10–11.

3. E.g., Harris 2008: 79–81.

Demosthenes went to court by *probole* and formally charged Meidias with offenses concerning the festival.[4]

He probably did not proceed immediately to trial after the hearing in the theater, because either he considered the vote of condemnation to be a sufficient punishment or he was concerned that a jury might have regarded the actual offenses committed during the festival to be fairly minor. In fact, he fails to provide us with any specific details about his physical confrontation with Meidias. Certainly if he had been injured, he would have told us (cf. **Dem. 54.8, 11–12**). So in all likelihood, the scuffle, which was the main justification for the *probole* against Meidias, was not as serious as Demosthenes implies. Meidias, however, continued to harass him, in spite of the Assembly's censure, with charges of desertion and murder and by trying to prevent Demosthenes from serving on the Council (**102–16**). Demosthenes, therefore, decided to pursue further his *probole*. He was likely to win at least one-fifth of the jury's votes, since the Assembly had already censured Meidias, and so the action entailed limited risks. If he won, he would have sent a strong warning to Meidias about the consequences of continuing to harass him. Even if he lost, the trial provided him with another opportunity to rail against Meidias and publicly embarrass him, and he would have made it clear that he was not going to take any future attacks lying down. On the other hand, a jury might have regarded the actual offense at the festival less seriously after this long hiatus. So Demosthenes had to focus his attention on the question of impiety and outrage in order to convince the jurors of the seriousness of Meidias' misconduct and prepare them for the penalty that he would be required to propose, since this action did not have a fixed penalty. While he insisted that Meidias deserved to be sentenced to death (e.g., **12, 21, 118, 142, 201**), he might have been hedging his bets, since he also suggested that confiscation of Meidias' property would suffice (**152**).

Although Aeschines (3.52) claims that Demosthenes sold his prosecution of Meidias for thirty minas, one must be wary of accepting this statement at face value. Since they were bitter rivals, Aeschines is not our most objective source. On the one hand, there are elements of the speech that suggest Demosthenes left it unfinished and that lend credence to Aeschines.[5] On the other hand, the speech also shows that Demosthenes had a thorough knowledge of Meidias' defense; so the preliminary hearing must have taken place. If he had dropped the case, he would have suffered partial disfranchisement and would have been fined one thousand drachmas, making

---

4. MacDowell 1990: 16–17; Rowe 1994.

5. E.g., the loan metaphor is repeated (**101, 184–85**) and Meidias' supporters are listed twice (**208, 215**), but the lists do not match up. See Dover 1968: 172–73; MacDowell 1990: 23–28.

thirty minas not much of an incentive (see Harris 1989: 132–34). It is more likely that Aeschines is either lying or misrepresenting the outcome. Perhaps Demosthenes proposed the penalty of thirty minas because he barely won a conviction and did not expect the jury to accept a more severe penalty. Thirty minas might not have been a hefty fine for Meidias, but for most Athenians it was a substantial sum of money. He was probably spared an even greater fine only because the skirmish between the two men was fairly minor.

Some suggest that this speech was never intended for court but was circulated privately to demonstrate how Demosthenes would have attacked Meidias (see Dover 1968: 174). If so, we should understand his awareness of Meidias' defense as an elaborate fiction rather than as evidence that a preliminary hearing had taken place. Yet this too is unlikely. Why would Demosthenes have bothered drafting the speech? What message would he have been circulating throughout Athens if he had refused to go after Meidias publicly in court? Meidias was one of his most bitter enemies. He had helped Demosthenes' guardians avoid returning the property Demosthenes had inherited from his father, and the two men had been pursuing their grievances against each other both in and out of the courts for some sixteen years (**77–122**). It is hard to imagine that Demosthenes would have been satisfied with any form of retaliation that did not involve public sanctions, especially when Meidias continued to bully him even after the Assembly's censure. For Demosthenes, the festival was just the tip of the iceberg. This is why he spends so much time in his speech describing how their quarrel had evolved over the years and how Meidias' behavior had impacted others. Demosthenes truly believed that Meidias was guilty of outrage and he was a threat not just to his personal enemies but to all Athenians. For this reason, Demosthenes uses words that have "*hybris*" as their root 130 times in the speech, approximately once for every two sections.

The speech has, as a result, become an important source for our knowledge of the Athenian law on *hybris*. It is a concept difficult to translate into English, and had a rather different meaning for the Athenians than it does today when it is used in discussions on drama. There remains disagreement about the full range of its meaning and about which connotations were core and which were ancillary, but *hybris* generally refers to an act that dishonors another. It is an attack on the dignity of the victim, and for this reason it is often violent and sexual, and thus rape may have been a form of *hybris*. Physical assault, however, is not necessarily an act of *hybris*. As Demosthenes explains:

> The blow did not provoke his anger, but the dishonor did, since it is not so terrible for free men to be struck (although it

is terrible) but to be struck with outrage (*hybris*). The one who strikes, men of Athens, could do many things that the victim could not express to another, with his body language, his facial expression, and his voice, when he commits outrage, when he acts out of enmity, when he throws punches, when he strikes the face. These things stir men, they make them lose control of themselves when they are not used to being abused. No one, as he describes these actions, men of Athens, could make the horror from the outrage be as vivid to his listeners as it appeared at the very moment to the victim and the witnesses. (**72**)

Hybris is the offense of a man who thinks too much of his own worth and too little of his victim and who acts in ways that shame, humiliate, and dishonor others. For this reason, *hybris* can be viewed as a threat to the democracy, and according to Demosthenes, this is why even slaves were formally protected by the law on *hybris*. The Athenians were not concerned about slaves per se; rather they extended such protection to prevent *hybris* from occurring in the first place (**46**).[6]

Given the extent to which Meidias and Demosthenes relied on legal procedures to retaliate against each other, the speech has also become an important source to show how the Athenian legal system provided a stage for enemies to pursue and publicly air their grievances against each other, thus serving to fuel further litigation.[7] The quarrel between Meidias and Demosthenes began some sixteen years before the incident in the Theater of Dionysus. In 364/3 Demosthenes began legal action against his guardians for confiscating funds and misappropriating property that belonged to him and that he should have inherited from his father. Acting in collusion with the guardians, Thrasylochus attempted to stop the suits by calling for an exchange of property (*antidosis*), which would have required Demosthenes to either perform the liturgy that had been assigned to Thrasylochus or exchange property with him. If the latter had happened, Demosthenes could not have continued his suits, since his father's estate would no longer have been his. Apparently Thrasylochus along with his brother, Meidias, entered Demosthenes' home as though Demosthenes had already agreed to the exchange, and the three of them engaged in an altercation inside of Demosthenes' home and in front of his mother and sister. Following this hostile encounter, Demosthenes agreed to perform the liturgy so that he could continue his suits against his guardians, but he retaliated against Meidias by lodging a suit of slander against him (**78–81**). It appears that Demosthenes did not

---

6. For further discussion on *hybris*, see MacDowell 1976; Fisher 1992; Cairns 1996.
7. See Cohen 1995; contra Herman 2006.

take legal action against Thrasylochus, probably because the *antidosis* permitted his entry into the home in spite of Demosthenes' assertions to the contrary. The young man had been legally outmaneuvered and had no grounds for proceeding against Thrasylochus; so he had to set his target on Meidias.

In a series of complicated legal maneuvers, Meidias first delayed the charge of slander from coming to an arbitrator, then he did not show up when the arbitration finally took place, and after the arbitrator decided against him by default, he had the decision set aside so that he did not have to pay the fine that the arbitrator had imposed (**81–87**). The quarrel between Demosthenes and Meidias appears to have subsided for some time. But then in 349 Athens began some military operations in the North to prevent the growth of Macedonian power. Demosthenes and Meidias both participated in the debates over the appropriate Athenian response and joined in some of the military missions that followed (**132–35, 161–74, 197–200**). It appears that the private animosity that had been festering for so many years heated up again as they took the public stage, which perhaps unintentionally became a venue for them to go after each other in front of a large audience. So when Demosthenes volunteered to produce the men's chorus for his tribe at the Dionysia in 348, there was no love lost between the two men, who already had quite a history of staged hostility before their fellow citizens. In some ways, the confrontation at the Dionysia—even if it resulted in merely a slap or punch—was all the more embarrassing for Demosthenes because everyone knew that Meidias had been able to hound him for years and Demosthenes had been unable to put a stop to it. So too one cannot help but wonder whether the fact that their drama played out in the theater, where the Athenians watched tragedies and comedies, made it all the more sensational.

Key Information

Speaker	Demosthenes prosecuted Meidias for hitting him at the Dionysia and for other offenses committed against him while he was serving as a chorus producer (*choregos*).
Defendant	Meidias.
Other Individuals	Thrasylochus, brother of Meidias, challenged Demosthenes to either perform the liturgy that he had been selected to do or accept an exchange of property (*antidosis*).
	Strato, serving as a public arbitrator for a dispute between Demosthenes and Meidias, lost his civic

rights after Meidias lodged a complaint against him over the arbitration.

Euctemon allegedly accepted a bribe from Meidias to charge Demosthenes with desertion.

Although Aristarchus, son of Moschus, killed Nicodemus, Meidias allegedly attempted to convince Nicodemus' relatives to prosecute Demosthenes instead for the murder.

Polyzelus, Euaeon, and Euthynus were mentioned by Demosthenes as examples of men who were subjected to outrage (*hybris*).

Euandrus, Ctesicles, and Aristophon were mentioned by Demosthenes as examples of men who committed offenses concerning the festival that were actionable by the procedure of *probole*.

Action	Public action for wrongs concerning a festival, lodged first by *probole* before the Assembly and then taken to court.
Punishment	If the jury found Meidias guilty, Demosthenes and Meidias each had to propose a penalty, and the jury then had to decide which of the two penalties to impose.
Date	347/6.

Against Meidias

[1] The brutality, men of the jury, and the outrage[8] to which Meidias always subjects everyone, I believe, are not unknown to any of you or to the rest of the citizens. I, however, did just what each of you would have also chosen to do if you had been a victim of outrage. I lodged a *probole*[9] against him for committing an offense concerning the festival, not only

---

8. *Hybris* is difficult to translate into English, but because it appears so frequently in the text (130 times), we have decided that it would be too cumbersome to leave it untranslated even if there is no English equivalent. For further discussion, see the introduction to this speech.

9. Offenses committed during the Dionysia were heard immediately following the festival, in a special session of the Assembly held in the theater by the procedure

because I received blows from him at the Dionysia, but also because I suffered many other acts of violence during the entire time I was a chorus producer.[10] [2] Acting correctly and fairly, the people[11] were so angry, so upset, and so concerned about the wrongs that they were aware I had suffered that even though he and some others on his behalf tried everything they were not persuaded to pay attention to his wealth and promises but condemned him with one resolve. Afterwards, men of the jury, many approached me, from both those of you who are now in the courtroom and the rest of the citizens. They bid and encouraged me to pursue the suit and hand him over to you, as it seems to me, men of the jury, for two reasons: by the gods, they both thought that I had suffered terribly, and at the same time they wanted him to pay the penalty for what they had seen him doing on other occasions—being bold, outrageous, and completely unstoppable. [3] And so I turned to the law to protect all of your interests that ought to have been protected, and I am present, as you see, to prosecute when the official introduces the case, refusing, men of Athens, much money—although I could have accepted it so as not to prosecute—and enduring many entreaties and promises and, yes, even threats. [4] What remains for you to do after this is as follows: the more this one has bothered many with his lobbying (for I saw what he was doing just now before the courts), the more I expect to receive justice. I would not accuse any of you of being careless about that matter for which I received your support or of voting under oath for anything other than what he believes is just so that Meidias may commit outrage with impunity for the rest of his life.

[5] If, men of Athens, I were going to prosecute him for proposing illegal decrees or for misconduct on an embassy or some other such charge, I would not think it right to ask for anything in addition, since I think that in such trials the prosecutor should only prove his case while the defendant can make an additional appeal.[12] He, however, corrupted the judges

---

of *probole*. The vote of the Assembly was only prejudicial, since a law court still had to hear the complaint in order for the perpetrator to receive a punishment.

10. Wealthy Athenians were required to perform public services, called liturgies, in rotation. The *choregia* was a liturgy performed by the chorus producer (*choregos*), who was responsible for paying the expenses to perform either a dramatic or lyric chorus. The trierarchy was the most costly liturgy. It was performed by the trierarch, who was responsible for the maintenance and command of an Athenian warship, known as the trireme because it had three banks of oars.

11. Litigants often referred to the Assembly as the "people" (*demos*), which we sometimes translate as "Assembly" for clarity; cf. **6, 16, 18, 68, 180, 206**.

12. Here Demosthenes cautiously prepares the jurors for his request that they feel sympathy for him for the wrongs that he has suffered. It is more typical for the defendant to seek the jury's pity.

at the competition so that my tribe was unjustly deprived of the tripod,[13] [6] and I myself received blows and suffered outrageous treatment such as I do not know whether any other chorus producer has ever endured. And since I bring to court the vote of condemnation that the people cast in the Assembly because they were upset with and shared in my anger over his actions, I will not shrink to make also this request. If I can say it, I am now a defendant, should it be my misfortune not to obtain justice after I have been treated with outrage. [7] Therefore, I beg and implore all of you first to listen favorably to me as I speak and then, if I show that Meidias, the man before us, has committed outrage not only against me, but also against you and the laws and everyone else, to help me and yourselves. Here, men of Athens, is how the issue stands: I was then treated with outrage and my body abused, but the matter will now be contested and decided whether or not he ought to be permitted to do such things and with impunity commit outrage against anyone of you who crosses his path. [8] So if anyone of you before supposed that this suit derives from some prior disagreement, let him consider now how it is not in the public interest to permit anyone to do such a thing; let him listen carefully, since the matter concerns the public; and let him vote for what seems to him to be most just.

He[14] will first read to you the law that establishes *probolai*. Next I will attempt to explain the other matters. Read the law.

LAW

The prytaneis[15] convene the Assembly in the precinct of Dionysus on the day after the Pandia.[16] At this meeting, they conduct business first on sacred matters, then let them bring forth the probolai that there are for the procession or the contests at the Dionysia and whichever have not been paid for.[17]

---

13. This was the prize for winning the men's chorus competition. Demosthenes is accusing Meidias of bribing the judges of the contest so that they would vote in favor of a rival chorus.

14. I.e., the court secretary.

15. This is the title of those fifty councilors who acted as the steering committee for the Council of Five Hundred. A councilor served as one of the *prytaneis* for one-tenth of the year (called a prytany) together with the other councilors from his tribe.

16. A festival in honor of Zeus held after the Dionysia (see Parke 1977: 136).

17. The *probolai* presented before the Assembly did not include those for minor offenses that were settled if the accused paid a small fine set by the Council (MacDowell 1990: 228–29).

[9] This is the law, men of Athens, for which there are *probolai,* and it states, as you have heard, to convene the Assembly in the precinct of Dionysus after the Pandia, and here, after the presiding officers (*proedroi*)[18] bring to a consideration matters that the archon[19] oversees, to deliberate also about the offenses or violations anyone has committed concerning the festival. This law is good, men of Athens, and useful, as the dispute itself shows. When some men are not less visibly insolent with this fear looming, what would one expect such men to do if there were imminent no trial or peril?

[10] Now I wish to read to you also the next law so that the discretion of the rest of you and the daring of this one will become clear to you all. Read the law.

LAW

Euegorus proposed: During the procession to Dionysus in the Piraeus and the comedies and the tragedies, and the procession at the Lenaea[20] and the tragedies and the comedies, and the procession at the City Dionysia and the boys' choruses and the revel and the comedies and the tragedies, and at the procession and the contest of the Thargelia,[21] no one may distrain[22] or seize[23] something else from another, not even from debtors in default, on those days. And if someone violates any of these restrictions, let him be liable to prosecution by the victim, and let there be probolai against him, in the Assembly in the sacred precinct of Dionysus, as the offender, just as it has been prescribed for other offenders.[24]

[11] Consider, men of the jury, that, while there is a *probole* in the former law against those who commit offenses concerning the festival, you established *probolai* in the latter law against those who exact payment from

---

18. Nine *proedroi* chaired the meetings of the Council and Assembly. They were selected by lot each day from the members of the Council so that each tribe was represented except for the one in prytany.

19. The archon (also known as the eponymous archon because the year was named after him) was in charge of the Dionysia.

20. A festival in honor of Dionysus held in January.

21. A festival in honor of Apollo held in the spring.

22. "Distrain" is to seize a security on a defaulted debt. For further discussion on loans and security, see the introduction to **Demosthenes 32**.

23. E.g., to seize the actual debt that is owed.

24. MacDowell (1990: 230–31) considers the law authentic, while Harris (2008: 90) believes this law and the previous one (**8**) are later insertions by a scribe who did not have access to the actual laws.

overdue debtors or take anything from someone else or use force. Because you believed that no one's body should be subjected to outrage on those days, nor the preparation someone personally contributed for his liturgy, you even permitted property belonging by law and by your vote to the prosecutors who won to remain with the defendants who lost and were the original owners, for at least the duration of the festival.[25] [12] Men of Athens, you have reached such a degree of generosity and piety that you refrain on those days from exacting punishment for even past offenses. Meidias, however, will be shown to have committed offenses on those days that deserve the most severe punishment. After describing each of the things that I suffered from the beginning, I want to speak also about the blows he finally laid on me. For everything that he has done, it will be shown that he deserves to die.

[13] Two years ago when the chorus producer had not been appointed for the Pandionis tribe and the Assembly convened, at which the law requires the archon to allot[26] flute players to the chorus producers, there was discussion and recrimination, with the archon accusing the managers of the tribe and the managers of the tribe the archon.[27] Then I came forward and promised voluntarily to be the chorus producer. When lots were cast and I drew the lot to be the first to select a flute player, [14] you, men of Athens, were all as pleased as possible at both my promise and the lucky drawing, and you shouted and applauded with what had to be your approval of and delight in the outcome. But Meidias, this man before us, was the only one, as it seemed, to be upset, and he hounded me throughout the entire time of my liturgy, constantly causing me troubles, great and small.

[15] How much he annoyed me with his opposition to the release of my chorus from military duty or his nomination and campaigning in the election for manager of the Dionysia,[28] I will not mention. I know that

---

25. A prosecutor who won a suit that awarded him damages had the responsibility of collecting the sum from the defendant, but the cited law indicates that he could not do so during these festivals.

26. The lottery determined only the order for the selection of flute players. Each producer chose for himself which flute players he wanted for his chorus.

27. Each tribe provided a men's and boys' chorus to perform at the Dionysia. In addition to overseeing the selection of the chorus producers, the three managers conducted sacrifices for the tribe and took care of the tribe's funds. Since the boys' chorus was less expensive to produce, the problem was probably with assigning a chorus producer to the men's chorus (MacDowell 1990: 236–37).

28. The archon had ten managers of the Dionysia (not the same as the managers of the tribe discussed above) who assisted him in preparations for the festival and were apparently still elected (see MacDowell 1990: 238–39). Meidias'

each of these acts stirred up in me, who was then attacked and treated with
outrage, the same anger as any other of the most terrible offenses, but for
the rest of you, who have no part in this dispute, they would perhaps not
in themselves appear worthy of a trial. What, however, will upset all of you
alike, I will mention. [16] What he did next, as I will discuss, has surpassed
everything, and still I would not have attempted to prosecute him now if
I had not convicted him then at the meeting of the Assembly. The sacred
clothing (for I consider all clothes that one prepares for a festival to be
sacred until used) and the golden crowns, which I had made to adorn the
chorus, he attempted, men of Athens, to destroy as he entered my goldsmith's house at night. He destroyed them, but not completely, because
he couldn't. And there is no one who says that he has ever heard anyone
attempting or accomplishing such a thing in the city. [17] This, however,
was not enough for Meidias, but he even, men of Athens, corrupted[29] the
director of my chorus. And if then Telephanes, the flute player, had not
been my best ally, and if he had not felt obligated to choreograph and direct the chorus himself after he drove the man away when he recognized what
the director was doing, we would not have had even a chance of winning
the competition, the chorus would have gone on stage untrained, and we
would have suffered the greatest humiliation. This was not the limit of his
depravity, but there was so much left in him that he tried to corrupt the
crowned archon and drive the chorus producers against me; with shouts
and threats he stood beside the judges[30] as they swore their oaths; he blocked
and nailed up the side-scenes,[31] although they were public property and he
was a private citizen; and he continually caused me unspeakable troubles
and problems. [18] As for what occurred in the Assembly[32] or before the
judges in the theater, you, men of the jury, are all my witnesses.[33] Certainly
those statements must be considered the most honest, which the audience
can bear witness to the speaker that they are true. After corrupting the
judges for the men's contest in advance, he topped off, as it were, all of his

---

"campaigning" probably entailed promises to the Assembly about the financial
support that he would provide for the festival if elected. Perhaps his intent was to
outdo Demosthenes with his own personal generosity.

29. See **5** n.

30. The archon oversaw the selection by lot of ten men to judge the performances
(Isoc. 17.33–34; Plu. *Cim.* 8.8).

31. This presumably disrupted the entrance of the chorus by blocking its entry and
forcing it to take a circuitous route.

32. See **2** n.

33. Cf. **36, 120, 171, 176**; see **Lys. 12.36** n.

youthful feats with these two acts: he subjected my body to outrage, and he was the main reason why the tribe with the best performance did not win.

[19] These, men of Athens, are the brutal acts that he committed against me and my tribesmen and the offenses that he carried out concerning the festival, on account of which I lodged a *probole* against him, and there are many other offenses that I will immediately describe to you as much as I can. I can also speak about the multitude of his other wicked and outrageous actions against many of you and the many terrible and shameless acts of this cursed man. [20] Some of his victims, men of the jury, kept silent because they feared him and his boldness and his friends and his wealth and everything else that he has in addition; some attempted unsuccessfully to receive legal compensation; and some reached a settlement with him, perhaps because they believed that it was in their interest. So those who were persuaded to settle gained compensation for themselves, but of that owed to the laws, which he violated when he wronged those men and now me and everyone else, you are the heirs. [21] Accordingly, set one penalty, whichever you believe to be just, for all of these offenses together. I will first show how I have been treated with outrage and then how you have. Next I will go over the rest of his life and will show that he deserves to die many times and not just once. Please take first the testimony of the goldsmith and read it.

[22] TESTIMONY

{*I, Pammenes, son of Pammenes, have a goldsmith's shop in the agora, where I live and practice the trade of a goldsmith. Demosthenes, for whom I testify, hired me to make a golden crown*[34] *and a gold-embroidered cloak in order to wear them at the procession for Dionysus. When I finished them and had them ready in my house, Meidias, whom Demosthenes is prosecuting, broke into my house at night with others, and he attempted to destroy the crown and cloak and he damaged some of them, but was unable to destroy them completely because I prevented him when I appeared.*}

[23] Now I can speak much, men of Athens, also about the offenses he committed against others, as I said in the beginning of my speech, and I have assembled a list of his acts of outrage and his shameful deeds, all of which you will hear right away. The list was easy to assemble since his victims came to me. [24] But I wish to speak first about the ways in which I have heard that he will attempt to deceive you, since I believe that it is

---

34. Since Demosthenes mentions multiple crowns elsewhere (**16**, **25**), this reference to only one crown helps show that the testimony is spurious.

especially important for me to warn you of his deceit and especially useful for you to hear about it. Why? Because this part of my speech, which prevents you from being deceived, will ensure that you cast a vote that is just and in accordance with your oath. Most of all, you must pay attention to this part of my speech, remember it, and reject each part of his when he speaks. [25] From what has been reported to me by some whom he approached privately, he clearly will say first that if I had truly suffered what I am claiming, I should have brought private cases of damage[35] against him for the destruction of the cloaks and the golden crowns and for all of his mistreatment of the chorus, and a case of outrage for the insolence, which I allege that he committed against my body, and should not, by Zeus, have prosecuted him publicly[36] and proposed a punishment for him to suffer or a fine for him to pay. [26] But this I know well, and so should you, that, if I had not lodged a *probole* against him but a private suit, I would have been immediately confronted with the opposite argument. If any of my assertions were true, I ought to have lodged a *probole* and sought retribution at the time of the very offenses since it was the city's chorus, the clothes were all prepared for the festival, and I, the victim of these violations, was a chorus producer. Therefore, who would have preferred any other form of redress than the one permitted by the law against those who commit offenses concerning the festival? [27] I know well that he would have said all of this then. It is, however, typical of a defendant who is guilty, I believe, to try to evade the legal procedure that is being used to punish him, by saying that the legal procedure that is not used ought to have been, but it is the trait of wise jurors to ignore such claims and punish whomever they catch committing brutal offenses. [28] Do not allow him to say that the law grants me the right to bring private cases or a public case for outrage. It certainly does, but let him show that he has not done what I have accused,

---

35. By the law on damage (*dike blabes*), an individual could bring a private suit against another for damage to property. It covered both physical and financial loss as well as the failure to repay a debt. See MacDowell 1978: 149–53; Todd 1993: 279–82.

36. The distinction here is between (1) standard dicastic suits, such as (a) cases for damage, which are private (*dikai*), and (b) cases for outrage (*hybris*), which are public (*graphai*); and (2) the *probole,* which is first heard "publicly" (i.e., before the Assembly [*demos*]); cf. MacDowell 1990: 247; contra Harris 2008: 96 n. Demosthenes insists that however he pursued his grievance Meidias would have responded that he should have used a different legal procedure for seeking redress. So if he had prosecuted Meidias for damage or outrage rather than lodged a *probole,* Meidias would have insisted that Demosthenes should have brought a *probole* before the Assembly immediately following the incident if he were in fact guilty of an offense concerning the festival.

or he has, but he is not guilty of committing a wrong concerning the festival. This is why I lodged a *probole* against him, and this is the matter for which you will now cast your vote. And if I give up the reward that comes with private suits and concede the penalty to the city and I chose this suit for which I cannot receive any gain, thanks, I suppose, would be fitting for me to receive from you, not harm.

[29] Now I know that he will also make much use of this argument: "Don't surrender me to Demosthenes, don't destroy me because of Demosthenes. Because I am at war with him, will you destroy me?" I know that he will voice such sentiment many times, wishing to instill some malice against me through these statements. [30] This isn't how it is done, not even close. You do not surrender any offender to any prosecutor. Whenever someone is wronged, you do not fix the penalty as each victim persuades you but rather you enacted the laws before the offenses, when it was not known who would be the offenders and who would be the victims. What do these laws do? They promise to all in the city that if anyone is wronged, he will be able to obtain justice through them. Well then, whenever you punish someone who has violated the laws, you do not surrender him to the prosecutors but you uphold the laws for your own interests. [31] With regards to his claim, "Demosthenes has been subjected to outrage," there is a response that is just and universal and impacts everyone: his brutality was directed not only against me, Demosthenes, on that day, but also against your chorus producer. You can best understand this point from the following. [32] You know, of course, that none of the *thesmothetai*[37] has the name *thesmothetes,* but each has his own name, whatever it may be. So if someone commits outrage or says slanderous remarks against any of them acting in his private capacity, he will be a defendant in a public suit for outrage or a private suit for slander, but if he does so against a person acting as a *thesmothetes,* he will be permanently disfranchised.[38] Why? Because the man who does so also commits an act of outrage against the laws and your public crown and the name of the city, since *thesmothetes* is a name that belongs to no man but to the city. [33] The same applies also to the archon: if someone strikes or slanders him when he is crowned, the individual is disfranchised, but if he does so against the archon in his private capacity, he is liable to a private suit. Not only for these individuals is this the case

---

37. They were six of the nine archons, with the primary duty of overseeing the law courts. The other three were the *basileus* (king archon), the polemarch (war archon), and the archon, mentioned in **9, 33**.

38. In contrast to state-debtors who regained their civic rights once they paid off their debt to the city, an individual found guilty of injuring a public official was permanently disfranchised; cf. **87**.

but also for whomever the city bestows the right to wear a crown or some other honor. And so it also applies to me: if Meidias had committed any of these offenses against me in my private capacity on some other day, it would have been appropriate for him to pay the penalty by a private suit. [34] If, however, he clearly committed outrage in all of his offenses against me when I was your chorus producer during a sacred time, it is just for him to incur public anger and suffer a public punishment. The chorus producer was treated with outrage at the same time as Demosthenes, and this concerns the city, and it took place on those days on which the laws prohibit it. When you are enacting laws, you must consider what their purpose is, but once you have enacted them, you must preserve them and apply them since this is the requirement of your oath and is otherwise just. [35] Long ago you had the law on damage, the law on battery, the law on outrage.[39] So if it were enough for those who committed any of these infractions at the Dionysia to pay the penalty by those laws, this additional law would not have been necessary. But it was not enough. Here's the proof: you established a sacred law for that god during sacred days. And so, if someone is liable under those laws, which existed beforehand, as well as this law, which was established after them, and all the other laws, for that reason is such a man not going to be punished, or would it be just for him to receive an even greater punishment? I believe a greater one!

[36] Someone told me that he was going around assembling a list and finding out whoever has happened to suffer outrage, and that he intends to name them and describe to you, men of Athens, their misfortunes, such as the *proedros* whom, they say, Polyzelus struck in front of you,[40] and the *thesmothetes* who was recently struck as he was removing the flute girl, and some others like them. And if he shows that many other men suffered much terrible treatment, he hopes that you will be less angry at what I suffered. [37] I think, men of Athens, that it would be right for you to do the opposite if you ought to care about what is best for the public. Who of you does not know that the failure to punish those who are guilty is the reason why there are many such offenses, and the exacting of the appropriate punishment every time an individual is caught would be the only reason why no one would commit outrage in the future? If it is useful to deter others, he ought to be punished also for their offenses, and more so, inasmuch as their offenses are many more and much worse. But if it is useful to incite him and everyone, let him go. [38] Moreover, we will find that he does not have the same grounds for forgiveness as they. First,

---

39. For the law on damage, see **25** n.; for battery, see the introduction to **Demosthenes 54**.

40. I.e., at a meeting of the Assembly.

the man that hit the *thesmothetes* had three excuses: drunkenness, sexual desire, and lack of recognition, since it took place in the darkness of night. Second, Polyzelus struck by mistake, in anger and without thinking, because he was hotheaded. The man was not his enemy, and he did not act with the intent of committing outrage. Meidias, however, cannot say any of these excuses, since he was my enemy, he knowingly treated me with outrage in broad daylight, and not only on this occasion but on every occasion he clearly chose to treat me with outrage. [39] And besides, I see no similarity between my actions and theirs. First, the *thesmothetes* clearly had no care for nor felt any anger on behalf of you and the laws, but was privately induced by some sum of money to drop his suit. Second, the man whom Polyzelus struck did the same thing: accepting a private reconciliation and saying goodbye to the laws and you, he did not even prosecute Polyzelus. [40] Well, if one wants to prosecute them now, he must speak about these matters. But if Meidias wants to defend himself against the charges of which I have accused him, he must speak about everything else first. I acted entirely the opposite of these men. It will be clear that I neither received nor attempted to receive anything, but I justly preserved the right to exact punishment on behalf of the laws, the god, and you, and I have now handed him over to you. Therefore do not permit him to say this, and if he persists, do not believe that his claim is just. [41] If this is your decision, he does not have an argument, not one. What excuse, what plea, reasonable and deserving of compassion, will appear for his actions? Anger? Perhaps he will even make this claim. But whatever someone has been induced to do on the spur of the moment without thinking, even if his actions are insulting, can be said to have been done in anger. Not only are whatever acts one is caught doing illegally for a long period of time, continuously, over many days, done without anger but it is clear that such an individual has also intentionally committed outrage.

[42] Well, since he clearly has done as I charge and has done so insolently, you ought now to consider the laws, men of the jury, for you have sworn an oath to judge according to them.[41] Consider how much they view those who intentionally commit acts of outrage as deserving more anger and a greater punishment than those who offend in some other manner. [43] First, all the laws concerning damage—to begin with them—order, if one intentionally causes damage, to pay double the amount, but if one does so unintentionally, to pay the amount of the damage. This is appropriate, since it is just for the victim to receive help in every instance, but the law

---

41. Litigants regularly reminded the jurors of the Heliastic oath that they swore at the beginning of the year, following the annual sortition, requiring them to vote in accordance with the laws (see Dem. 24.148–51).

did not mete out the same anger for an individual acting intentionally as
one acting unintentionally. Next, the laws on homicide punish those who
intentionally kill with death, permanent exile, and confiscation of property,
but they considered those who unintentionally kill to be deserving of forgiveness and much compassion.[42] [44] Not only from these suits can one
recognize that the laws are severe in the case of those who intentionally
commit outrage, but from all suits. Why on earth is it the case that if someone loses a private suit and does not pay the fine the law does not render
the suit of ejectment[43] a private matter, but sets an additional penalty owed
to the city? And again, why on earth is it the case that if someone obtains
a talent or two or ten by mutual consent and commits fraud, the city has
no claim against him, but if an individual obtains something worth a very
small amount and he takes it away by force, the laws prescribe an additional
payment to the city equal to that owed to the individual? [45] Because the
lawgiver believed that all acts of violence are public offenses and impact
those who are not parties to the dispute. Whereas a few have strength, the
laws belong to everyone, and the one who is persuaded needs a private
remedy while the one who suffers violence requires public assistance. He,
therefore, permitted everyone who wanted to bring public suits for outrage, but he awarded the entire penalty to the city. He believed that the
one attempting to commit outrage harmed the city and not just the victim,
and justice was sufficient compensation for the victim, who ought not
to receive money for himself from such offenses. [46] He went to such an
extreme as to allow a public suit even in the case of a slave whom someone
subjects to outrage, since he believed that one ought not to take into consideration who the victim is but what sort of an offense it is.[44] And when
he discovered that it was detrimental, he enjoined that the offense could

---

42. The Athenians distinguished only between intentional and unintentional
homicide, not degrees of intent and not whether the murder was premeditated or
without forethought; see Loomis 1972; Carawan 1998; Phillips 2008: 59 n. 4. In
the case of intentional homicide, the accused was permitted to go into voluntary
exile at any point before he delivered his second speech in order to avoid execution.
If found guilty, the defendant had his property confiscated in addition to suffering
the penalty of death or exile. A person found to be guilty of unintentional homicide
was required to go into exile; see the introduction to **Antiphon 6**.

43. If a defendant lost a private suit and refused to surrender the property or pay
the sum awarded to the prosecutor, the prosecutor could bring a suit of ejectment
against the defendant. If the prosecutor won the suit, he was granted the right to
use force to secure the amount that he had been awarded in the original suit, and
the defendant received an additional fine, which he had to pay to the city. See
MacDowell 1978: 153–54; Todd 1993: 144–45.

44. Cf. **Aesch. 1.17–18**.

not be committed either against a slave or at all. Nothing, men of Athens, nothing at all is more intolerable than outrage, nor does anything deserve your anger more. Please read the law on outrage, since there is nothing like hearing the very law.

LAW[45]

[47] *If someone commits outrage against another, whether it be a child or woman or man, whether free or slave, or commits some other offense against another, let him whoever wishes of those Athenians who are permitted lodge a public suit before the thesmothetai, and let the thesmothetai bring it to the Heliastic court within thirty days from the indictment, if public business does not prevent it, but if it does, as soon as first possible. Whomever the Heliastic court condemns, let it immediately impose a penalty on him, whichever it thinks he deserves to suffer or pay. Whoever lodges a public suit in accordance with the law and does not go to court or going to court fails to receive one-fifth of the votes, let him pay a fine of one thousand drachmas to the city. If he is fined for outrage, let him be imprisoned, if he committed outrage against a free individual, until he pays it.*[46]

[48] You hear, men of Athens, the generosity of the law, which does not even deem it right for slaves to suffer outrage. By the gods, what are we to conclude? Suppose someone should bring this law to the barbarians, from whom slaves are imported to Greece, and praising you as he describes the city, should say to them, [49] "There are some Greeks so civilized and so humane in their ways that although you have often wronged them and they have inherited a natural animosity to you nevertheless they do not deem it right to treat with outrage even those slaves whom they have acquired by purchasing them but have publicly established this law to prevent it, and they have already sentenced to death many who have violated it." [50] If the barbarians should hear and understand these words, don't you think that they would publicly make all of you their representatives?[47] Since the law not only is well esteemed among the Greeks but would even seem

---

45. For the law's authenticity, see MacDowell 1990: 263–64; contra Harris: 2008: 103–4 nn. 94–95, 97–98.

46. I.e., a defendant who is found guilty of committing outrage against a free person and receives a fine as a penalty must be imprisoned until he pays the fine.

47. *Proxenoi* were local citizens who represented the interests of a foreign state and performed many of the functions that modern ambassadors and consuls now carry out.

so among the barbarians, consider what penalty the man who violates the law will pay if he is to pay an appropriate one.

[51] So if, men of Athens, I had not suffered these injuries at the hands of Meidias while I was a chorus producer, one would only have found him guilty of committing outrage. But as it turns out, I think that one would be right to find him guilty even of impiety. You know, of course, that you perform all these choruses and hymns for the god, not only as mandated by the laws concerning the Dionysia but also by the oracles, in all of which— from Delphi as much as from Dodona—you will find that the city has been ordered to establish choruses in accordance with ancestral custom, fill the streets with the smell of sacrifice, and wear crowns. [52] Please take the very oracles and read them.

ORACLES

I proclaim to you, the sons of Erechtheus, who inhabit the town of Pandion and set festivals in accordance with ancestral laws, to remember Bacchus and all together give thanks[48] along the broad streets to Bromius for the fruits of the season and make the altars smell of sacrifice, covering your heads with crowns.

For health, sacrifice and pray to Zeus the highest, Heracles, and Apollo the protector; for good fortune, to Apollo of the street, Leto, and Artemis. Arrange bowls of wines and dances along the streets, wear crowns, and, in accordance with ancestral custom, lift up your right and left hands to all the Olympian gods and goddesses and remember their gifts.

ORACLES FROM DODONA

[53] *To the people of Athens, the oracle of Zeus orders, because you have disregarded the times for sacrifice and for the sacred embassy, to send nine chosen envoys; and without delay they are to sacrifice to Zeus Naeus three oxen and two pigs with each ox, and to Dione an ox, and to set up a bronze table as a votive offering which the people of Athens gave.*

The oracle of Zeus orders to perform sacrifices at Dodona to Dionysus at public expense, to mix bowls of wine, to arrange choruses, for free men and slaves to wear crowns, and to hold a holiday for one day. To Apollo the averter of evil, sacrifice an ox; to Zeus the protector of property, a white ox.

---

48. I.e., to perform dances; see MacDowell 1990: 271.

[54] Men of Athens, the city has these and many other good oracles. What should you conclude from them? In addition to commanding you to perform the sacrifices to the gods indicated in each oracle, they also order you, by all the oracles whenever they are sent, to arrange choruses and wear crowns in accordance with ancestral custom.[49] [55] So, clearly all of us who perform in choruses or are chorus producers wear crowns on behalf of you, in accordance with these oracles, for those days during which we engage in contests, regardless of whether we will win or come in last place. The winner, however, wears a crown on his own behalf for the day of his victory celebration. So if one subjects one of the chorus members or chorus producers to outrage out of enmity and he does so during the actual contest in the sacred precinct of the god, will we say that he does anything other than commit impiety? [56] You know that you do not want a foreigner to participate in the contest, but you do not at all permit any chorus producer to accost and question members of the chorus. If one does, you require him to pay fifty drachmas, and if he orders a chorus member to sit down, then one thousand drachmas.[50] Why? So that no one accost, harass, or maliciously subject to outrage an individual wearing a crown and performing a liturgy to the god on that day. [57] When the individual who legally accosts a chorus member will not go without a fine, will not the man who so clearly violates the law by striking a chorus producer pay the penalty? It is useless to establish laws, which are good and humane for the many, if those who disobey and violate them do not bear your anger every time you are entrusted with legal authority.

[58] Please consider also the following. I will ask you not to get upset with me if I mention by name some men who have suffered misfortune.

---

49. This tendentious inference allows Demosthenes to use the fact that he wore a crown at the Dionysia as proof that he was performing a religious duty when Meidias struck him, and therefore Meidias was guilty of impiety.

50. The Athenians apparently passed a law to deter a rival from interfering with a choral performance by questioning a chorus member about his citizenship and demanding his removal from the chorus if his answers were inadequate. The fees mentioned in this section would have been recovered if, following the performance, he brought his complaint to court and won. Demosthenes' claim that the law applied also to chorus producers is tenuous. Though there could have been reason to doubt the citizenship of chorus members, there would not have been reason to doubt the citizenship of the chorus producer, given his status and standing in the community. Moreover, any such objection would not have interfered with the performance and could have been raised long before the festival. See MacDowell 1990: 275–77.

I will do so, by the gods, not because I want to cast reproach on anyone but to show how all the rest of you avoid committing violent and outrageous acts and other such offenses. Sannion is, as you know, a director of tragic choruses, and he was convicted of evading military service and paid the consequences.[51] [59] After this misfortune, a chorus producer of tragedies—Theozotides, I believe—hired him because he desired to win. At first the other chorus producers were angry and said that they would stop him. But when the theater was full and they saw the crowd gathered for the contest, they hesitated, they tolerated it, no one laid a hand on him. One could see so much restraint in each of you, out of reverence for the gods, that to this day he is directing choruses and none of his private enemies stops him, much less the chorus producers. [60] There is another man, Aristeides from the tribe of Oeneis, who suffered a similar fate, and although he is now old and perhaps not that good as a chorus member, he was once the chorus leader for his tribe. You know, of course, once you take away the leader, the rest of the chorus goes. Nevertheless none of the chorus producers—although there were many who desired to win—ever saw to this advantage or dared to remove or stop him. Since one could only do so by taking him by the hand, and one could not summon him to the archon, just as one would do if he wanted to remove a foreigner, everyone avoided being seen as personally responsible[52] for this wanton violence. [61] Therefore, isn't it terrible, men of the jury, and shocking? Of those who believed that they could win this way, although they often spent all their possessions on their liturgies, not one ever dared to touch those whom the laws permitted them to, but they were so careful, so pious, so reserved that—although they spent their money and were competing—nevertheless they held themselves back and gave priority to your wishes and your eagerness for the festival. Meidias, by contrast, although he was a private citizen and spent nothing, because he was angry at someone who was his enemy (although this man was spending his own money, was serving as your chorus producer, and possessed all the rights of a citizen), Meidias abused him and struck him and thought not of your festival or your laws or what you would say or of the god.

---

51. He was disfranchised, and as result he was liable to arrest by the procedure of *apagoge* (as Demosthenes indicates in **59–60**) if he was caught enjoying privileges or appearing in public places from which he had been barred; see Hansen 1976a: 55–74; Todd 1993: 116–18, 42–43.

52. *Autocheir* literally means "one who does so with his own hand" and can be used to refer to the perpetrator of an offense, such as in this passage, but it also commonly means "murderer" (cf. **106, 116, 119, 121**); see MacDowell 1990: 332.

[62] Although there are, men of Athens, many men who are enemies of one another not only for personal reasons but also from political disagreements, no one has ever gone to such a degree of shamelessness as to dare to do this sort of thing. Yet they say that once the well-known Iphicrates was involved in a rather heated dispute with Diocles of Pithus and, as it also turns out, Teisias, the brother of Iphicrates, happened to be a chorus producer in competition against Diocles. Iphicrates had many friends and much wealth, and he thought as highly of himself as one would expect from a man who had his reputation and had received the honors that he had received from you.[53] [63] Nevertheless, he did not go into goldsmiths' houses at night, nor did he rip up cloaks that were prepared for the festival, corrupt the director, prevent the chorus from practicing, or do any of the other things that this man carried out. Instead he deferred to the laws and the wishes of the rest of you, and he endured watching his enemy win and be crowned. As was fitting, he thought that he ought to concede in such matters to the community under which he knew his good fortune rested. [64] Or take, for example, Philostratus of Colonus. We all know that he prosecuted Chabrias when he was on trial for a capital offense concerning Oropus, and he was the fiercest prosecutor.[54] Afterwards, Philostratus produced a boys' chorus at the Dionysia and won, but Chabrias did not strike him nor take the crown away from him nor go anywhere at all where he was not allowed. [65] I could mention still many more men and the many reasons why they were enemies of one another, but I have never heard or seen anyone who has gone to such a degree of insolence as to do this sort of thing. I know that none of you can recall a time in the past when a man—because he was in a private or public dispute with someone else—stood before the judges as they were called forth or dictated an oath to them when they were sworn in or revealed his animosity on any such occasion. [66] If a chorus producer does any of these sorts of things, men of Athens, because he desires to win, he deserves some sympathy. But if he persecutes someone

---

53. Iphicrates was an Athenian general most known for his use of peltasts (light-armed troops) to defeat a Spartan contingent during the Corinthian War (395–387). He was awarded the same honors as the descendants of Harmodius and Aristogeiton (i.e., the right to eat in the Prytaneum at public expense).

54. Chabrias was an Athenian general and contemporary of Iphicrates. He scored a decisive victory against the Spartan fleet at Naxos in 376, which allowed Athens to expand the Second Athenian League; see **[Dem.] 59.33**. In 366, Oropus, which was on the border between Attica and Boeotia, was taken by Thebes (Aesch. 3.85; Dem. 18.99; D. S. 15.76.1; Xen. *Hell.* 7.4.1). Chabrias was probably accused of betraying the town to the Thebans.

out of enmity, intentionally and on every occasion, and if he shows that he is personally more powerful than the laws, by Heracles, the situation is grave, it is unjust, and it is not to your advantage. Should it become clear to each of the chorus producers first that I will be deprived of my victory if so-and-so is my enemy (Meidias or some other equally conceited and wealthy man), even if I do better in the competition than someone else, and then that I will be defeated on every occasion and continually humiliated, who would be so irrational or so foolish as to spend willingly one drachma? [67] No one, of course. But I think what makes all men desire honor and willing to spend their money is that each believes that he has an equal share of justice under a democracy. Well I, men of Athens, did not enjoy this privilege because of that man, and in addition to being treated outrageously I was also deprived of my victory. Yet, I will show clearly to all of you that Meidias could have caused me distress and competed for honor legally without doing anything malicious, without committing outrage, and without striking me, and I would not have even been able to open my mouth about him. [68] When I undertook in the Assembly to be the chorus producer for Pandionis, he should have, men of Athens, then stood up on behalf of Erechtheis,[55] his own tribe, and undertaken to compete against me, and placing himself on equal terms and spending his own money, just as I did, he should have deprived me of victory in that way, but even then he should not have subjected me to such outrageous treatment and struck me. [69] But as it turns out he did not act in a way that would have honored the people or engage in any youthful daring of this sort.[56] As for me, whether one wants to think, men of Athens, that I undertook to be chorus producer because I am crazy (for perhaps it is crazy to do something beyond one's power) or because I desired honor, I was hounded by Meidias, who carried out such conspicuous and vile attacks that he did not keep away from sacred cloaks or the chorus until at last he did not keep his hands from my body.

[70] If, however, any of you, men of Athens, feels less anger for Meidias than you would if you believed he must be sentenced to death, you are mistaken. It is not right or fitting for the discretion of the victim to contribute to the acquittal of the man who does not shrink from acts of outrage. But it is fitting to punish the latter, since he has caused all kinds of irreparable harm, and thank the former by coming to his defense. [71] Furthermore, one cannot even say that there have never been any dire consequences from such actions and I am now overstating the significance of this matter

---

55. Demosthenes' and Meidias' tribes were respectively named after Pandion and Erechtheus, the legendary kings of Athens (see **52**).

56. Cf. **18**.

and making it terrifying. This is far from the truth. Everyone knows, or at least many, what Euthynus, once a famous wrestler, did as a young man to Sophilos, the pancratiast,[57] a strong dark man—I believe that some of you know whom I am talking about. While he was in Samos at some party and private gathering, because he believed that he had been treated outrageously, he put up such a defense that he ended up killing him. Many know that Euaeon, the brother of Leodamas, killed Boeotus at a dinner because of one blow. [72] The blow did not provoke his anger, but the dishonor did, since it is not so terrible for free men to be struck (although it is terrible) but to be struck with outrage. The one who strikes, men of Athens, could do many things that the victim could not express to another, with his body language, his facial expression, and his voice, when he commits outrage, when he acts out of enmity, when he throws punches, when he strikes the face. These things stir men, they make them lose control of themselves when they are not used to being abused. No one, as he describes these actions, men of Athens, could make the horror from the outrage as vivid to his listeners as it appeared at the very moment to the victim and the witnesses. [73] In the name of Zeus and all the gods, consider, men of Athens, and judge for yourselves how much more I deserved to be angry for what I suffered at the hands of Meidias than did that Euaeon at the time when he killed Boeotus. He was struck by a friend, who was drunk, in front of six or seven men, and they were friends, who would have reproached Boeotus for what he had done and would have praised Euaeon afterwards if he had held back and stopped himself, and what's more, Euaeon went to a house for a dinner where he did not have to go. [74] I, by contrast, was subjected to outrage by an enemy, who was sober, in the morning, acting insolently and not under the influence of wine, and in front of many people, both foreigners and citizens, and what is worse, it occurred in a sacred precinct where I had to go, since I was a chorus producer. I believe, men of Athens, that my response was prudent, or rather fortunate, when I held myself back at that time and was not provoked to do anything that could not be undone, but I have much sympathy for Euaeon or anyone else who comes to his own defense when he is dishonored. [75] I think that many jurors for that trial had the same opinion. I am told that he was convicted by only one vote in spite of the fact that he did not cry, ask the jurors for anything, or provide them with any act of kindness whatsoever, whether great or small. Therefore let us suppose the following: those who found him guilty condemned him not because he defended himself but because the manner of

---

57. The *pankration* was a rather savage athletic contest, which included elements of boxing and wrestling. Although the competitors could not bite their opponents or poke them in the eye, they could kick them, strangle them, and break their bones.

his defense resulted in another's death, while those who voted for acquittal granted this additional amount of retribution to one who had his body subjected to outrage. [76] What follows? After I have been so careful to avoid doing any irreparable harm that I did not even defend myself, from whom should I receive satisfaction for my sufferings? From you and the laws, I believe, and an example ought to be made to everyone else, not to defend himself in an act of anger against those who commit outrage and are brutal but to bring them before you, since you guarantee and insure that the laws protect the victims.

[77] I suppose that some of you, men of the jury, desire to hear about the animosity that existed between us, since some think that no one would inflict such brutality and violence on any citizen unless he was owed some great retribution. So I wish to tell you about it from the beginning and describe it in full so that you might realize that he clearly deserves to be punished also for these offenses. My discussion of them will be brief even though I may appear to be starting from the beginning. [78] When I brought the lawsuits against my guardians over my inheritance, I was just a young man and did not know whether Meidias was alive or who he was—would that I did not know him now! Three or four days before my suits were then to appear in court, he and his brother rushed into my house and began carrying out an exchange[58] of property over a trierarchy. Although Thrasylochus initiated the challenge in his own name, Meidias was responsible for all of their acts and actions. [79] First, they broke down the doors of the rooms under the pretense that they were already theirs by virtue of the challenge.[59] Then, in front of my sister, who at that time was still inside the house and was a young girl, they spoke as shamefully as such men would—but I could not bring myself to tell you any of the things that were said—and shouted out insults, which can and cannot be

---

58. When a wealthy Athenian assigned to perform a liturgy (see **1** n.) believed that there was a richer Athenian, who had not recently performed a liturgy and was not exempt, he could challenge that individual either to perform the liturgy in question or exchange property (*antidosis*). If the other party accepted the challenge but refused to carry it out, then the parties could settle the question by the procedure of *diadikasia* and a court would decide which party would perform the liturgy. It appears that Demosthenes wanted neither to perform the liturgy nor to exchange the property and be forced to give up his suits against his guardians. He therefore first agreed to the exchange but then refused to carry it out so as to force a *diadikasia* to occur (see Dem. 28.17).

59. Since Demosthenes subsequently sued Meidias for slander and not for breaking and entering, Thrasylochus and Meidias may have legally entered the house in order to conduct an inventory of Demosthenes' property as part of the ongoing *antidosis*.

repeated, at my mother and me and all of us. But what was most terrible was not what they said but what they then did: they dropped the suits against my guardians, claiming that the property was theirs. [80] Although this occurred long ago, nevertheless I believe some of you remember, since the entire city was aware of the exchange and this plotting of theirs at that time and their brutality. Because I was then all by myself and just a young man and since I expected to receive not how much I was able to recover but how much I knew that I had been deprived of, I gave them twenty minas, which was the amount that they had paid to have the trierarchy performed,[60] so that I might not be robbed of the possessions that were in the hands of my guardians.[61] These were the acts of outrage that they committed against me at that time. [81] But later I lodged a suit of slander against Meidias and won it by default since he was absent.[62] Although his debt became overdue and remained so, I never laid a hold on any of his belongings, but I lodged a suit of ejectment, and to this day I have not yet been able to bring my case to trial.[63] He has found so many techniques and excuses to evade me. While I am so careful to do everything in accordance with justice and by the laws, he, as you hear, believed that he ought to

---

60. An individual assigned a trierarchy could hire someone else to perform it on his behalf if he did not want to take up his time to prepare the ship and risk the danger of commanding it.

61. Demosthenes downplays how he had been legally outmaneuvered. By refusing to carry out the exchange, he would have had to postpone his suits against the guardians until the *diadikasia* was settled. Then, at the *diadikasia*, he would have had to argue that the value of his estate either included or excluded what he alleged his guardians illegally possessed. If he argued the former, then he would have lost the *diadikasia,* since the size of his estate was such that he would have been obligated to perform the liturgy (cf. **157**). If he argued the latter, then he would have lost his suits against his guardians, since he would have in effect conceded that he had no legal claim against them. Therefore, in the best-case scenario, Demosthenes would have lost the *diadikasia* and would have delayed his suits against his guardians. It is quite likely that Thrasylochus and Meidias knew that the *antidosis* created such a dilemma. So when they made the challenge, they probably did not expect that it would end the lawsuits over the inheritance; rather, their intent was merely to free Thrasylochus from the burden of performing the liturgy, distract Demosthenes from his suits over his inheritance, and cause Demosthenes to suffer financial difficulties so that he was less capable of pursuing his case against his guardians.

62. If a party failed to show up to a hearing, the judgment went against him by default and was recorded accordingly to reflect his absence.

63. A defendant, found guilty in a private suit and ordered to pay the defendant a fine, had to do so within a specified period of time or the prosecutor could pursue a suit of ejectment against him (see **44** n.)

subject not only me and my family to brutal outrage but also members of my tribe, because of me. [82] To testify that I speak the truth, please call forth the witnesses of this so that you may know that I have suffered such additional acts of outrage, as you have heard, before I received satisfaction for my previous injuries.

TESTIMONY

{*We, Callisthenes of Sphettus, Diognetus of Thoricus, and Mnesitheus of Alopece, know that Demosthenes, for whom we testify, lodged a suit of ejectment against Meidias, whom Demosthenes now is also publicly prosecuting, and eight years have already passed since that suit, and Meidias is responsible for the entire delay with his constant excuses and delays.*}[64]

[83] Hear what he has done, men of Athens, concerning the suit, and consider each instance of his insolence and his arrogance. In the suit, I mean the one in which I won a conviction against him, Strato of Phalerum was the arbitrator, a poor man, uninvolved in the affairs of the city, although not otherwise bad,[65] but even very good. It is not right or just but very disgraceful that this was the cause of his destruction. [84] This man, Strato, was our arbitrator when the appointed day arrived, and when all legal delays had been used up, oaths by proxies and countersuits,[66] and there was nothing else remaining, first he asked me to suspend the arbitration, then to postpone it until the next day. Finally, since I did not agree and Meidias did

---

64. Frequently the statements of witnesses are spurious insertions added later by scribes, either for sake of clarification or to add further realism to the speech (cf. **94, 107, 121, 168**). The use of non-Attic forms for the testimony in section **82** indicate that the original document was not preserved.

65. Cf. MacDowell 1990: 304–5 and Wilson 1991:180. Although Demosthenes' use of the adverb *allos* ("otherwise") suggests that Strato's poverty as well as his political inactivity could carry negative connotations unless qualified, it does not imply that the jury would necessarily have assumed the worst of him simply because of his social status. Rather, Demosthenes was on the defensive because a court had found Strato guilty of misconduct, and he was arguing against that ruling (cf. Dover 1974: 34 n. 1; Ober 1989: 210–11; 1996: 100). In the end, Demosthenes' depiction is quite positive and has a leveling effect since he calls Strato *panu chrestos* ("very good"), which is a trait commonly associated with aristocrats.

66. A litigant unable to attend a hearing because he is ill or away from Athens can send a proxy on his behalf who would declare as much under oath (*hypomosia*); countersuit (*paragraphe*) is a procedure by which the defendant can challenge the legality of the suit lodged against him (MacDowell 1990: 305–8). For an example of a countersuit, see **Demosthenes 32**.

not show up, and it was late, Strato ruled against him. [85] But when it was already night and dark,[67] this man, Meidias, arrived at the magistrates' office and came upon them as they were exiting and Strato was already outside, after giving a ruling against him by default,[68] as I learned from one of the bystanders. At first he tried to persuade Strato to declare that his arbitration was for the defendant, which he had ruled in favor of the prosecutor, and the officials to change the record, and he offered them fifty drachmas. [86] But when they became upset at his suggestion and he failed to persuade either of them,[69] he threatened and insulted them, and what did he do after he left? Observe his wickedness. Moving to have the arbitration annulled, he did not swear an oath, but he allowed it to remain in force against him, and his appeal was returned as unsworn.[70] Because he wanted his plans to remain a secret, he waited until the arbitrators' last day, on which some are present and some are not.[71] [87] He persuaded the chief arbitrator to put the matter to a vote illegally, without recording the name of even one witness to the summons. Accusing the arbitrator in his absence and with no one present, he had him removed from the list of arbitrators and disfranchised. And now because Meidias lost a suit by default, an Athenian is deprived of all his civic rights and is permanently disfranchised.[72] It is not safe to prosecute Meidias if one is harmed or to serve as his arbitrator or even, so it seems, to walk on the same street!

[88] You ought then to examine this matter in the following way: consider what on earth it is that Meidias suffered, which is so horrible that he plotted to exact such a penalty against a fellow citizen because of it. If it is something truly terrible and outrageous, he deserves forgiveness, but if it isn't, consider what violence and cruelty he inflicts on all who happen upon him. So what is it that he suffered? Perhaps one would say he owed

---

67. Since all public business had to be completed before nightfall, Demosthenes is careful to stress that Meidias did not show up until the sun had set and therefore the ruling against him was valid.

68. See **81** n.

69. I.e., Strato to change his ruling and the other officials to change the record.

70. A party to an arbitration that receives a ruling by default can appeal the decision on the grounds that his absence was unavoidable, provided that he swears an oath to such an effect. Meidias, however, allowed his appeal to elapse by failing to swear an oath so that the original ruling against him remained in force.

71. Since it was their last day, arbitrators could not be assigned new disputes, which they would not be able to settle on that day. As a result, arbitrators who did not have pending business sometimes did not appear (MacDowell 1990: 310).

72. See **32** n.

such a large fine that he lost all his possessions.[73] But it was only one thousand drachmas. [89] Fair enough, but even that stings, someone could say, when one is required to pay a fine because of an injustice that also caused the fine to become overdue without his knowledge.[74] Meidias, however, was aware of the hearing on the very day, which is the greatest proof that the man had in no way treated him unfairly, and he has not yet paid one drachma. But more on this matter later. [90] He could, of course, have moved to have the arbitration annulled and brought the dispute against me, who was the original party of the suit, but he did not wish to do so. So that Meidias might not have to be a party in a lawsuit with a fixed penalty of ten minas,[75] which he did not attend although he was required, and either pay the penalty, if found guilty, or not, if acquitted, an Athenian had to be disfranchised and offered neither forgiveness nor the right to speak nor any form of fairness, all of which are provided even to the actual perpetrators. [91] But after he disfranchised whom he wanted to, you granted him this favor,[76] and he satisfied his shameless desire, which drove him to do these things, did he do what was required, did he pay the penalty that caused him to ruin the man? Not even a penny, not yet to this day, but he remains a defendant in an outstanding suit of ejectment. And so one man has been disfranchised and completely ruined while the other has suffered nothing whatsoever, but confounds the laws, the arbitrators, and whatever else he wants. [92] The ruling against the arbitrator, which he devised without a summons, he makes valid for his own advantage, but the ruling in his suit with me, which he lost because he was summoned and knew about it but did not attend, he makes invalid. Yet if he thinks that he deserves to exact such a penalty from those who rule against him by default, what penalty ought we to receive from him, who openly and insolently violates your laws? If disfranchisement and loss of legal protection and the use of the courts and all other rights are a fitting penalty for that offense, death will

---

73. A hypothetical response (cf. **41**, **98–99**).

74. I.e., Meidias might argue that he was unaware of the arbitration, and so he lost by default and became an overdue debtor because he did not even know that the arbitrator had fined him (MacDowell 1990: 313).

75. For some offenses, the prosecutor proposed a penalty after the defendant was convicted and the defendant proposed an alternative penalty. Since the suit against Meidias had a fixed penalty, Meidias knew that the most he would have had to pay was ten minas.

76. Litigants regularly address the jury to refer to previous court decisions (cf. **11**, **176**, **180**, **182**; **Dem. 54.39**). Since Strato appealed the arbitrators' decision (cf. Arist. *Ath. Pol.* 53.6) and the jury ruled against him, Meidias' case was stronger than Demosthenes admits.

appear to be a minor penalty for his outrage. [93] To testify that I speak the truth, please call forth the witnesses of this, and read the law on arbitrators.

TESTIMONY

{*We, Nicostratus of Myrrhinous and Phanias of Aphidna, know that Demosthenes, for whom we testify, and Meidias, whom Demosthenes is prosecuting, chose Strato to be their arbitrator when Demosthenes brought a suit of slander against Meidias, and when the day appointed by law arrived, Meidias was not present at the arbitration, but he forfeited the case.[77] After a ruling was made against Meidias by default, we know that Meidias tried to persuade Strato, the arbitrator, and us, who were officials at that time, to declare the arbitration in his favor, and he offered us fifty drachmas. But when we refused, he threatened us and left. We also know that this is the reason why Meidias had Strato punished and disfranchised, contrary to all justice.*}

[94] Read also the law on arbitrators.

LAW

{*If some parties are in a dispute with each other over private contracts and they want to choose anyone to be an arbitrator, let them be allowed to choose whomever they want. And when they have agreed on their choice, let them adhere to the decisions of that man, and afterwards let them not transfer the same charges from him to another court, but let the decisions of the arbitrator stay in force.*}[78]

[95] Call also Strato, the very man who has suffered such a plight; for, I suppose, he will be allowed to stand. This man, men of Athens, is perhaps poor, but he is by no means wicked. Although he is a citizen who has served on all campaigns when he was of military age and has done nothing terrible, he now stands silent, deprived not only of all other privileges commonly enjoyed but even of the right to utter a sound or lament. Whether he has suffered justly or unjustly, he cannot even tell you. [96] He has endured this from Meidias and from the wealth and arrogance of Meidias

---

77. Since litigants were assigned a public arbitrator by lot, the mistake in this sentence shows that this testimony is spurious.

78. A description of the law on private arbitration has been wrongly inserted here where the law on public arbitration should have been read.

on account of his poverty and isolation and because he was only one man from the multitude. If he had violated the laws, accepted the fifty drachmas from Meidias, and declared that his arbitration, which he had ruled in favor of the prosecutor, was for the defendant, he would be a full citizen, would not have suffered any harm, and would enjoy the same rights as the rest of you. But since he paid attention to what was just rather than Meidias and feared the laws more than this man's threats, he has fallen into such a great and terrible misfortune because of this man. [97] When he is so savage and so hard hearted and metes out such retribution for wrongs that he alone says that he suffered (but he didn't, actually), will you let him go after you have caught him subjecting a citizen to outrage? And when he pays no heed to festivals, sacred places, the law, or anything else, will you not convict him? [98] Will you not make an example out of him? And what will you say, men of the jury? What just or fair excuse, in the name of the gods, will you be able to say? Will you say that he is brutal and detestable? This is true, but of course, you ought, men of the jury, to hate such men rather than save them. Or will you say that he is wealthy? But you will find that this is the main cause of his insolence so that you ought to deprive him of the source of his insolence rather than save him because of it. If you allow a bold and detestable man, such as him, to possess great wealth, you have given him resources to use against you. [99] What other reason remains? Perhaps you will say pity. He will bring forth his children, and he will cry and ask to be pardoned for their sake. This is what remains. But you know, of course, that you ought to pity those who unfairly suffer what they cannot endure, not those who pay the penalty for the terrible wrongs that they have done.[79] And who could fairly pity Meidias' children when he sees that that man did not pity Strato's children? In addition to their other problems, they also see no relief from their father's plight. Strato cannot pay a fine in order to regain his citizenship, but he has been permanently disfranchised by the force of Meidias' anger and insolence. [100] Who will stop committing acts of outrage and be stripped of the wealth that causes him to do so, if you will pity this man as though he has suffered terribly, and if there is a poor man, who is not guilty of any crime and has fallen into the worst misfortune because of Meidias, and you will not even be moved to share in his anger? It must not happen. It is not right for anyone to receive pity who pities no one or forgiveness who does not forgive.

---

79. Although defendants regularly ask the jury to pity them, such appeals do not typically imply an acknowledgment of guilt. Thus, as Demosthenes suggests here, pity is an appropriate emotion to evoke in the case of a defendant who is unjustly on trial, and differs from the concept of mercy, which justifies sparing a guilty individual who has expressed remorse (see Konstan 2001: 27–48).

[101] For I believe that all men recognize that they give a contribution[80] from their own resources for the benefit of their own life in everything that they do. Say, for example, I am moderate in my behavior to all, feel pity, and perform services for many. It is appropriate for everyone to give the same contributions to such a man, if ever the occasion or need occurs. Say another is a violent individual, showing no one pity or considering him at all human. He deserves to receive the same contributions from everyone. Meidias, since you have given such a contribution for your own benefit, you deserve to receive the same.

[102] Now I believe, men of Athens, that even if I could not lodge any other accusation against Meidias, and even if what I am going to mention was not worse than what I have said, it would be right for you to convict him on the basis of what has been said and to sentence him to the worst punishment. The matter, however, does not rest here, nor do I think that I will be at a loss as to what to say next, such an abundance of accusations he has provided me. [103] I will not discuss how he fabricated an indictment of desertion against me and hired that cursed and incredibly unscrupulous man, the filthy Euctemon, to lodge it. That malicious accuser[81] did not bring the suit to the preliminary hearing, nor did Meidias hire him for any other reason than to post publicly in front of the Eponymous Heroes[82] so that all might see: "Euctemon of Lousia indicted Demosthenes of Paeania for desertion." And I think that he would have gladly added, if it were somehow possible, that Meidias hired him to prosecute Demosthenes. I, however, am not going to mention this incident, since I have enough compensation and do not need more for an accusation that caused that one to disfranchise himself because he did not pursue it. [104] But I will mention what I think he has done which is a terrible and shocking act of impiety that concerns the public and is not just a personal offense. When a horrible and grievous accusation was brought against that pitiful and miserable man, Aristarchus, son of Moschus, men of Athens, he first went

---

80. *Eranos* is a type of loan whereby the borrower raises the full amount of the loan by collecting separate contributions from individual friends, and it is usually repaid in installments without interest or with a very favorable interest rate. Each lender can be said to benefit from the contribution that he gives, since the borrower is obligated to repay the favor in kind at some future date when the lender is in need. The point of this metaphor is to suggest that Meidias should receive what he gives. Its repetition in **184–85** has led many to conclude that the speech could not have been delivered in its present form; see the introduction to the speech.

81. For the meaning of "sykophant," see **Lys. 12.5** n.

82. Public notices were placed in the agora in front of the statues of the ten heroes representing the tribes of Athens.

around the agora and dared to say impious and terrible stories about me, how I was responsible. But when he did not accomplish anything from these allegations, he approached those who lodged the charge of homicide against Aristarchus—the relatives of the deceased—and he promised to give them money if they would charge me with the offense. Neither the gods nor divine law nor anything else stood in the way of such talk, nor did he hesitate. [105] Before those whom he spoke, he did not even feel shame for illegally bringing so great and such a serious charge against someone. Instead he made it his one goal to destroy me in any way, and he thought that he ought to stop at nothing as though it were necessary—if someone should suffer outrageous treatment from him and think that he ought to receive compensation and not remain silent—that he be ruined by banishment and in no way let off but be convicted of desertion, accused of murder,[83] and all but nailed up.[84] Yet, when he has been shown to have carried out these acts in addition to the outrage that he committed against me as a chorus producer, what forgiveness or pity will he justly receive from you? [106] I believe, men of Athens, that he perpetrated my destruction by these acts. While before, at the City Dionysia, he subjected my preparations, my body, and my expenses to his insolence, through his subsequent acts and deeds he targeted those and everything else—my city, my family, my civic rights, my hopes. If any of his plots had been successful, I would have been deprived of everything and would also have suffered the fate of not being buried at home. Why, men of the jury? If someone will endure this or some other similar treatment because he tries to protect himself after he has been illegally subjected to outrage at the hands of Meidias, it will be best to bow down before those who commit outrage, just like the barbarians do, and not to defend oneself. [107] But to testify that I speak the truth and that all these acts have also been done by this disgusting and shameless man, please call forth the witnesses of this.

WITNESSES

{*We, Dionysius of Aphidna and Antiphilus of Paeania, after our relative Nicodemus died a violent death at the hands of Aristarchus, son of Moschus, charged Aristarchus with murder. When Meidias, who is now being prosecuted by Demosthenes, for whom we testify, became aware of*

---

83. The alternative translation, "banished for murder," is less preferable, since Demosthenes has already referred to exile.

84. Criminals were executed by being nailed to boards.

this, he tried to persuade us with the offer of money to allow Aristarchus to go unpunished and instead indict Demosthenes with murder.}

Now, please also take the law concerning bribes.

[108] While he is looking for the law, men of Athens, I want to speak briefly to you, and I ask, in the name of Zeus and the gods, for all of you, men of the jury, to keep the following question in mind in everything that you hear. What would any one of you do if you were to suffer this misfortune, and what anger would you feel for the man responsible? Although I am particularly bothered by the outrage I endured during my liturgy, I am by far more upset, men of Athens, and more angry at what happened next. [109] For what would someone say is truly the limit of depravity, or what shamelessness, savagery, and insolence exceed this, if a man should commit many really terrible offenses against another, and instead of paying compensation for them and showing remorse, he should afterwards carry out other wrongs in addition, still much more terrible, and use his wealth not in order to increase his own private possessions without harming someone but for the opposite purpose, so that he can illegally banish and humiliate anyone and then be proud of himself because of his wealth? [110] Well, men of Athens, all these actions he has committed against me. He brought against me the charge of murder, which was false and did not at all concern me, as was clear from the actual outcome, and he indicted me for desertion, although he abandoned his post three times. As for the problems in Euboea—I almost forgot to mention them—which his ally and friend Plutarch had caused, he tried to place the blame on me until it became clear to all that Plutarch was responsible.[85] [111] And finally, he brought an accusation against me at my scrutiny[86] when I had been selected by lot to be a councilor, and I was in a very dangerous predicament. Instead of receiving compensation for what I had suffered, I risked being punished for matters that did not at all concern me. Since I am suffering this misfortune and being persecuted in this way, as I am now describing to you, when I am not completely without friends or entirely without resources, I do

---

85. In 349, Plutarch, tyrant of Eretria (not to be confused with the author), sought assistance from Athens to secure his control of Euboea. The Athenians sent a force, under Phocion's command, that was able to defeat the enemy at Tamynae despite some initial setbacks (**161–62**; Plu. *Phoc.* 12–13). The force later received relief from the cavalry that had first been sent to Argoura (**132**, **164**). Phocion was replaced, and when his successor was captured, the Athenians were forced to recognize Euboea's independence (Plu. *Phoc.* 14).

86. All candidates for public office, whether selected by lot or elected, had to pass a scrutiny (*dokimasia*) to establish their eligibility before their term began. See the introduction to **Lysias 16.**

not know, men of Athens, what I ought to do. [112] If I can now say something also about this, the rest of us do not have a share in the equal protection of the law in disputes with the rich, not a share, not at all. They are given whatever dates they want for their trials, and the charges against them come to you stale and cold, but as for the rest of us, if anything happens, each is tried freshly caught. They have witnesses ready and all their cospeakers[87] prepared to oppose us while some of my witnesses, as you see, are not even willing to testify to the truth. [113] One could wear himself out, I believe, lamenting this. But please read next the law that I began to mention. Read it.

LAW

If any Athenian receives something from someone or himself gives something to another or corrupts someone with promises, to the harm of the people or individually to any one of the citizens, by any manner or device whatsoever, let him and his children be disfranchised and his property confiscated.

[114] Well then, this man is so impious, so polluted, and so eager to say and do anything—without drawing any distinction whatsoever, whether it is true or false, for an enemy or friend, or so forth—that he charged me with murder and brought such a serious matter against me. Yet afterwards he allowed me to perform the inaugural rites on behalf of the Council, make the sacrifices, and initiate the rites on behalf of you and the whole city. [115] He allowed me to serve as the *architheoros* and lead the sacred embassy on behalf of the entire city to Zeus of Nemea. He overlooked that I was elected from all of the Athenians to be one of the three *hieropoioi* and initiate the rites for the Revered Goddesses.[88] If he had even a jot or a trace of proof for the accusations he concocted against me, would he have allowed me to do any of these things? I don't think so. This clearly proves that insolence drove him to seek my banishment from my fatherland.

[116] When he could not in any way bring a charge against me, although he turned it inside and out, he then openly brought a malicious accusation against Aristarchus to attack me. I am not going to mention the other things that he did, but when the Council convened and examined this matter, he came forward and said, "Members of the Council, don't you know the

---

87. Although litigants were required to speak on their on behalf, they were allowed to share the time allotted to them with cospeakers (*synegoroi*), who were regularly their relatives and friends. *Synegoroi* were prohibited from receiving money for their assistance. See Rubinstein 2000.

88. I.e., the Furies.

situation? Although you have the perpetrator," meaning Aristarchus, "do you wait, are you still investigating, are you crazy? Won't you execute him? Won't you go to his house? Won't you arrest him?" [117] This vile and shameless creature made such statements, even though he had left Aristarchus' house the day before and was on the same terms with him as anyone else would have been until that day, and despite the fact that Aristarchus had gone to greater lengths than everyone else to reconcile Meidias with me before this incident. If he made these remarks because he thought that Aristarchus committed any of the acts that caused his ruin and he believed the accusers' allegations, he still should not have done so. [118] To end a friendship is an appropriate penalty in the case of friends thought to have done something terrible; to seek revenge and to prosecute are reserved for victims and enemies. Yet, one could forgive a man like Meidias for this. But if it will be shown that he had a conversation with Aristarchus under the same roof,[89] as though he had done nothing, and then made these allegations and charges in order to bring a malicious accusation against me, how does he not deserve to die ten times, or rather ten thousand times over? [119] To testify that I speak the truth, I will also call forth for you witnesses who were present to the following. On the day before he made these allegations, he entered Aristarchus' house and spoke with him, and then on the next day—this, men of Athens, this act of impurity cannot be topped—he went back to Aristarchus' house and sat next to him as close as this. Taking his hand in front of many witnesses, after he said in the Council that Aristarchus was the perpetrator and accused him of the most terrible things, Meidias then swore upon his own destruction that he had said nothing damning about Aristarchus, and he did not care that he swore falsely or that there were people present aware of his lies, and he even asked Aristarchus to negotiate a reconciliation with me. [120] And yet, men of Athens, how is it not terrible, or rather impious, to say that Aristarchus was a murderer and then deny under oath having said so, and accuse him of murder and then sit under the same roof as him? If I let him go and surrender your vote of condemnation, it seems, I am not at all guilty. But if I prosecute him, I have abandoned my post, I am an accomplice to murder, I must be taken away. I, however, believe that the opposite is true: if I had let him go, I would have abandoned, men of Athens, the post of justice, and it would have been appropriate for me to prosecute myself for murder, since my life would certainly not be worth living after I had acted in such a way. [121] To testify that I speak the truth, please call forth also the witnesses of this.

---

89. Since a murderer was considered polluted, it would have been dangerous to be in a confined area with him. For that reason, cases of homicide were tried in the open air; see Ant. 5.11; Arist. *Ath. Pol.* 57.4.

TESTIMONY

{*We, Lysimachus of Alopece, Demeas of Sunium, Chares of Thoricus, Philemon of Sphettus, and Moschus of Paeania, know that when a denunciation was made to the Council against Aristarchus, son of Moschus, that he murdered Nicodemus, Meidias, who is being tried by Demosthenes for whom we testify, came to the Council and alleged that no one other than Aristarchus was the murderer of Nicodemus, and he was the perpetrator, and Meidias advised the Council to go to Aristarchus' house and arrest him. He made these allegations to the Council, even though he had dined the day before with Aristarchus and us. And we know that after Meidias made these allegations and left the Council, he went again into Aristarchus' house and took his hand and swore upon his own destruction that he said nothing damning against him before the Council, and he asked Aristarchus to negotiate a reconciliation with Demosthenes.*}

[122] What can top this? What wickedness is or could be comparable to his? He believed that he had to bring a malicious accusation against an unfortunate man, although the man had not wronged him (I leave off that he was a friend), and he asked Aristarchus to negotiate a reconciliation with me. He did this and spent his money in order to cause me to be exiled unjustly together with Aristarchus.

[123] This practice and this art, men of Athens, of overwhelming those who justly pursue complaints on behalf of themselves with still greater problems, ought not to anger and disturb me, while the rest of you disregard it. Far from it. All of you ought to be equally upset as you consider and observe how it is easy and most likely for the poorest and the weakest of you to be victims of mistreatment, while loathsome men armed with riches are most likely to commit acts of outrage and not be punished after doing so but even hire men who will create problems[90] in return. [124] You should not ignore such behavior or think that the person who prevents any of us through fear and intimidation from receiving compensation from him for wrongs suffered is doing anything other than depriving us of our share of equal speech and liberty. Perhaps I drove back the lies and malicious accusations (and someone else might be able to), and I have not been destroyed. But what will you, the many, do if you do not make everyone publicly afraid to misuse his wealth for such purposes? [125] One should first make his case and stand trial for accusations that someone has lodged and then retaliate against those who unlawfully attacked him. One should not snatch them away beforehand, seek to avoid trial by bringing false charges, or be

---

90. I.e., by lodging countersuits.

upset for paying the penalty rather than see to it from the beginning that one does not commit an offense.

[126] How I have suffered outrage during my liturgy and in my person and how I have escaped from every kind of plot and mistreatment, men of Athens, you have heard. But I leave out many incidents, since it is perhaps not easy to mention everything. Yet, it is the case that he has not committed a single offense for which I am his only victim. In the wrongs inflicted against the chorus, my tribe—a tenth of you—has also been injured; in his acts of outrage and his plots against me, the laws, which protect each of you; and in all of these actions, the god, for whom I was appointed chorus producer, and that hallowed law, holy and divine, whatever it may be. [127] If you want to exact from him the right punishment fitting for his offenses, you ought not to be indignant, as though I speak only on my own behalf. Believing instead that the laws, the god, and the city have all together been injured at the same time, you ought to punish him accordingly and suppose that those who help him and are his followers not only speak on his behalf, but even approve of his actions.

[128] Now if, men of Athens, Meidias had been upstanding and moderate in other regards, had not harmed any other citizen, and had only been so brutal and violent to me, first I would have considered this to be my misfortune, and then I would have been afraid that he would have avoided paying the penalty for the acts of outrage that he inflicted by showing how the rest of his life was moderate and humane. [129] But as it is, he has committed so many and such terrible offenses against many of you that I am free from this worry, and fear instead that, when you hear the many terrible offenses that others suffered from him, the following thought may come to you: "What is your point? Are you angry because you suffered something worse than everyone else?" I could not say to you everything that he has done nor would you bear to hear it. Even if all of our time—mine along with his—were allowed for the rest of my speech, it would not be enough, but I will mention the worst and most obvious offenses. [130] Rather, I will do the following: I will read out to you all of my notes, and I will mention first whatever you want to hear first, then your next preference, and the rest in the same way as long as you want to listen. They are of all sorts: many forms of outrage, wrongs against his family, and acts of impiety against the gods. In every arena, you will discover that he has committed many offenses worthy of death.

NOTES ABOUT MEIDIAS' OFFENSES

[131] Such are the offenses, men of the jury, that he has done every time he has encountered someone. I have left out other incidents, since no one could mention at one time all the acts of outrage that he has carried out

over so much time and without interruption throughout his entire life. It is, however, worth observing how arrogant he has become by escaping punishment for all of these offenses. It seems to me that he does not believe anything someone does to another is noteworthy or manly or deserving of admiration, but unless he humiliates an entire tribe, the Council, and a whole group of people while at the same time harassing the multitude of you all together, he does not consider life worth living. [132] I will not speak about the rest, although countless are the stories that I could tell. As for the cavalry serving with him at Argoura, all of you know, I suppose, what he said to you in the Assembly after he returned from Chalcis, when he denounced the army and said that the expedition was an embarrassment to the city. You also remember the reproach that he cast on Cratinus in this matter, who, as I understand, is now going to help him. How much wickedness and audacity ought one to believe motivated him to instill such anger, for no reason, in so many citizens assembled together? [133] Are they, Meidias, an embarrassment to the city, who crossed over in military order with the equipment necessary to march out against the enemy and join allies, or is it you, who prayed that you not be selected to participate in the mission when you were casting lots, who never put on a breast-plate but rode on a silver-ornamented chair,[91] bringing woolen cloaks, cups, and jars, which the tax collectors tried to seize?[92] This was reported to those of us who were hoplites; for we did not cross over at the same place as the cavalry. [134] So then did you persecute all of them because Archetion or someone else poked fun at you about this incident? If you did, Meidias, what your fellow cavalry say you did and what you accuse them of saying about you, you deserved the reproach, since you endangered and disgraced them as well as the men here today and the entire city. But if some people fabricated this lie about you and you didn't do it, and the rest of the soldiers did not reproach them but took pleasure in your embarrassment, they clearly thought you were capable of doing what was said about you, based on the rest of your life. Therefore you should have shown more self control and not have slandered them. [135] But you threaten everyone, and you go after everyone. You demand that others consider your wishes, even though you do not consider what you will do to avoid upsetting them. What I think is most shocking and the greatest

---

91. The *astrabe* was normally mounted on donkeys for female riders.

92. Imported and exported merchandise was subject to a 2 percent tax; failure to pay the tax resulted in confiscation of the goods. The point of this reference is to ridicule Meidias for appearing more like a trader than a soldier. Since Demosthenes raises doubts about the accuracy of this gossip in the next sentence, the alleged incident probably did not take place; see MacDowell 1990: 353.

proof of your insolence is the fact that you, cursed creature, came forward and accused so many men all at once. Who would not have shuddered at doing such a thing?

[136] When I see, men of the jury, all other men charged with one or two offenses, they have plenty of the following arguments at their disposal: "Who of you is aware of me doing such a thing? Who of you ever saw me carrying it out? No one. They bring false charges against me out of enmity. I am a victim of false testimony," or similar sorts of arguments. The opposite applies to this man. [137] I think that all of you know his disposition, the brutality and arrogance in his life, and I believe that some have been wondering for a while why they are not hearing now from me about what they know. But I see that many of his victims are even unwilling to testify to all their injuries because they fear his violence, his meddling, and the resources that make this despicable man mighty and frightening. [138] Whenever power and wealth spur on a wicked and insolent man, he has a buttress to protect himself from suffering any onrush. So if Meidias is deprived of his wealth, perhaps he will not continue to commit acts of outrage, or if he does, you will not even consider him worthy of the smallest amount of consideration. He will utter reproaches and shout in vain, since he will pay the penalty just like the rest of us if he commits some violent transgression. [139] But as it turns out, I believe, he is shielded by Polyeuctus, Timocrates, and the filthy Euctemon. Such are the mercenaries at his side. There are others in addition to these men, a gang[93] of witnesses banded together. They do not openly annoy you, but they silently and without hesitation nod in agreement to his lies. By the gods, I do not think that they gain anything from him, but some have the knack, men of Athens, for being corrupted by the rich, waiting on them, and serving as their witnesses. [140] All of this, I believe, terrifies the rest of you as each one tries individually to make a living as best as he can. Therefore unite, since individually each of you has fewer friends and less wealth and is weaker in every other way than they, but united you can be stronger than each of them and put an end to their acts of outrage.

[141] Perhaps the following question will be said to you, "Why is it that so-and-so did not receive legal compensation from me although he suffered this and that?" or "Why did not so-and-so?" as he names perhaps another victim. I think that all of you are aware of the reasons why each one

---

93. *Hetaireia* literally means "a group of companions," which consisted of rich and noble Athenians who socialized together and served as political allies. By the fourth century, this term carried mainly negative connotations because *hetaireiai* had organized and carried out the oligarchic revolutions of 411 and 404. See **Lys. 12.43, 55**.

fails to defend himself: lack of free time, reluctance to become involved in litigation,[94] inability to speak, lack of resources, and countless other reasons. [142] I, however, believe that he should not now say this, but prove that he has not done any of those things that I have accused him of doing, and if he cannot, then he deserves to die all the more. If someone is so powerful that he can deprive each one of us individually of receiving justice from him for such conduct, now together by all and on behalf of all, since he has been caught, he ought to be punished as a common enemy of the state.

[143] It is said that Alcibiades[95] lived in Athens during her golden age. Consider what sort of services he performed for the people and how your forefathers dealt with him when he felt compelled to act in a vile and outrageous fashion. I recall this episode not because I want to compare Meidias to Alcibiades (I am not so foolish or dense), but so that you may know, men of Athens, and understand that there neither is nor will be anything—not birth, not wealth, not power—that you must put up with, when it is accompanied by insolence. [144] That one, it is said, men of Athens, was a descendant of the Alcmaeonids on his father's side.[96] They say that they were banished by the tyrants for stirring up revolution against them on behalf of the people, freed the city by borrowing money from Delphi, and expelled Pisistratus' sons.[97] On his mother's side, he is said to be a descendant of Hipponicus and from that house, which performed

---

94. *Apragmosyne* generally means "an unwillingness to be involved in public affairs" (cf. **83**), but here refers more specifically to litigation. Cf. MacDowell 1990: 304.

95. Nephew of Pericles, Alcibiades advocated the disastrous military expedition against Syracuse in 415. After the fleet arrived in Sicily, he was forced into exile because of accusations raised against him concerning the profanation of the Eleusinian Mysteries (see Thuc. 6.15–18, 27–29, 61; And. 1). He fled first to Sparta and then to Persia, where he gave Athens' enemies important military advice, but then he helped the democratic fleet while the Four Hundred were in power. Because of his services, he was allowed to return to Athens in 407. Under his leadership, the Athenians regained some of their lost allies and won key naval victories, but he again fell under suspicion and went into exile in 406. He eventually found his way to Phrygia where he was received by the Persian satrap Pharnabazus and was murdered sometime after the Thirty seized control of Athens.

96. It was actually his mother, and not his father, who was an Alcmaeonid.

97. I.e., the Alcmaeonids used the advance on their payment for rebuilding the temple to fund their campaign to remove the tyrants. In Herodotus' version (5.62–63), the Alcmaeonids won over the oracle by spending more to rebuild the temple than they were required by the contract to spend, and in return the Spartans received oracles calling on them to free Athens from the tyrants.

many great services for the people.[98] [145] Besides these honors, he took up arms on behalf of the people, twice in Samos and a third time at Athens, by which he displayed his patriotism with his body, not with his money or his speeches. In addition, there were his horse races at Olympia and his victories and crowns. He was thought to be the best general and, as they say, the most skilled speaker. [146] Nevertheless, your forefathers did not allow him to subject them to outrage because of any of these distinctions, but they banished him and forced him to live in exile. Although the Spartans were then a threat, they endured that Decelea be fortified against them, the capture of their fleet, and everything else, because they believed it was better for them to suffer anything unwillingly than willingly submit to outrage.[99] [147] Yet what act of outrage did Alcibiades do that is comparable to what Meidias has now been shown to have done? He struck Taureas when he was serving as a chorus producer. Fair enough, but Alcibiades was a chorus producer when he hit a chorus producer, and he was not in violation of the law, since it had not yet been enacted. He imprisoned the painter Agatharchus; for that's what they also say. However, they also say that he caught Agatharchus as he was committing an offense; so it is not worthy of reproach. He mutilated the Herms. All acts of impiety, I believe, merit the same degree of anger. Yet, completely destroying sacred objects differs from mutilating them, and Meidias has been shown to have done the former.[100]

[148] Let us, by contrast, consider what sort of person Meidias is and what upset[101] him so that he did these things. When you catch a man who is a nobody and the son of a nobody being wicked and violent and insolent,

---

98. Alcibiades' wife, not his mother, was the daughter of Hipponicus. He was famous for his wealth and was a member of the Ceryces family, which shared with the Eumolpidae priestly responsibilities for the Eleusinian Mysteries.

99. The Spartans fortified Decelea in 413, upon the recommendation of Alcibiades, and captured the Athenian fleet at the Battle of Aegospotami in 405, after the Athenian generals had ignored his warnings.

100. Since Demosthenes indicated earlier in the speech that the goldsmith prevented Meidias from completely destroying the sacred clothing (**16**), he must be distinguishing Alcibiades' intent from that of Meidias (MacDowell 1990: 364). During the investigation to discover who was responsible for the mutilation of the Herms, Alcibiades was accused of profaning the Mysteries, but no evidence was brought against him to suggest that he had any part in desecrating the Herms. Given Demosthenes' other mistakes in his discussion on Alcibiades, this error could be unintentional. Alternatively, he may have intentionally made this error for the sake of the comparison with Meidias.

101. Our translation is based on MacDowell's correction to the text: *epoiesen daknomenos*.

do not, men of the jury, consider it fair or right or pious for descendants of such ancestors to deem him worthy of any forgiveness, kindness, or favor. Why would you? Because of the occasions when he was a general? But he does not even merit any consideration for his time as a private soldier, much less as a leader of others. Because of his speeches? He never said anything for the public good, but he says many terrible things about everyone individually. [149] Because of his birth, perhaps? But who of you does not know that this man's unmentionable birth is like something from tragedy? Two of the most opposite extremes befell him: his actual mother, who gave birth to him, was the smartest person, while his reputed mother, who raised him as her own, was the most foolish woman. Here is the proof: the former sold him as soon as he was born while the latter bought him at the price for which she could have bought a better son. [150] As a result, he holds property that does not belong to him and has acquired a fatherland known more than all other cities for being governed most closely in accordance with the laws. He cannot, however, in any way put up with or practice them, but that part of his nature, truly barbaric and hateful to the gods, drags him about with violence and makes it obvious that he treats his belongings as though they do not belong to him, which they don't.

[151] Although this disgusting and shameful man has lived a life filled with so many and such terrible crimes, some of his friends, men of the jury, approached me and advised that I abandon and drop this suit. But when they could not convince me, they did not dare deny that he had committed many terrible offenses and deserved to pay any penalty whatsoever for them. Instead, they turned to this approach, "He has already been convicted and received a vote of condemnation. What penalty do you expect the court to impose on him? Don't you see that he is wealthy and he will speak about his trierarchies and his liturgies? Watch out that he does not plead for leniency through such appeals and laugh at you for paying much less to the city than what he is offering you." [152] In the first place, I do not accuse you of anything ignoble, nor do I suppose that you will impose on him a punishment less than that which, when paid, will end his outrage; ideally, this is death, or else confiscation of all his property. In the second place, I consider his liturgies and his trierarchies and such claims as follows. [153] If this is a liturgy, men of Athens, to say to you at every meeting of the Assembly and everywhere else, "We are the men who perform liturgies, we are the men who pay you the *proeisphora*,[102] we are the rich"—if a liturgy is to say these sorts of things, I admit that Meidias is the most notable

---

102. *Eisphora* was a tax that the wealthy paid on occasion, typically in times of war. In order to collect the tax quickly, the wealthy were grouped into symmories, and the wealthiest of each symmory had to pay in advance the entire amount (*proeisphora*)

citizen in Athens. He wears us down with his unpleasant and distasteful behavior at every meeting of the Assembly as he makes such statements. [154] If, however, you ought to consider what on earth are the liturgies that he truly performs, I will tell you, and I will compare him to myself so that you may see how fairly I scrutinize him.

Although Meidias, men of Athens, is about fifty years old or a little less, he has not performed for you more liturgies than I, who am thirty-two.[103] Moreover, I served as a trierarch as soon as I was an adult and at a time when we performed the duty in pairs, paid all the expenses out of our own pockets, and manned the ships. [155] This man did not yet begin to perform liturgies until he reached the age I am now, and he only undertook to do so when you first established twelve hundred joint-contributors, from whom these men collect a talent and contract the trierarchies out for a talent.[104] Furthermore, the city provides the crew and equipment so that it turns out that some of them actually spend nothing, and since they have purportedly performed a liturgy, they are exempt from other liturgies. [156] What more? This man has once been a chorus producer for tragedies, while I for a men's chorus, but everyone knows, I suppose, that the latter is much more expensive than the former. In addition, I volunteered while he was appointed after a challenge to exchange property, and therefore it would certainly not be right for anyone to owe him thanks. What else? I have given a feast for my tribe and served as a chorus producer for the Panathenaea. He has done neither. [157] For ten years, I have led my symmory[105] for you, paying as much as Phormio, Lysitheides, Callaeschrus, and the richest, assessed not from the property in my possession (since I had been deprived of it by my guardians) but from the amount that my father was

---

that his symmory was required to contribute. He would then be reimbursed by the members of his symmory for the amount that they owed.

103. This could not have been Demosthenes' age at the time of the speech, since he was born in either 385/4 or 384/3. MacDowell (1990: 370–71) suggests that the text originally read "thirty-seven" but was corrupted to "thirty-two" in a subsequent copy. Alternatively, Demosthenes is lying about his age in order to make his liturgical record appear that much more impressive in comparison to that of Meidias (Harris 1989: 121–25).

104. In 357, the Athenians reduced the financial burden of the trierarch by grouping wealthy Athenians into symmories to share the costs of maintaining the triremes. According to Demosthenes, Meidias manipulated this system so that he had his joint-contributors paid all of the expenses, including the costs to hire a deputy, and he did not have to command the trireme or pay for someone else to command it on his behalf.

105. See **153** n.

known to have left and that I was legally entitled to receive when I became an adult. This is how I have behaved towards you. But how has Meidias behaved? He has not yet to this day led a symmory, although no one has deprived him of any of his inheritance. He has received much property from his father.

[158] What is his munificence? What are his liturgies and his majestic expenses? One cannot see them unless one gazes at the following: he has built a house at Eleusis so big that it casts a shadow on everything in its vicinity; he leads his wife to the Mysteries,[106] and wherever else he wishes, by a pair of white horses from Sicyon, and he clears a path through the agora with three or four attendants as he speaks of cups, drinking horns, and drinking bowls so that the passers-by hear. [159] I do not know how all that Meidias acquires for private luxury and personal gain helps the many of you. I see, however, how the acts of outrage, which his possessions spur him on to commit, affect many of us ordinary people. You should, therefore, bestow honor and show admiration not whenever someone behaves in such a fashion, and you should judge the desire for distinction not from those instances when someone builds a magnificent home or has acquired many servants and fine furniture but when someone gives lavishly and strives for distinction in that which all of you, the many, enjoy. You will discover that this is not the case for Meidias.

[160] But, by Zeus, he donated a trireme. I am sure that he will blather on about it, and he will say, "I have donated a trireme to you." So respond accordingly. If, men of Athens, he donated it out of a desire for distinction, be grateful and thank him as is fitting for such generosity, but do not allow him to engage in acts of outrage. Such license should not be conceded because of any act or deed. If, on the other hand, he will be shown to have done it because of cowardice and lack of manliness, do not be deceived. How will you know? I will tell you about this as well, and I will start from the beginning since the story is short. [161] Donations were first offered to you for Euboea. Meidias was not one of the volunteers, but I was, with my fellow trierarch, Philinus, son of Nicostratus. Donations were next proposed for Olynthus. Meidias was not one of those to volunteer. Yet a generous person ought to volunteer every time. When donations were offered a third time, then he donated. How? Although he was present as donations were being received in the Council, he did not volunteer then. [162] But when it was reported that the soldiers[107] stationed at Tamynae

---

106. Initiates of the Eleusinian Mysteries performed in secret ceremonies and fertility rites in honor of Persephone and Demeter and were promised eternal happiness for their devotion.

107. This was the force sent under Phocion's command; see **110** n.

were being besieged and the Council drafted a motion to dispatch all of the remaining cavalry, of which he was a member, then, because he was afraid of this expedition, he came at the next meeting of the Assembly and offered a donation even before the presiding officers (*proedroi*)[108] sat down.

How is it so clear that even he cannot deny it, that the desire to avoid the expedition, and not an eagerness for distinction, prompted him? By that which he did next. [163] First, as the Assembly proceeded and speeches were made, and it was decided that assistance from the cavalry was no longer needed and the motion in favor of an expedition was abandoned, he did not board the donated ship but sent out an Egyptian metic, Pamphilus, while he remained here and committed the offenses at the Dionysia for which he is now on trial. [164] But when the general Phocion had called on the cavalry from Argoura to relieve the deployed force and Meidias' ploy had been exposed, then this cursed coward abandoned his post, went onto his ship, and did not join the cavalry, whom he thought himself worthy to command in Athens. If, however, there had been some danger at sea, he certainly would have gone ashore. [165] This was, by no means, the case for Nicostratus, son of Nicias, although he was an only son, childless, and in very bad health, nor so for Euctemon,[109] son of Aesion, nor Euthydemus, son of Stratocles. Each of them willingly donated a trireme and did not avoid the expedition. Each provided the city with a seaworthy ship as a gift and an act of generosity, but where the law stationed them, there they thought it right for them to perform their liturgies in person. [166] But this was not the case for the hipparch Meidias. Although he abandoned his post assigned by law, for which he ought to pay the city a penalty, he will count this act as a form of public generosity. And yet is it fitting to call a trierarchy such as this tax farming, a 2 percent exemption,[110] desertion, evasion of military duty, and something of this sort, or the desire for distinction? Unable to find an exemption from military service by any other way, he has discovered this new 2 percent exemption from the cavalry.[111] [167] Consider also this: when all of the other trierarchs brought you home from Styra on the triremes they donated, he alone did not, but he neglected you in order to ship vine-stakes, cattle, and doors to his home, and wood to the silver mines. This despicable man performed his trierarchy as

---

108. See **9** n.

109. Probably not the same man mentioned in **103** and **139**.

110. Those Athenians who collected the 2 percent tax on imported and exported goods were exempt from military duty; cf. **133**.

111. That is to say, Meidias avoided cavalry duty by donating a trireme and thus found an exemption comparable to that which those collecting the 2 percent tax receive.

a business venture, not a liturgy. That I speak the truth, you mostly know. Nevertheless, I will also call forth witnesses for you.

WITNESSES

[168] {*We, Cleon of Sunium, Aristocles of Paeania, Pamphilus, Niceratus of Acherdous, Euctemon of Sphettus, when we sailed from Styra to Athens with the entire fleet, were trierarchs along with Meidias, who is now being tried by Demosthenes, for whom we testify. When the entire fleet sailed in formation and the trierarchs were instructed not to separate until we landed in Athens, Meidias abandoned the fleet and loaded his ship with wood, vine-stakes, cattle, and some other things. He landed alone in the Piraeus two days later and did not join the other trierarchs in bringing the fleet back.*}

[169] Now if, men of Athens, his liturgies and his actions were really as he will claim and boast to you very soon and not as I show, of course it would be wrong even then for him to evade punishment for his acts of outrage because of his liturgies. I know that many have performed many good deeds for you, not like the liturgies of Meidias. Some have won naval battles, some have conquered cities, and some have set up many fine trophies on behalf of the city. [170] Nevertheless, you never granted nor would grant any of them this gift—permission for each of them to subject his private enemies to outrage whenever he wants to and in whichever manner he can. This privilege was not even granted to Harmodius and Aristogeiton, whom you awarded most extraordinary gifts for their exceptional services. You would not have even tolerated it if someone added on the inscription, "They are also permitted to subject whomever they wish to outrage."[112] This is why they received their other privileges, because they stopped those who were committing acts of outrage.

[171] I also wish to show you that he has received sufficient gratitude from you, men of Athens, not only for the liturgies he has performed (for they were trifling), but also for the most remarkable liturgies, so that you may realize that you do not owe this despicable man anything. You, men of Athens, elected him treasurer of the *Paralus*[113] (in spite of who he is),

---

112. The right to dine in the Prytaneum was awarded to the descendants of Harmodius and Aristogeiton for their failed attempt to end the Pisistratid tyranny in 514 through the assassination of the sons of Pisistratus, Hippias, and Hipparchus. As the plan was being carried out, the conspirators panicked and were only able to kill Hipparchus before Hippias captured and executed them.

113. The *Paralus* and the *Salaminia* were ships used for sacred functions, such as the transportation of Athenian envoys to religious festivals, and had their own officials,

also a hipparch (although he could not ride in the processions through the agora), the manager of the Mysteries, a performer of a sacrifice, a purchaser of sacrificial cattle, and so on. [172] Then, by the gods, do you suppose it is a small gift and favor for a man naturally wicked, cowardly, and base to be redeemed through these offices, honors, and elections, thanks to you? And if someone were to deprive him of the right of saying, "I have been a hipparch, I have been the treasurer of the *Paralus*," how much is he worth? [173] But you surely know that when he was treasurer of the *Paralus* he took more than five talents from some Cyzicenes, and so as not to be punished, he pushed the men around and persecuted them in every way, and he played havoc with the treaty and made Cyzicus hostile to Athens, and he kept the money for himself. When he had been elected hipparch, he harmed the cavalry by establishing rules that he later denied he had enacted. [174] When he was treasurer of the *Paralus* at the time of your expedition against the Thebans in Euboea, you ordered him to spend twelve talents of public money. When you asked him to set sail and convey the soldiers, he did not assist but arrived only after the truce was in effect that Diocles had made with the Thebans. A privately funded trireme even sped past him: this is how well he had furnished the sacred trireme! Can you believe what else he did when he was a hipparch? This illustrious and wealthy man did not dare to buy a horse, not even a horse, but led the processions on one that he borrowed from another person, Philomelus of Paeania. All the cavalry know about this as well. To testify that I speak the truth, please also call forth the witnesses to this.

WITNESSES

[175] Now I would also like to speak to you, men of Athens, about the men whom you found guilty of committing offenses concerning the festival after the people cast a vote of condemnation against them, and to explain what some of them did and how angry you were with them, in order for you to compare their actions with those of Meidias. Let me first discuss the most recent conviction: the people cast a vote of condemnation against Euandrus of Thespiae, for an offense concerning the Mysteries, when Menippus, a man from Caria, lodged a *probole* against him. The law concerning the Mysteries is the same as the one concerning the Dionysia, which was enacted first. [176] What did Euandrus do, men of Athens, to cause you to cast your vote against him? Listen to this. Since he won a mercantile suit against Menippus and could not find him beforehand, so

---

including treasurers. Because of their speed, they were also often used in war to convey messages.

he alleged, he seized him when Menippus was in Athens for the Mysteries. Because of this offense and for no other reason whatsoever, you voted against Euandrus in the Assembly. When he came to court, you wanted to sentence him to death, but since the man lodging the *probole* gave in, you forced Euandrus to forfeit the entire sum of two talents, which he had won in the previous suit, and you fined him in addition for the damages Menippus calculated he had suffered by waiting in Athens for the trial after the vote of condemnation in the Assembly. [177] This one man, from a private dispute, although he was not also guilty of committing an act of outrage, paid such a great penalty for violating the law. This is right, since you must protect the laws and your oath. You, who happen to be serving as jurors, hold them like a deposit from the rest of us, which must be kept safe for all who come to you with a just case. [178] There was another man you once decided was guilty of committing an offense concerning the Dionysia. Although he was serving as an assessor[114] to his son, the archon, you cast a vote of condemnation against him because he seized and removed someone from the theater as he was taking a seat.[115] This man was the father of that most distinguished archon, Charicleides. [179] The man lodging the *probole* seemed to you to have a strong case when he said, "If I was taking a seat, mister, and ignored the proclamations, as you allege, what are you and the archon legally authorized to do? You are permitted to instruct attendants to bar me, but not to hit me yourself. If even then I do not obey, you may fine me, and do anything other than grab me by your hand. The laws have established many measures to prevent each individual from having his person subjected to outrage." This is what he said, and you voted against the accused. He did not, however, go to court, because he died before the trial. [180] Then there was another man against whom the entire people cast a vote of condemnation for an offense concerning the festival, and when he appeared in court, you sentenced him to death (I am talking about Ctesicles). Why? Because he was marching in a procession with a whip, and in a drunken state, he struck an enemy with it. It was decided that insolence, not wine, motivated him to strike, but he used the procession and his intoxication as a pretext for committing the offense of treating freemen like slaves. [181] Now, I am quite aware, men of Athens, that everyone would say that Meidias' offenses are much worse than the offenses of each of these men, one of whom evidently forfeited the sum awarded to him while the other was sentenced to death. Although Meidias was not marching in a procession, had not won a lawsuit, was not serving

---

114. The three senior archons—the *basileus,* polemarch, and (eponymous) archon— each appointed two assessors (*paredroi*) to assist them in their duties as archon.

115. Some of the seats in the theater were reserved for dignitaries.

as an archon's assessor, and had no excuse other than insolence, he acted as none of these men did.

[182] I will leave off there about them. There was also Pyrrhus, men of Athens, one of the Eteobutadae,[116] who was indicted for serving on the jury while in public debt. Some of you believed that he ought to be sentenced to death, and he died after you convicted him. Yet need, not insolence, made him attempt to obtain jury pay. I could talk about many others: some were executed, and some were disfranchised for acts that were much less serious than those of Meidias. You, men of Athens, fined Smicrus ten talents and Sciton a similar amount for proposing an illegal decree, and you did not pity their children, friends, relatives, or any of their supporters. [183] Therefore, do not show yourselves to be so angry if someone proposes an illegal motion, and then so compassionate if someone does, rather than says, something illegal. No term or word is as grievous to the many of you as the acts of outrage that someone inflicts if one of you crosses his path. So do not, men of Athens, bear such proof against yourselves that if you catch some ordinary individual committing any offense, you will not pity or let him go, but you will either execute or disfranchise him, and when some wealthy man commits an act of outrage, you will forgive him. Don't do it, since it is not just; but show that you mete out your anger the same way in all cases.

[184] Now after I have said and briefly discussed what I consider to be no less necessary than what I have already told you, I will step down. Your tendency, men of Athens, to be lenient provides a great advantage to all who commit offenses. Hear me tell you why you ought not to be lenient to Meidias. I think that all men give contributions throughout their lives for their own benefit, not only those that some collect and for which there are contributors, but there are also other kinds.[117] [185] Say, for example, one of us is moderate and generous and feels pity for many. He deserves to receive the same from everyone if he is ever in need or appears in a dispute. Say there is another person who is shameless, subjects many to acts of outrage, and considers some men beggars, some garbage, and others to be nothing. He deserves to receive in return the same contributions that he has given to others. Now if you happen to consider it, you will find that Meidias has given the latter kind of contribution and not the former.

[186] Now I know that he will have his children beside him as he wails and delivers a long and humble speech, crying and making himself as

116. One of the aristocratic families, known as the "Eupatrids," that ruled Athens before the reforms of Solon in 594 and retained their ancestral priesthoods after they lost their political prerogatives.

117. See **101**.

pitiable as possible. But as much as he now makes himself more humble, so much more is it fitting for you to hate him, men of Athens. Why? If he was so brutal and so violent in the past because he was not at all able to be humble, it would be fitting to let go of your anger a little bit, since he was this way by nature and by chance. But if he knows how to conduct himself modestly when he wants to, but he chose to live in the opposite way, it is clearly the case that, if he now evades punishment, he will again be that man whom you know him to be. [187] So you ought not to pay attention or place more weight or trust in the present circumstances, which this one intentionally fabricates, than in all of his past, which you know for yourselves. I do not have children, nor could I set them before you as I cry and lament over the acts of outrage that I suffered. For this reason, will I, the victim, receive less of your concern than the perpetrator? Of course not. [188] But when he has his children beside him and asks you to cast your vote for them, then imagine that I stand before you with the laws beside me, asking and beseeching each of you to vote for them. For many reasons, it would be more just for you to side with the laws than with him. You have sworn, men of Athens, to obey the laws, you enjoy equality because of the laws, and all the benefits that you have are because of the laws, not because of Meidias and not because of Meidias' children.

[189] "This man is an orator," perhaps he will say, speaking about me. If an orator is a person who gives advice that he believes is useful to you, and he does so without upsetting or pressuring you, neither would I refuse nor deny the title. If, however, an orator is like some of those speakers whom I and you also see—shameless men who have grown rich from you—I could not be one, since I have not taken anything from you but have spent on you all that I have except for a very little. And yet even if I were the most wicked of them, I must be punished according to the laws and not be subjected to outrage for the performance of my liturgies. [190] Moreover, not one of the orators is helping me. I do not blame them, since I never spoke before you for the sake of any of them. I have simply set out to say and do what I believe is useful to you. But very soon you will see all the orators alongside him, one right after another. And yet, how is it fair for him to attach this label to me as a form of reproach and ask to be saved by these men?

[191] Well perhaps he will also say this sort of retort, that everything I am now saying has been thought over and prepared. I admit it, men of Athens, and I would not deny that I have thought over and practiced as much as I could. I would be pitiful, if—in spite of that which I have suffered and still am suffering—I didn't consider what I was going to say to you. [192] However, Meidias is the one who has written my speech. The person who did what is the subject of the speech would deserve most of

all to hold the blame, not the man who has thought about and cares to say now what is just. The latter, men of Athens, I admit to doing. It is likely, however, that Meidias never thought in all of his life about what is just. If it had occurred to him to think about such things for even a little bit, he would not have gone so far astray.

[193] Then I believe that he will not even hesitate to accuse the people and the Assembly, and what he dared to say then at the *probole,* he will say here, that the Assembly consisted of people who stayed behind, although they should have gone on the expedition, and those who had abandoned the forts, and that choristers, foreigners, and such sorts of men had cast a vote of condemnation against him. [194] He then came to such a degree of daring and shamelessness, men of Athens, as those of you who were present know, as to believe that he could terrify the entire people with his aspersions and threats and by eyeing whichever section of the Assembly was making a commotion. It would therefore be appropriate for his tears now to appear ridiculous. [195] What are you saying, cursed creature? Will you ask them to pity your children or you or to be concerned about your belongings, when they have been abused by you in public? Will you alone of men who are alive be so conspicuously full of so much arrogance towards everyone throughout your life that even those who have no business with you are upset when they observe your audacity, your tone, your appearance, your followers, your wealth, and your acts of outrage, and then once on trial, will you immediately receive pity? [196] You would have discovered an extraordinary power, or rather skill, if you could elicit for yourself two completely opposite reactions in such a short time: indignation for the way that you live and pity for the lies that you tell. In no way do you warrant any pity, not even a little bit, but rather hatred, indignation, and anger. These are the responses that you deserve to receive.

But I will return to my previous point, that he will accuse the people and the Assembly. [197] When he does so, consider among yourselves, men of the jury, that this man came before you in the Assembly and accused those men who had served in the cavalry with him when they crossed over to Olynthus.[118] Now, however, in spite of the fact that he remained in Athens, he will accuse the Assembly in front of those men who went on the expedition. Will you admit that you are the sort of men whom Meidias declares you to be, whether you remain here or march out? Or is it entirely the opposite, that he is always and everywhere a vile fiend? I believe that he is that sort of man; for what should one call a person whom the cavalry, his colleagues, and his friends cannot stand? [198] I swear by Zeus, Apollo, and Athena—for it will be said regardless of the consequences—that when

---

118. See **132.**

he went around with a story about how I had dropped the case, it was clear to me that some of his closest associates were upset. By Zeus, they have a good excuse since the man is unbearable. He claims to be the only one who is rich, the only one who can speak; and all others are for him garbage and beggars and not even human. [199] When the man has come to this degree of arrogance, what do you expect him to do if he is now acquitted? I will tell you how you will know: consider as evidence what he did after the vote of condemnation. Wouldn't any man who had been condemned for impiety concerning a festival—even if no other trial or danger were imminent—have laid low for this reason alone and behaved with self-control at least up until the trial, if not for all time thereafter? There is no one who would not have. [200] But not Meidias. From that day forth, he talks, he reproaches, he shouts. There is an election. Meidias of Anagyrous is a candidate. He represents the interests of Plutarch, he knows the secrets, the city is too small for him. He clearly does all of these things to prove nothing other than that "I have suffered nothing from the vote of condemnation, and I am not frightened or afraid of the upcoming trial." [201] Men of Athens, doesn't the man who believes that it is shameful to appear to fear you and manly to care not at all about you deserve to die ten times over? He thinks that you cannot handle him. He is rich, bold, arrogant, loud, violent, and shameless. Where will he be captured if he escapes now?

[202] But I believe that he deserves to suffer the worst punishment if for nothing else, than for the speeches that he makes every time in public and for the occasions that he makes them. Of course you know that if some urgent news is announced to the city that everyone welcomes, Meidias never appears among those who share in the pleasure and joy of the people. [203] But if there is some bad news, which no one else wants, right away he is the first to stand up, and he delivers a speech, taking advantage of the opportunity and reaping the benefit of the silence that comes to you from your distress at the situation to say: "This is the sort you are, men of Athens. You do not go on expeditions, and you do not believe that you ought to contribute money. Then do you wonder if your affairs turn out badly for you? Do you believe that I will pay the eisphora[119] and you will distribute it? Do you think that I will serve as trierarch when you will not board the ships?" [204] From such insults, the bitterness in his soul and the malice, which he has for the multitude of you and which he keeps in secret to himself as he walks around, he brings to light on this occasion. Therefore, men of Athens, when he tries to deceive and trick you with his crying and lamenting and pleading, you must respond to him as follows: "This is the sort of man you are, Meidias. You commit acts of outrage, and you do not

---

119. See **153**.

want to keep your hands to yourself. So, are you surprised if you, who are evil, will come to an evil end? Do you think that we will put up with you and you will keep hitting us? Do you think that we will acquit you and you do not have to stop?"

[205] Those speaking on his behalf are going to help him, by the gods, not so much because they want to do him this favor but because they want to harass me because of the personal enmity that this man[120] says exists between us, whether or not I admit it. He insists it is the case, and he is incorrect. But it sometimes turns out that a person who is too successful becomes too difficult to bear. When I am treated badly and do not admit that he is my enemy, and this man does not let me go although I have let him go, and he opposes me in other people's disputes and now will stand before you and ask that I be deprived of the protection of the laws shared by all, how isn't he now too difficult to bear and too powerful to be of any use to each of us? [206] Moreover, men of Athens, Eubulus was present and seated in the theater when the people cast a vote of condemnation against Meidias, and even though Meidias called him by name and begged and beseeched him, as you know, he did not stand up. And if Eubulus believed that the *probole* had been lodged against an innocent man, of course he ought to have spoken then on behalf of his friend and assisted him. But if he knew then that Meidias was guilty, and for that reason he did not respond, but now, because he is angry with me, he will intercede on behalf of Meidias, it is not fair for you to grant him this favor. [207] Let no one be so powerful in a democracy that through his advocacy he causes one man to endure acts of outrage and another to avoid punishment. But if you want to harm me, Eubulus—although, by the gods, I do not know why— you are powerful and you are involved in politics. Inflict on me whatever punishment you want, in accordance with the laws, but do not deprive me of vengeance for the outrage that I suffered in violation of the laws. But if you cannot harm me in that way, this too is proof of my innocence since, although you easily prosecute other men, you have no basis to do so to me.

[208] Now I have also learned that Philippides, Mnesarchides, Diotimus of Euonymon, and some other wealthy trierarchs will plead on his behalf, beseech you, and ask you to grant them this favor. I would not say to you anything disparaging of them (for I would be crazy to do so), but what you ought to ponder and consider when they make their entreaties, I will tell you. [209] Consider, men of the jury, if these men (may it not happen, nor will it happen) should be in charge of the government, along with Meidias

---

120. I.e., Eubulus, an influential politician and rival of Demosthenes, who is best known for his management of the theoric fund and for his efforts to prevent the use of this fund for military expenditures (see **[Dem.] 59.4**).

and men like him, and one of you, the majority of ordinary men, were to wrong one of them—not like what Meidias did to me, but something else—and should you go to a court filled with these men, what forgiveness or pity do you think that you would obtain? They would readily grant you this favor (wouldn't they?), and they would pay attention to one of the many entreating them. Or wouldn't they immediately say, "The fiend, the scoundrel: he commits an act of outrage and he breathes. If he is allowed to live, he should be happy"? [210] Therefore, men of Athens, do not treat them any differently than they would treat you. Admire not their wealth or reputation but yourselves. They have many goods, which no one prevents them from possessing. So do not let them prevent us from possessing the protection that the laws bestow to us as common property. [211] Meidias will be suffering nothing terrible or worthy of pity if he holds the same rights as the many of us whom he now subjects to outrage and calls beggars but is deprived of that superfluous wealth that now incites him to engage in outrage. Of course it is not right for these men to ask the following of you: "Men of the jury, do not deliver a verdict in accordance with the laws; do not come to the aid of the individual who has suffered terribly; do not obey your oaths; grant us this favor." If they ask for anything on behalf of Meidias, this is what they will ask for, even if they do not use these words. [212] If, however, they are his friends, and they believe that it will be terrible for Meidias not to be wealthy, well they are very wealthy, and that is fine; but let them give him their own money so that you can deliver a verdict that is just and in accordance with the oaths you swore before entering the court, and they can grant him this favor at their own expense, not at the expense of your honor. But if they have money that they would not give up, how is it fair for you to give up your oath?

[213] Many wealthy men are assembled, men of Athens, who have acquired the reputation for being important because of their fortune, and they will come forward to entreat you. Do not, men of Athens, surrender me to any of them, but just as each of them will look after his own private interests and those of Meidias, so look after yourselves, the laws, and me, who has taken refuge with you, and adhere to that resolution that brings you here.[121] [214] If, men of Athens, when the *probole* took place, the people had voted in favor of Meidias after it heard what had happened, it would not be so terrible, since one could comfort himself much by saying that outrage had not been committed, there had not been an offense concerning the festival, and so on. [215] But as it is, this would be the worst thing to happen to me: if you revealed yourselves to be so angry, resentful,

---

121. I.e., the jury should give a verdict in support of the vote of condemnation that the Assembly delivered against Meidias.

and upset at the very time of the offense that you shouted out to me not to let him go when Neoptolemus, Mnesarchides, Philippides, and another of those very wealthy men were beseeching you and me. And when Blepaeus the banker approached me, you thought that I was going to accept money and cried out, "This is it!" [216] I was, as a result, startled by your ruckus, men of Athens, I let my cloak fall, and I was almost naked, with just a tunic, while I was trying to escape from him as he was grabbing me. Afterwards, you approached me and said, "See to it that you prosecute that cursed man and do not settle; the Athenians will be watching you to see what you will do," and similar sorts of things. When it has been determined that his action was outrage, and those passing judgment delivered their opinion while they were sitting in a sacred precinct, and I remained steadfast and betrayed neither you nor myself, then will you acquit him? [217] Never, since such an outcome is disgraceful, and I do not deserve such treatment from you, men of Athens, (for how could I?) when I prosecute a man who is as violent and insolent as his reputation holds him to be and who has committed a brutal offense at a public festival, making not only you witnesses of his insolence but all the Greeks who were in Athens. The people heard what he had done. What happened? They voted against him and handed him over to you. [218] So it is impossible for your verdict to go unnoticed or be hidden or for you not to be asked what was the verdict that you delivered when the dispute came to you. If you punish him, you will be considered prudent and noble men who despise villains. If you acquit him, it will be thought that you succumbed to some other influence. The accusation is not politically motivated, nor is it like when Aristophon stopped the *probole* by handing over the crowns. Meidias is on trial because of an act of outrage and because he cannot make amends for any of the things that he has done. So is it better to punish him in the future or now? I believe now. This is a public suit, and all the offenses for which he is on trial are public.

[219] Moreover, he did not hit only me, men of Athens, or intentionally subject only me to outrage at that time when he committed those acts but all who are thought to be less able than I to obtain satisfaction for themselves. You all were not struck or harassed while serving as chorus producers; you know, of course, that you do not all serve as chorus producers at the same time, and no one could assault all of you at the same time with one hand. [220] But when one victim does not obtain justice, everyone ought then to expect to be the next victim and ought not to disregard these offenses or wait until they happen to him, but be on the lookout as far ahead as possible. Perhaps Meidias hates me, but each of you is hated by somebody. Should you then give any enemy the power to do to each of you what Meidias has done to me? I do not think so. Therefore, do not, men of Athens, hand me over to him. [221] Think about it: very soon, when the

court is adjourned, each of you will go home, perhaps one more quickly, another more slowly, not at all concerned, not turning his head around, and not afraid whether some friend or enemy will cross his path, whether the man will be tall or short, strong or weak, or any such sort of thing. Why not? Because he knows in his heart and holds trust and confidence in the community[122] that no one will seize him, subject him to outrage, or hit him. [222] If you walk freely, without fear, will you not guarantee the same to me before you go? Why should I think that I will survive after I have suffered this plight, if you will abandon me now? "Don't worry," someone might say, "you will not be subjected to outrage again." And if I am, will you then show your anger at the perpetrator when you now let him go? Do not, men of the jury, do not betray me, yourselves, or the laws.

[223] If you would like to consider and examine why those of you who happen to be serving as jurors are powerful and have authority over all matters of the city, whether the city convenes two hundred, a thousand, or however many, you would discover that it is not because you are the only citizens drawn up with weapons, nor because you are physically the best and the strongest, nor because you are the youngest, nor for any such reason, but because the laws make you powerful. [224] But what makes the laws powerful? If one of you suffers a wrong and calls out, will the laws run to you and be at your side to help. No, since they are written texts and cannot do such a thing. So what makes the laws powerful? You do, if you enforce them and authorize them every time someone needs them. So the laws are powerful because of you, and you because of the laws. [225] You must, therefore, come to their aid just as everyone helps himself when he is wronged, and you must believe that legal violations are a public matter in every instance when they are discovered, and neither liturgies, nor pity, nor any man, nor any skill, nor any other thing has been found that will permit a person to violate the laws and not have to pay the penalty.

[226] Those of you who were at the Dionysia hissed and booed at him as he entered the theater and gave all the signs of your hostility to him although you had not yet heard anything about him from me. So before the matter was heard, you were angry, you called for the victim to seek retribution, you applauded when I lodged a *probole* against him before the Assembly. [227] But when he has been convicted, and the people sitting

---

122. Literally, *politeia* means "government" or "constitution," but here "community" is a better translation because Demosthenes is suggesting that his fellow citizens
adhere to the laws, since they are also responsible for establishing and enforcing
them. For a modern audience, government is often viewed as an external force that
imposes its will on the citizens, but Demosthenes is emphasizing how the laws of
Athens are a shared responsibility.

in the sacred precinct have cast a preliminary vote of condemnation against him, and everything else that this cursed man did has been examined in addition, and you have been selected by lot to serve as jurors, and you have the power to settle everything with one vote, will you now hesitate to help me, to please the people, to make everyone else behave, and to live safely for the rest of your lives by making him an example to everyone else? Therefore, because of all that has been said, but especially for the sake of the god whose festival this man has been caught profaning, cast a vote that is pious and just, and punish him.

DEMOSTHENES 32

AGAINST ZENOTHEMIS

Introduction

The beginning of the Peloponnesian War marks when Athens started to become heavily dependant on imported grain.[1] Nearly a century later, at a time when the city was suffering serious grain shortages, maritime cases (*dikai emporikai*) were established so that merchants and shipowners could settle their suits promptly and continue on with their trade.[2] The terminology is slightly misleading, since maritime cases were not a new kind of suit but rather new procedures were established for disputes concerning maritime trade. A lender could still, for example, lodge a suit for damage (*dike blabes*) or a suit of ejectment (*dike exoules*) against a merchant who failed to hand over the security on a defaulted loan, but if the suit met certain conditions, he could in addition use procedures reserved for maritime cases (Isager and Hansen 1975: 84–85). They were brought before the *thesmothetai* regardless of the charge lodged against the defendant, and it appears that they were heard in the winter on a monthly basis when ships could not sail and many of the parties would be staying in Athens, where they would be making arrangements for the upcoming sailing season.[3] For a suit to qualify as a maritime case and follow the legal procedures afforded to such cases, it had to concern (1) a written document and (2) goods either shipped to or from Athens (see **1**). In contrast to other types of suits, maritime cases could be brought to court by foreigners, on an equal basis with Athenians, and it seems to be the case that this privilege was extended to foreigners in other cities as well (Dem. 35.45). If the defendant was a foreigner, he was required to post bail and those acting as his sureties had to pay the prosecutor the amount disputed should the defendant flee Athens before the trial (see **29**).

The reason for the requirement that maritime cases concern freight going to or from Athens is rather obvious, but it might seem surprising

---

Translated by Andrew Wolpert.

1. For the dating of Athenian dependency on imported grain, see Garnsey 1988: 89–164; Gallant 1991; Sallares 1991; Whitby 1998.

2. MacDowell 1978: 231–33; Lanni 2006: 150–51.

3. Cohen 1973: 23–59. Alternatively, maritime cases were only heard in the summer and had to be completed within a month of the summons; see Isager and Hansen 1975: 85.

that such cases had to concern a written document. This restriction has led some scholars to conclude that the standard of proof was higher for maritime cases, but the requirement was probably intended merely to limit maritime cases to disputes over business transactions on a scale that required loan documents. Professional shippers, lenders, and merchants engaging in international trade were responsible for the movement of substantial shipments of goods to and from Athens, and their business could not have been done without loans. The maritime loan stands out from other types of loans. It had a significantly higher interest rate because it also provided insurance to the borrower, who was required to repay the loan only if the ship carrying the cargo purchased by the loan arrived safely in harbor. Since the cargo served as security on the loan, it had to be surrendered to the lender if the borrower failed to repay the loan by a specified date. Therefore, maritime cases sometimes concerned insurance fraud and sometimes concerned disagreements over ownership of the cargo should the borrower fail to repay the lender as specified by the contract. In both instances, the contract was the primary focus of the dispute, and the stakes were quite high for the parties to such loans. Moreover the lender and the borrower would have had less capital at their disposal to facilitate and participate in maritime trade until their dispute over the contract was settled in court. The Athenians, as a result, had a vested interest in ensuring that these cases were settled promptly. So the creation of special procedures for maritime cases reflects not a new or fundamentally different approach to law but the importance of both maritime trade for securing the Athenian grain supply and the centrality of the contract for that trade.

The present speech was written for Demon, cousin of Demosthenes, whom Zenothemis accuses of illegally possessing property that belonged to him. Zenothemis alleges that the shipowner, Hegestratus, purchased the cargo in question with money that Zenothemis had loaned Hegestratus. When the ship arrived in Athens, Zenothemis claimed that it was his because Hegestratus defaulted on the loan when he was lost at sea (2). Since Demon had obtained possession of the cargo and refused to relinquish it, Zenothemis lodged a suit of ejectment (*dike exoules*) in order to force Demon to surrender the cargo to him, and he sought to have his suit proceed to court as a maritime case (1, 17–20). If successful, Zenothemis would have recovered the cargo and Demon would have had to pay a penalty to the city equivalent to its value. Demon, however, responded by lodging a countersuit (*paragraphe*). He claims that Zenothemis was not permitted to bring his action to court as a maritime case, since the two were not parties of a contract with each other (2), and Zenothemis had attempted to prevent the ship from sailing to Athens (22–23). Thus Zenothemis allegedly failed to meet the two conditions required for any suit to proceed to court as a maritime case.

In response to Zenothemis' claim of ownership, Demon argues that the cargo in question was purchased in Syracuse, not by Hegestratus, as Zenothemis alleges, but by Protus, with money that Demon had loaned him. After purchasing the cargo, Protus placed it on Hegestratus' ship, which was to sail to Athens. Once the ship arrived safely in port, Protus intended to sell the cargo and repay Demon the sum that he owed him from the loan (**12, 15**). Hegestratus and Zenothemis, however, allegedly engaged in an elaborate conspiracy to defraud their lenders. They secured loans by claiming that much of the cargo on the ship belonged to them, and they sent the money they had received from their lenders back to their home city of Massalia rather than use it to purchase cargo as specified in their contracts. Of course, this meant that Hegestratus and Zenothemis could not have repaid their lenders. So they attempted to sink the ship when it was at sea and thus free themselves from the terms of their loans. The passengers, however, noticed that the ship was taking in water and took action to stop it from sinking. As they pursued Hegestratus, he leapt into the ocean and drowned. Realizing that his fraud would be discovered if the ship finished its intended journey, Zenothemis attempted to divert the ship when it reached Cephallenia, but he was unsuccessful (**4–9**). When the ship finally arrived in Athens, Zenothemis became embroiled with Protus over ownership of the grain. The merchants, who had loaned Zenothemis money, sided with him, since they knew that this was the only way they would recover their losses. Zenothemis then proceeded to take legal action against Protus, perhaps suing him for damage. Protus allegedly relented only after the price of grain had fallen, because then he could not have repaid Demon the amount he owed if he had sold the cargo in the market. So he reached an agreement with Zenothemis and fled town, and Zenothemis won, by default, the suit that he had lodged against Protus (**14–19, 24–28**). Next, it appears that Demon took the grain from Zenothemis (**20**). In response, Zenothemis attempted to recover the grain by lodging a suit of ejectment, which takes us to the present case, Demon's countersuit (*paragraphe*).

The speech is perhaps most noteworthy for the elaborate insurance fraud that Hegestratus and Zenothemis had allegedly plotted and for the vivid depiction of the panic that occurred on the ship as the passengers realized that the ship was in trouble and as Hegestratus attempted to escape from the retribution that was sure to follow if the passengers were able to seize him. In order to convince the jury that Zenothemis had no right to the cargo, Demon must explain why so many individuals sided with Zenothemis even after what he had done in Syracuse and at sea. Demon presents himself as a victim against a whole gang of individuals who knowingly assisted

Zenothemis in his fraud because they would have benefited materially from their complicity (**11–12, 24–27**). Demon offers an artful balance in his depiction of Protus and the lenders of Zenothemis both as victims and as co-conspirators.[4] Although Demon apparently had partners who also suffered losses from the loan that they had made to Protus (**21**), he does not provide many details about them, perhaps so that he might garner greater sympathy from the jury if he should appear isolated. It might also seem more believable that Zenothemis could have succeeded in such a grand scheme of deception if Demon lacked the necessary support to oppose him.

Zenothemis probably responded to Demon's countersuit by insisting that he had grounds to proceed with his complaint as a maritime case since the cargo in question was under contract and it did not matter who were the parties to that contract. Even if the jury sided with Demon and concluded that both parties to a maritime case had to be the signatories of the contract in question, Zenothemis could still have proceeded with his original suit, but he would have had to take the case to court by the regular procedure (MacDowell 2004: 86). And while Demon could point to his contract with Protus, Zenothemis also had a contract of his own, and he could easily call into question the validity of Demon's contract by pointing out how Protus had been convicted of wrongdoing, albeit in absentia. So much of Demon's case depended on the effectiveness of his characterization of Protus and the lenders of Zenothemis. If he could convince the jury that he lacked witnesses to confirm his allegations because Zenothemis had co-opted them, he could win. If the jury found this elaborate conspiracy far fetched, his case might unravel. So even though the dispute concerns business transactions, Demon frames his arguments in ways that follow patterns that we see in other types of suits. He builds his case around arguments of probability and relies heavily on characterization to persuade the jury.

Key Information

Speaker	Demon, cousin of Demosthenes, blocked the suit that Zenothemis lodged against him by claiming that Zenothemis had no right to bring the action to court as a maritime case.
Defendant	Zenothemis brought a suit of ejectment (*dike exoules*) against Demon, alleging that the cargo in question belonged to him and not Demon.
Other Individuals	Hegestratus, a shipowner and captain, allegedly conspired with Zenothemis to defraud their

---

4. For the rhetoric of conspiracy in Demosthenes 32, see Roisman 2006: 35–38.

lenders. Several days after the ship left the harbor of Syracuse, Hegistratus was caught attempting to sink it, jumped overboard, and drowned.

Protus borrowed money from Demon in order to purchase cargo in Syracuse. He allegedly made a deal with Zenothemis when he returned to Athens regarding the cargo in question and then fled town.

Aristophon was asked by Demon to help him recover the grain but allegedly assisted Zenothemis.

Action   Countersuit (*paragraphe*) to determine whether Zenothemis could lodge his suit of ejectment against Demon as a maritime case or whether Zenothemis had go to court through the regular procedure.

Date   c.354–340.

Against Zenothemis

[1] Men of the jury, because I have brought a countersuit[5] that the action is inadmissible, I would like to speak first about the laws that are the basis for my objection. The laws permit, men of the jury, shipowners and merchants to bring suits over contracts regarding cargo going to and from Athens and for which there are written agreements.[6] And if someone brings a suit that violates these requirements, it is inadmissible. [2] The fact that Zenothemis did not enter into a contract or a written agreement with me, he even

---

5. If a defendant believed that the prosecutor had lodged an unlawful accusation, he could bring a countersuit (*paragraphe*) against the prosecutor. The court then heard the countersuit to decide whether the original suit might proceed to trial.

6. According to Demon, a suit had to meet two conditions in order to proceed to court as a maritime case (*dike emporike*): (1) the dispute had to concern cargo transported either to or from Athens, and (2) there needed to be a written agreement concerning the cargo. If the cargo was not transported to or from Athens, or if there was no written agreement concerning the cargo in question, then the suit could not follow the special procedures afforded to maritime disputes (see Cohen 1973: 100–114). Since Zenothemis, by his own admission, never signed a contract with Demon and he never intended for the ship to arrive in Athens, Demon maintains that the suit cannot go to trial as a maritime case (see the introduction to this speech).

acknowledges in his charge. He claims to have made a loan to Hegestratus, the shipowner, but when he was lost at sea, we took his cargo. This here is his charge. Now, from my very same speech you will learn that Zenothemis' suit is inadmissible, and you will find out all about the plotting and the depravity of this man who is here before us. [3] I ask you all, men of the jury, if ever you paid close attention to any matter, to do so also in this case. You will hear about the man's audacity and his extraordinary wickedness if with any luck I can express to you what he has done, as I believe I can.[7]

[4] Zenothemis—this man before you—was the assistant[8] to Hegestratus the shipowner, and he planned this crime with Hegestratus, who was lost at sea, as he indicated in his charge; although he did not say how, I will tell you. They borrowed money in Syracuse. Hegestratus assured those loaning money to Zenothemis, if anyone asked, that much of the grain on the ship belonged to Zenothemis, and Zenothemis assured those loaning money to Hegestratus that the cargo on the ship was Hegastratus'. Since one was the shipowner and the other was the passenger, it was reasonable for lenders to believe what the two men were saying about each other.[9] [5] After they received the money, they sent it to Massalia[10] and brought nothing onboard the ship. Since their contracts specified, as is typical of all contracts, that they are to repay the loans when the ship pulls into harbor safely, they plotted to sink the ship in order to defraud the lenders. So when two or three days passed after they had sailed away from land, Hegestratus went down into the hold of the ship during the night and drilled through the bottom of the ship. This man before us, as though unaware, was spending his time with his fellow passengers on the deck. There was a noise, and those on the ship realized that there was some problem in the hold of

---

7. It is typical for litigants appearing before the courts to present themselves as inexperienced speakers both in order to convey to the jury that they are not litigious and so that the jury might overlook any deficiencies in their arguments as merely the result of this inexperience rather than as weaknesses in their case; cf. **Lys. 12.3**; **Dem. 41.3**; **[Dem.] 53.13**; **59.14**.

8. This term serves either to indicate Zenothemis' low social status or to prejudice the jury against him.

9. The grain that was already on the ship, some of which was actually purchased by Protus with money Demon lent him, served as security for the loans that Hegestratus and Zenothemis were seeking in Syracuse. The creditors would have attempted to confirm ownership of the cargo by making inquiries with men who were knowledgeable about the ship's content and who were not parties to the loan. Since Hegestratus and Zenothemis were pursuing separate loans, the individual creditors loaning money to the one had no reason to believe that the other man would be lying when they spoke with him.

10. I.e., Marseilles.

the ship, and they headed down to help. [6] Since Hegestratus had been caught and suspected that he would pay the penalty, he fled, and as they were chasing him, he dove into the water. He missed the rowboat because it was night, and he drowned. So that terrible man met a terrible death just as he deserved, suffering what he had planned to do to others. [7] This man here, his partner and accomplice, at first when he was on the ship, immediately at the moment of the crime, as though he had no knowledge of it but was himself terrified, tried to persuade the lookout man[11] and the sailors to board the rowboat and abandon the ship right away, under the pretense that there was no hope for safety and the ship was at that very moment about to sink. By this he hoped he could finish what they had planned—the ship would be lost, and they would have robbed their lenders of the money owed to them from the contracts. [8] But he failed in this objective, since our man,[12] who was onboard, opposed him and promised the sailors large rewards to save the ship. When it safely reached Cephallenia,[13] thanks mostly to the gods and also to the effort of the crew, then he tried, with the help of the Massaliotes, Hegestratus' fellow citizens, to prevent the ship from sailing back to Athens, claiming that he and the money were from Massalia and the shipowner and the lenders were Massaliotes. [9] But he failed also in this objective since the officials in Cephallenia ruled that the ship was to sail back to Athens, where it began its journey. Although no one would have believed that he would have dared to come here after such schemes and actions, this man, men of the jury, excels so much in shamelessness and audacity that not only has he come here but even has made a claim to my grain and lodged a suit against me.

[10] What on earth is his reason? What on earth has induced him to come here and lodge this suit? I will tell you, men of the jury, although—by Zeus and the gods—it troubles me to say, still I must. There is a gang of wicked men in the Piraeus[14] who are in cahoots with each other and whom even you would recognize if you saw them. [11] When Zenothemis was trying to prevent the ship from sailing back to Athens, we decided in our deliberation for one of these men to be our agent. He is quite well-known but inasmuch as we did not know what sort he was, this was no less a misfortune, if I can say it, than our having to get involved with these wicked men in the first place. The man whom we sent—Aristophon is his name—and who managed the affairs of Miccalion (this we now know)

---

11. The sailor who stood at the bow and gave signals.

12. This is probably a reference to Protus (**15**), who allegedly borrowed money from Demon to purchase the grain.

13. An island just west of the entrance to the Corinthian gulf.

14. The main port of Athens.

made the job his own and bid his services to Zenothemis. He is the one who is taking care of the whole matter, and Zenothemis has gladly received his assistance. [12] Since Zenothemis failed to destroy the ship and he could not repay his lenders (How could he? He did not put anything onboard in the first place), he laid a claim to our property, and he said that he loaned money to Hegestratus on the security of the grain that our man, sailing on board, had purchased.[15] The lenders, having been deceived from the start and seeing that instead of their money they have a wicked man as a borrower, and nothing else, hope that they will recover their loans from my property if you are deceived by him.[16] Although they know that he is spreading lies against me, they are forced to support his case because it is profitable to them.

[13] This, in short, is how the case, for which you will cast your vote, stands. After first providing you with witnesses to what I have said, I would like to instruct you about the rest of the case. Please read their testimonies.

TESTIMONIES

[14] So the ship arrived in Athens since the Cephallenians ruled, in spite of this man's opposition, that it had to sail back to the port where it began its journey. Then those who had lent money on the security of the ship immediately took possession of the ship, while the man who had bought the grain had it in his possession, and this was the man who had borrowed money from us. Next Zenothemis came with Aristophon, whom we had sent as our agent, and made a claim to the grain, alleging that he had loaned money to Hegestratus.[17] [15] "What are you saying, mister?" asked Protus immediately—that's the name of the man who imported the grain and borrowed money from us. "Have you given money to Hegestratus even though you joined him in a scheme to deceive others so that he might borrow money, and despite the fact that he told you many times that his lenders would lose their money? So when you knew this, would you have

---

15. This sentence reveals the main issue in the dispute. Demon claims ownership of the grain as security on his loan to Protus. Zenothemis, by contrast, argues that the grain served as security for his loan to Hegestratus. So when Hegestratus drowned, thereby defaulting on the loan, the grain belonged to him in accordance with the terms of their contract.

16. Zenothemis' lenders were allegedly forced to back his claim in court so that he would have the means to repay them.

17. This part of the dispute is quite confusing in part because of the legal wrangling that took place between the two parties and in part because Demon quickly passes over some details that undermine his argument.

offered him your own money?" "Yes," he said. The man was shameless. "Then, if you are really telling the truth," a man who was there replied, "your partner and fellow citizen, Hegestratus, so it seems, has deceived you, and having sentenced himself to death for his crimes, is dead." [16] "Yes," another man who was present said, "and this man collaborated in all of his crimes, as I will prove to you. Before he attempted to drill through the bottom of the ship, Zenothemis and Hegestratus entered[18] into a written agreement with one of the passengers. If you loaned money based on trust, why did you receive guarantees before the crime, and if you didn't trust him, why didn't you, like others, take legal precautions before the voyage?" [17] Why should one go on about this matter? It was no use to us at all, in spite of what we were saying. He kept the grain. Protus and his partner, Phertatus, tried to eject him.[19] He refused to be ejected, and expressly said that he would not be ejected by anyone except me.[20] [18] Protus and

---

18. So Isager and Hansen 1975: 140. MacDowell (2004: 90 n.) suggests this contract held the passenger liable for the loan in the event of a shipwreck. It is hard to imagine why the passenger would have agreed to such terms unless he received a favorable interest rate by accepting this condition. Alternatively, the text can be read to mean "deposited a written agreement with one of the passengers" (see Pearson 1972: 263–64).

19. In certain instances, when one party either refuses to hand over or takes away property which a second party is legally entitled to possess (e.g., by a court ruling or in the case of a defaulted loan secured by the property in question), he is said to have ejected (*exagein*) the second party. The second party can then seek redress by lodging a suit of ejectment (*dike exoules*) against the first party. If found guilty, the defendant must return the property to the rightful owner and pay a fine to the city equivalent to the value of the property in question (Harrison 1968: 217–18; Isager and Hansen 1975: 144–46; MacDowell 1978: 153–54).

20. This part of the dispute, as Isager and Hansen (1975: 146–47) explain, can be interpreted in two different ways. First, Protus retains possession of the grain, and Zenothemis demands that he release it. When Protus ejects him (i.e., refuses to surrender the grain), Zenothemis then can bring a suit of ejectment against Protus, but he chooses (for whatever reason) not to do so. Later Protus hands over the grain to Demon because he is unable to repay his loan. Zenothemis then again attempts to recover the grain and Demon ejects him (i.e., refuses to surrender it); so he lodges a suit of ejectment against Demon. Alternatively, Zenothemis takes the grain away from Protus, perhaps during their initial argument on the ship (**14–15**). Protus later attempts to recover it, but Zenothemis says that he will only allow Demon to eject him (i.e., take the grain away from him). Eventually the price of grain drops, and Protus decides to leave town with the grain still in Zenothemis' possession because he can no longer recover the cost of his loan by selling the cargo. So Demon is forced to eject Zenothemis (i.e., take the grain from him), who then brings a suit of ejectment against Demon. The Greek is worded in such a way that

I then challenged him to go before the authorities in Syracuse, and if it is established that Protus bought the grain and paid the taxes,[21] and he was the one who made the payments, we demanded that Zenothemis be punished as a villain; if not, we would pay him for his expenses and give him a talent in addition, and we would abandon our claim to the grain. Although these were terms of the challenge that Protus and I proposed, it was of no use, and my choice was to either eject him or lose my property after it had arrived safely. [19] Protus then called on us to eject Zenothemis, giving his assurance that he was willing to sail back to Sicily, but if we surrendered the grain in spite of his willingness, then the matter was not his concern.[22] That I speak the truth, and that he said he would not be ejected by anyone but me, and that he did not accept the challenge to sail back to Sicily, and that he made a written agreement on the ship, read the testimonies.

TESTIMONIES

[20] So when he refused either to be ejected by Protus or to sail back to Sicily for a legal resolution, and it was evident that he knew in advance about all the crimes that Hegestratus committed, it remained for us, who had made the contract in Athens and had received[23] the grain from the man who lawfully purchased it in Sicily, to eject Zenothemis. [21] What else could we have done? My partners and I did not suspect at all that you would ever rule that he was the owner of the grain, which he tried to persuade the sailors to abandon so that it would be destroyed when the ship sank. This is the greatest proof that it does not at all belong to him. Who would have tried to persuade those seeking to save his grain to abandon it? Who would not have accepted the challenge and sailed to Sicily where one could establish ownership definitively? [22] And we certainly would not

---

the second scenario is a more natural reading. If this is the case, Demon glosses over the fact that Protus voluntarily relinquished the grain because such an admission would have supported Zenothemis' case.

21. I.e., export taxes.

22. By this declaration, Protus states his intent to default on the loan, and he declares that he has no legal obligation to reimburse Demon for failing to hand over the grain, which served as security on the loan, since he had done everything in his power to recover it. Therefore, Demon must either pursue legal action against Zenothemis or abandon his claim, and Protus is allegedly free from all financial obligations (contra **30**).

23. I.e., Demon now has a legal claim to the grain, because Protus defaulted on the loan. However, in order to acquire possession of the grain, he must still eject Zenothemis.

accuse you of ruling his suit admissible over goods whose admission[24] into Athens he tried in many ways to prevent: first when he tried to persuade the sailors to abandon them, and then when, in Cephallenia, he tried to stop the ship from sailing here. [23] How would it not be shameful and terrible if the Cephallenians ruled that the ship was to sail here so that Athenian goods might be saved, and if you, although you are Athenians, should decide to give citizens' goods to those who wanted to sink them, and if you should vote admissible what he tried to prevent from arriving here at all? Don't—by Zeus and by the gods—do so! Please read my countersuit.

COUNTERSUIT

Please read the law.

LAW

[24] That my countersuit is in accordance with the laws and that his action is inadmissible, I believe to have sufficiently shown, but you will hear about the trick of that sly man, Aristophon, who devised the entire scheme. When they realized from the facts of the case that their claim had absolutely no merit, they made offers to Protus and attempted to persuade him to entrust his affairs to them. It appears that they did so from the beginning, as we now know, but they could not persuade him. [25] As long as Protus believed he would make a profit when the grain arrived, he held on to it and preferred the profit to be his and to repay us what was owed rather than become their partners, make them shareholders in his spoils, and swindle us. But when he came here and was dealing with this business, the price of grain fell, and he immediately changed his mind. [26] At the same time—I must, men of Athens, tell you the whole truth—the lenders and I were at odds with him, and we were bitter because we were incurring the loss from the grain[25] and blamed him for bringing us this malicious prosecutor[26] instead of our money. So Protus, clearly not an honest man by nature, went over to their side, and he allowed it to happen that he lose,

---

24. In this and the next sentence, Demon plays upon the double meaning of *eisasgogima,* which can refer to a suit that is admissible or to goods that are imported.

25. Since Protus defaulted on the loan, the lenders could claim the grain, which served as security, but the price of grain had dropped, and so they could not have recovered the full amount of their loan.

26. I.e., sykophant (see **Lys. 12.5** n.).

by default,[27] the suit that Zenothemis lodged against him before they came to their agreement. [27] If Zenothemis had dropped his suit against Protus, it would have been immediately revealed that his prosecution against us was malicious. Protus did not allow himself to be present when the court ruled against him so that, if Zenothemis did as they had agreed, all might be well and good, and if not, he could challenge the judgment by default.[28] But why did it matter? If he did as Zenothemis alleges in his complaint, it seems to me that justice would require him not simply to lose his case but to be put to death. If during a bad storm he kept drinking so much wine like a madman, what doesn't he deserve to suffer? Or if he stole documents and opened them up? [28] But how these matters stand, you will decide for yourselves, but Zenothemis,[29] don't you confuse that suit with mine. If Protus has wronged you in word or deed, you have, as it seems, justice. None of us stood in your way or now pleads on his behalf. If you have brought a malicious prosecution against him, we are not meddling. [29] "Yes, but the man is gone."[30] Sure, thanks to you, so that we might be deprived of our testimony and now you can say what you want to say against him. If it is not your doing that the suit be decided by default, you would have summoned him and demanded bail before the polemarch, and if he had provided sureties, he would have been forced to stay in Athens, or you would have had those who would have paid you the sum.[31] If he did not provide sureties, he would have gone to jail. [30] But as it turns out, you are his partner, and Protus believes that he will not have to pay

---

27. Zenothemis prosecuted Protus and won his suit by default when Protus failed to show up for the trial.

28. Demon is forced to explain why Zenothemis would have continued with his suit against Protus although the two had reached a private settlement. If Zenothemis had dropped the suit, then his claim to the grain would have been shown to have been dubious. Yet Protus, for his part, did not want to appear in court because he did not fully trust Zenothemis. He therefore allegedly had the judgment go against him by default. Then if Zenothemis did not adhere to their agreement, Protus could appeal the ruling on the grounds that his absence was unavoidable (see Pearson 1972: 272–73; MacDowell 2004: 93 n.),

29. After addressing the jury, Demon now speaks directly to Zenothemis.

30. This is a hypothetical reply.

31. A foreigner, who was a defendant in a lawsuit, could be required to appear before the polemarch and provide sureties—typically friends or associates of the defendant—who then had to pay the penalty should the defendant flee Athens. If the defendant did not provide sureties, he was imprisoned until trial.

the interest that has accumulated, thanks to you,[32] and you believe that you will gain ownership of our belongings by accusing him. Here's the proof: I will summon him to be a witness; you, however, neither demanded bail nor will you now summon him.

[31] There is still another way that they hope that they will deceive and trick you. They will make an accusation against Demosthenes, saying that I ejected Zenothemis because I trust him. They assume that their accusation is believable because Demosthenes is a well-known orator. Demosthenes, men of Athens, is related to me (I swear by the gods that I tell you the whole truth), [32] but when I approached him and asked him to be on my side and help me, "Demon," he said, "I will do as you ask, since it would be terrible if I didn't. However, you must consider your situation and mine. From the moment I began to speak about public matters, I never came forward in a private case, but . . ."[33]

---

32. Demon alleges that Protus is responsible for the interest that has accumulated on the loan during the time that Zenothemis has kept the grain in his possession.

33. The manuscript breaks off at this point.

DEMOSTHENES 41

AGAINST SPUDIAS

Introduction

The speech *Against Spudias* provides a wealth of information on the role of women in the Athenian family and their involvement in the economic activities of the ordinary household. While women are often depicted in the sources as lacking the authority to act officially in their own capacity and without the consent of their guardian (*kyrios*), this speech shows that they had a greater ability to administer and manage the property of a house and participate in economic transactions than has been normally assumed. The speech is also an important source for our understanding of lending practices, the use of written contracts for mortgages, rules governing inheritance and estates that lack a male heir, and questions related to women's literacy. Not only does the matriarch of the family lend substantial sums of money in her own right, but she also keeps in her possession documents that concern legal transactions, and she is said to have the power to verify their authenticity (**9, 21, 24**). So, too, her daughters verify legal documents and even disburse significant sums of money. They act as witnesses to a will, and, as it turns out, one husband did not even attend the reading of the will, since he apparently entrusted his wife to inform him of its contents (**17–19**).[1]

The dispute concerns the estate of Polyeuctus. By Athenian law, sons inherited equally, and if a man had no children, then the next closest male relative was the heir. Since Polyeuctus had two daughters and no sons, he adopted Leocrates, his wife's brother, and gave his younger daughter in marriage to Leocrates so that he could serve as the heir. The marriage, however, did not last. Leocrates divorced Polyeuctus' daughter and forfeited his right to be the heir of the estate. The prosecutor, who does not tell us his name, apparently married the older sister, and Spudias, the defendant, became the second husband of the younger sister (**3–5**). For whatever reason, Polyeuctus decided to adopt neither the speaker nor Spudias, perhaps because his daughters had children (cf. Dem. 43.4, 65), who by Athenian law were the heirs since he had neither a natal or adopted son. So when he passed away, his estate belonged equally to them, and until

---

Translated by Konstantinos Kapparis.

1. See also the discussion in Cohen 1998: 53–57.

they reached adulthood, their fathers managed it. But as the present speech shows, Polyeuctus' daughters were more involved in its management than Athenian law would seem to allow.[2]

The speaker lodged a complaint against Spudias concerning property worth thirty minas. This was a substantial sum of money, equal to an average dowry, or over fifteen years of wages for an unskilled worker. By law, all revenue had to be divided equally between the heirs for the husbands to manage after all debts had been paid. The speaker claims that Polyeuctus had promised to pay him a dowry of forty minas. Thirty were given upon marriage and ten were to be given later. As he was dying, Polyeuctus set up a will, which instructed that a house was to be mortgaged after his death so as to pay the speaker the ten minas that were still outstanding. This required the estate either to pay the speaker the ten minas or to surrender the property in question. Until the debt was paid or the property was surrendered, rents were owed to the speaker (**5–6**). Spudias, however, denied that the speaker had not been paid the full amount of the dowry and challenged the legitimacy of the term in the will that called for the property in question to be mortgaged (**16, 25–28**). He insisted that the property was unencumbered and therefore it belonged equally to Polyeuctus' heirs.

In addition to the ten minas the speaker claimed the estate owed him, he argued that Spudias had debts still outstanding that he had to pay to the estate. Since Spudias' wife was Polyeuctus' daughter, this would have required Spudias to surrender only half the sum that he allegedly owed to the estate. According to the speaker, Spudias had purchased a slave for two minas from Polyeuctus, but never paid his father-in-law the sum owed. Polyeuctus even asserted as much on his deathbed before Aristogenes, who seems to have acted as an executor of his will (**8, 22**). Spudias also borrowed some eighteen minas from Polyeuctus' wife, after the death of her husband; she was in charge of the loan and only had her brothers present to serve as witnesses. From the speaker's account, she appears to have been quite a capable widow, who kept close track of the family finances and diligently maintained the records (**9, 20–21**). Finally, the speaker mentions some articles that Spudias and his wife took from the estate (**11**). Since the speaker does not specify the articles' value, it is not clear whether he expects the jury to award the estate a sum for the loss of these items or his discussion is merely intended to make his other arguments and his characterization of Spudias appear more plausible.

---

2. For Athenian law on inheritance and adoption, see MacDowell 1978: 92–103; Rubinstein 1993.

Key Information

Speaker	The prosecutor married Polyeuctus' older daughter and was promised a dowry of forty minas.
Defendant	Spudias was the second husband of Polyeuctus' younger daughter.
Other Individuals	Polyeuctus died without sons, leaving his estate in dispute.
	Leocrates was the brother of Polyeuctus' wife and the first husband of Polyeuctus' younger daughter.
	Aristogenes was present when Polyeuctus' will was read and served as the executor.
Action	The speaker lodged a suit against Spudias in order to recover (a) ten minas of the dowry that were still owed to him and (b) twenty minas owed to Polyeuctus' estate.
Date	c.340

Against Spudias

[1] Spudias, this man here, and I, men of the jury, are married to sisters, the daughters of Polyeuctus. Since Polyeuctus died leaving no male children, I am forced to lodge a suit against this man over his estate.[3] If I had not made every effort and shown a willingness to come to an arrangement and defer our differences to the arbitration of our friends, I would blame myself for choosing trials and trouble instead of absorbing a modest financial loss. [2] But in this case, the more I was accommodating and generous in my discussions with him, the greater was his contempt. Now I am in danger of

---

3. The original is more dramatic: it states that Polyeuctus died "childless," and then adds "of male issue." In the absence of sons, a daughter, if childless, was required to marry her father's closest male relative when he passed away, but neither she nor her husband owned his estate. If she were to have sons, they became his heirs and their father managed the property until they reached adulthood. If the daughter was already married and had children before her father died, they were his heirs. To avoid these complications, Polyeuctus adopted Leocrates and married his younger daughter to him. But when Leocrates divorced her, he was no longer Polyeuctus' heir. It is not clear why Polyeuctus did not then adopt either the speaker or Spudias, but his daughters probably had children before he died.

entering into an uneven contest with him, because it is easy for him, since he comes here often, and I am afraid that in my inexperience I might not be able to express myself well. But listen to me, men of the jury.[4]

[3] There was a man named Polyeuctus from Teithras, whom some of you may have known. This Polyeuctus, since he had no male children, adopted Leocrates, the brother of his wife.[5] Polyeuctus had two daughters from the sister of Leocrates; the elder he betrothed to me with a dowry of forty minas and the younger to Leocrates.[6] [4] After these arrangements, Polyeuctus had a quarrel with Leocrates over something that I see no reason to explain; he took back his daughter and betrothed her to Spudias here. Leocrates was furious and sued Polyeuctus and Spudias here, and he forced them to account for everything. Finally they reached an agreement on the condition that Leocrates was to take back everything that he had brought into the estate and end his hostilities with Polyeuctus, and both were to drop all claims. [5] Why did I mention all this, men of the jury? Because I did not receive the dowry in its entirety, but it was agreed that one thousand drachmas[7] would be paid after the death of Polyeuctus. As long as Leocrates was the heir of Polyeuctus, my contract was with him; however, when Leocrates walked away and Polyeuctus was ill, then, men of the jury, I had this house as mortgage for the ten minas, the rents from which Spudias is trying to stop me from collecting.[8]

[6] First I will summon for you witnesses, who were present when Polyeuctus betrothed his daughter to me with a dowry of forty minas; then I will show that I did not receive one thousand drachmas, and in addition, Polyeuctus always acknowledged that he owed me the sum, and

---

4. Litigants regularly comment on their inexperience in litigation in order to win the jury's sympathy; cf. **Lys. 12.3**; **Dem. 32.3**; **[Dem.] 53.13, 59.14**.

5. Since the main purpose of adoption in classical Athens was to provide an heir, adoption could only occur if a man had no legitimate sons by birth and the adopted son was Athenian. The adopted son was typically either a relative or from the family of a close friend. After the adoption, the adoptee severed formal ties with his natal family and, for all legal purposes, became the son of the adopter, with the same rights and obligations as a legitimate son by birth.

6. It was not uncommon in Athens for a niece to marry her uncle; cf. **[Dem.] 59.2**.

7. One thousand drachmas equal ten minas.

8. After his divorce, Leocrates was no longer Polyeuctus' heir and therefore no longer obligated to pay the remaining amount of the dowry owed to the speaker once Polyeuctus passed away. So Polyeuctus mortgaged, to the speaker, the property that was appraised at one thousand drachmas in order to guarantee that the speaker would receive the remainder of the dowry owed to him.

he introduced Leocrates as the guarantor,[9] and when he was dying, he willed that pillars[10] were to be set up before the house for one thousand drachmas towards the dowry for me. Please call the witnesses.

WITNESSES

[7] This is the first of the charges that I am bringing against Spudias, men of the jury, and regarding this matter, how could I come before you standing on more solid ground than the law itself, which does not allow either the parties themselves or their heirs to engage in litigation over mortgaged properties? The claim of Spudias goes against this fair law.

[8] The second of the charges, men of the jury, concerns two minas, which, according to the testimony of Aristogenes, Polyeuctus mentioned on his deathbed as owed to him by Spudias, with interest (this debt is the price of a slave, whom he bought from Polyeuctus, but he neither paid for the slave nor included the value in the inventory of the common property).[11] Then there are eighteen hundred drachmas, and I cannot think of anything just that he could say about it. [9] He had borrowed this money from the wife of Polyeuctus, and there are documents, which she left when she died, and the woman's brothers were witnesses present throughout all this, and they inquired about everything so that there would be no animosity between us.[12] Is it not terrible and appalling, men of the jury, if for

---

9. When Leocrates married Polyeuctus' younger daughter, he pledged, as Polyeuctus' heir, to give the remaining sum of the dowry owed to the speaker after Polyeuctus passed away.

10. Stone pillars (*horoi*) were placed on property that was mortgaged or pledged, indicating the amount owed and the terms of the debt. They were removed when the debt was paid and the property was no longer encumbered or if the property was surrendered to the lender because of a failure to pay back the loan. Thousands of such stones have been found all over Attica; see Finley 1952. Coincidentally, one thousand drachmas was the median value in *horos* inscriptions (Sickinger 1995: 333).

11. Each of the two husbands was due to receive forty minas as a dowry; then after Polyeuctus' death, his remaining property was to be distributed equally to the heirs of his estate. An inventory needed to be created of the common assets, which included any outstanding loans owed to Polyeuctus by either of the two sons-in-law. These loans would then be deducted from their shares of the estate. The speaker claims that he included all his outstanding loans, but Spudias failed to declare very substantial debts to Polyeuctus.

12. This passage provides important information about the economic rights of women in classical Athens and their legal capacity to perform transactions in their own right. Although, customarily, large transactions were performed by men in public places and women were said to be prohibited from involvement in contracts

everything that I bought from Polyeuctus or received from his wife when they were alive I have paid the full amount with interest, and anything that I still owe I have now added to the inventory of the common property? [10] He, on the other hand, does not care about your laws or the terms of Polyeuctus' will or the documents left behind or the witnesses but comes to court to dispute everything. Please first take the law that does not permit litigation against those holding mortgaged properties, then the documents left behind and the testimony of Aristogenes.

LAW, DOCUMENTS, TESTIMONY

[11] I wish now, men of the jury, to explain to you each of the other charges. They took a bowl from the wife of Polyeuctus and pawned it along with some jewelry; this they have not recovered or included in the inventory, as Demophilus, to whom it was pawned, will testify.[13] They also have a tent, which they do not mention, even though they took it, and many more items like this. Finally, my wife brought to the Nemesia[14] a silver mina and spent it in memory of her father, and he would not even contribute his share to this, but he is keeping what he has already taken, receiving his due part of everything else and refusing so blatantly to return things. In order to avoid any omissions, please take the testimonies for all of this.

TESTIMONIES

[12] Maybe Spudias will not object to any of this, men of the jury (because he will not be able to do so, although he is clever). He will blame Polyeuctus and his wife and will say that I talked them into giving me all this, and that, by Zeus, he has suffered grave injustice and has sued me. This is what he tried to say before the arbitrator, too. [13] First, men of the jury, I do not think that this is a fair or appropriate defense, when someone is caught

---

with sums greater than one bushel of barley (Isae. 10.10), this passage shows that women sometimes managed complicated economic transactions and became involved in legal contracts that far exceeded the value of one bushel of barley, acting in their own capacity and not under the supervision of a guardian (*kyrios*). For further discussion, see Schaps 1979: 52–56; Hunter 1994: 20–29; Foxhall 1989; Harris 1992; Cohen 1998.

13. Bowls were a sign of wealth (Dem. 22.75), and this was especially true for those made of gold or silver or superior craftsmanship. Since such objects were precious, they were often pawned for quick cash (Dem. 49.22.)

14. The Nemesia was a festival of the dead, celebrated in September.

lying, to turn things around and become an accuser and make malicious accusations. But where he has suffered injustice, he will receive restitution, and where he has committed injustice, he will pay the price. How could I fight their slander if I were to abandon the claims on which you are about to vote? [14] Then I wonder why on earth, if he ever had any true and fair claim, when our friends wanted to resolve our differences and he had so many chances to explain himself, he was not capable of abiding by their decision.[15] Who could better detect false claims entered either by him or by me than the men who were present in all these instances, those who knew the facts no less than we did, persons who were common and impartial friends to both of us? [15] It is clear that he would not benefit from a resolution reached through this kind of examination. Do not think, men of the jury, that those who know all this would now be testifying in my favor at their own risk, but during the arbitration they would have given different evidence under oath.[16] But even if you did not have all this evidence, still it would not be hard to decide who is telling the truth.

[16] Regarding the house, if he claims that I induced Polyeuctus to order the placement of pillars for one thousand drachmas: I did not induce the witnesses too, Spudias, to give false testimony in my favor, those who were present during the betrothal, those who know that I received less dowry, those who heard him agree that he owed me and gave instructions for the payment, and finally those present when he made his will. It would be impossible for all these men to be doing me a favor, risking a lawsuit for false testimony if they gave testimony that was not true. Let us move on. [17] [To Spudias] What would you[17] say to this? You will need to explain it to them very precisely. [To the jury] If he does not, you should all insist that he does. When Polyeuctus gave instructions in his will, the wife of Spudias was present, and obviously she was going to report to him the will of her father, especially if the distribution was unequal and he got a smaller share in everything. He was invited, too, so that he could not say that we did this

---

15. The speaker is referring to attempts by relatives and friends to resolve his differences with Spudias through private arbitration. There was no specific time limit, women could give evidence in person, and the arbitrators could and often would cross-examine the witnesses. The primary purpose of a private arbitration was to produce a resolution acceptable to both parties, and thus effect a reconciliation, but if this was not possible, the arbitrators could find in favor of one party.

16. Evidence given before a private arbitrator was not subject to a lawsuit for false testimony (*pseudomartyrion*) in contrast to evidence given in a *dikasterion*. In this respect giving such evidence was risk free, but witnesses could be cross-examined before the arbitrator, making it easier to detect a lie.

17. I.e., Spudias.

hidden and in secret from them. When he was asked, he said that he was too busy and that it would be sufficient if his wife were present. [18] What happened next? When Aristogenes reported everything to him in detail, it seems that he did not say a word, and although Polyeuctus survived for more than five days after this, he did not storm in full of indignation or raise any objections, nor did his wife, who was present from the beginning for all of these discussions. So since Polyeuctus was not persuaded by me, it would seem that you did this favor for me.[18] Keep this in mind, men of the jury, and if he tries now to say anything slanderous, stand up to him. But first, in order that you might know exactly how the issue is, hear the witnesses. Read.

WITNESSES

[19] Thus, men of the jury, Polyeuctus mortgaged the house for a thousand drachmas, a debt that was legally binding, and Spudias and his wife (in addition to the other witnesses) testify to this fact, since they gave their consent then by not arguing with Polyeuctus, although he lived for so many more days, or with Aristogenes as soon as they heard about the will. If the mortgage was lawful, you must keep in mind the law and cannot acquit Spudias, at least as far as this part of the case is concerned.

[20] Consider also the twenty minas, which he has not returned; in this instance, too, he will be my strongest witness, not with the words, by Zeus, that now he is saying (for this constitutes no proof at all), but from his conspicuous actions. Doing what, men of the jury? Pay close attention, so that, if he dares to say something disparaging about the mother of our wives or about the documents, his words cannot deceive you, because you already know.[19] [21] These documents were left by the wife of Polyeuctus, as I mentioned shortly before. Both Spudias' wife and mine acknowledged the seals and were present with both of us when we opened them and made

---

18. The meaning of "it would seem" (*hos eoiken*) is ironic. Since Spudias and his wife did not complain about the will, they accepted its terms, so "it would seem," as a favor to the speaker.

19. Written contracts and financial documents became more common from the middle of the fourth century, and although seals were used to confirm their authenticity, still the presence of witnesses confirming the content and verifying their authenticity was indispensable to legal proceedings; for further discussion see Thomas 1989. The present passage is important evidence regarding the literacy of Athenian women, proving that some could read and had acquired this important skill because their ability to keep books and accounts was crucial for good household management.

copies; then we sealed them again and deposited them with Aristogenes. [22] Hear this, men of the jury, by the gods. The two minas were in there, the price of the slave, and it was not only Polyeuctus on his deathbed who was claiming the two minas, and the eighteen hundred drachmas were in there too. If it had nothing to do with him and what was written was not true, then when he read them would he not immediately react with indignation to all this? Why did he agree to reseal documents that were incorrect and untrue? This is not something that someone would do if he did not agree with the content of all these documents. [23] It would certainly be terrible, men of the jury, if they are now allowed to reopen the debate on matters to which they have already agreed and you are expected to overlook the fact that, when someone makes untrue or unjust claims, all people are accustomed not to keep quiet but to object right away, and if they do not do so, but start arguing later, they appear to be wicked sykophants. [24] Spudias knows this as well as I, and maybe even better, since he is in the habit of appearing before you frequently, and still he is not ashamed to say things that contradict his own actions. And yet many times when you detected only one fabricated claim, you used it as evidence against all the other charges; in this case, however, he has proven everything to be a lie by himself. Please take the testimony that his wife verified the seals of the documents and now they are deposited after they were resealed by Spudias.

TESTIMONY

[25] When such solid proof has been provided, I believe there is no need to say anything else. I am in the position to produce laws and witnesses for everything that I said, and even my opponent agreed with me. So why is there a need for lengthy speeches? But if he appears indignant about the dowry and claims that he is defrauded of one thousand drachmas, he will be lying. He is laying a claim to this sum although he received not less, but more, as it will become immediately apparent to you. [26] But even if all of this were true, still it would not be fair for me to be denied the agreed dowry if the laws are of any use at all; if Polyeuctus wanted to give less dowry to one of his daughters and more to the other, he should not be retroactively prevented. You had the option, Spudias, not to take her unless one thousand drachmas were added to match the sum that I received.[20]

---

20. According to the speaker, Spudias either needed to negotiate the dowry at the betrothal if he wanted a greater sum or he had to refuse to marry her if he was not satisfied with the amount that her father offered. Once he was married, he had no grounds for complaint if the dowry was less than that of the speaker's wife. The

But you did not receive any less dowry, as I am going to explain. Please first take the testimony concerning the terms of his wife's betrothal to him.

TESTIMONY

[27] How does he not have any less, someone might say, if in his case the jewelry and the clothes worth one thousand drachmas were included in the value of the forty minas while the additional ten minas were to be paid to me separately? I will explain this right away. Spudias, men of the jury, received his wife from Leocrates, with her jewelry and clothes,[21] and Polyeuctus paid to Leocrates, for this purpose, more than one thousand drachmas.[22] However, one will find that whatever is in my possession that Polyeuctus sent to me, apart from the dowry, is roughly equal in value to that given to Spudias, not including the one thousand drachmas.[23] [28] He understandably included in the forty minas the value of the gold and jewelry, for which he paid Leocrates, and they were much more than what I received.[24] Please first take this inventory and read to them what each one

---

estate, by contrast, had to be divided equally between the heirs, but only after all outstanding debts were first paid.

21. The speaker seems reluctant to explain in detail the quarrel of Leocrates with Polyeuctus, which resulted in the marriage of the younger daughter of Polyeuctus to Spudias. This section of the text seems to contradict his previous assertion that Polyeuctus took back his daughter after he had an argument with Leocrates and then betrothed her to Spudias (4). On the basis of parallels (e.g. Isae. 3.45), we can infer that Leocrates did not want to stay married to the younger daughter of Polyeuctus and he chose to betroth her to Spudias. Maybe this was one of the reasons why he fell out with Polyeuctus and ended up walking away from the adoption.

22. Murray (1939: 23) translates the last clause as "Polyeuctus set a value to Leocrates of more than a thousand drachmae." However, the verb used means "paid in addition" (*prosapeteisen*). Sometimes jewelry and articles of clothing that a wife brought with her to her marriage were part of her dowry and had to be returned to her guardian if the couple divorced. Sometimes they were not part of the dowry and the husband did not have to return the articles should they divorce (see Wyse 1904: 245–26, 314; Lacey 1968: 109–10). It appears that the articles in question were not part of the younger daughter's first dowry. So Polyeuctus had to pay Leocrates an additional one thousand drachmas in order to recover them. But then when she married Spudias, Polyeuctus included them as part of her dowry.

23. I.e., whatever articles the two daughters brought to their marriages that were not part of their dowry were roughly of the same value.

24. I.e., the jewelry and clothing worth one thousand drachmas were part of the younger daughter's dowry because of their value. Since the total amount of her

of us has in his possession, and then read the testimony of the arbitrators so that they can see that he has much more money; Leocrates was making demands about this, and this was the decision of the arbitrators. Read it.

INVENTORY, TESTIMONY

[29] Is it not obvious? He had a dowry worth forty minas long ago, while I possess thirty minas, as does he, but not only did I not receive one thousand drachmas but even now I risk litigation about them on the grounds that I have them illegally in my possession. For these reasons, men of the jury, Spudias did not wish to entrust the case to the arbitration of our friends and resolve our differences, because he knew that he would be exposed; men who had been present through all these events and had clear knowledge of them were not going to let him say whatever he wanted. However, he thinks that he will prevail over me, although I am telling the truth, by lying to you. [30] Concerning all my charges, I have offered you clear proof for everything as best as I could. He avoided those who know because he did not think that he could deceive them. Do not, men of the jury, allow him to lie and slander, but remember what has been said. You know how everything happened, unless I forgot something, since I only had such a short period of time to speak.

---

dowry was forty minas, Spudias received a far greater dowry than the speaker, if one were to exclude the sum of one thousand drachmas that was owed to the speaker from the mortgaged property.

[DEMOSTHENES] 53

APOLLODORUS AGAINST NICOSTRATUS

Introduction

Internal references to Apollodorus' young age (**9**), inexperience (**13**), and his service as a trierarch (**6**) indicate this was one of his earliest speeches, delivered around 366 (Trevett 1992: 32–33). When Pasion died in 370, he left a will specifying that Phormio, who was the manager of his bank and had been freed by him, was to marry his widow, serve with Nicocles as a guardian for Apollodorus' younger brother, Pasicles, and manage the estate until Pasicles reached adulthood, at which time it was to be divided between Pasion's two sons. This arrangement was strictly illegal. Apollodorus was twenty-four years old and should have received his portion of the estate upon his father's death, but because of Apollodorus' extravagance, Pasion did not have faith in the ability of his older son to manage the family fortune. Apollodorus took immediate action to protect his inheritance, but in the protracted litigation that ensued, he ended up losing much money and becoming alienated from his relatives.[1] The present litigation began while he was in the middle of the legal proceedings against Phormio (**9**), and it is obvious from the outset that revenge was the primary objective.

The narrative begins when Pasion died and the feud between Apollodorus and his relatives forced him to take residence in the sumptuous country manor of the family. There he apparently began a mutually convenient friendship with one of the neighbors, a man called Nicostratus. Apollodorus had someone to look after his estate when he was out of town, and in return Nicostratus without a doubt enjoyed financial benefits from his rich and generous neighbor.[2] At some point Nicostratus left Athens in order to recover some runaway slaves, when, ironically, he was captured by a foreign warship and sold as a slave in Aegina. Apollodorus was asked by Nicostratus' brother, Deinon, to help with the travel expenses to Aegina, and generously provided Deinon three hundred drachmas, initially as a loan. Deinon went to Aegina and arranged the release of his brother by paying a substantial ransom secured through a short-term loan. Since Nicostratus had only thirty days to repay the

---

Translated by Konstantinos Kapparis.

1. For the dispute between Apollodorus and his relatives, see Thompson 1981; Trevett 1992: 8–15.

2. As Christ (1998: 176–77) observes, Apollodorus downplays the fact that Nicostratus worked for him.

lenders or he would owe them twice the amount of the loan, he went to his
rich neighbor and friend for help. Apollodorus forgave Deinon's debt of three
hundred drachmas, gave Nicostratus a substantial sum of money to help him
pay off part of the short-term loan, and used one of his properties as collateral
for a high-interest loan to pay the rest that was still outstanding. Nicostratus
was then to secure an interest-free loan (*eranos*) by collecting separate contributions from friends and relatives so that he could then within a year pay
off the amount that Apollodorus owed from the high-interest loan (**4–12**).

Apollodorus says that this was the moment when his relationship with
Nicostratus turned sour. Nicostratus started avoiding him and sided with
Apollodorus' relatives because he did not want to pay back the loan. As part
of a deal with them, Nicostratus had Apollodorus registered as a state debtor
by wrongly winning his conviction when he failed to respond to a summons.
This prevented Apollodorus from further pursuing any legal action against
his relatives until he discharged his debt to the state (**13–14**). But if Nicostratus and his brothers thought they could intimidate him, they were certainly
wrong. Perhaps they did not even suspect at the time that they were dealing
with someone whose reputation for litigiousness was destined to last into pos-
terity. By the time Apollodorus was done with them, Arethusius, seemingly
the richest of all the brothers, had lost all of his property and his civic rights,
and the rest of the brothers were struggling to recover whatever they could.
Apollodorus first settled his debt to the public treasury, and then took Arethusius to court, winning a conviction against him for falsely testifying that he
had witnessed the summons, and the jury fined Arethusius one talent. He lost
everything: his property was confiscated, and his civic rights and his ability to
conduct financial transactions were seriously restricted (**15–18**). Apollodorus
was then on the offensive. After securing Arethusius' conviction, he lodged
the present legal action—*apographe* (literally, "inventory"), which was used to
authorize the confiscation of property belonging to a state debtor.[3] He alleged
that Nicostratus had two slaves in his possession, who were actually owned by
Arethusius and therefore should be surrendered, since Arethusius was still in
debt to the city. If Apollodorus won, the slaves would be auctioned, he would
receive one third of the proceeds, and the rest would go to the city (**1–2**).

Although this is one of the first speeches that Apollodorus delivered, it exhibits all the characteristic traits of his technique. As with most of his speeches,
the main thrust of the argument comes from the colorful, dramatic narrative,
which provides the details of the case and paints a vivid picture of the events,
which the orator would like the jurors to remember when it comes time for
them to cast their vote. The portrayal of the main parties to the dispute is
consistent and serves well the purposes of the orator. Apollodorus felt deeply
injured by the conduct of Nicostratus and his brothers; he hated them, and
wanted revenge. He does not hide this goal or disguise his motives in any

---

3. For the confiscation of property owned by a state debtor, see **[Dem.] 59.7** with n.

way, and he successfully portrays them as ungrateful scoundrels. Throughout his narrative the themes of injury, betrayal, anger, retribution, and revenge figure prominently and generate an overall impression of honesty in order to enhance the rhetorical appeal of the speech. As a source for Athenian social history, this speech vividly calls to our attention the real dangers of sea travel, helps us understand some of the reasons why friends and families became involved in protracted legal disputes, and reveals valuable information on the ancient economy and the social factors that influenced lending and borrowing, as Apollodorus outlines four different loans that Nicostratus received.

Key Information

Speaker	Apollodorus, son of Pasion, prosecuted Nicostratus for possessing slaves that were subject to confiscation.
Defendant	Nicostratus claimed that he, and not his brother Arethusius, owned the slaves in question.
Other Individuals	Arethusius, brother of Nicostratus, was a state debtor whose property was subject to confiscation. Deinon, Nicostratus' other brother, secured his release when captured by pirates.
	Cerdon and Manes were slaves allegedly owned by Arethusius.
Action	*Apographe* (literally, "inventory") was a public action to authorize the confiscation of property belonging to a state debtor.
Penalty	Cerdon and Manes would be auctioned off. As prosecutor, Apollodorus would receive one-third of the proceeds, and the city the rest.
Date	c.366.

Against Nicostratus: Regarding the Ownership of the Slaves of Arethusius

[1] I did not enter this claim (*apographe*) over the ownership of the slaves because I am a sykophant but because I have been injured and subjected to outrage (*hybris*) by these men and I felt that I should seek retribution.[4]

---

4. The Greek term *apographe* (literally, "inventory") refers to the legal procedure to authorize the confiscation of property belonging to a state debtor, the inventory

The mere size of the claim and the fact that I entered it myself provide firm proof of this.[5] If I had wanted to lodge a malicious accusation against someone, I would neither have entered a claim over some slaves worth only two and a half minas, according to the assessment of the opposing litigant, nor risked a fine of one thousand drachmas and my right to bring public prosecutions against anyone in the future. [2] I was not so poor or so deserted of friends to the point that I could not have found someone willing to enter this claim. However, I would have considered it as the most terrible among human affairs if I were the injured party and yet I allowed someone else to initiate legal proceedings on my behalf. They would have used it as proof that I was lying when I talked to you about the hostility between us and said that if I was the injured party, the claim would not have been entered by someone else; for that reason I entered the claim personally. If, after entering the claim, I prove that the slaves belong to Arethusius, as stated in my inventory, I will leave to the city the one-third reward, which by law belongs to the person who began the confiscation proceedings; it will be sufficient for me to have my revenge.[6] [3] If I had enough time to tell you from the beginning how many benefits they have enjoyed from me and what they have done to me in return, I know for certain that you would be more forgiving of me for my anger at them and you would consider them to be the worst people. But as it is, not even twice the time would be sufficient. So, I will give you an account of the

---

of the property proposed for confiscation, and also any counterclaim to items of that inventory by a third party. Depending on the context and meaning, we have translated it into English as "claim," "confiscation proceedings," or "inventory." *Hybris* was an offense that had a wide range of meanings and was used to describe the excessively degrading and abusive treatment of another person in a manner not fitting for free persons (see the introduction to **Demosthenes 21**).

5. Since Apollodorus lodged a public action, he risked paying a fine of one thousand drachmas (i.e., ten minas) if he failed to secure one-fifth of the jury's votes. Thus the fine was four times the value of the slaves, which he was trying to recover for the public treasury, and twelve times the amount that he would have personally received if he won (see **2** n.). He clearly did not take such a risk for financial reasons but took it for revenge, as the last act in a vicious and protracted feud with the family of Nicostratus.

6. The manuscripts read "three-quarters," but this is probably an error, since it would mean that the prosecutor would have received more than the state from the auctioning of confiscated property. In other similar legal actions the prosecutor was awarded only one-third of the proceeds (see Osborne 1985: 44–45).

worst and most notorious of their crimes and how this claim was entered, but I will leave out most of the details.[7]

[4] Nicostratus here, men of the jury, was a neighbor of mine in the countryside and of my same age. I knew him for quite some time, but when my father died and I took residence in the country house, where I still live, we saw more of each other, since we were neighbors and of the same age. As time went by, we became close friends, and I felt so close to him that I never denied him whatever he needed, and in turn he helped me by taking care of and supervising my things. Every time I was out of town, whether to serve as a trierarch for the city or on some private business, I left him in charge of everything on the farm. [5] Then I happened to serve as trierarch off the Peloponnese, and from there I had to take the ambassadors elected by the people to Sicily. So I had to set sail quickly. I sent him a letter saying that I had to sail and would not be able to come home so as not to delay the ambassadors; I instructed him to take care of my affairs at home and run things as he had done before. [6] While I was away, three slaves escaped from his farm, two whom I had given him and one whom he had purchased. As he went after them, he was seized by a trireme and brought to Aegina where he was sold as a slave.[8] When I returned home from my service as trierarch, Deinon, his brother, came to me and told me about Nicostratus' misfortune.[9] He said that although Nicostratus had been sending him letters, he could not go to him because he lacked travel money; he also told me he had heard that Nicostratus was not doing at all well. [7] When I heard this, I was upset over his misfortune, and straightaway I sent to him his brother Deinon, supplying him with three hundred drachmas for travel expenses. As soon as Nicostratus returned, he came to me first, embraced me, and praised me for supplying his brother with the travel expenses. He complained about his misfortune, and while he blamed his own family, he asked me to help him, as I had been a true friend to him in the past; he was crying and saying that he had been ransomed for twenty-six minas, and he asked me to make a contribution towards the ransom. [8] As soon as I heard this, I pitied him, seeing that he was in a bad way, and he showed me the wounds from the shackles on his calves; he still has the scars, but if you ask him to show you,

---

7. It is a characteristic technique of Apollodorus to promise the jury that he is going to tell them everything from the beginning; he also frequently promises more details, if he has any time left, that he usually does not offer.

8. Although Greek cities had laws with severe penalties to prevent the enslavement of freeborn persons, the possibility of being captured and sold into slavery was very real. In such a case, the family might be able to ransom the enslaved person, and if they could not afford to pay the full ransom, they might seek help from friends and relatives.

9. The trierarchy can be dated to 368 (see Trevett 1992: 33).

he will not be willing to do so. I answered that in the past I was a true friend to him and now I was going to offer help in his misfortune. I said that I would forgive the debt of three hundred drachmas, which I had given his brother for the travel expenses when he went to him, and on top of that I was going to contribute one thousand drachmas towards his ransom.[10] [9] And these were not just promises that were uttered and never translated into actions, but since I did not have an abundance of cash because I was involved in litigation with Phormio, who had deprived me of my paternal inheritance, I brought to Theocles, who was in charge of a bank at that time, some cups and a golden crown, which happened to be in my possession from my father's estate, and I asked him to give Nicostratus one thousand drachmas. This money I gave to Nicostratus as a gift, and I freely admit that I did so. [10] A few days later he came back to me, crying and saying that the foreigners who had lent him the money for the ransom were demanding the remaining sum, and it was in the contract to pay them back within thirty days or his debt would be doubled, and the piece of farmland next to mine no one wanted either to buy or to accept as collateral for a mortgage. He said that his brother Arethusius, to whom the disputed slaves in this case belong, would not let anyone buy or mortgage it because Nicostratus still owed him money.[11] [11] "Give me the remaining sum," he said, "before the thirty days go by, so that I do not lose even the money that I have already paid, the one thousand drachmas, and become liable to a lawsuit. Then," he said, "after I pay off the foreigners, I will collect a loan and pay back what you have lent me.[12] You know," he said, "that the laws state that the person who has been ransomed from the enemy is to belong to the person who ransomed him, if he fails to pay back the money for the ransom." [12] Listening to this, I believed that he was not lying and answered him like a young man and a friend who never contemplated the possibility that he might be wronged: "Nicostratus, I have been a true friend in the past, and in your present

---

10. This was a substantial gift, amounting to ten minas and more than one-third of the twenty-six minas that he owed the lenders. In addition, as Apollodorus indicates below, he agreed to mortgage an apartment complex at a 16 percent interest rate in order to secure a loan of sixteen minas so that Nicostratus could pay off the remainder of the short-term loan.

11. Apparently Nicostratus had used the field as collateral to borrow money from his brother, and Arethusius required that he first be reimbursed before Nicostratus could either sell it or use it again as collateral for another loan.

12. Nicostratus promised to reimburse Apollodorus for the additional sixteen minas that he was requesting by procuring an *eranos* loan. This was a kind of loan that the borrower received by collecting separate contributions from friends and relatives, with either no interest or a favorable interest rate, and often with greater than usual leeway in the time frame for repaying the loan (see **Dem. 21.101** n.).

misfortune I have helped as much as I could. Now, since you cannot find all
the money and I do not have any more to give you myself, I will let you use
any of my property you wish as collateral for the remaining sum of the
money that you need, interest free for a year, to pay back the foreigners.
Then, once you collect a loan, as you say you will, you can pay my debt."
[13] He heard this, thanked me, and suggested that we should do so as soon
as possible before the deadline when he said the money for the ransom was
due. So I mortgaged the apartment complex for sixteen minas to Arcesas of
Pambotadae, whom Nicostratus had introduced to me, with an interest rate
of eight obols per mina for each month.[13] He took the money, and instead
of being grateful for the favor, he immediately started plotting to deprive me
of the money and became hostile so that I would not collect the money from
him, for which the apartment complex was mortgaged, but I would let him
keep it. He thought that because I was young and inexperienced I would not
know what to do. [14] First he plotted with my legal adversaries and pledged
his allegiance to them; then when I became involved in legal proceedings
with them, he revealed to them my arguments that he knew and succeeded
in having me registered as a debtor to the state for six hundred and ten drachmas, without a summons, for failing to produce certain articles, and he carried out the trial through Lycidas the miller.[14] As witnesses to the summons,
he put down his brother Arethusius here, to whom these slaves belong,[15] and
someone else. If I proceeded with the preliminary hearing of the lawsuit that
I had brought against those of my relatives who had wronged me, they were
prepared to indict me as a debtor to the state and throw me into prison.[16]

---

13. This was an annual interest rate of 16 percent, which was rather high since the
regular rate was 12 percent. Probably the urgency of the loan forced them to accept
unfavorable terms.

14. This is a difficult passage to put into English, since the charge lodged against
Apollodorus is obscure, and he avoids discussing the details of the trial probably
because he lost. However, the fact that Arethusius was later convicted for false
testimony (see **17**) suggests that Apollodorus' objections were not without merit.
Apparently Nicostratus lodged a suit against Apollodorus so that Apollodorus'
conviction would temporarily prevent him from continuing some kind of legal
action that he was pursuing against his family.

15. It is a classic rhetorical technique of Apollodorus to take for granted what needs
to be proven. He repeats over and over again that the slaves belonged to Arethusius
(and not to Nicostratus, as his opponents claim) before he provides the evidence
to prove this assertion (**19–26**) so that the jury will listen more favorably to the
evidence when he introduces it.

16. The Athenian legal system had limited uses for prison. It was mostly used as
a short-term holding place but could also be used for temporary imprisonment of
debtors to the state.

[15] Moreover {Arethusius} the man who had me convicted without a summons and fined <six hundred> and ten drachmas, listing <false> witnesses to the summons, forcibly broke into my house, removed all the furniture, worth more than twenty minas, and left nothing.[17] When I thought that I should retaliate and had paid my debt to the state, I found out about the plot and went after the person who testified that he had witnessed the summons, namely, Arethusius, according to the law on false summons. Then he came into my field at night and cut all the grafts implanted into the fruit trees and the vines climbing on the trees, and he broke up all the olive trees planted around the garden beds with such ferocity as not even the enemy would have exhibited. [16] In addition to this, they sent a citizen boy during the day—since they are my neighbors and their field is next to mine—and told him to pluck the buds off the rose bush so that, if I caught him, I would tie him up or strike him like a slave and then they could prosecute me for outrage. When they failed, because I supplied witnesses to what was done to me and did not wrong them in any way, they conceived the worst plot against me. [17] After the preliminary hearing was already conducted and the case on the false summons was just about to come to trial, he waited for me near the quarry as I was coming up from the Piraeus late in the evening. He punched me with his fists, grabbed me by the waist, and was trying to push me into the quarry, but some people passing by heard me shouting and rushed to my aid. A few days later I went to court on the appointed day, proved that he had lied about the summons and was guilty of all the other offenses that I mentioned, and had him convicted. [18] During the assessment of the penalty, the jurors wanted to sentence him to death, but I pleaded with them not to do such a thing on my account, but I agreed with their proposed penalty of one talent.[18] This I did not because I cared whether

---

17. The text appears to be damaged at this point as several rather obvious errors can be seen. For example, in the manuscripts, Arethusius is said to have prosecuted Apollodorus; however, we have already been told that he was only a witness and that Nicostratus prosecuted Apollodorus with Lycidas' help. Since Athens did not have regular law enforcement, the successful litigant needed to secure for himself any property or money awarded to him by the court. If the defeated litigant refused to comply, his opponent could lodge a suit of ejectment, authorizing the use of force to secure the judgment in question (see **Dem. 21.44, 81**). Such self-help, although legally sanctioned, had to be the last resort and beyond suspicion since the Athenians considered the private home off limits to strangers (cf. **Lys. 12.8**), thus making Nicostratus' actions appear even more reprehensible.

18. For this offense, the two parties proposed a penalty after the defendant was found guilty, and the jury then decided which of the proposals to accept. Far from being a light sentence, a fine of one talent was crippling and undoubtedly suggests that the jury believed Apollodorus and agreed that the testimony on the summons

Arethusius dies (for he had done things to me worthy of the death penalty), but because I, the son of Pasion and a citizen by decree, did not want to kill an Athenian citizen.[19] That I have told you the truth, I will present witnesses to all this.

WITNESSES

[19] I have explained to you, men of the jury, the wrongs they have done to me, on account of which I entered this claim. That these slaves belong to Arethusius and that I listed them in the inventory as part of his estate, I will prove to you. He brought up Cerdon from early childhood, and I will present persons who know that he belonged to Arethusius.

WITNESSES

[20] I will now present witnesses who know where he worked, that Arethusius was the one receiving payments for his work and also received or paid compensation if something had gone wrong, since he was the master.

WITNESSES

As for Manes, Arethusius lent money to Archepolis of Piraeus, but since Archepolis was unable to pay back either the interest or the principal, he handed him Manes as compensation. That I am telling you the truth, I will present witnesses of this.

WITNESSES

[21] Furthermore, you will be able to realize from this, men of the jury, that the slaves belong to Arethusius. When these men bought the fruit

---

was false. If Apollodorus had insisted on the death penalty, he would have risked losing the second vote, since death for false summons might have seemed to many jurors to be excessive. So his decision to propose a penalty of one talent was not as merciful as he suggests.

19. Apollodorus was born in 394, when his father was still a metic, and so he was not an Athenian citizen at his birth. A few years later Pasion was granted Athenian citizenship as a benefactor to Athens, and as was the custom in such cases, the decree extended the citizenship award to his descendants. Thus Apollodorus became a citizen, most likely before reaching adulthood, by the decree that awarded citizenship to his father.

or were contracted to harvest or undertook some other agricultural task, Arethusius was the man who conducted the sales and entered into contracts on their behalf. That I am telling the truth, I will present you with witnesses to this too.

WITNESSES

[22] I have provided you with as many witnesses as I could that the slaves belong to Arethusius. I would like, however, to talk to you about the challenge that they presented to me and I presented to them. They challenged me at the time of the preliminary hearing, saying that they were ready to hand over the slaves to me in order to question them under torture, because they wanted this offer to serve as testimony of some sort on their side.[20] [23] I answered them, before witnesses, that I was ready to meet them at the Council House and take the slaves in the presence of members of the Council or the Eleven. My argument was that if I had brought a private lawsuit against them and they were willing to deliver the slaves, I would have taken them; now, however, the slaves and the confiscation proceedings were public, and for that reason they should be tortured, with the involvement of the state. [24] I did not think that it was appropriate for me, a private citizen, to torture public slaves. Neither had I been put in charge of the torture, nor was I in the position to judge whether what these men were saying was true. I thought that the magistrate or appointed members of the Council should write down and seal the testimony extracted from the slaves under torture and present it to the court so that, on the basis of what you heard from them, you could make up your minds. [25] If the slaves had been tortured privately by me, my opponents would have disputed every single word of theirs; however, if the torture was public, we would sit quietly, and the magistrates or the appointed members of the Council would have tortured them for as long as

---

20. Here we follow closely the translation of Bers (2003). He correctly observes that Apollodorus would have implicitly recognized Nicostratus' ownership of the slaves if he had accepted the challenge. This is why Nicostratus offered up the slaves for torture and Apollodorus could not accept the offer. Apollodurus' counteroffer to involve the Council or the Eleven was equally calculating, since it would have compelled his opponents to agree implicitly that the slaves now belonged to the city along with the remaining property of Arethusius. As is usually the case, such challenges often were intentionally framed in ways so that they would be rejected and then the challenger could raise questions about the unwillingness of his opponent to accept his challenge once the parties appeared in court. For the rhetorical use of such challenges, see Gagarin 1996; Kapparis 1999: 424–30.

they saw fit. This is what I wanted, but they did not agree to submit the case to the magistrate nor did they wish to follow me to the Council. That I am telling the truth, call for me the witnesses of this.

WITNESSES

[26] It seems to me that they are shameless on so many levels when they claim what belongs to you, and not least of all, as I will demonstrate to you, by your own laws. When the jury wanted to sentence Arethusius to death, they pleaded with the jurors to punish him with a fine and with me to consent, and they agreed to contribute to the payment. [27] Now, far from paying according to their guarantee, they also lay claims on what is yours. And yet the laws state that the property be confiscated of that man who guaranteed money owed to the city but did not secure the payment. So even if the slaves were theirs to begin with, they ought to belong to the state, if the laws are any use at all. [28] Before he became a debtor to the state, Arethusius was said to be the richest of the brothers. But from the moment the laws ordered that his property belonged to you, all of a sudden Arethusius is portrayed as poor, and some of his property is disputed by his mother, and some by his brothers. What they should have done, if they wanted to be fair to you, is first disclose all of his property, and then, if someone had listed something that belonged to them, they could claim it. [29] Remember that there is never going to be a shortage of people laying claims on what is yours. They will invent orphans and heiresses and plead for your pity, or they will speak of old age and the maintenance expenses of their mother and moan in the hope that they will deceive you most effectively in their attempts to deprive the city of its due. If you ignore all this and vote against them, you will be making the right decision.

DEMOSTHENES 54

AGAINST CONON

Introduction

The hostilities between Conon's sons and Ariston began at Panactum, where they were stationed, probably in 357 or 343 (see **3** n.), when Conon's sons attacked Ariston after he and his messmates told the general about their failure to adhere to military discipline. The young men allegedly spent their days getting drunk and engaging in the kind of rowdy and violent behavior that was more commonly associated with symposiasts acting against passers-by than with soldiers on military duty. During one of their drinking binges, Conon's sons shouted at Ariston's slaves and dumped their chamber pots on them as they were preparing dinner in the next tent. They then attacked Ariston for reporting the confrontation to the general. In recalling the fight that broke out the following evening, Ariston seems to imply that he got the worst of it before the general and taxiarchs put a stop to the fighting (**3–5**). Although this incident, as Ariston admits, was the cause of the lasting enmity between himself and Conon's sons, apparently nothing more happened until two years later, long after they had returned to Athens, when Ariston was enjoying an evening stroll through the agora with a friend. They came upon Ctesias, a son of Conon, who was drunk. According to Ariston, Ctesias then got his father and some men with whom he was drinking, and the group of them brutally beat up Ariston when they found him in the agora in nearly the exact same spot. When Ariston recovered, he lodged a private suit of battery (*dike aikeias*) against Conon, as the principal attacker. Although the testimony from the trial is not preserved, Ariston's summary of it suggests his wounds were quite serious (**11–12**).

The evidence for the attack is less straightforward. While Ariston goes over at length the wounds he suffered and the commotion that was created when he returned home from the fight, he only briefly summarizes the testimony of the witnesses who saw the attack. It is not entirely clear whether the bystanders arrived as he was being attacked or after the attackers left (**9, 32**). While one could understand how the group with Conon could overpower Ariston and his friend, it is hard to imagine that they could inflict such serious wounds and then leave with Ariston's cloak

---

Translated by Andrew Wolpert.

if bystanders had been present when the fight had started. So there seems to be good reason to doubt whether Ariston had sufficient evidence to prove that Conon's group started the fight and that Conon participated in it. Similarly, Ariston may have exaggerated the misconduct of Conon's sons at Panactum (**3–6**). They only received a reprimand from the general even though, as Ariston alleges, they spent most of their days drunk; and after they attacked a fellow soldier, no further action appears to have been taken either at the fort or when they returned to Athens.[1]

The speech is a key source for discussions on violence in Athens, since the speaker states how he did not pursue legal grievances after the assault on him at Panactum (**7**) and alleges that Conon will claim in defense that such fights are common among young men and should not result in lawsuits (**14**).[2] Ariston may be attributing to Conon an argument that the jurors would have found reproachable in order to prejudice them and provoke their anger so that they might be more prone to convict the defendant. Similarly, he may be exaggerating both his own refusal to respond in kind to the violence of Conon's sons and his own steadfast adherence to the law in order to establish Conon as the aggressor. If Ariston appeared ready to defend his honor when insulted, then the jury might have found Conon's defense more believable should he maintain that he was merely trying to break up the fight and did not actually strike Ariston.[3] So it is difficult to judge from Ariston's remarks how much the Athenians tolerated fights among young men or expected their disputes to be settled peacefully through the courts, since he had good reason to exaggerate the violent behavior of Conon and downplay how his own actions were confrontational.

The speech also shows how private and social considerations come into play when a litigant chooses which legal procedure to use since, as Ariston explains, he decided that it was inappropriate to lodge a suit of outrage (*hybris*) against Conon because of his age (**1**).[4] Ariston's motives

---

1. For a summary of the strengths and weakness of Ariston's case, see Carey and Reid 1985: 69–74.

2. While Cohen (1995) argues that the Athenians tolerated private fights between men as long as such infractions remained minor and did not negatively impact public interests, Herman (2006) suggests that any violation of the law had to be resolved through the law courts and that violent forms of retaliation and retribution were not tolerated.

3. At several points in his speech, Ariston seems to allude to such a defense, perhaps even mischaracterizing it (see **14**, **31**, **35**).

4. See Osborne 1985. For the meaning of *hybris,* see the introduction to **Demosthenes 21**.

may, however, have been less honorable. While the prosecutor of a public suit was not compensated if he won and was fined if he failed to
receive one-fifth of the votes, the successful prosecutor of a private suit
received the fine imposed on the defendant and he did not suffer a penalty if he lost. Even if financial considerations were not his main concern,
perhaps Conon chose to lodge a private suit to avoid the consequences
should he fail to receive the requisite number of votes. So too we must
bear in mind that Ariston may have alleged that Conon was guilty of a
more serious offense in order to justify the action that he brought against
him. By convicting Conon of battery, the jury was actually being lenient,
since his actions deserved a more severe penalty. This way, the jury
did not have to side either with the prosecutor or with the defendant.
A conviction helped both, while an acquittal would be all that much
more of an injustice. The speech provides, in addition, an interesting
commentary on the role of law in Athenian society and the relevance of
mitigating factors (**18–19, 21–23**).[5] The penalties escalate, we are told,
according to the severity of the offense in order to prevent conflicts from
escalating and to encourage the injured party to seek a legal resolution
for his grievance rather than retaliate in kind. Finally, the speech shows
how litigants manipulate testimony to avoid revealing the weaknesses of
their case and is an important source for understanding the use of expert
witnesses.[6]

Key Information

Speaker	Ariston charged Conon for the wounds that he received from a fight in the agora.
Defendant	Conon.
Other Individuals	Phanostratus of Cephisia was walking in the agora with Ariston when they ran into Ctesias, son of Conon, who then got his father and some men drinking with him, and together they allegedly attacked Ariston.
Action	Private suit of battery (*dike aikeias*).

---

5. Lanni (2006) provides an excellent overview of Athenian conceptions of justice
and the impact they had on the types of arguments that litigants presented in the
various courts.

6. For the use of witness testimony, see Humphreys 1985, Todd 1990a, Carey
1995b, Mirhady 2002, Thür 2005.

Penalty   A monetary fine set by the jury.[7]
Date   357 or 343.

Against Conon

[1] I was subjected to so much outrage,[8] men of the jury, and such injuries at the hands of Conon, this man before you, that for a very long time neither any of my relatives nor the doctors expected me to survive, but after I regained my health and recovered, contrary to expectations, I lodged this suit of battery against him. All my friends and relatives whom I consulted, said that he was liable to summary arrest[9] as a robber and to public suits for outrage for what he had done. They advised and recommended, however, that I neither undertake a burden greater than I could handle nor appear to bring a charge for my injuries that was beyond my age. I acted accordingly and lodged a private suit because of their advice, but I would have preferred most of all, men of Athens, to try this man for a capital offense. [2] I know very well that all of you will forgive me for this once you hear what I have suffered. Although the outrage that happened then was terrible, the violent acts of this man afterwards were no less serious. I therefore ask and request all of you alike first to listen favorably as I say what I have suffered and then, if you think that I have been injured and my injuries are in violation of the law, to help me as is just. I will tell you from the beginning everything that happened, as briefly as I can.

[3] Two years ago I went to Panactum,[10] where I was posted to guard. The sons of Conon pitched their tents near mine. I wish that this had not happened because, as you will learn, this was where our animosity and the attacks began. These men drank the entire day, beginning as soon as they had finished their lunch, and every day for as long as we were at the fort. We, however, kept to a schedule there that we had in Athens. [4] So when

---

7. See MacDowell 1978: 123.

8. The meaning of *hybris* is discussed in the introduction to **Demosthenes 21**.

9. Clothes-stealers fall under the category of wrongdoers (*kakourgoi*), who were subject to summary arrest (*apagoge*) and brought before the Eleven. If they were caught in the act and confessed, they were summarily executed. See MacDowell 1978: 148–49.

10. A fort bordering the Boeotian border, which was manned in 357 and 343. Since Ariston states that he was ordered to guard the fort, it is unlikely that he is referring to the regular military training of ephebes (Carey and Reid 1985: 69, 78).

it was time for the rest of us to have dinner, they were by then already acting like drunks, mostly with attacks on the slaves who served us, but even ending with attacks on us. Accusing our slaves of smoking them out with their cooking and claiming everything that the slaves said was insulting, they beat them, dumped their chamber pots on them, and urinated on them, leaving out no act of violence or outrage whatsoever. After we saw with irritation what they did, we first reproached them, but when they mocked us and did not stop, all of my mess as a group approached the general and told him about the matter—I did not do so alone. [5] He reprimanded and rebuked them not only because of their licentious behavior toward us but also for everything else that they were doing in the camp. Yet they were so far from stopping and being ashamed at their conduct that, once it became dark that evening, they immediately rushed against us. They began by hurling abuses and finished by pelting me with blows, creating such a noisy ruckus around the tent that the general and taxiarchs came along with some other soldiers and prevented us from suffering irreparable harm or doing anything in return for the drunken violence of those men. [6] After the confrontation had progressed to this point, we returned home, as one would expect, bitter enemies of one another. Still, I swear by the gods, I thought that I shouldn't bring legal action against them or take to heart any of their offenses. Instead, I simply decided from then on to watch out and take care to avoid those men. I wish first to provide you with testimony from witnesses of what I have said and then to show you what I have suffered at the hands of this very man in order that you might recognize how he should have shown his disapproval for their first offenses rather than taken the lead in carrying out much more terrible crimes.

TESTIMONIES

[7] These are all of their offenses, which I decided to take in stride. Not much later I was walking around, as was my custom, one evening in the agora with Phanostratus of Cephisia, a friend of my own age. Ctesias the son of Conon came upon us by the Leocorion[11] near Pythodorus' premises. When he saw us, he shouted and spoke incoherently to himself as one would expect from a person who was drunk, and then he went up to Melite.[12] There at the house of Pamphilus, the fuller, they were drinking

---

11. A monument in honor of the daughters of Leos, located in the agora; see Carey and Reid 1985: 81–82.

12. A deme just west of Athens.

(as we learned later), Conon, the man before us, a man by the name of Diotimus,[13] Archebiades, Spintharus son of Eubulus, Theogenes son of Andromenes, and many others. Ctesias rounded them up and led them to the agora. [8] We happened to be turning back from the temple of Persephone and were walking again somewhere by the Leocorion when we came upon them.[14] When we drew near, one of them, a person I didn't recognize, went after Phanostratus and held him down while Conon, his son, and Andromenes' son attacked me. They first stripped me; then they knocked me down and threw me into the mud. They leapt on me and treated me so brutally that they caused my lip to split and my eyes to close shut. They left me in such a weak condition that I could not stand up or even speak, and while I lay there I heard them say many terrible things. [9] Many of their remarks were profane, and I would shrink from saying some of them to you, but I will tell you what the evidence is that this man committed outrage and proof that the attack was entirely his doing. He crowed like a rooster having won a cock fight while the others called out to him to flap his elbows against his sides like wings. Afterwards, some passers-by carried me naked,[15] since those men had left taking my cloak.[16] When I came to the door of my house, there was crying and shouting from my mother and the female slaves, and after they brought me with great difficulty to the bath and washed me, they showed me to the doctors. That I speak the truth, I provide you with witnesses to this.

WITNESSES

[10] Well then, men of the jury, Euxitheus of Cholleidae, who is here today and is my relative, and Meidias, who was with him, happened to be returning from a dinner somewhere, when they found me then near my house, and they followed me as I was carried to the bath and were present when the doctor was led in.[17] Since I was so weak and they did not want

---

13. "Theotimus" is in the manuscripts, but Mensching emends the text to read "Diotimus," since he appears as a witness in **31** (Carey and Reid 1985: 82–83).

14. So that the jury does not think that he may have provoked the confrontation, Ariston makes it clear that he was neither waiting for Ctesias nor expecting him to return.

15. I.e., without a cloak.

16. Alternatively, "and those men left taking my cloak."

17. After mentioning multiple doctors, Ariston now switches to the singular, but it may be the case that one primary physician was providing the evidence for the medical team that cared for him.

me to be carried a long distance home from the bath, those present decided
to carry me to Meidias' house for the evening, and that is what they did.
Take also their testimonies in order that they might know that there
were many people who were aware of the outrage that those men inflicted
on me.

TESTIMONIES

Take also the testimony of the doctor.

TESTIMONY

[11] Such was then my immediate condition from the blows and outrage
that I incurred, as you have heard and has been testified to you by all who
saw me immediately afterwards. Later, the doctor said that he was not too
concerned about the swelling on my face and my wounds, but I had constant fevers and very severe pain over all of my body, but especially along
my sides and in my stomach, and I had no appetite. [12] And as the doctor said, if not for the purging, which happened spontaneously,[18] from the
great amount of bleeding while I was in great pain and distress, I would
even have died from an abscess. But it turns out that the blood loss saved
me. That I also tell you the truth about this, and that my wounds became
so serious from the blows that those men inflicted on me that I was reduced
to a life-threatening condition, read the testimony of the doctor and those
who visited me.

TESTIMONIES

[13] I think that it is clear to you, for many reasons, that I have lodged a
suit that falls far short of what they deserve when one considers how I received blows that were not minor or insignificant, but rather I was reduced
to this most dire condition because of the outrage and violence of those
men. I suppose some of you wonder what on earth Conon will dare to say
about this matter; so I want to warn you about what I have learned that
he has prepared for his defense. He will attempt to distract you from the
outrage of their actions by making the incident into a prank and joke. [14]

---

18. This blood loss was natural and not induced. Until modern times, bloodletting
was commonly practiced as therapeutic. Apparently Ariston's doctors believed
that the blood emitted from his wounds made it unnecessary to prescribe such a
treatment.

He will say that there are many in the city, sons of good and noble men,[19] who in jest, as young men do, give themselves various nicknames, such as the "Ithyphalloi" and the "Autolekythoi,"[20] and some of them are in love with courtesans, and his son is one of them, and often they give and receive blows over courtesans, and this is typical of young men. He will concoct a story about my brothers and me, how we are all drunk and insolent men, and also rash and spiteful. [15] Although I find the injuries that I have suffered, men of the jury, to be grievous, I would be no less upset and I would consider myself to have been subjected to just as much outrage—if I do not seem to be going too far—should you think that Conon is speaking truly about us, and if you are so mistaken as to consider a person to be such as he claims for himself or as his neighbor accuses him of being, while those men of self-restraint will find no advantage whatsoever from their daily life or their habits. [16] No one saw us drunk or engaging in outrage, nor do we believe that we are doing anything rash if we seek to receive justice for our injuries in accordance with the laws. I concede that his sons are the "Ithyphalloi" and the "Autolekythoi," and I pray to the gods that this and all of their other similarly impious acts recoil on Conon and his sons. [17] They are the men who initiate each other in the rites of the "Ithyphallos," and what they do brings much shame on men with self-restraint just to say it, not to mention if they were to do it.

How does this concern me? I am amazed if any excuse or pretext has been found for you by which a person will not have to pay the penalty after he has been proven guilty of committing outrage and battery. The laws take entirely the opposite view, and they have planned in advance with regard to excuses based on necessity so that they do not lead to even more serious offenses. For example (I was forced to investigate and learn

---

19. *Kaloi kagathoi* (literally, "beautiful and good men") are moral terms often used in reference to aristocrats, as is the case here.

20. The *ithyphallos* ("with an erect penis") can refer to the *phallos* carried at fertility rituals in honor of Dionysus. Used in such a profane context here, this nickname reveals the irreverence of these young men, and, by extension, the sons of Conon (see **16**). It also serves to bring to mind the abuses of those young aristocrats who mutilated the ithyphallic Herms and profaned the Mysteries during the Peloponnesian War (see **Dem. 21.143–47**). *Autolekythoi* (literally, "those who carry their own flask") refers to poor men who do not have slaves to pour them wine, and thus it can be translated as "beggars" or "bums" (see Carey and Reid 1985: 87). It is hard to imagine that Conon would not have recognized how these nicknames could have offended the jury even if they were used in jest by young aristocratic Athenians at dinner parties. So in all likelihood, Ariston attributes such remarks to Conon or at least distorts his defense in order to prejudice the jury against him.

about this because of Conon), there are suits for slander. [18] It is said that they exist for the following reason: in order that men not be induced to strike each other when they are being insulted. There are also suits for battery, and I am told that they exist so that if someone is losing a fight, he does not defend himself with a stone or some other weapon but waits for legal compensation. There are also public suits for wounding in order that murders not occur when people are inflicting wounds.[21] [19] Precautions are in place for the least serious offense, I believe, slander, to prevent the last and most serious one, murder, and that men not be spurred on little by little from slander to blows, blows to wounds, and wounds to murder, but the law has penalties for each of these offenses so that the judgment is not based on the anger or whim of the individual.[22]

[20] So this is how our laws are. If Conon says, "We are members of the 'Ithyphalloi,' and in our love affairs we strike and strangle whomever we please," will you then laugh it off and acquit him? I don't think so. None of you would have been laughing if you were there when I was dragged, stripped, and subjected to outrage, or when I returned home on a stretcher to the house, which I had left healthy, and my mother rushed out, and there was such crying and shouting from the women in the house, as if someone had died, so that some of our neighbors sent inquiries to us to find out what had happened. [21] Generally speaking, men of the jury, it is not right for anyone to have such an excuse or such an indemnity when he appears before you that will permit him to commit outrage. But if it is permitted for anyone at all, then those doing so because of their youth ought to have this haven reserved for them, not so that they escape being punished but so that they pay a penalty less than what is usual. [22] But when a man more than fifty years old appeared with younger men, his own sons, and he not only failed to dissuade or prevent them but was their leader, the principal and the most savage assailant, what penalty would be enough for him to pay for his actions? I believe not even death. If he had done nothing, but stood by while his son, Ctesias, acted as he has now been shown to have done, it would have been right for you to hate him. [23] If he has raised his own children to commit offenses in front of him and to feel neither shame nor fear when the penalty is death for some of their offenses, what do you think wouldn't be appropriate for him to suffer? I

---

21. This is important evidence to prove that intentional wounding, although heard before the Areopagus, was a public suit, in contrast to homicide, which was a private suit; see Phillips 2007: 93–98.

22. While this rationale for the ascribed penalties may be self-serving, Ariston correctly lists the offenses in order of severity since the penalties also escalate (Todd 1993: 268–69).

believe that this proves that he did not respect his own father. If he had honored and feared his father, he would have demanded his children do the same for him.

[24] Please also take the law on outrage and the law concerning clothes-stealers. You will see that they are liable by both these laws. Read them.

LAWS

Conon is liable for his actions by both of the laws. He committed outrage and stole clothing. If I chose not to pursue legal action by these laws, I would deserve to be acknowledged for not being overly litigious[23] and for showing self restraint. Conon, however, remains equally base. [25] If, however, anything had happened to me, he would have been liable for murder and the most severe punishment. Although it was acknowledged that the father of the priestess at Brauron did not touch the man who died, the council of the Areopagus rightly decided to banish him, because he encouraged the man who struck to do it. If, instead of preventing those who are about to commit an offense because they are drunk, out of anger, or for some other reason, the bystanders will goad them on, there is no hope of safety for the man who falls in with villains. Until they are exhausted, he will be treated to outrage, and this is what happened to me.

[26] What they did at the arbitration, I would like to tell you, since it will also reveal to you their licentiousness. They kept it going past midnight by refusing to read the testimony of their witnesses and hand over copies, leading our witnesses who were present, one by one, to the stone,[24] making them swear an oath, and writing down testimonies that were irrelevant—that his son's mother was a courtesan and he has been a victim of this and that, which, by the gods, men of the jury, everyone present found objectionable and annoying until at last they were even annoyed with themselves. [27] Once these men were worn out and had enough of this, they submitted a challenge[25] that they were willing to hand over

---

23. Although *apragmon* literally means "not meddling" and is typically used to refer to those who avoided politics, here Ariston means that he is not excessively litigious (cf. **Dem. 21.141**) since he could have prosecuted Conon for a more serious offense, such as outrage or clothes-stealing, but he chose not to do so.

24. This is where the arbitrators and the witnesses swore their oath; see Arist. *Ath. Pol.* 55.5.

25. Evidence from a slave was only formally admissible in court if submitted under torture (*basanos*). The litigant had to present a challenge (*proklesis*) by which he either offered his own slaves or requested those of the opposing litigant to undergo torture and which indicated the questions that were to be asked. The opposing

their slaves and wrote down the names of the slaves in order to delay the proceeding and so that the jars[26] would not be sealed. And now I suspect they will speak at length about this. I think, however, that you should consider the following: if they presented the challenge for the torture of slaves to occur because they had confidence in the merit of this evidence, they should not have made the challenge when the arbitration was then being decided, when it was night, and when they had no other excuse remaining. [28] But right away—before the suit was lodged, when I was ill and did not know if I would survive and I was denouncing to all my visitors the man who first struck me and was responsible for most of the outrage that I suffered—then he should have come to my house with many witnesses, and then he should have handed over his slaves and sent for members of the Areopagus to observe, since the case would have come before them if I had died. [29] But if he did not know about my condition—and although he had this proof of his innocence, as he is now going to say, he did not make any preparations to avert so great a danger—then when I had recovered and summoned him, at our first meeting with the arbitrator, he should have readily handed over his slaves. He did none of this. That I speak the truth and the challenge was for the purpose of delay, read the testimony. It will be obvious from this.

TESTIMONY

[30] With regard to his call for torture, bear in mind that at that time when he issued the challenge he did so to delay the proceedings, but on the first occasion he made it clear that he did not want his case to be based on such evidence, since he neither issued a challenge nor called on me to issue one. Well then, all of the evidence at the arbitration, which is the same as is now being considered, refuted him and clearly showed all that he was guilty

---

litigant was then free to accept or reject the challenge, or issue a counterchallenge in response. Although litigants frequently issued such challenges, there is not a reference in the extant orations to one that had been accepted and carried out. Litigants clearly expected their challenges to be rejected and regularly worded them in such a way as to ensure that they would be rejected so that they could then accuse their opponents of lying. For further discussion on judicial torture of slaves, see Gagarin (1996).

26. Once the arbitrator made his decision, all the documents (i.e., witness testimony, challenges, and laws) that the parties provided were sealed in jars, one for the prosecutor's case and the other for the defendant's. If a party appealed the arbitrator's decision, the litigants could have only documents from the sealed jars read in court; see Arist *Ath. Pol.* 53.2–3.

of the charges. [31] As a result he deposited false testimony and recorded the names of witnesses, which, I think, you will recognize when you hear them: "Diotimus son of Diotimus of Icaria, Archebiades son of Demoteles of Halae, and Chaeretius son of Chaerimenes of Pithus testify that they were returning from dinner with Conon, and they came upon Ariston and the son of Conon fighting in the agora, and Conon did not strike Ariston." [32] As if you would immediately believe them and could not surmise the truth! First of all, Lysistratus, Paseas, Niceratus, and Diodorus, who have expressly testified that they saw me being hit by Conon, stripped of my cloak, and subjected to all the other acts of outrage that I suffered, would never have been willing to give false testimony when they did not know me and they witnessed the fight by chance, if they had not seen what I suffered.[27] Second, if he had not inflicted this harm on me, I would never have let go of those men who beat me, as even my opponents concede, and preferred to take first to court the man who did not even touch me. [33] Why would I? The man who first struck me and subjected me to the worst outrage, he is the one I charge, the one I hate, and the one I prosecute. Since it is so clear that all my statements are true, he would not have had one argument if he had not furnished these witnesses, but he would have been convicted right away without speaking. As to be expected, his drinking companions and his partners to these crimes give false testimony. If this is how it is going to be, if some have no shame at all and dare to give patently false testimony, and there is no help from the truth, it will turn out dreadfully.

[34] Surely they are not men of this ilk.[28] Yet, many of you know, I think, Diotimus, Archebiades, and Chaeretius, that man with the grey hair over there, that they look morose in the day, they say that they are imitating the Spartans, and they wear short cloaks and shoes with thin soles.[29] When they get together and spend time with each other, there is not one terrible or shameful act that they leave untried. [35] They will resort to this wonderfully bold defense: "Can't we testify for each other? Isn't this what

---

27. This delay in discussing the details of their testimony, which was read in section **9**, raises questions about the accuracy of Ariston's summary of it. There is also some vacillation in the wording ("they saw me being hit" versus "if they had not seen what I suffered"); see Carey and Reid 1985: 70–72, 97.

28. This is a hypothetical reply.

29. This affectation began among wealthy Athenians in the fifth century and apparently continued on in the fourth even though many of their fellow citizens disapproved of such behavior and considered this exuberant fondness for Sparta as proof that such individuals were hostile to the democracy and the rule of the many. Cf. **Lys. 16.18**.

friends and comrades do?[30] What is so damning about the evidence that he
will furnish against you? Some say that they saw him being beaten? But
we will testify that you did not touch him at all. He was stripped of his
cloak? We will testify that they did it first. His lip was stitched together?
We will say that you had your head bashed in or some other bone broken."
[36] Whereas I provide my doctors as witnesses, men of the jury, this is
not the case for them. In fact, they will not have a witness against us for
anything other than what they witness for themselves. In the name of the
gods, I could not even begin to say why and how far they are ready to do
anything whatsoever. But so that you might know what sort of things they
go about doing, read[31] to them these testimonies, and stop the water clock.

TESTIMONIES

[37] If they break into houses and beat up men whom they come upon, do
you think that they would hesitate to write down false testimony on a piece
of paper for each other when they are partners of so great and so much
viciousness, wickedness, shamelessness, and cruelty? I think that all of these
characteristics are manifested in the actions of these men. Although they
have committed some other crimes even more terrible than these, I could
not find everyone whom they harmed.

[38] As for the most shameful thing of all that I hear he intends to do,
I think it is best if I warn you. They say that he will bring forth his own
children and swear an oath upon them, invoking such dreadful and disturb-
ing curses as to shock the man who heard and reported them to me. Such
shamelessness, men of the jury, is impossible to defeat, I believe, since the
most honorable men and those who would be least likely to lie are most
likely to be deceived by such men. They ought, however, to draw their
conclusions by looking at his life and his ways. [39] I will tell you about his
disdain for such matters, as I have learned by necessity. I hear, men of the
jury, that a man by the name of Bacchius, whom you sentenced to death,[32]
and Aristocrates, the man with bad eyes, and other men of that sort were

---

30. After referring to Conon's associates as drinking companions (**33**) and now
as comrades (*hetairoi*) who admire Sparta (**34**), Ariston all but says that they were
members of a political club (*hetaireia*) conspiring against him. For *hetaireiai,* see **Lys.
12.43** n.; **Dem. 21.139** n.

31. After addressing the jury, Ariston then asks the clerk to read out the testimonies.

32. Litigants regularly address the jurors when referring to previous trials even
though only a few if any could have been in attendance (cf. **Dem. 21.91**). Ariston
does so here in order to co-opt the jury by claiming that it has already expressed its
disapproval of Conon and his associates.

Conon's comrades when they were young, and they had the nickname, "Triballoi."[33] Each time they dined together, they collected the offerings to Hecate[34] and pigs' testicles,[35] which are used for purification whenever there is going to be a meeting of the Assembly, and they more easily swore oaths and perjured themselves than anything else. [40] So a man such as Conon is not to be trusted if he swears an oath, far from it. Instead, the man who would not even swear an honest oath and would not think of swearing upon his children any oath that is not in accordance with your custom, but would prefer instead to suffer anything whatsoever, and if it is necessary to swear an oath, he swears an oath in accordance with your custom—he is more trustworthy than the man who swears an oath upon his children and goes through fire.[36] Well then, I, who would deserve in every regard to be considered more trustworthy than you, Conon, was willing to swear this oath, not so that I could evade punishment in whatever I do, as is the case for you, but for the sake of the truth and so that I might not again be treated to outrage, since I will not lose this case through your perjury. Read my challenge.

CHALLENGE

[41] I was then willing to swear this oath, and I now do so by all the gods and all the goddesses, for your sake, men of the jury, and that of the

---

33. The Athenians considered this tribe of Thracian men to be savage and barbaric. Ariston mentions this nickname in order to convey to the jury the lawlessness of Conon's gang in much the same way as the nicknames used by Ctesias and his friends (**14**).

34. Offerings were placed at crossroads every month for Hecate (Ar. *Pl.* 594–97). She was a chthonic deity with magical and sinister powers, associated with the ghosts of the dead. To take her offerings was a remarkably irreverent act, which showed that the culprit had no qualms.

35. Since the pigs' testicles had been used in a purification ritual for the Assembly, they were polluted, and therefore Conon and his associates should not have taken them, let alone eaten them. In fact, the carcasses were normally thrown into the sea after the ceremony in order to purify them (see Carey and Reid 1985: 101). This is yet another shocking example of Conon's willingness to violate traditional religious conventions.

36. The translation of this sentence is based on Carey and Reid (1985: 102). Although the text is rather convoluted here, Ariston's main point is that the jury should place its trust not in someone willing to swear any and every kind of oath, but in the individual who is more circumspect and shows that he adheres to religious convention.

bystanders.[37] I swear that because I suffered, at the hands of Conon, these injuries for which I am bringing a suit, because I was beaten and my lip was so cut up that it had to be stitched, and because I was subjected to outrage, I pursue this legal action. And if I swear an honest oath, may I prosper and may I never suffer anything similar again, but if I swear falsely, may I and what I either now possess or will possess be utterly destroyed. But I do not swear falsely, even if Conon says so until he bursts. [42] Since I have presented to you my entire case and I have in addition given you my pledge, I ask you, men of the jury, just as each of you would hate the perpetrator if you were the victim, to feel the same anger for Conon on behalf of me, and do not regard as a private matter anything that could possibly happen to another. But whenever it happens to someone, help him and give him justice, and hate those men, who are bold and reckless when they carry out their crimes and shameless and base when they are in court, and who think not about honor, custom, or anything else other than evading of justice. [43] But Conon will beg to be let off and he will cry. So consider who is to be pitied more: the man who has suffered what I have suffered at the hands of Conon if I will leave the court and will be treated to this additional act of outrage should I not obtain justice, or Conon if he will pay the penalty? Does it benefit each of you to permit assault and outrage or not? I think not. If you acquit him, there will be many more like him, but if you convict him, there will be fewer.[38] [44] I could speak at length, men of the jury, about how useful we have been, both my father for as long as he was alive and I, when we were trierarchs and served in the army and did what we were ordered, and how neither the defendant nor his family ever did anything. But there is not enough time, and the speech does not concern such matters. If we were by our own admission even more useless and more wicked than they, we ought not, I suppose, to be beaten or subjected to outrage. I do not know what more I need to say. I believe that you understand all that I have said.

---

37. For a discussion on the audience of Athenian trials, see Lanni 1997.

38. This is a common form of the consequentialist *topos;* see Lanni 2004.

[DEMOSTHENES] 59

AGAINST NEAERA BY APOLLODORUS

Introduction

Delivered around 342, this is the last and longest of Apollodorus' speeches. It was part of a series of lawsuits and counter-lawsuits between Apollodorus, a political supporter of the anti-Macedonian faction, and Stephanus, a supporter of the pro-Macedonian faction seeking accommodation with Philip. The feud between the two men started in 348/7, shortly before or after the fall of Olynthus, when Stephanus successfully prosecuted Apollodorus for proposing an illegal decree (*graphe paranomon*), and then a couple of years later he was unsuccessful in his prosecution of Apollodorus for homicide. The prosecution of Neaera, the concubine of Stephanus, a year or two after the homicide trial is Apollodorus' response to the attacks he had sustained. What makes this case particularly malicious is that the attack focused not on Stephanus but on Stephanus' elderly life partner, a former courtesan, whom he took as his concubine approximately thirty years before this trial. Apollodorus had never met Neaera and had no personal grudge against her, but he did not hesitate to use her in order to retaliate against Stephanus. He accused her of living with Stephanus as though she were his lawfully wedded wife. Since it was forbidden for aliens to marry Athenians and there was no doubt that Neaera was an alien, Apollodorus only had to prove that she had usurped the privileges reserved for Athenian women. If convicted, Neaera would have been sold into slavery and Stephanus would have had to pay a fine of one thousand drachmas.

The main argument of the prosecution was that Stephanus and Neaera had introduced their children into the citizen body under the pretense that they were properly born offspring of a lawfully married Athenian couple. It was not illegal for an Athenian citizen to live with an alien woman or have children with her, but it was illegal to present their children as citizens. The defense acknowledged that Neaera was an alien, but disputed the parentage of the children and maintained that they were the children of Stephanus from a previous marriage to a citizen woman and therefore were legitimate and permitted to exercise all the rights reserved for Athenian citizens (**119**). For some reason that is not entirely clear, it was not Apollodorus but his brother-in-law, Theomnestus, who formally lodged the complaint against Neaera. He begins the case for the prosecution by explaining the reasons

Translated by Konstantinos Kapparis based on his 1999 version published by de Gruyter.

for the previous hostility between his family and that of Stephanus, which led him to prosecute an elderly woman whom he had never met (**1–15**). Then, as a supporting speaker (*synegoros*), Apollodorus finishes their case (**16–126**). One would expect his speech to focus almost entirely on the status of the children, but this is not the case. Nearly one-third of the speech is dedicated to Neaera's career as a courtesan; one-third to the two marriages and divorces of Phano, allegedly a daughter of Neaera; and one-third to a lengthy digression about the Plataeans and the argumentation of the speech. No evidence is offered regarding the status of the three boys who allegedly were the sons of Neaera, and the evidence about Phano, if anything, inadvertently confirms her citizen status.

Apollodorus begins his speech with the recital of the law under which the prosecution was made and then goes back to the beginning of the fourth century, when Neaera was bought by a famous pimp as a young slave girl in order to become a courtesan. He mentions a number of well-known men who had been her lovers when she was at the height of her career and explains how she was freed from slavery, met Stephanus, and was mistreated by the men who were attracted to her undoubtedly considerable charms. His narrative about Neaera essentially ends in section **48**, when she becomes the exclusive concubine of Stephanus. Afterwards she is only briefly mentioned in reference to the marital adventures of her alleged daughter, Phano, who thereafter is the focus of the narrative.

Phano was first given in marriage to a bad-tempered miser called Phrastor, but the marriage lasted less than a year. Apollodorus maintains that Phrastor divorced her because he discovered that she was the daughter of Neaera and thus an alien, but Apollodorus later unintentionally reveals that this was probably not the reason. This austere manual worker, Phrastor, had no time for the airs and graces to which Phano was apparently accustomed; they argued a lot, and she was unwilling to play the meek and obedient wife. Phrastor not only divorced her but also blackmailed Stephanus in order to keep the dowry. He accused Stephanus of betrothing to him the daughter of an alien woman. The risk was great for Stephanus, who would have lost his civic rights and all his property if convicted. In the face of such danger, Stephanus understandably abandoned any claim to the dowry and let Phrastor keep it on condition that he withdraw his lawsuit. Phano, however, was pregnant at the time of the divorce, and this may also have induced her father to give up on the lawsuit, hoping that the birth of Phrastor's child might effect a reconciliation between him and his wife. Although no such reconciliation was ever reached, Phano gave birth to a boy whom Phrastor accepted as his son and took into his house after a while. Now the allegations that he had made against his former wife came to haunt Phrastor. When he tried to enroll his son in his *genos*, the citizen status of the boy was called into question because of Phrastor's previous actions. Phrastor then had to sue the *genos* and, ironically, defend the citizen status of his former wife before the arbitrator in order to have his son accepted as a citizen. Apollodorus employs several cheap tricks, such as verbal ambiguity, in order to conceal the fact that throughout this process the citizen status of Phano was confirmed and finally the arbitrator found that she was of Athenian birth and her son legitimate (**49–63**).

The second marriage of Phano, this time to Theogenes, the *basileus* (king archon), was motivated by the political ambitions of Stephanus, who wanted to be appointed an assessor (*paredros*). A marriage in this case, apart from providing a husband for Phano, served to consolidate the friendship between Stephanus and Theogenes and secure his appointment to the office of assessor to the *basileus*. However, an ancient law prohibited the wife of the *basileus* from being previously married, because of her religious role in the festival of the Anthesteria (see note 55), when she was to be presented as a bride to Dionysus. The Areopagus found out and punished Theogenes with a modest fine. Theogenes, stunned by the revelations, confessed that he had been deceived, expelled Stephanus from office, and divorced Phano. Apollodorus claims that the Areopagus discovered that Phano was an alien of loose morals, but there is no doubt that if this had been the case a modest fine would not have been an appropriate punishment. The least the Areopagus would have done would have been to demand that Theogenes divorce his alien wife and bring Stephanus and Phano before a court, with charges of impiety. The Areopagus clearly could not prove that Phano was an alien and probably did not even suggest that she was (**72–84**).

In between her marriages, Phano seems to have had an extramarital affair with a mature man, an old lover of Neaera and friend of the family, which Apollodorus pushes in opposite directions to suit his argument. Sometimes he treats it as proof that prostitution was still practiced in the house of Stephanus, and sometimes he treats it as a genuine situation of seduction with all the legal disabilities that this entailed for the woman (**64–72**).[1]

---

1. *Moicheia* is translated in our text as "seduction" rather than "adultery" because it was illegal for a man to have a sexual relationship with a respectable Athenian woman without the consent of her guardian. Thus *moicheia* was in some ways broader in scope than adultery, since it applied even to unmarried Athenian women; and in other ways it was narrower, since an Athenian man could have an extramarital affairs and not be guilty of *moicheia* if the woman was a prostitute or the relationship was not with a respectable Athenian woman. Neither "seduction" nor "adultery" adequately conveys how serious an offense *moicheia* was for the Athenians. See the introduction to **Lysias 1**.

After the discussion on the second marriage of Phano, the narrative essentially ends, and next follows a digression on the Plataeans. The orator contrasts these worthy recipients of a mass citizenship award, in the years of the Peloponnesian War, with Stephanus and Neaera, who tried to steal citizenship rights for their offspring (**88–106**). The short argumentation of the speech reiterates the themes that the orator had explored in his narrative, adds to the emotional charge, and tries to amplify this case into something fundamentally important that concerns the entire city and the gods themselves (**107–25**).

Blass (1888) believed that the speech was the creation of an inferior orator who overemphasized the narrative because he did not know how to use proofs, properly based on reason or arguments that would appeal to a more sophisticated audience, such as expounded by Aristotle, Cicero, Quintilian, and experts on rhetoric. And yet the speech has been popular throughout the centuries and remains to this day at least as popular as any of the best speeches of Demosthenes or Cicero. It had a profound impact upon authors in later antiquity, most notably Procopius, in his saucy tales about Empress Theodora (*Anecdota,* Ch. 9). Recent studies offer convincing explanations to account for the way Apollodorus frames his case, and they see a clear purpose and intent in the rhetorical strategies he employs. Far from being weak oratory, the speech both offers a portrayal of Neaera that conforms to Athenian assumptions about the behavior of women of such a class and appeals to the anxiety and concerns of the jury. The plan was to win a weak case by distracting the jury with a good story, by drawing on familiar quotes from history and religion, and by constructing a portrait of a villainous woman who had deceived the entire city and posed a threat to two social institutions that the Athenians regarded as the foundation of their democracy—marriage and citizenship. Whether Apollodorus was successful or not is unknown, and the strengths or weaknesses of the case by themselves do not allow us to safely draw any conclusions about the outcome. Aeschines won an even weaker case against Timarchus merely with rumor and innuendo (see introduction to **Aeschines 1**). Apollodorus has done something similar, and he may well have been equally successful.

Key Information

Speaker	Theomnestus, brother-in-law of Apollodorus, lodged a public action against Neaera.
Supporting Speaker	Apollodorus, son of Pasion, gave a speech, on behalf of his brother-in-law, which provided the main arguments of the prosecution.
Defendant	Neaera, former slave and prostitute, was the concubine of Stephanus.

Other Individuals	Stephanus was both the political rival of Apollodorus and Neaera's lover. Apollodorus retaliated against him by prosecuting Neaera.
	Phrynion paid for Neaera to be freed and brought her to Athens.
	Phano was allegedly Neaera's daughter and illegally treated by Neaera and Stephanus as a legitimate Athenian, born of a lawful marriage.
	Phrastor was Phano's first husband and the father of her son.
	Theogenes was Phano's second husband.
	Epaenetus allegedly had a sexual relationship with Phano. He charged Stephanus with wrongful imprisonment.
Action	A public suit against Neaera for living with Stephanus as his lawful wife, although she was a foreigner.
Penalty	If convicted Neaera would have been sold into slavery and Stephanus would have been fined one thousand drachmas.
Date	c.342.

Against Neaera

The Speech of Theomnestus

[1] I had strong motives, men of Athens, when I decided to bring this lawsuit against Neaera and appear before you. My father-in-law, myself, my sister, and my wife have all suffered grave injury at the hands of Stephanus and have been placed in serious danger by this man. So in this trial I will be acting not as the instigator but as the punisher, because he was the one who started the hostilities although we had never said or done anything wrong to him. First I would like to relate to you how we were harmed by him and faced the danger of exile and disfranchisement, so that you can forgive me if I am trying to defend myself.

[2] After the Athenian people decreed that Pasion and his descendants were to be Athenian because of his services to the city,[2] my father, in line

2. Pasion, the father of Apollodorus, was born a slave, but from his success as a bank manager, he earned the trust of his masters, was liberated, and ultimately inherited

with the gift of the people, betrothed to Apollodorus, son of Pasion, his daughter—my sister, by whom Apollodorus had his children. Since Apollodorus treated my sister and the rest of us well and earnestly believed that as relatives we should be sharing everything, I took the daughter of Apollodorus—my niece—as my wife.[3] [3] Later on Apollodorus was selected as a member of the Council. After his scrutiny and the customary oath, a serious crisis and war befell the city. In this situation, either you would be the greatest power among the Greeks, if you won, and doubtless recover all your possessions and decisively defeat Philip, or, if you delayed the dispatch of aid and abandoned the allies, with the army disbanded because of the lack of resources, you would lose them and appear untrustworthy to the other Greeks and risk losing the rest: Lemnos, Imbros, Scyros and the Chersonese.[4] [4] As you were preparing to march out in full force to Euboea and Olynthus, Apollodorus as a councilor proposed a decree in the Council and brought it to the Assembly,[5] suggesting that the people should decide by show of hands whether the surplus of the administration should be directed to the military or the theoric fund.[6] The laws stated that in times of war the surplus of the administration should go to the military fund; moreover, he thought that the people should have the power to dispose their own money as they wished, and as a councilor he had taken an oath to act in the best interests of the Athenian people, as you

---

their bank. He became very wealthy, and after generous donations to the city of Athens he was given citizenship around 385 (see Trevett 1992: 24-5).

3. Marriage between relatives was common, as Athenian fathers often looked for husbands for their daughters among people they knew, such as the wider family and their friends (see Just 1989: 76–104).

4. Theomnestus is referring to events that happened between 351 and 348. Philip besieged and captured Olynthus in the summer of 348. Athens tried to assist Olynthus, but the relief force was delayed by strong northern winds and did not arrive on time.

5. For a proposal to be considered at a meeting of the Assembly, it first had to be presented to the Council of the Five Hundred (*boule*), which then decided whether and in what form it should be placed on the agenda for the Assembly to discuss.

6. In the fourth century the theoric fund was used for all spectacles and public works in the city, while the military fund was used to finance wars; transfers between the two funds were forbidden. In an effort to secure additional financing for the war against Philip, Apollodorus attempted to win the Assembly's approval for surplus revenue to be transferred to the military fund. This move still seemed bold in the summer of 348 and eventually lost popular support (see Hansen 1976b). The imminent threat from Philip in the late 340s renewed support for such a proposal and eventually led to legal reforms allowing such transfers by a decree of Demosthenes in 339.

all agreed at the time. [5] When the vote took place, no one objected to the use of these funds for military purposes, and even to the present day, if anyone talks about this, everybody agrees that although he gave the best advice, he suffered unjustly. So one should be angry with the man who deceived the jurors, not with those who were deceived. Stephanus here filed a lawsuit, alleging that the decree was illegal,[7] came to court, and won with false witnesses and many irrelevant accusations. [6] If he thought it best to do so, we are not complaining. However, when the jury was about to assess the penalty, despite our pleas he did not wish to reach a compromise.[8] He proposed a penalty of fifteen talents, in order to have Apollodorus and his children disfranchised and my sister and the rest of us thrown into extreme poverty and complete deprivation. [7] The estate of Apollodorus was barely worth three talents, and he was not able to afford such a huge debt; but if the debt was not paid by the ninth prytany, it would be doubled and Apollodorus would be listed as owing thirty talents to the treasury. Once he was listed as a debtor to the state, the rest of his possessions would be catalogued as public property, and after their sale everyone would be cast in extreme poverty, Apollodorus himself, his children, his wife, and all of us.[9] [8] Moreover, the other daughter would remain unmarried, because who would ever marry without a dowry the daughter of a poor man who owes money to the state? So he was the cause of such trouble for all of us, even though he was never injured by us. But I am very grateful to the jurors of that trial for this matter at least, that they did not sit back and watch him be ruined but fined him one talent, which he could barely manage to pay. So it is only fair that we return "the favor" to him.

[9] But this was not the only way he tried to destroy us; he even tried to have Apollodorus expelled from his homeland. He brought false charges against him, alleging that once he came to Aphidna searching for a runaway

---

7. A proposal could be blocked as unlawful on grounds of content or procedure. This process (*graphe paranomon*) was introduced near the end of the fifth century in order to add accountability to the decisions of the Assembly but, as is to be expected, it was sometimes misused for political purposes in subsequent years.

8. For some offenses, the penalty was fixed, but for others, as is the case here, each party proposed a penalty after the defendant was convicted. The jury then chose which of the two penalties to accept for the present case (see **[Dem.] 53.18**).

9. Unpaid debts to the state were routinely doubled at the end of the third quarter of the financial year (i.e., the ninth prytany). Someone who owed money to the state lost his civic rights (*atimia*) until he repaid the entire sum. If a state debtor owned property but failed to pay his debt, he could have his property catalogued and auctioned (*apographe*). The citizen who initiated this process was rewarded with a third of the proceeds that the state recovered (see the introduction to **[Demosthenes] 53**).

slave of his, and there he struck a woman, and she died from the blow. He brought together some slaves of his, disguised them as Cyreneans, and made a proclamation for homicide against him at the Palladium.[10] [10] Stephanus here acted as prosecutor in the trial and testified under oath—calling destruction upon himself and his family and his household if he lied—that Apollodorus had killed the woman with his own hands, which, of course, had never happened, and he had never seen or heard from anyone else.[11] However, after he was caught perjuring himself and bringing false charges, it became obvious that he had been paid by Cephisophon and Apollophanes to have Apollodorus expelled or disfranchised.[12] He only won a few votes out of an expense of five hundred drachmas, and he went away leaving behind the impression that he was a perjurer and a bad man.

[11] Think about it, men of the jury, and consider the possibilities. What was I supposed to do with myself, my wife, and my sister if Apollodorus happened to fall victim to the plots of Stephanus here, either in the first or in the second trial? What kind of shame and misfortune would not have befallen me? [12] Everyone was coming to me privately—urging me to go after him for all that he had done to us—and putting me to shame, saying that I was going to be the biggest coward if I did not exact vengeance on behalf of those closest to me—my sister, my father-in-law, my nieces, and my wife—and if I did not bring her before you and prove convincingly that she is guilty, this woman who has committed crimes against the gods and treated our city with insolence and our laws with contempt, so that you can deal with her as you see fit. [13] And just as Stephanus here tried to take my family away from me in defiance of your laws and decrees, I have come forward to prove that he is living with a foreign woman as his wife, against the law, and has introduced into the phratry and the deme someone else's children; given in marriage the daughters of courtesans as if they were his own; committed impiety against the gods; and taken away

---

10. The Palladium tried cases of murder of a slave or foreigner and could impose either exile or a fine as a penalty (see Boegehold 1995: 48).

11. For the religious significance of Athenian homicide law, see the introduction to **Antiphon 6**. A person accused of homicide was required to refrain from public life from the moment of his prosecution until the trial. Thus Stephanus calculated that if he lost he would have succeeded in removing Apollodorus from politics for at least a few months, which was during the critical period when the controversial peace of Philocrates between Athens and Philip was under negotiation (346). If he won, then—all the better—he would have secured the exile of a fierce opponent.

12. Both Cephisophon and Apollophanes were political figures in favor of the peace of Philocrates. Theomnestus alleges that they bribed Stephanus with five hundred drachmas to bring the homicide charges against Apollodorus.

from the city the authority to make someone a citizen if it wishes, because who would ask from the city the favor of becoming a citizen, with a great deal of expense and trouble, if they can get exactly the same favor from Stephanus for much less?

[14] I have told you what I suffered from Stephanus before I brought this lawsuit. Now you need to hear that Neaera here is an alien, and she lives with Stephanus here as his wife, and that she has committed many crimes against the city. Therefore I am asking you, men of the jury, what I think I should be asking as a young man and an inexperienced speaker—to allow me to invite Apollodorus as my advocate for this trial. [15] He is older and has more experience in the laws, he has paid close attention to all these matters, and he suffered injustice at the hands of Stephanus; so he has every right to punish the man who started it. And you must vote according to the truth, once you listen to the finer points of the prosecution and the defense, on behalf of the gods, and the laws, and justice, and yourselves.[13]

The Speech of Apollodorus

[16] Theomnestus has spoken to you, men of Athens, about all the wrongs that I have suffered at the hands of Stephanus, which made me come forward and accuse Neaera here. Now I will demonstrate clearly to you that Neaera is a foreigner and that she lives illegally with Stephanus as his wife. But first the clerk will read for you the law, in accordance with which Theomnestus brought this prosecution and the case has been introduced before you.

LAW

If an alien man lives in marriage with a citizen woman, by any means or device, any Athenian who has the right can bring a prosecution against him to the thesmothetai. If he is convicted, he and his property are to be sold, and one-third of the sale is to be given to the successful prosecutor. The same applies if an alien woman lives in marriage with a citizen man, and the man living in marriage with the convicted alien woman is to owe a fine of one thousand drachmas.[14]

---

13. The law recognized that some citizens might not be capable of speaking for themselves and allowed them to receive the assistance of a supporting speaker (*synegoros*), provided that he did not receive financial compensation for his help. It was not uncommon for speakers to call relatives or friends as advocates for a variety of reasons (see Rubinstein 2000 as well as the introduction of **Isaeus 12**).

14. This law was probably introduced around 380 in order to prevent Athenians from marrying non-Athenians. Apollodorus correctly interprets the spirit of this law

[17] You heard the law, men of Athens, which prohibits an alien woman from living in marriage with a citizen man, and a citizen woman with an alien man, or having legitimate children, by any means or device. If someone acts contrary to this, the law provides for a prosecution before the *thesmothetai* against the alien man and the alien woman, and if they are convicted, the law orders they are to be sold. So now I would like to show you in detail that Neaera here is an alien, and I will go back to the beginning.

[18] Nicarete, a freedwoman of Charisius of Elis, and wife of his cook, Hippias, acquired seven little girls from a very young age. She was very skilled in discerning the potential for beauty in very young children and knew how to bring them up and train them skillfully, since she was an expert in this trade and made her livelihood from it.[15] [19] She pretended that they were her daughters in order to exact the largest possible fees from those who wished to be with them under the pretext that they were free women; and after she had enjoyed the profits from each of them from the prime of their lives, she sold all seven of them, Anteia, Stratola, Aristocleia, Metaneira, Phila, Isthmias, and Neaera here.[16] [20] And who bought whom and how they were set free by the men who bought them from Nicarete, I will tell you later in my speech, if you want to hear it and I have enough time. But I wish to come back to the point when Neaera, while still under the ownership of Nicarete, was earning with her body from those men who wanted to be with her. [21] Lysias the sophist, who was a lover of Metaneira, wanted, in addition to the money he was already spending on her, to pay for her initiation into the Mysteries.[17] His

---

as an attempt to stop the introduction of non-Athenian children into the citizen body (see **122**; Kapparis 1999: ad loc.).

15. The education of women destined for marriage mostly consisted of household skills and training in good manners and moral behavior (Xen. *Oec.* 7). However, the education of courtesans consisted of skills which would help them enchant and entertain their lovers, such as dancing, music, and even philosophy and literature (see Athen. 13).

16. There is further evidence from comedy and other literature to confirm the claim of Apollodorus that these women were famous courtesans in their heyday (see Kapparis 1999: ad loc.).

17. This passage is a good example of how the word "sophist" did not necessarily have negative connotations and initially meant "teacher of rhetoric" or "orator." Plato is largely responsible for the negative meaning that became predominant in later centuries. The fact that a man in his 60s was with a young courtesan would not have sounded offensive per se for an Athenian audience. Gagarin (2002: 49) points out that this passage generated four more references to Lysias as a sophist in later antiquity and also a fictitious letter from Lysias to Metaneira. The Mysteries was a celebration in honor of Demeter and Persephone which attracted visitors from all

thinking was that the rest of the money went to her owner, but what he was going to spend during the festival and the Mysteries would be a personal favor to the woman. So he asked Nicarete to come to the Mysteries, bringing along Metaneira in order to be initiated, and promised to bear the expenses for her initiation. [22] When they arrived, Lysias did not take them into his own house out of respect for his wife, the daughter of Brachyllus and his niece, and for his elderly mother, who was living in the same house. He took Metaneira and Nicarete to the house of Philostratus of Colonus, a friend of his who was still a bachelor, and Neaera here was with them, already working with her body, although she was too young and not yet in the prime of her life. [23] To prove that I am telling the truth, that she belonged to Nicarete and came along with her and was accepting money from any man willing to pay, I summon as a witness Philostratus himself.

TESTIMONY[18]

{*Philostratus, son of Dionysius, of Colonus, testifies that he knew that Neaera belonged to Nicarete, to whom Metaneira also belonged, and they stayed in his house when they came for the Mysteries from Corinth where they were living, and Lysias, the son of Cephalus, a friend and companion of his, brought them into his house.*}

[24] Later on, men of Athens, Simus of Thessaly came here for the Great Panathenaea, and Neaera here was with him. Nicarete was following, and they lodged at the house of Ctesippus, son of Glauconides, of Cydantidae; and Neaera here was feasting and drinking in the presence of a number of men as a courtesan.[19] And to prove that I am telling the truth, I am calling witnesses for you. [25] Please call Euphiletus, son of Simon, of Aexone, and Aristomachus, son of Critodemus, of Alopece.

---

over Greece. Initiation was open to everyone, and eternal happiness was promised to the initiates.

18. Since the testimonies of private citizens, like that of Philostratus, no longer existed when the manuscripts were later transcribed, scribes subsequently added spurious insertions, such as this one, to eliminate the gaps in the text.

19. Apollodorus is suggesting that the mere presence of Neaera at the symposium in the company of men proves that she was a courtesan. Properly brought up women would not have participated in symposia; however, courtesans, flute players, and other prostitutes regularly provided entertainment for the guests.

WITNESSES

{*Euphiletus, son of Simon, of Aexone, and Aristomachus, son of Critodemus, of Alopece, testify that they know that Simus of Thessaly arrived at Athens for the Great Panathenaea, and along came Nicarete and Neaera, who is now on trial; and they lodged at the house of Ctesippus, son of Glauconides, and Neaera was drinking with them as a courtesan while a number of other men were present and joined the drinking party at the house of Ctesippus.*}

[26] Later on, when she was working in Corinth as a notorious prostitute, she met other lovers, including Xenocleides the poet and Hipparchus the actor, who hired and kept her.[20] I would not be able to produce the testimony of Xenocleides because the laws do not allow him to testify. [27] The reason is that when you sent aid to the rescue of the Spartans, persuaded by Callistratus, he opposed this rescue plan in the Assembly because he had purchased the right to collect the 2 percent tax on grain in peacetime and had to make payments in the Council house every prytany.[21] Although by law he was exempt from service when he did not join this expedition, still he was prosecuted by Stephanus here for evasion of military service, slandered in court, convicted, and disfranchised.[22] [28] Do you not find it is terrible if Stephanus here has deprived from the right to speak those who are citizens by birth and legitimate participants in the city while, in violation of the law, he forces on you those who have no right to be Athenians? But I will call Hipparchus himself and compel him to testify to you or

---

20. Xenocleides was disfranchised and left Athens in 369 to go to Macedonia, where he served as a poet in the court of the king. Philip was offended when Xenocleides hosted some Athenian envoys without permission, and sent him back to Athens in 343. Evidently this speech was delivered after 343, since Xenocleides was away from Athens until that time. Hipparchus was a well known actor who won the Lenaea (see **Dem. 21.10**) at least six times.

21. Each shipment of grain into Attica was subject to a 2 percent tax. The state auctioned the collection of the tax at the beginning of the financial year, and the highest bidder paid a lump sum to the public treasury and then collected the tax throughout the year, certainly with considerable profit.

22. Callistratus was a brilliant orator and a dominant figure in Athenian politics in the 370s and early 360s, but he was prosecuted for the loss of Oropus and condemned to death. There were undoubtedly political motives for the prosecution of Xenocleides, since he had opposed Callistratus' plan to offer aid to Sparta.

deny under oath any knowledge, or I will issue an official summons to him.[23] Please call Hipparchus.

TESTIMONY

{*Hipparchus of Athmonon testifies that Xenocleides and he hired, in Corinth, Neaera, who is now on trial, as one of the courtesans for hire, and that Neaera was drinking with him and Xenocleides the poet in Corinth.*}

[29] After this, two men became her lovers—Timanoridas of Corinth and Eucrates of Leucas. Since Nicarete was extravagant in her demands, expecting them to pay all her household costs, they put down thirty minas, the price for Neaera's person, and bought her outright from Nicarete, according to the law of the city, to be their own slave. And they kept and used her as long as they wanted. [30] But when it was time to get married, they told her that they did not wish to see someone who had been their own courtesan working in Corinth or under a pimp, and they would happily accept on her behalf less money than they paid and see something good happen to her.[24] So they said that they would contribute, towards her freedom, one thousand drachmas—five hundred each—and asked her to find the other twenty minas and pay them off. When she heard that from Eucrates and Timanoridas, she sent for some of her former lovers to come to Corinth, among them Phrynion of Paeania. He was the son of Demon and brother of Demochares and lived an extravagant life of pleasure, as the elders among you may still remember. [31] When Phrynion arrived, she explained to him what Eucrates and Timanoridas had told her and gave him whatever money she had collected in the form of contributions from other lovers as a loan towards her freedom, and all her personal savings. She asked him to supplement the remaining amount towards the twenty minas and pay off Eucrates and Timanoridas on her behalf so that she would be free. [32] He was very glad to hear what she said. He took the money that her other lovers had contributed, added the rest, and paid the twenty minas

---

23. A witness was obliged either to confirm or to deny under oath what the litigant asked him. If he refused to do one or the other he could be summoned formally to do so, and if he still refused he was punished with a fine of one thousand drachmas (MacDowell 1978: 243–44).

24. The prospect of working in the miserable conditions of a cheap brothel would have been very unappealing to a courtesan accustomed to a life of luxury like Neaera. This is why the proposal of Eucrates and Timanoridas was satisfactory for both parties. They got a fair price for Neaera, who was now in her twenties and less valuable, and Neaera gained her freedom.

to Eucrates and Timanoridas, on her behalf, towards her freedom, on the condition that she could not work as a prostitute in Corinth.[25] To prove that I am telling the truth, I call for you the witness who was present. Please call Philagrus of Melite.

TESTIMONY

{*Philagrus of Melite testifies that he was present in Corinth when Phrynion, the brother of Demochares, paid twenty minas for Neaera, who is now on trial, to Timanoridas the Corinthian and Eucrates the Leucadian, and as soon as he paid the money, he left, bringing Neaera with him to Athens.*}

[33] When he brought her here, he treated her in a lewd and rough manner, and taking her with him to the dinner parties, he brought her everywhere he drank. He was partying with her all the time and openly had sex with her whenever and wherever he wanted, showing off his power over her in front of an audience. In addition to the many other houses he took her to for parties, he went to the house of Chabrias of Aexone when he won the Pythian victory in the archonship of Socratides with the four-horse chariot, which he had bought from the sons of Mitys the Argive, and on his return from Delphi, he celebrated with a victory banquet at Colias.[26] There, many others had sex with her while she was drunk and Phrynion was asleep, including the servants who had served the food of Chabrias. [34] To prove that I am telling the truth, I will present for you witnesses who were present and saw it. Please call Chionides of Xypete and Euthetion of Cydathenaeum.

---

25. The manumission of a slave was completed in a variety of ways, but typically it required a written or oral contract in the presence of witnesses. Neaera's manumission was carried out with an oral contract. Philagrus probably was the witness for Phrynion and Neaera, while some Corinthian citizen would have been the witness for her masters. Sometimes certain conditions were added to the terms of a manumission contract, like the obligation for the freed slave to stay with his or her former master for a period of time. The terms of Neaera's manumission were unusual in that she was obliged to stay away in the future not only from her former masters but from Corinth altogether.

26. Chabrias, the victorious general at the battle of Naxos (376), was given life-long tax exemption in return for his services to the city. He accumulated substantial wealth, which allowed him to pursue expensive sports, such as the four-horse chariot race (see Nepos *Chabrias,* passim). The party probably took place at his villa, situated on the promontory of Colias, which is near modern Phalerum (Pollux 9.36). Socratides was archon in 374.

TESTIMONY

{*Chionides of Xypete and Euthetion of Cydathenaeum testify that they were invited by Chabrias to dinner when he was celebrating the chariot victory, and the party was at Colias. They know that Phrynion was present at this dinner with Neaera, who is now on trial. They themselves went to sleep and so did Phrynion and Neaera, and they noticed that a number of men woke up and went to Neaera during the night, including some servants who were the domestic slaves of Chabrias.*}[27]

[35] Since she was insolently abused by Phrynion and not loved as she expected, and he did not do her bidding, she put together some items from his household and all the clothes and jewelry that he had bought for her, and two servant-girls, Thratta and Coccaline, and escaped to Megara.[28] This was the year when Asteius was archon in Athens and you were fighting the second war against the Spartans. [36] She spent two years in Megara, the year of Asteius' archonship and that of Alcisthenes, but her earnings from prostitution were not enough to maintain the entire household. (She was extravagant while the Megarians were mean and petty, and there were not many foreign visitors because there was a war and the Megarians were on the side of Sparta, and you ruled the seas. But she could not go back to Corinth because she had been set free by Eucrates and Timanoridas on the condition that she could not work in Corinth.) [37] So when peace was concluded in the archonship of Phrasicleides and the battle was fought at Leuctra between the Thebans and the Lacedaemonians,[29] it was then that Stephanus here went to Megara and stayed with her, since she was a courtesan, and they became close.

---

27. The testimony, which is almost certainly a forgery, provides a different version of events from that of the text of the orator. In the version of Apollodorus, everything happens in full view of the guests. First Phrynion is showing off his power over Neaera by having sex with her in public. Then, as he passes out, she ends up sleeping with other men while the party is still ongoing. This behavior was perhaps inconceivable for a Hellenistic grammarian, and he toned down this version by converting what was essentially an orgy into a somewhat more respectable, secretive activity in the dark and attributing the lewd behavior exclusively to Neaera.

28. Neaera chose to go to Megara because it was a flourishing center for prostitution. Apollodorus' assertion that this market would normally have many visitors is probably true, since all other centers of prostitution in the Greek world, such as Corinth and Athens, tended also to be major commercial cities (see also Kapparis 1999: ad loc.).

29. Neaera left Athens in the year of Asteius' archonship (373), stayed in Megara during the year of Alcisthenes' archonship (372), and returned to Athens during

She told him about everything that had happened and the abusive behavior of Phrynion and entrusted to him all that she had taken when she
left Phrynion's house. She wanted to live in Athens but was afraid of
Phrynion because she had wronged him and he would be very angry with
her, and she knew that his manner was arrogant and reckless; and so she
placed herself under the protection of Stephanus. [38] He encouraged her
with his words, in Megara, and boasted that Phrynion would bemoan his
fate if he laid so much as a finger on her; he was going to take her as his
wife and introduce the children she already had into his phratry, as if they
were his own, and make them citizens, and nobody would harm her.
So he brought Neaera from Megara with her three children, Proxenus,
Ariston, and a daughter, whom they now call Phano.[30] [39] He put her
and the children into the small house that he owned near the statue of
Whisperer Hermes, between the houses of Dorotheus of Eleusis and of
Cleinomachus, the one that Spintharus has now bought from him for
seven minas.[31] So this was the property that Stephanus owned and nothing else, and he brought her with him for two reasons: in order to have
a beautiful courtesan for free and to have her make money and support
his household, since he had no other income except perhaps whatever he
could make from his sykophantic activities.[32] [40] When Phrynion found
out that she was in town and staying in Stephanus' house, he took a number of young men with him, went to the house of Stephanus, and tried to
take her. And when Stephanus gained her release as a free woman in accordance with the law, Phrynion demanded sureties before the polemarch.[33]

Phrasicleides' archonship (371). The battle of Leuctra, which signaled the end of
Spartan power, occurred in the summer of 371.

30. This information from the orator does not add up, but provides an important
clue for the overall understanding of the case against Neaera. It is difficult to believe
that Neaera had three children in two years from unknown men and, on top of
that, she was trying to make a living as a highly paid courtesan.

31. This property, although small, must have been quite desirable, if we judge from
the fact that the neighbor of Stephanus, Dorotheus, was quite a rich man, and
Spintharus, who later bought the house from Stephanus, was the son of Eubulus,
the most prominent Athenian politician of the time. Maybe Stephanus was not so
destitute that he needed to pimp Neaera in order to secure a living for himself and
his family.

32. See **43** n.

33. Phrynion essentially abducted Neaera, as a though she were a runaway slave,
perhaps hoping that Stephanus would not stand up for her. But when Stephanus
went to the polemarch, the magistrate who oversaw foreigners living in Attica, and
provided sureties to guarantee that Neaera would not leave Athens until a trial was
set to determine her status, Phrynion had to surrender Neaera to Stephanus.

To prove to you that I am telling the truth, I will produce for you as a witness the man who was the polemarch at that time. Call Aeetes of Ceiriadae for me.

TESTIMONY

Aeetes of Ceiriadae testifies that when he was polemarch, sureties were demanded for Neaera, who is now on trial, by Phrynion, the brother of Demochares; and the men who volunteered as sureties for Neaera were Stephanus of Eroeadae, Glaucetes of Cephisia, and Aristocrates of Phalerum.

[41] When sureties had been provided by Stephanus, and while she was living in his house, she continued with her work as usual, though she received higher fees from men wishing to be with her. The excuse was that she already belonged to someone and was living with a man as his wife. He was her accomplice, and if he caught some rich, naive, foreign lover of hers, he trapped him in his house as a seducer[34] and extracted large sums of money, as you can imagine. [42] Neither Stephanus nor Neaera had any property to be able to cope with their daily expenditures, while their spending in the household was endless. She had to support him, herself, the three children she had when she came to him, two servant girls and a manservant, and, of course, she was accustomed to a certain lifestyle, as other men were spending on her in the past. [43] Moreover, Stephanus had no serious income from his political activities; he was still only a sykophant—one of those who make noise near the rostrum and, for a fee, initiate indictments and denunciations and introduce the proposals of others under their own name—and had not yet become a politician until Callistratus of Aphidna took him under his wing.[35] How this happened and for what reason, I shall tell you after I show that Neaera here is an alien and has committed grave offenses against you and impiety against the gods [44] so that you can see that this man too deserves no lesser punishment than Neaera here, but a much greater one. For someone who claims to be an Athenian, he has held the laws and you and the gods in such contempt. And he has the insolence not to keep quiet out of shame for his wrongdoings, but, by slandering others and me, he has brought

---

34. For the law on seduction, see the introduction to **Lysias 1**.

35. Certain citizens, whom the Athenians called sykophants, were believed to make it a practice to pursue malicious lawsuits, often for financial gain. Apollodorus accuses Stephanus of having engaged in such litigation because of his poverty, until he later became a wealthy politician under the patronage of Callistratus.

upon her and himself a trial that has revealed who she is and exposed him as an evil man. [45] When Phrynion began legal proceedings against him on the grounds that he had improperly secured the release of Neaera here as a free woman and that he had received the goods which she had stolen from his house when she left, their friends brought them together and persuaded them to submit the case to arbitration.[36] Satyrus of Alopece, the brother of Lacedaemonius, sat as an arbitrator on behalf of Phrynion, and Saurias of Lamptrae on behalf of Stephanus, and in common they chose Diogeiton of Acharnae. [46] When they met at the temple and heard what both of them and the woman herself had to say about the facts, they pronounced judgment by which all the parties abided. The woman herself was to be free and her own mistress, but everything Neaera had taken from the house of Phrynion when she left, except her clothes, jewelry, and slaves, which had been bought as personal gifts, should be returned to Phrynion. She was to live an equal number of days with each of the two men, but if they came to a different arrangement this should be valid, too; maintenance for the woman was to be provided by the man with whom she was at the time, and in future they should remain friends and bear no grudges.[37] [47] This was the settlement between Phrynion and Stephanus concerning Neaera here, as determined by the arbitrators. To prove that I am telling you the truth, the clerk will read for you the testimony on these facts. Please call Satyrus of Alopece, Saurias of Lamptrae, and Diogeiton of Acharnae.

---

36. The procedure used in this case was an *aphairesis eis eleutherian* (literally, "removal to freedom"), which gave a third party the right to secure the release of a person who had been seized as a runaway slave (see **Lys. 23.9** n.; cf. **Aesch. 1.62**). This was a dangerous lawsuit for Neaera, despite the fact that Phrynion had no true and legitimate claim against her. So, it was sensible for both parties to resolve their differences out of court, through private arbitration. The arbitrators could simply produce a ruling in favor of one side, but they usually tried to work out a compromise and reconcile the two parties, as is the case here.

37. It is obvious that the arbitrators did not expect this unusual arrangement to last long, and this is why they incorporated stipulations that allowed for future amendments to their ruling by mutual agreement. Their immediate aim was to calm the two men down and prevent further animosities from arising between them by allowing each of them to share Neaera's company. Clearly they considered her to be a *hetaira*. The arbitrators probably judged the situation correctly, since Phrynion seems to have been satisfied by the arrangement and did not pursue the matter further. It would be reasonable to assume that Neaera persuaded him to let her live with Stephanus.

TESTIMONY

Satyrus of Alopece, Saurias of Lamptrae, and Diogeiton of Acharnae testify that they reconciled Phrynion and Stephanus over Neaera, who is now on trial, as appointed arbitrators. The settlement in accordance with which the dispute was settled is the one presented by Apollodorus.

SETTLEMENT

{They brought a settlement between Phrynion and Stephanus on these terms: each man would use Neaera for an equal number of days every month, unless they came to a different arrangement between themselves.}[38]

[48] Once the reconciliation had been effected, those who had stood by each party in the arbitration and the whole affair did what I think usually happens, especially when the quarrel is about a courtesan: they went to each other's house for parties every time each man had Neaera, and she was dining and drinking with them as a courtesan. To prove that I am telling the truth, please call as witnesses those who were with them, Eubulus of Probalinthus, Diopeithes of Melite, Cteson of Cerameis.

WITNESSES

{Eubulus of Probalinthus, Diopeithes of Melite, and Cteson of Cerameis testify that when the reconciliation over Neaera took place between Phrynion and Stephanus, they often dined and drank with Neaera who is now on trial, when Neaera was in the house of Stephanus and also when she was in the house of Phrynion.}

[49] That she was initially a slave, sold twice, performed the bodily work of a courtesan, escaped from Phrynion to Megara, and, when she returned, sureties were demanded on her behalf before the polemarch, since she was an alien, I have shown in my speech and supported through testimonies. Now I wish to prove to you that Stephanus himself has testified against her that she is an alien. [50] The daughter of Neaera here, whom she brought to him as a small child and they used

---

38. On the grounds of content, it is likely that the first of the documents announcing the second is genuine, while the second is a forgery.

to call Strybele but now they call Phano,[39] was betrothed by Stephanus here, as his own daughter, to an Athenian—Phrastor of Aegilia; and he gave with her a dowry of thirty minas.[40] When she came to Phrastor, a hard worker who had amassed his property through miserly savings, she did not know how to adjust to Phrastor's ways but was still following her mother's habits and lax morals because, I think, she was brought up with such license. [51]. Phrastor saw that she was not properly behaved and did not wish to obey him, and he had obtained reliable information that she was not Stephanus' daughter but Neaera's, and he had been deceived when he married her as a daughter of Stephanus and not Neaera, but born to him by a citizen woman before he took Neaera as his wife. So he became enraged by all of this, and believing that he had been insulted and deceived, he threw the woman out of the house while she was pregnant, ending a marriage that lasted about a year, and he refused to return the dowry.[41] [52] Stephanus initiated legal proceedings against him at the Odeum[42] for the interest of the dowry in accordance with the law that states that if a man divorces his wife, he must return the dowry or else pay interest at the rate of nine obols and the legal guardian of the woman may sue for the interest at the Odeum on her behalf. Phrastor, in return, indicted Stephanus here before the *thesmothetai* in accordance with the following law, on the grounds that he had given to him as a wife the daughter of an alien woman, pretending that she was related to him. Please read it.[43]

---

39. Apollodorus is implying that they changed her name from one that was servile to one suitable for a well-born Athenian woman.

40. Thirty minas is an average dowry; Phano was given in marriage to a husband who was well-off but apparently mean and miserly.

41. Apollodorus wants the jury to believe that Phrastor divorced his wife because of doubts about her citizen status, but he also hints at irreconcilable differences. Since Phrastor was later prepared to go to court and assert that she was a legitimate Athenian, it is likely that their divorce had nothing to do with any doubts about his wife's status.

42. The Odeum was a roofed theater, which during the day functioned as a court for lawsuits regarding unpaid interest on loans.

43. Regardless of his reasons for the divorce, Phrastor was obligated to return the dowry. By failing to do so, the dowry became in essence a loan with a monthly interest rate of 18 percent, which he was required to pay to her guardian for her maintenance (*sitos*) until he relinquished the dowry. Phrastor's withholding of the dowry was undoubtedly unlawful; he resorted to blackmail in order to intimidate Stephanus into giving up his claim.

LAW

If anyone betroths an alien woman to an Athenian man under the pretext that she is related to him, he is to be disfranchised and his property confiscated, and one-third is to go to the successful prosecutor. Let those who are entitled bring a prosecution before the thesmothetai, as in the case of a prosecution for being an alien.

[53] He read to you the law under which Stephanus here was indicted by Phrastor before the *thesmothetai*. Since he knew that he was in danger of suffering severe penalties if convicted for the betrothal of the daughter of an alien woman, he came to terms with Phrastor and abandoned his claim to the dowry; he dropped the lawsuit for the interest, and then Phrastor withdrew his prosecution from the *thesmothetai*. To prove that I am telling the truth, I call Phrastor himself as a witness to these events, and I will compel him to testify in accordance with the law. [54] Please call Phrastor of Aegilia.

TESTIMONY

{*Phrastor of Aegilia testifies: When he realized that Stephanus had betrothed to him an alien woman under the pretext that she was his own daughter, he brought an indictment before the thesmothetai in accordance with the law, and threw the woman out of his house and was no longer living with her. When Stephanus started legal proceedings for the interest against him at the Odeum, Stephanus reached a settlement with him under the terms that the indictment before the thesmothetai was to be withdrawn as well as the lawsuit for the interest, which Stephanus initiated against me.*}[44]

[55] Now, if you wish, I will present another testimony, from Phrastor and the members of his phratry and *genos,* that Neaera here is an alien. Not long after Phrastor divorced the daughter of Neaera, he fell ill and was in a terrible condition and very needy. As there was an old feud with his family and

---

44. Phrastor was an unwilling witness because any doubt cast upon the status of Phano would have raised questions about the citizenship of his son, who was probably a teenager or perhaps even an adult and already recognized as a legitimate citizen by the time of this trial. Since Phrastor would only have agreed to testify about his divorce from Phano and would have refused to confirm statements that were incriminating and that called into question the legitimacy of his son, the document inserted at this point is almost certainly spurious.

a lot of anger and hatred, and he was childless, too, Neaera and her daughter were comforting him in his illness. [56] They were going to his house when he was unwell and had no one to look after him, bringing along what was good for his condition and keeping an eye on him—and you know yourselves how valuable a woman is in sickness, looking after an ill man. He was finally persuaded to take back the baby and acknowledge him as his legitimate son whom Neaera's daughter had after he threw her out when she was pregnant, because he found out that she was not Stephanus' daughter but Neaera's, and he was very angry at her deception. [57] His thinking was human and understandable: he was unwell and there was little hope of survival, so he acknowledged the boy as his legitimate son and took him back, in order to stop his relatives from inheriting his property and to avoid dying childless. And I will prove to you with substantial and indisputable evidence that he would never have done so if he had been healthy. [58] As soon as Phrastor recovered from this illness and got back on his feet and felt better, he married a citizen woman, the legitimate daughter of Satyrus of Melite and sister of Diphilus.[45] This should prove to you that he did not take back the boy willingly but was forced by illness, childlessness, and hostility towards his family so that he could stop them from inheriting his property if something happened to him. And this will be better illustrated by what followed. [59] When Phrastor was ill, he introduced his son by the daughter of Neaera to his phratry and the *genos* of the Brytidae, to which he belonged, and the members of the *genos* voted against the boy and refused to enroll him. I believe they knew who the woman was whom Phrastor had married first—the daughter of Neaera—and that the woman was cast out and that in his illness he had been persuaded to take back the boy.[46] [60] When Phrastor sued them over their refusal to enroll his son, the members of the *genos* challenged him before the arbitrator to take an oath that he considered him to be his son by a citizen woman whom he had married according to the law. When the members of the *genos* addressed this chal-lenge to him before the arbitrator, Phrastor declined the oath and did not

---

45. The orator suggests that Phrastor remarried in order to have legitimate children because he knew his son from Phano was illegitimate; however, Phrastor's subsequent actions prove otherwise.

46. The phratry and *genos* were traditional religious bodies with significant community functions. Since only legitimate Athenians were admitted, membership offered proof of citizenship, albeit not definitive. All Athenian men still had to be enrolled in a deme when they reached adulthood in order to exercise the rights of citizenship, and it was this vote of the deme that determined whether an individual was of Athenian descent (see the introduction to **Isaeus 12**).

swear it.⁴⁷ [61] To prove that what I say is true, I will provide witnesses from the Brytidae for you.

WITNESSES

Timostratus of Hecale, Xanthippus of Eroeadae, Eualces of Phalerum, Anytus of Laciadae, Euphranor of Aegilia, and Nicippus of Cephale, testify that they and Phrastor of Aegilia are members of the genos called Brytidae, and when Phrastor requested the enrollment of his son into the genos, they put obstacles to the introduction of Phrastor's son because they had personal knowledge that he was the son of Phrastor by the daughter of Neaera.

[62] So I provide solid proof to you that even the closest relatives of Neaera here have testified against her that she is an alien: Stephanus here, her keeper who lives with her as her husband, and Phrastor, who took her daughter. Stephanus has done so by being unwilling to go to court to defend the interests of her daughter and by giving up the dowry and failing to reclaim it when Phrastor prosecuted him before the *thesmothetai* on the grounds that he had betrothed an alien woman to him, an Athenian man. [63] Phrastor has done so by divorcing the daughter of Neaera here as soon as he found out that she was not the daughter of Stephanus, without returning the dowry. Later he was persuaded to acknowledge the boy as his legitimate son and introduce him to the *genos* because of his illness, childlessness, and enmity towards his relatives. However, when the members of the *genos* voted to reject him and challenged him to take an oath, he did not want to swear an oath but chose to avoid perjury, and he later married a citizen woman in accordance with the law. These actions, because they are so visible, provide important testimony against them, that Neaera here is a foreigner.

---

47. Without a doubt the oath that the *genos* challenged Phrastor to take is misrepresented here. He would have had no difficulty swearing that the boy was legitimately born from a citizen woman, since this was the normal requirement for admission to the *genos*. Most likely the *genos* had phrased the oath so that Phrastor had to refuse to swear it. This weak evidence clearly did not carry any weight with the arbitrator, whose decision Apollodorus neglects to mention for obvious reasons. If Phrastor had lost, he certainly would have called attention to the arbitrator's decision because then he would have had substantial proof that Phano was not an Athenian. So we can assume from his omission that the arbitrator found in favor of Phrastor.

[64] Just consider the greed and wickedness of this man Stephanus and you will see from this too that Neaera here is not a citizen. Epaenetus of Andrus, who was a former lover of Neaera and had spent a lot of money on her and stayed with them every time he was in Athens because of his friendship with Neaera, fell victim of a plot by Stephanus here. [65] He was invited to the country under the pretext of a sacrifice, and he was caught seducing the daughter of Neaera here, and after much intimidation, he was compelled to agree to a compensation of thirty minas. Then he accepted as sureties Aristomachus, a former *thesmothetes,* and Nausiphilus, son of Nausinicus, the former archon, and set him free in order to return with the money.[48] [66] When Epaenetus was set free and became master of himself again, he indicted Stephanus here before the *thesmothetai* for wrongful imprisonment in accordance with the provisions of the law, which lays down the following: if anyone wrongly imprisons a man as a seducer, the victim may bring an indictment before the *thesmothetai* on the grounds that he was wrongly imprisoned, and if he secures the conviction of the man who imprisoned him and it is judged that he was the victim of an unjust plot, he is to be innocent and the sureties are to be free from liability; but if he is judged to be a seducer, it is laid down that the sureties must hand him over to the successful litigant, and he is to inflict upon him in the courtroom any punishment he wishes, without using a knife, as one would with a seducer.[49] [67] Epaenetus indicted him in accordance with this law, admitting that he had used the woman but not that he was a seducer. His arguments were that she was not the daughter of Stephanus but Neaera's, and her mother was aware of her relation with him, and he had spent a lot of money on them and provided for the entire household when he was staying with them. He produced the law on the subject, which forbids accusations of seduction with one of those women established in brothels or visibly practicing any form of prostitution, claiming that this place too, the house of Stephanus, was

---

48. Other than the assertion of Apollodorus that Stephanus and Neaera treated Phano as a courtesan, there is no evidence to support this version of the events. Her treatment as a courtesan was incompatible with the relentless attempts of her family to secure a dowry and find a husband for her. More likely this was a genuine case of seduction.

49. This law was introduced in the classical period in order to deal with abuses of the seduction laws with a view to profit. Someone who had imprisoned a person as a seducer and forced him to agree to a settlement might need to face him in court and convince the jury that seduction had been committed before he could claim the settlement money.

a brothel, and this was their trade, and they were doing very well from it.⁵⁰ [68] While Epaenetus was using such language and had submitted the indictment, Stephanus here, knowing that he would be exposed as a brothel-keeper and a sykophant, proposed to Epaenetus to submit the dispute to the arbitration of the same men who had served as sureties on condition that they were to be released from liability and Epaenetus was to withdraw the indictment. [69] Epaenetus was persuaded to accept these terms and withdrew the indictment against Stephanus, for which he was plaintiff. When a meeting was held and the sureties sat as arbitrators, Stephanus had no rightful claim to make. He begged Epaenetus for some contribution towards a dowry for the daughter of Neaera, going on about his own poverty and the woman's earlier misfortune with Phrastor and saying that he had lost the dowry and he would not be able to find a husband for her again. [70] "You have used the woman," he said, "and doing something good for her would be the right thing," and other deceptive words like these, which someone in need would say from a position of weakness. The arbitrators listened to both of them and reconciled them and persuaded Epaenetus to contribute one thousand drachmas towards a dowry for the daughter of Neaera. To prove that everything I am saying is true, I call for you as witnesses the same men who served as sureties and arbitrators.

WITNESSES

[71] *Nausiphilus of Cephale and Aristomachus of Cephale testify that they served as sureties on behalf of Epaenetus of Andrus when Stephanus claimed that he caught Epaenetus seducing his daughter; and when Epaenetus went away from the house of Stephanus and became his own master, he indicted Stephanus before the thesmothetai on the grounds that he had unlawfully confined him; and serving as conciliators, they reconciled Epaenetus and Stephanus. The terms of the settlement are those produced by Apollodorus.*

---

50. If Stephanus had gone to court, he would have in effect made his entire household the subject of ridicule and public gossip. This is why he readily agreed to arbitration, which was a more appropriate procedure for his purposes. Epaenetus was then persuaded to accept a compromise and make a contribution of ten minas, which was one-third of the initially agreed sum of thirty minas, to be used as part of Phano's dowry. This suggests that he recognized that Phano was not a courtesan but a poor Athenian woman in need of a dowry.

SETTLEMENT

{*The conciliators reconciled Stephanus and Epaenetus on these terms: no reference should be made to the events surrounding the confinement; however, Epaenetus should give Phano one thousand drachmas towards a dowry because he has used her many times, and Stephanus should hand over Phano to Epaenetus whenever he is in town and wishes to have intercourse with her.*}[51]

[72] Although she was openly regarded as an alien and he dared to seize the man whom he caught with her as a seducer, Stephanus and Neaera here reached such a degree of insolence and shamelessness that they could not be content with the claim that she was a citizen. When they saw that Theogenes of the Coironidae, a man of noble birth but poor and inexperienced in public affairs, had been selected as *basileus,* Stephanus here offered support and financial assistance during his scrutiny and earned his favor and bought from him the office of his assessor. Moreover, he gave him this woman, the daughter of Neaera, to be his lawful wife, betrothed like his own daughter.[52] Such was the level of contempt he felt for you and the laws. [73] And this woman performed the most secret rituals on behalf of the city and saw what, as an alien, she should not have been allowed to see. Although she was a disreputable woman, she entered where no other Athenian may enter, except the wife of the *basileus,* and administered the oath to the Venerable Women, who serve the temples, and was given as a wife to Dionysus, and performed the holy and secret traditional rites for the gods on behalf of the city. How could it be within the boundaries of piety if any woman at all can perform rites that it is not permissible for everyone even to hear, especially if that woman is of this character and has done such things?[53]

---

51. It would be absurd if Epaenetus retained conjugal rights after providing Stephanus with a substantial contribution for a dowry that was to be offered to her future husband, and this is the primary reason against the authenticity of this settlement.

52. Stephanus was willing to support the new *basileus* and even give him his daughter in marriage because he wanted to be appointed as his assessor (*paredros*). The two assessors of each of the three senior archons (*basileus,* polemarch, eponymous archon) were directly appointed by the archons themselves.

53. In this digression Apollodorus describes the festival of Anthesteria (see **76** n.), a discussion that is irrelevant as far as the legal facts of the case go. However, by reminding the jurors of those sacred rituals, he seeks to impress upon them how her actions were also offenses against the gods and cannot be overlooked because the whole city might be punished for them.

[74] But let me return to the beginning and speak to you about each one of these issues in greater detail so that you can administer a more severe punishment and see that you are not only about to vote on behalf of your-selves and the gods but also for religious observance, by imposing penalties for the impious acts and punishing the offenders. In ancient times, men of Athens, the city was a monarchy, and the kingship traditionally belonged to those most distinguished, because they were autochthonous.[54] The *basi-leus* used to make all the sacrifices while some very solemn and secret rites were performed by his wife, naturally because she was the *basilinna*.[55] [75] However, when Theseus unified them and established the democracy and the population of the city increased, the people nonetheless elected the *basileus,* on merit, from preselected candidates, and they introduced a law prescribing that his wife should be a citizen woman who had not had intercourse with another man; she should be a virgin when he married her. The purpose of this was that the secret rites would be performed on behalf of the city in accordance with the ancestral custom, and what was due to the gods would be performed with piety, without omissions or innova-tions. [76] This law they inscribed on stone and placed in the sanctuary of Dionysus at the Marshes, next to the altar (and this stone is standing to this day, while the inscription in faint Attic characters is still legible). The people offered the god this contract of piety, and that heritage was passed on to future generations, stating that "we expect the woman who will be given to you as your wife and perform the rituals to be of this quality." The reason why it was placed in the oldest and most holy sanctuary of Dionysus at the Marshes is that not many people would know the content of the inscription, because the sanctuary is open only one day a year, the twelfth of Anthesterion.[56] [77] So you should be concerned, too, men of Athens, about the holy and solemn rites of which your ancestors took such great

---

54. For the myth of autochthony—that the Athenians were born from the ground and had always lived in Attica—see Rosavich 1987, Loraux 1993, Shapiro 1998.

55. This was probably an ancient title of the wife of the *basileus*, which survived into the classical period.

56. The festival of the Anthesteria (literally, "flower festival") was a fertility festival celebrated in February in honor of Dionysus, when the trees were in full blossom and the new wine was ready. On the first day of the festival the jars with the new wine were opened; the second day there was a central celebration in downtown Athens, with the magnificent rituals of the sacred marriage of Dionysus to the *basilinna* and a marital procession of a wooden statue of the god and his new wife to the old residence of the *basileus*, the Boukoleion. The third day was devoted to the dead and the gods of the underworld, typically associated with fertility in Greek and oriental myth. As the *basilinna* Phano would have been given as a wife to Dionysus during the ritual. See Hamilton 1992.

care with so much splendor. And they, who so insolently have shown their contempt for your laws and so impudently their disrespect for the gods, deserve to be punished for two reasons: so that they may suffer the consequences for their actions and so that others may be cautioned and be wary of committing crimes against the gods and the city. [78] I would also like to call for you the sacred herald, who assists the wife of the *basileus* when she administers the oath to the basket-bearing Venerable Women by the altar, before they touch the sacrifices, so that you may hear the permissible parts of oath and realize how solemn and holy and ancient these rites are.

OATH OF THE VENERABLE WOMEN

I live a holy life, and I am clean and pure from anything that is unclean, including intercourse with a man. And I celebrate the Theoinia and Iobaccheia for Dionysus in accordance with the ancestral custom and at the appointed times.[57]

[79] You have heard the oath and the ancestral rituals that are permitted to mention and how the woman, whom Stephanus betrothed as his own daughter to Theogenes when he was *basileus,* performed these rituals and administered the oath to the Venerable Women, and not even the women who see these rites are permitted to divulge them to anyone else. Let me now provide for you testimony that is secret but evidently true, as I will demonstrate from the facts themselves. [80] When these celebrations were over and the nine archons went up to the Areopagus on the appointed days, without delay the council of the Areopagus, the most worthy body in the city in matters of piety, launched an inquiry on the wife of Theogenes and started investigating. It was concerned about the rituals and was inclined to fine Theogenes within the limits of its authority, but in secret and discreetly, since the council does not have unlimited authority to punish an Athenian in any way it wishes.[58] [81] There was an argument, and the

---

57. The Venerable Women (*gerairai*) were respectable priestesses. This oath seems to signify their entry to office, since they promise to celebrate other Dionysiac rituals, too, in the future. The oath was probably administered at the beginning of the sacred marriage ceremony; afterwards the *gerairai* would assist the *basilinna* with the ritual.

58. The nine archons joined the Areopagus for life at the end of their year in office. Thus the Areopagus would treat the current archons as provisional members and might require of them the same degree of respectability that it required from its permanent members. The Council, like most Athenian authorities, had the right to impose modest fines on the spot for minor offenses and could also bring offenders

council of the Areopagus was unhappy and wanted to fine Theogenes because he had taken a wife of this sort and let her perform the secret rituals
on behalf of the city. Theogenes started pleading with them and implor-
ing, saying that he did not know she was the daughter of Neaera. He said
that he had been deceived by Stephanus when he married her, believing
that she was his legitimate daughter in accordance with the law, and it was
because of his own inexperience in public affairs and his innocence that
he appointed Stephanus as his assessor, so that he could handle the challenges of his office with a friend at his side, and for this reason he became
his son-in-law. [82] "And I will show you," he said, "that I am not lying,
with clear and unambiguous proof: I will cast out of my house the woman,
since she is not Stephanus' daughter but Neaera's. If I do this, you should
believe me that I was deceived; if I don't, punish me as a wicked man who
has committed crimes against the gods." [83] Since Theogenes was making such promises and pleading, the council of the Areopagus felt sorry for
him because of his naivety and believed that he had been truly deceived by
Stephanus; so it cancelled the fine. As soon as Theogenes left the Areopagus, he
immediately expelled this woman, the daughter of Neaera, from his house
and dismissed Stephanus, the man who had deceived him, from office. So
the Areopagites ended their proceedings against Theogenes and were not
angry with him, and they forgave him because he had been deceived.[59]
[84] To prove that what I am saying is the truth, I call Theogenes himself
as a witness to these events, and I will compel him to testify. Please call
Theogenes of Erchia.

TESTIMONY

{*Theogenes of Erchia testifies that when he was basileus, he married
Phano as a daughter of Stephanus, but when he realized that he had been
deceived, he divorced the woman and was no longer living with her, and*

---

to court for more serious offenses. At the time of Neaera's trial, the Areopagus
functioned primarily as a court for cases of deliberate homicide, but it retained
the right to perform its own investigations and provide reports (*apophasis*) to the
Assembly.

59. Apollodorus suggests that Theogenes was fined by the Areopagus because it
discovered that his wife was a courtesan of foreign descent. If so, a modest fine
was certainly insufficient. Such a fairly lenient treatment would only have been
justified if Theogenes was truly unaware of her previous marriage. Still, he could
have chosen to pay the fine and remain married to her, but under no circumstances
would he have been permitted to do so if the Areopagus believed that she was
an alien.

dismissed Stephanus from the office of assessor and no longer allowed him to be his assessor. }[60]

[85] Now take the law on these matters and read it, so that you can see that a woman of this sort, who had committed such acts, ought to keep away not only from these rites but also from all other rites in Athens, from viewing and sacrificing and performing traditional religious duties on behalf of the city. For a woman with whom a seducer has been caught is not allowed to enter any of the public temples, into which the laws admit even the alien woman and the slave who comes as a spectator or a suppliant. [86] The only women barred by the law from entering public temples are those caught with a seducer. If she enters and breaks the law, she can suffer anything whatsoever, except death, at the hands of anyone who wishes, and that person will not be punished. The law allows anyone who wishes to inflict the punishment for such offenses. That is why it allows any other form of humiliation, without the right of redress, except death, in order to prevent pollution and impiety in the temples and inspire sufficient fear among women to live properly and refrain from mischief and meticulously perform their household duties. It teaches her that, if she commits a crime like this, she will be expelled from her husband's house and from the temples of the city at the same time. [87] And you will know that it is so after hearing a reading of the law. Please take it.

LAW OF SEDUCTION

After he catches the seducer, the man who caught him shall not be permitted to continue living with the woman in marriage. If he continues living with her in marriage he is to be disfranchised. And whoever is caught with a seducer shall not be permitted to enter the public temples. If she enters, she is to suffer whatever humiliation she suffers, except death, with impunity.

[88] Now I will provide for you, men of Athens, testimony of the Athenian people, showing how much importance it attaches to these rituals and how much care has been provided. Although the Athenian people is the sovereign authority over everything in the city and can do whatever it wishes, it considered becoming an Athenian citizen to be such a fine and solemn gift that it imposed laws on itself with which it must comply if it wishes to make someone a citizen. These laws have now been abused by Stephanus here and by those who have conducted marriages in a similar manner. [89] Once you hear these laws, you will understand them better and realize how they have ridiculed the finest and most solemn gifts, reserved for

---

60. The pointless repetitions in this document suggest that it is spurious.

the benefactors of the city. First there is a law for the people, which states that it is not possible to make someone an Athenian unless he deserves to become a citizen because of good service to the Athenian people.[61] Next, once the people is convinced and grants the award, it does not allow the naturalization to become valid before it is approved in the next Assembly by secret ballot of at least six thousand Athenians.[62] [90] The law orders the presidents to place the ballot boxes and allow the vote as the people are coming in, before the foreign visitors enter and the fences are removed, so that each person may consider in private who the man is who is going to be made a citizen and whether he is worthy of the gift.[63] After this it allows any Athenian who wishes to initiate an indictment for illegal proposal, and it is possible to come to court and prove that the man does not deserve the gift but has become an Athenian contrary to the laws.[64] [91] And already there have been cases where, although the people offered the gift, deceived by the words of those who proposed it, a prosecution for an illegal proposal was brought before the court, the beneficiary of the award was judged unworthy of it, and the court took it away. It would be difficult to go through a lot of old cases, but you all remember Peitholas of Thessaly and Apollonides of Olynthus, who were made citizens by the people but the court removed the award. [92] These events did not happen that long ago to be forgotten. In addition, although the laws regulating citizenship awards and the steps for someone to become an Athenian are so well and firmly laid down, there is another, very important law attached to all these. Such great

---

61. Service to the city of Athens remained the only pathway to citizenship throughout the classical period, but it was more liberally interpreted in the fourth century, when rich foreigners became citizens because of their generous donations to the public treasury and foreign potentates were offered citizenship for diplomatic reasons.

62. Since a citizenship award was essentially viewed as legislation for one person (*ep andri*), the standard procedure for such decrees was followed, which required a quorum of six thousand citizens voting in secret.

63. This passage is difficult to understand. Portable fences were probably placed at the entranceway to the Assembly and directed citizens into an area where they could vote in secret; then they were removed before the meeting began.

64. Any decree proposed in the Assembly could be challenged as unconstitutional. Thus a citizenship award could be revoked any time, even years later, as political and personal alliances and circumstances changed. The case of Apollonides, the leader of the anti-Macedonian faction of Olynthus, who was awarded citizenship on account of his political activities against Philip, is a clear example. As the anti-Macedonian faction fell in and out of favor in the messy politics of the 340s, Apollonides seems to have been the victim of a changing political climate, and he lost his citizenship in court.

care has the people taken, for its own sake and for the gods, to make sure that the sacrifices on behalf of the city are performed properly. Naturalized Athenian citizens are explicitly banned by law from becoming one of the nine archons or holding any priesthood. However, the people has allowed its offspring an equal share in all rights and privileges with the additional clause: "if they are born of a citizen woman, betrothed in accordance with the law."[65] [93] I will show you with clear and compelling proof that I am telling the truth. I would like to go back to the origins of this law and explain to you how it was introduced and for whose benefit. These were good men, loyal friends of the people. Through all this you will realize that the gift reserved for the benefactors of the people was abused and that many important privileges have been snatched from your control by Stephanus here and those who have conducted marriages and fathered children in the same manner as he did.[66]

[94] The Plataeans, men of Athens, alone among the Greeks offered you help at Marathon, when Datis—the general of king Darius—left Eretria after he subdued Euboea, landed in our territory with a large force, and began to ravage it. To the present day the painting in the Stoa Poikile stands as a reminder of their bravery, for each one has been depicted as helping out as fast as he could, . . . the ones wearing Boeotian caps.[67] [95] Again when Xerxes came after Greece, while the Thebans medized, the Plataeans did not dare to abandon their friendship with you, but, alone among the Boeotians, half of them lined up with the Lacedaemonians and Leonidas at Thermopylae against the attacking barbarians and fell with them, while the rest embarked on your triremes, as they did not have vessels of their own, and fought by your side in the sea battles at Artemisium and Salamis.[68] [96] They also participated in the final battle at Plataea against Mardonius, the king's general, with you and those who liberated Greece, and they gained freedom as a common prize for the other Greeks. Later on, Pausanias, the king of

---

65. This restriction was for religious reasons and had minimal impact upon the life of a new citizen (see Kapparis 1995: 359–78).

66. In the following sections, the orator compares and contrasts the way the Plataeans obtained citizenship with the allegedly illegal maneuvers of Stephanus and Neaera. From a legal point of view this very long digression is irrelevant, but the emotional impact of this famous historical incident was potentially tremendous.

67. Besides oral tradition, Apollodorus relies on a famous painting on the Painted Stoa in the Athenian agora as a source for the battle of Marathon. Unfortunately it seems that a sentence or two have dropped out of his description in our manuscripts.

68. The narrative at this point is based on oral tradition with certain inaccuracies, in order to amplify the contribution of the Plataeans (e.g., the Plataeans did not participate in the battle of Thermopylae).

the Lacedaemonians, tried to insult you and was not satisfied with the fact that the Lacedaemonians alone were honored by the Greeks with leadership while our city in reality was the champion of freedom of the Greeks but out of courtesy did not stand up against the Spartans in order to avoid arousing jealousy among the allies. [97] Pausanias, the king of the Lacedaemonians, swollen with arrogance inscribed on the tripod in Delphi, which the Greeks who fought the battle at Plataea and the naval battle at Salamis jointly made and dedicated to Apollo as a memorial of the victory against the barbarians:

> Leader of the Greeks, because he destroyed an army of Medes,
> Pausanias dedicated this monument to Phoebus

as though this accomplishment and the dedication were his own and not the joint enterprise by the allies.[69] [98] The Greeks were furious, and the Plataeans, on behalf of the allies, brought an indictment against the Lacedaemonians, before the Amphictyony, for one thousand talents and compelled them to erase these verses and inscribe the names of the cities that had taken part in the undertaking. This was the main reason why enmity ensued from the Lacedaemonian side, and the royal houses in particular. At the time, the Lacedaemonians could not decide how to deal with them, but about fifty years later Archidamus, son of Zeuxidamus, king of the Lacedaemonians, attempted to seize their city in peacetime.[70] [99] He carried out this attack from Thebes through Eurymachus, son of Leontiades, one of the Boeotarchs, while Naucleides and some others with him opened the gates during the night, after receiving bribes. When the Plataeans sensed that the Thebans had entered during the night and that their city had been suddenly seized in peacetime, they started coming together and preparing for battle. At daybreak they saw that there were not many Thebans, since only the first wave had come in. Heavy rain during the night had prevented the bulk of them from entering. The river Asopus was running high, and it could not be easily crossed, and in addition it was night. [100] When the Plataeans saw the Thebans in the city and realized that part of the invading force was absent, they attacked, defeated them in a battle, and destroyed them before the

---

69. The differences from the written accounts of this incident are considerable (e.g., Thuc. 1.132). Apollodorus is probably drawing on oral tradition and using his own memory of the tripod at Delphi.

70. Without a doubt, Apollodorus has used Books 2 and 3 of Thucydides as a source for his discussion on the siege and capture of Plataea. However, he has condensed the account and changed the details to make it more exciting and flattering for the Plataeans and the Athenians. The events described here took place between 431 and 427. The attack on Plataea is considered by Thucydides to be the opening act of the Peloponnesian War.

others could come to their aid. Then they sent a messenger to you to tell you about the event, announce that they had won the battle, and ask for help in case the Thebans ravaged their land. When the Athenians heard about these events, right away they sent aid to Plataea, and when the Thebans saw, they went home. [101] Because the Thebans failed in this attempt and the Plataeans killed the men they had captured alive in the battle, the Lacedaemonians, motivated by anger, marched out against the Plataeans without any justification. They ordered all the Peloponnesians except the Argives to send two-thirds of each city's army, and called upon all the other Boeotians, the Locrians, the Phocians, the Malians, the Oetaeans, and the Aenians to march out in full force. [102] They besieged the walls of Plataea with large forces and proposed terms, stating that if they surrendered the city to them they could keep the land and have the benefit of their possessions, and they should give up their alliance with Athens. When the Plataeans did not agree but responded that they would do nothing without the Athenians, they besieged them, enclosing the city with a double wall for ten years, using multiple devices of all kinds. [103] When the Plataeans became desperate and had nothing left and could not think of any salvation, they cast lots among themselves. One group remained and continued the effort of the siege, while the other watched for a night with heavy rain and strong wind, came out of the city and climbed over the enclosing wall of the enemy, escaping the attention of the army after they slaughtered the guards, and arrived here unexpectedly, in a terrible state. But of those who stayed behind, once the city had been taken by force, the adult males were slaughtered while the children and the women were sold into slavery, whoever had not escaped to Athens when they saw that the Lacedaemonians were on their way. [104] Now think again how you awarded citizenship to those men who proved so abundantly their love for the people and left everything behind—their belongings, children, and wives. Your own decisions will shed light upon the law, and you will know that I am telling the truth. Please take this decree and read it out to them.

DECREE CONCERNING THE PLATAEANS[71]

Hippocrates proposed that the Plataeans be Athenians from this day, fully enfranchised like the other Athenians, and they will have a share in

---

71. The decree, which should have been preserved on the Acropolis at the time of this trial, was Apollodorus' only source. As someone who was granted citizenship when he was a teenager through the decree naturalizing his father, Apollodorus was probably fairly knowledgeable about citizenship legislation and this famous award to the Plataeans.

everything that the Athenians have a share in, both sacred and secular,
except for any hereditary priesthood or rite, . . . nor the nine archons, but
their offspring. . . . The Plataeans are to be distributed among the demes
and the tribes. Once they have been distributed, no other Plataean is to
become an Athenian unless this award is granted by the Athenian people.[72]

[105] You see, men of Athens, what a fair and just proposal the orator made for the Athenian people. He demanded that the Plataeans receiving the award should first be scrutinized individually in court to determine whether each man was a Plataean and one of the friends of our city, so as to prevent many people from obtaining citizenship under this pretext. Second, he ordered that the names of those who had passed their scrutiny should be inscribed on stone and set up on the Acropolis near the goddess so that the award is preserved for future generations, and one could check whose relative an individual might be. Finally, he does not allow anyone to become an Athenian, [106] who did not receive the award at that time and undergo a scrutiny in court, in order to prevent many people from obtaining citizenship by fraud, claiming that they were Plataeans. Then on behalf of the city and the gods, he also defined in the decree the law that applied to them, that none were to be allowed to be selected by lot as one of the nine archons or hold any priesthood but that their offspring could if they were born from a citizen woman legally betrothed.

[107] Isn't this outrageous? For your neighbors, and admittedly the most loyal friends of Athens among the Greeks, you set everything so well and precisely concerning the terms of the award. Now, are you going to allow this woman, who has prostituted herself all over Greece so shamelessly and recklessly, to insult the city and offend the gods without punishment, a woman who neither inherited citizenship from her ancestors nor was made a citizen by the people? [108] Where has she not worked with her body? Where has she not gone for her daily pay? Has she not been all over the Peloponnese, in Thessaly and Magnesia with Simus of Larisa and Eurydamas, the son of Medeius,[73] in Chios and most of Ionia accompanying Sotadas of Crete, hired out by Nicarete when she was still her slave? And what do you think a woman who is under the power of others and following the man who is paying her does? Does she not serve her clients with any form of pleasure? Are you then going to vote that a woman like this, whom everyone knows well that she has worked her way around the

---

72. This is probably a partial quotation from the decree.

73. From other sources we know that Simus and Eurydamas were the offspring of rich and powerful families who gained prominence in Larissa in later years. Sotadas of Crete was a well-known athlete.

entire map of the earth, is a citizen? [109] And what good are you going to say has been accomplished when someone asks you? Of what disgrace and crime against the gods are you going to be able to absolve yourselves? Before this woman was indicted and brought to trial and everyone could find out who she really was and what offenses against the gods she had committed, she was guilty of these crimes, but the city was guilty of negligence. Some of you did not know, and those who had found out expressed their indignation but were unable to take action themselves, as nobody had brought her to trial or put her on vote. Now, since you all know and she is in your hands and you have the power to punish her, the impiety against the gods becomes yours if you do not punish her. [110] If you acquit her, what is each one of you going to say to your wife or daughter or mother when you go back to your house and she asks, "Where have you been?" and you say, "We were trying a case"? "Whose?" she will ask then. "Neaera," you will naturally say (will you not?), "because she is illegally living with a citizen in marriage although she is an alien, and because she betrothed her daughter, who was caught with a seducer, to Theogenes the former *basileus,* and that woman performed the secret rites on behalf of the city and was given as a wife to Dionysus," and you will relate the other charges against her as diligently and carefully as the prosecution has laid them down, one by one. [111] Listening to this they will say, "And what did you do?" and you will reply, "We acquitted her." The most respectable women will be furious with you because you allowed her to share with them the same privileges in public life and religion. On the other hand, to those who do not have sense you are showing that they can do as they please, since you and the laws have granted them total license. Thus with your negligence and laxity you will give the impression that you approve of her ways. [112] So it would have been far better if this trial had not taken place at all rather than it result in an acquittal now that it has. There will be total freedom for whores to marry anyone they like and claim that the father of their children is any man that happens to be around. The laws will become useless, while the ways of the courtesans will have the license to do as they please. Besides, be mindful of citizen women, so that the daughters of the poor will not be left unmarried. [113] Right now, when a woman is poor, the law supplies her with sufficient dowry, even if nature has given her modest looks. However, if the law is cast aside by you, through her acquittal, and becomes invalid, without a doubt the work of whores will reach the daughters of the citizens, the ones unable to be betrothed because of poverty. On the other hand, the privilege of free women will go to the courtesans if they can bear children as they wish and take part in the rites and sacrifices and honors of the city. [114] So each one of you should consider that he is casting his vote for his wife, or daughter, or mother, or the city and its laws and its rites, so that these women may not seem to be held in equal esteem with this whore, and so that those who were brought up by their families with great decency and care and lawfully betrothed may not seem to be equal to this woman, who has been with many men many times each day, in many and shameless ways, as each man wanted. [115] Consider that the dispute is not between myself, the speaker, and the citizens who will defend and support her, but between the laws and Neaera here, about her actions. And when you are considering the prosecution, listen to the laws of the city, according to which you have sworn to judge what they state and how the defendants have broken them. When you consider the defense, remember the accusations of the laws and the proof presented in my speech, then look into her face, and ask only these questions: whether she is Neaera and whether she has done these things.

[116] It is worth remembering this, too, men of Athens: that you punished Archias the hierophant after he was found guilty of impiety because he had performed sacrifices contrary to the ancestral custom. Among else, he was accused of sacrificing for the courtesan Sinope a victim she had provided, on the altar in the courtyard of the sanctuary at Eleusis during the Haloa, although it was not permissible to sacrifice victims on that day, and the sacrifice was not one of his functions but the priestess's. [117] Is this not terrible? A man from the *genos* of the Eumolpidae and a citizen with worthy ancestry was punished for a minor transgression of the traditional ritual. Neither the pleas of his relatives and friends nor the liturgies he and his ancestors had performed for the city nor the fact that he was a hierophant did him any good, but you punished him, nonetheless, because he appeared to have done something wrong. Will you not punish Neaera here, who has committed crimes against the same god and the laws—she and her daughter too?[74]

[118] I wonder what they will actually say to you during the defense. That Neaera here is a citizen and that she lives with him as his lawful wife? But witnesses have verified that she was a courtesan and a former slave of Nicarete. That she is not his wife, but he keeps her as a concubine in his house? But the children, who are hers and have been introduced into the phratry by Stephanus here, and the daughter, who was betrothed to an Athenian man, clearly prove that he keeps her as his wife. [119] I believe neither Stephanus nor any advocate of his will be able to prove that the accusations and the testimonies are not true and that Neaera here is a citizen. But I hear that he intends to build the defense around the

---

74. Archias was probably prosecuted and punished for political reasons, but some minor religious infraction provided the excuse for his prosecution.

argument that he does not keep her as his wife but as his concubine and that the children are not hers but his by another woman, a citizen and a relative of his, whom he claims he had married before.[75] [120] In order to respond to this shameless claim and the plots of the defense and the supporting witnesses that he has put together, I addressed a fair and appropriate challenge to him, which would allow you to find out the whole truth. I challenged him to hand over the slaves who were serving Neaera when she came to Stephanus from Megara, Thratta and Coccaline, and those whom she obtained later in his house, Xennis and Drosis. [121] They know for sure that Proxenus, the one who died, and Ariston, the one who is still alive, and Antidorides the sprinter, and Phano—who was the wife of Theogenes, the former *basileus*—are Neaera's. And if under torture it was revealed that Stephanus here had married a citizen woman and that the children were his by that woman, and not Neaera, I was going to withdraw from the case and not bring this indictment. [122] For a man, living in marriage means that he has children, introduces his sons into his phratry and deme, and gives his daughters to husbands as his own. We have courtesans for pleasure, concubines for the daily care of our body, and wives in order to have legitimate children and a reliable custodian of our household.[76] So if he had married a citizen woman in the past and the children were by her and not Neaera, he could have proven it with the most accurate proof, by handing over these slaves. [123] He will read for you the testimony and the challenge to verify that I challenged him. Read the testimony and then the challenge.

---

75. At this point the orator is trying to anticipate the arguments of the defense. Considering that in a public case, like this one, each side delivered only one long speech and there was no further opportunity to respond to the arguments of the opponent, so it was important to try and answer some of the points of the defense in advance. The preliminary hearing (*anakrisis*) would have provided some insight, and it was not uncommon for the litigant to learn of his opponent's legal strategy from some of his acquaintances. See, e.g., **[Dem.] 53.14**, where the former friends of Apollodorus reveal his line of argumentation to his opponents once they fall out with him. See Dorjahn 1935.

76. This statement has frequently been quoted as a definition of the social roles of women in classical Athens. In reality, this is a generalization, which may contain some truth but should not be considered as the golden rule on the division of women's roles in classical Athens. For example, it may be true that some Athenians kept courtesans for pleasure, and that often marriages were conducted with a view to good household management and the upbringing of legitimate children, but not all Athenians kept courtesans, and not all marriages were loveless arrangements.

TESTIMONY

Hippocrates, son of Hippocrates, of Probalinthus; Demosthenes, son of Demosthenes, of Paeania; Diophanes, son of Diophanes, of Alopece; Deinomenes, son of Archelaus, of Cydathenaeum; Deinias, son of Phormos, of Cydantidae; and Lysimachus, son of Lysippus, of Aegilia, testify that they were present in the agora when Apollodorus challenged Stephanus, demanding the servant girls for examination under torture concerning the accusations made by Apollodorus against Stephanus regarding Neaera, and that Stephanus refused to hand over the slaves. The challenge is the one produced by Apollodorus.

[124] Now read the actual challenge which I addressed to Stephanus here:

CHALLENGE

{This was the challenge that Apollodorus addressed to Stephanus concerning the reasons for which he indicted Neaera, that although she was an alien she was married to a citizen. He was prepared to take over for examination under torture the slaves of Neaera, those whom she had when she came from Megara—Thratta and Coccaline—and those whom she obtained in Stephanus' house—Xennis and Drosis. They know for sure about the children of Neaera, that they are by Stephanus: Proxenus, the one who has died, and Ariston, who is still alive, and Antidorides the sprinter, and Phano. And if they confirmed that these children are by Stephanus and Neaera, Neaera was to be sold, according to the laws, and the children were to be alien; but if they did not admit that the children are by her but by another woman, a citizen, I was willing to withdraw from Neaera's case; and if the slaves had suffered any injury from the torture I would pay whatever the damage cost.}[77]

[125] When I addressed this challenge, men of the jury, Stephanus here refused to accept it. So do you not agree, men of the jury, that a verdict has already been reached by Stephanus here himself, that Neaera is guilty of the charges that I have brought against her; and I have told you the truth, and the testimonies that I brought are true, and whatever this man here says will all be lies, and that he himself will prove that he is not saying anything

---

77. As with the other double documents, the first appears to be authentic, but the second without a doubt it is a forgery. Scholars have tried to correct its many flaws with numerous textual interventions, but it is easier to accept that it has been forged at a later time reflecting inaccurately many of the details from the context.

truthful by his refusal to hand over the slaves, whom I asked for examination under torture?

[126] I brought them to trial and placed them under your vote, men of the jury, avenging both the gods, against whom they have committed impiety, and myself. And you too should not think that the gods, against whom they have committed crimes, will not notice how each one of you will be voting. You must vote for justice and exact vengeance on behalf of the gods and then yourselves. If you do this, everyone will think that you have tried well and fairly this indictment that I brought against Neaera, that although she is an alien she is married to a citizen.[78]

---

78. Invoking the gods in the epilogue and trying to amplify this case into a matter of cosmic significance is a fairly common theme in the epilogue of Attic speeches (e.g., Dem. **21**, 22 and 26). The orator argues that Neaera and her family deserve punishment, or else the whole city might suffer from the anger of the gods.

AESCHINES 1

AGAINST TIMARCHUS

Introduction

Modern Greek still retains an expression—*anô potamôn*, "upstream"[1]—that Demosthenes made famous in his speech *On the False Embassy,* where he used it to describe the outcome of Timarchus' trial. The expression refers to something totally paradoxical, strange, and unexpected, such as a river changing its course and flowing backward toward its source. Demosthenes maintained that Timarchus' trial was such a bizarre affair because the claims of Aeschines were unfounded and totally untrue and yet he won and had Timarchus disfranchised. This must have been a tour de force from the underdog; for a minor politician to go against two of the most powerful political figures in the city and actually win an inherently weak case would indeed seem as surprising and paradoxical as Demosthenes suggests. Like most extant speeches of public lawsuits, Aeschines 1 is overtly political, stemming from Aeschines' part in the embassy that negotiated the controversial peace of Philocrates between the Athenians and Philip II in 346. When Aeschines was accused by Timarchus and Demosthenes of having betrayed the interests of Athens and consorting with Philip, he preempted them by bringing a suit against Timarchus for having illegally addressed the Assembly; the suit came to court around 345.[2] By law, an Athenian was prohibited from being a public speaker if he had prostituted himself, mistreated his parents, squandered his father's estate, or failed to take part in a military campaign (**27–32**).

Male prostitution was not illegal per se, but persons who had practiced it as adults were required to refrain from advising the Assembly and holding priestly offices, including those of the nine archons, undoubtedly because

---

Translated by Konstantinos Kapparis.

1. Dem. 19.287. This expression, used by Aeschylus (fr. 335 Radt) and Euripides (*Med.* 410) and subsequently by many authors, is probably considerably older.

2. See Harris 1985: 376–80; Fisher 2001: 6–8. Aeschines used the scrutiny of orators (*dokimasia ton rhetoron*) to lodge his complaint. Unlike other scrutinies, which took place before an Athenian was allowed to exercise the right in question (see the introductions to **Lysias 16** and **24**), the scrutiny of orators took place, for obvious reasons, only after the individual had exercised the right of speaking before the Assembly.

of the extensive religious duties required by these offices.[3] Most Athenians might find it distasteful for someone to sell his body, but they only imposed legal sanctions when that citizen became the voice of the city or held religious positions that required a decent lifestyle. In such a case, the prostitute could lose all his civic rights and suffer total disfranchisement (*atimia*). Many of the male prostitutes established in the numerous brothels of the city were undoubtedly slaves, some may have been free persons by birth, and most were probably in their teens. Since it was illegal for a parent or guardian to procure a citizen boy under eighteen years of age, we would not expect to find them in brothels. Those citizen boys that were prostituted would have garnered higher prices as exclusive companions, discreetly procured in higher social circles. Similarly, adult citizen men normally served as exclusive companions rather than worked as prostitutes in a brothel. This is why it was extremely difficult to prove that a citizen with such a high profile as Timarchus could have been a prostitute.

The difficulty of defining prostitution also complicated Aeschines' case. If, for example, two men chose to become long-term companions, and one of them was richer and maybe older, would their relationship be a form of prostitution? Aeschines repeatedly implies that it would, undoubtedly broadening the conventional definition to suit his purposes. For Aeschines to move beyond innuendo and unsubstantiated allegations, he would have had to convince one of Timarchus' disenchanted lovers to come forward and testify, and thereby ruin his own reputation and risk facing possible legal sanctions as a result of his testimony. Aeschines repeatedly recognizes the difficulty of producing such evidence, but he is not deterred. He knows that legally his case is extremely weak, and so he must use a different strategy to win.

The speech opens with recitations of several legal documents, most of which are not directly related to his lawsuit. Each one of them, however, is followed by commentary to explain its relevance to the case (**9–38**). Beyond the limited demonstrative power that such recitations might have, they served a much more important purpose: they were intended for the sake of *amplificatio,* namely, to present the case as an important matter that threatened to destroy the fabric of society and to impress upon the jury the gravity of Timarchus' misconduct. After this lengthy prelude, Aeschines begins with his main narrative, starting from the point where Timarchus had reached adulthood and was legally responsible for his own actions.

---

3. For Athenian laws on homosexuality and male sexuality more generally, see Dover 1978; Halperin 1990; Winkler 1990; Cohen 1991: 134–70, 1995: 143–62; Davidson 1998: 139–82, 2007; MacDowell 2000: 13–27; Foxhall and Salmon 1998; Lear and Cantarella 2008.

We first find him as an apprentice at a doctor's practice in the Piraeus where he was learning medicine (**40–52**). Aeschines discerns an improper motive, saying that he only went there to meet clients. His argument is that an exceedingly good-looking citizen boy from a wealthy family would not waste his time trying to learn medicine and that this was only a pretext. Although taverns, inns, and even bakeries might serve also as brothels, it is hard for us to imagine that a place as dreary and filled with as much pain and sickness as the practice of an ancient physician could serve at the same time as a brothel for a wealthy citizen boy, and this is why this allegation can be dismissed without hesitation. Timarchus, perhaps on a youthful whim, tried to learn medicine but then abandoned the idea shortly afterwards.

The affair with Misgolas did not last long, we are told, because Timarchus was hard to keep in line and enjoyed wild parties and gambling. This brought him in touch with Pittalacus, a man of humble origins, a former slave, who owned a gambling house, and for a while he became Pittalacus' lover. Aeschines presents him as the lowest of the low and Timarchus even lower for that, but without a doubt Pittalacus was an affluent metic. In the gambling house of Pittalacus, Timarchus met Hegesandrus, a more powerful and wealthy man, from a prominent Athenian family. They entered into a long-term relationship, and when Pittalacus tried to sabotage the affair he was subjected to violent and abusive behavior by Timarchus and his new lover. Then, we are told, the shameless couple pursued a life filled with intemperance and lewd behavior that was shocking to many decent people (**53–70**).

While Aeschines alleges that Timarchus enjoyed the company of these men, he also mentions how Timarchus enjoyed the company of female courtesans and spent much money on them. The modern reader might find such behavior contradictory, but this was not the case for the Athenians. It was not considered unexpected for a man to be sexually attracted to both men and women. So it was perfectly possible that Timarchus had genuine love affairs with these men while he also spent time with courtesans. Aeschines, however, seeks to persuade the jury that Timarchus was only able to afford this lavish lifestyle by prostituting himself to older, wealthy men. Still, all Aeschines proves in this lengthy section of the narrative, which takes up about a third of his speech, is that Timarchus was very attractive and popular and he had several friendships with a number of men. Aeschines does not secure any witnesses to confirm that these affairs were sexual and not just personal friendships, or even if they were sexual, that Timarchus was a prostitute who offered himself to these men for money. Recognizing the weaknesses of his case, Aeschines suggests that no one was willing to testify to such unsavory and illicit matters. This explanation is plausible, but nonetheless it cannot by any means be taken to constitute proof that Timarchus had in fact been a prostitute.

The second battery of charges against Timarchus was that he was a terrible son and nephew, who squandered his father's estate before turning to prostitution to fund his extravagant lifestyle. We are told that although his father left him a considerable fortune, he wasted it on whores, parties, and gambling. He even sold some land, which his mother wanted to use as her burial site, and he failed to look after his blind uncle. In order to support this accusation, Aeschines summons Arignotus to testify against his nephew. His testimony concerns an occasion when Arignotus did not appear before the Council on the appointed day to claim his disability benefit but turned up later begging for it as a suppliant. Timarchus, who was a member of the Council at that time, failed to defend his uncle, and a very resentful Arignotus appeared in the trial as a hostile witness (**95–105**). These charges were intended to demonstrate that Timarchus was not only shameless and heartless but also unfit to lead Athens, especially since every new official was asked at his scrutiny whether he had fulfilled his duties as a son by looking after his mother and father and properly managing his inheritance. The implication was that a person who did not perform his filial responsibilities could not be trusted to look after public funds.

Timarchus, however, was not a poor man at the time of this trial; so the charge that he had squandered his inheritance was unfounded. The liquidation of the property mentioned by Aeschines may simply have been an informed business decision. An ambitious young man who was moving in the better social circles of Athens and had political aspirations might not have had the time or inclination to supervise the work of slaves who were shoemakers and dress-weavers, or hold on to remote land for which he had no use. The testimony of Arignotus, on the other hand, could have had a devastating effect. Although Arignotus was only summoned to testify about an isolated incident of little significance for the trial, his presence as a blind uncle giving evidence against his own nephew was quite a dramatic moment, which probably stayed in the minds of the jurors much more than any argument or discussion about Timarchus' management of his property. This testimony, albeit irrelevant, would have left a lasting impression, especially among the older jurors.

The third set of accusations against Timarchus involved his conduct as a state magistrate, and here again Aeschines probably embellished rumors for his unfounded allegations. He informs us that Timarchus, despite his relatively young age, had occupied almost every available office, and he proceeds to discredit his conduct in all of them. He argues that Timarchus accepted bribes and harassed other magistrates during their auditing, but since he does not provide any specifics, one cannot take these claims seriously. He then proceeds to mention how Timarchus bought the office of archon on the island of Andros with money he had borrowed at a very high interest rate, alleging that he profiteered from the islanders. Although we are not certain about the details of this office, it sounds like a typical tax-collecting assignment. When Athens auctioned off the right to collect a tax, the highest bidder paid the state a fixed sum in advance and then kept however much of the tax that he was able to collect, usually at a considerable profit. Aeschines says that Timarchus had borrowed money at an annual interest rate of 18 percent in order to win the bid (**106–8**). This means that he had to tax the islanders quite heavily in order to pay off the loan and the interest and still make a profit.

The next accusation was that Timarchus, together with his alleged lover Hegesandrus had planned to embezzle money. An investigation by the Council acquitted them, understandably, because even if they were planning to commit an offense in the future, they had not yet done so at the time of the inquiry (**109–12**). The allegation that Timarchus had received a bribe to challenge someone's citizenship during the scrutiny of all citizens in 346 is also questionable.[4] The only substantiated accusation against Timarchus for all his years of public service concerns his actions as an inspector of mercenary troops in Eretria, for which he admitted that he had received a bribe and for which he was fined half a talent (**113**). But if we believe the orators, bribery of state officials in allied cities was one of the perks of political life in Athens and was not particularly unusual for a seasoned career politician like Timarchus.

The last third of the speech is filled with an analysis of events already mentioned and with further discussion of Timarchus' prostitution, which is taken for granted and further amplified. Aeschines mentions notorious male prostitutes in Athens, whose shameless acts were known from rumors and gossip, and contrasts them with boys whose conduct and reputation among male lovers was blameless. Finally a lengthy session of quotes from literature follows, to distinguish pure love and appropriate same-sex relationships from prostitution. Particularly memorable are the quotes from the *Iliad* where Aeschines contrasts the romantic relationship of Achilles and Patroclus with the shameless ways of Timarchus. This is not just entertaining reading intended to amuse the jurors but a powerful rhetorical strategy to show that the defendant did not adhere to their values.

If there was ever a court case where a defendant was convicted merely on the basis of innuendo, unfounded accusations, rumors, moral platitudes, and banalities, this must be it. The case against Timarchus was not just feeble, it was built out of thin air. Yet it succeeded, and two prominent political figures suffered the consequences. Timarchus' political career was over as a result of the trial, and Demosthenes was forced to postpone his

---

4. See **115** n. and the introduction to **Isaeus 12**.

suit against Aeschines for his conduct on the embassy, which he eventually lost. How are we to explain Aeschines' success? Was it envy for a man whose good looks were legendary? Was it resentment for someone who had held so many political offices over the years? Was it due to the adverse political climate following the peace of Philocrates? These factors cannot be discounted, but above all the power of this speech deserves to be recognized and credited. Aeschines was successful precisely because he turned the jury's attention away from the weaknesses of his case. He knew that he had no reliable evidence against Timarchus, no witnesses to confirm the charge of prostitution, and no prior convictions, except for the charge of bribery. So Aeschines focused on Timarchus' reputation to make his case against him seem plausible. Since Timarchus was exceptionally good looking and had attracted the attention of several wealthy men wanting to be his lovers, rumors would have circulated in Athens, regardless of whether they were true. If one were then to add Timarchus' fondness for an exciting social life—parties, courtesans, gambling and other such pleasures—and his reputation for being a playboy, there would have sufficient suspicion among many of the jurors to convince them that the allegations were true. Aeschines knew that his only chance of success in this trial was to manipulate the public image of Timarchus by embellishing rumors that were circulating in Athens and presenting them as well-known facts so that Timarchus appeared to have the same characteristics as a type of man that was well established in the Athenian social imaginary. Unfortunately for Timarchus, the jury put more faith in the compelling image of the corrupt politician—willing to sell his body and the interests of city, an image Aeschines so artfully composed and the Athenians so feared—than it did in the more complex and nuanced person that Timarchus really was.

Key Information

Speaker	Aeschines accused Timarchus of illegally addressing the Assembly.
Defendant	Timarchus.
Other Individuals	Demosthenes helped Timarchus prepare his defense.
	Euthydicus was a physician for whom Timarchus briefly served as an apprentice.
	Misgolas, Pittalacus, and Hegesandrus allegedly had affairs with Timarchus.
	Arignotus, Timarchus' uncle, was a poor invalid deprived of his disability benefit because Timarchus was allegedly unwilling to intervene.

Action	Scrutiny of orators (*dokimasia ton rhetoron*).
Outcome	Timarchus was found guilty.
Punishment	Loss of civic rights (*atimia*).
Date	c.345.

Against Timarchus

[1] No citizen has ever been prosecuted by me or harassed during his auditing, men of Athens.[5] On the contrary, I think I have conducted myself with reserve in such matters, but when I saw the city suffering great damage at the hands of this man, Timarchus, who keeps speaking in the Assembly contrary to the laws, and since I have been personally slandered (and how this happened I will explain later in my speech), [2] I came to the conclusion that it would be one of the most cowardly things ever if I did not help the entire city, the laws, you, and myself. With the knowledge that he is guilty of the charges that you have just heard the secretary read, I initiated this scrutiny against him. It seems, men of Athens, what is customarily said about public cases is not false: personal animosities very often set right public affairs. [3] It will be demonstrated that Timarchus has no one else to blame for this entire trial, not the city, not the laws, not you, not me, but only himself. The laws ordered him to refrain from addressing the Assembly because he has lived shamefully, and this command, in my judgment, is not too difficult to follow but, on the contrary, rather easy; if he had abided by it, I could have avoided his malicious attacks. I hope that my introduction on these matters sounds reasonable.

[4] I am not ignorant of the fact that what I am going to say first, men of Athens, will sound to you familiar from previous speakers. Nevertheless, I think it is an appropriate occasion for me to use the same words. It is agreed that there are three types of constitutions among all people: monarchy,[6]

---

5. All magistrates in Athens underwent an audit (*euthyna*) at the end of their year in office, and any citizen could step forward and make accusations concerning their conduct.

6. The actual wording of Aeschines (*tyrannis*) deliberately fuses the meaning of monarchy (*basileia*) with the dictatorial rule of one man who unlawfully seizes power by force (*tyrannos*). For a fourth-century Athenian orator who wanted to flatter a democratic audience, such distinctions would be too fine and meaningless: rule by one man was tyrannical by definition, regardless of the circumstances under which he had assumed his office. This fusion would be familiar to the audience from the plays of the fifth century (e.g., *Oedipus Tyrannos*), where the word

oligarchy, and democracy. Monarchies and oligarchies are governed by the whims of those in charge, but democratic states are governed by established laws. [5] You know well, men of Athens, that in a democracy the citizens and the state are preserved by the laws, but in monarchies and oligarchies by mistrust and armed guards. Oligarchs and those ruling on the basis of inequality must guard against those men seeking to subvert their state by the rule of brute force, while you who have a constitution based on laws and equality must guard against men who either speak or have lived their lives contrary to the laws. This shall be the source of your strength, when you use good laws and you do not allow those who break them to subvert the state. [6] I think it is appropriate, when we enact laws, to consider how we will establish laws that are good and beneficial to the state, but when we have enacted them, to obey the laws that are established and punish those who do not obey, if the city is to prosper. Think, men of Athens, how much care Solon, that ancient legislator, took on matters of propriety,[7] and so did Draco and the lawgivers of those times. [7] First they introduced laws about the proper conduct of our children and explicitly stated how the freeborn boy is to conduct himself and how he is to be brought up. Second, they spoke about the adolescents, and finally about each one of the remaining age groups, with reference not only to private citizens but also to public figures, and when they wrote down these laws, they entrusted them to you and made you their guardians. [8] So I would like to organize my speech to you in the same way as the lawgiver has the laws. First I will go through the established laws that regulate the appropriate conduct of our children, then the laws on the adolescents, and finally those about each one of the remaining age groups, with regard to not only private citizens but also public figures.[8] Thus I believe my speech will be easiest to understand. At the same time, men of Athens, I would like first to expound to you what are the laws of the city and then to contrast them with the ways of Timarchus. You will find that he has lived contrary to every single law.

---

tyrannos is frequently used in this ambiguous sense (e.g., Eur. *Andr.* 204, *Hec.* 809, *Med.* 308; Soph. *Ant.* 60, 506, *Elect.* 661, *OT* 514).

7. The Greek word, *sophrosyne* (literally, "sound-mindedness"), is difficult to translate because it has a broad semantic range of meaning that varies based on context (see North 1966). Given the sexual and moral undertones of Aeschines' speech, we have chosen "propriety" and its derivatives as a translation.

8. Aeschines presents the laws of Athens as a very logical and sequential system. In reality these early lawgivers did not introduce a systematic corpus of law. For the contrary view, see Gagarin 2008.

[9] First, the lawgiver mistrusted the teachers, to whom by necessity we have to entrust our children, even though their livelihood depends on good conduct and the lack of it brings poverty. He explicitly lays down first what time the freeborn boy must arrive at school, then with how many other boys he is to enter and when he needs to leave. [10] He prohibits the teachers to open the schools and the trainers the gymnasia before sunrise, and he has ordained that they close them before sunset, motivated by suspicion of deserted places and darkness. He also stipulates who should be attending these schools and what age they must be and the office that will oversee these matters, and specifies the oversight that there is to be of the slave attendants (*paidagogoi*) and for the Mouseia in the schools, the Hermeia in the fighting ring, and finally the associations of the children and the circular dances.⁹ [11] He ordains that the chorus producer (*choregos*), who is going to spend his own fortune on you, needs to be over forty years old when he undertakes this task so that he will be at his most prudent age when he deals with our children in this capacity.¹⁰ The secretary will read these laws to you, and you will see that the lawgiver was convinced that a well-brought-up boy will become a man useful to the city; however, when one's nature takes the wrong turn from the beginning through education, he was convinced that from badly brought up boys the citizens will indeed become like Timarchus here. Read these laws to them.¹¹

LAWS

[12] {*The teachers of the boys should open the schools not earlier than sunrise and close them before sunset. And no one above the age of the children is to enter while the children are present unless he is the son or brother or son-in-law of the teacher; if anyone enters in defiance of this law, he is to be punished by death. Those responsible for the Hermeia are not to*

---

9. Aeschines is the main source for all these regulations and institutions. As his father Atrometus was a schoolteacher, he would be familiar with these rules. The Mouseia were comparable to modern school plays. Students had the opportunity to showcase their learning through dramatic contests, dancing, and recitals. The Hermeia were annual athletic contests in the schools. Fisher (2001: 129–33), with good reason, does not believe that these laws date to the time of Solon but were most likely introduced later and were in force by the time of Aeschines. The *paidagogoi* were slaves who walked children to and from schools.

10. See the introduction to **Antiphon 6**.

11. Undoubtedly this document is a forgery, as many of the details are wrong and it relies much on the context.

allow anyone of adult age to participate; if he allows it and does not expel
him from the gymnasium, the manager of the gymnasium is to be personally
responsible in accordance with the law on the corruption of free persons.
The choregoi appointed by the people must be over forty years old.}

[13] After this he legislated on crimes which, although grave, still, I think, are taking place in the city; for the people of old introduced laws after someone had done something that was inappropriate. The law explicitly says that if a father or brother or uncle or guardian or any other person with legal authority procures a boy, there will be no prosecution against the boy himself but against the person who hired him and the one who hired him out—against the former because he hired him, against the latter, he says, because he hired him out. The penalty he made equal for both, and it is not obligatory for the boy who had been hired out as a prostitute to maintain his father or provide a dwelling for him once he reaches adulthood; however when the father dies, he must bury him and perform the rest of the traditional rites. [14] Think, men of Athens, how wisely the law deprives him of the benefits of having children while he is alive in the same manner as he has deprived the boy of freedom of speech, but when he dies and the beneficiary is no longer aware of the benefits, but the law and the gods are honored, the law orders that the son should bury him and perform the rest of the traditional rites.[12]

What other law did he establish to guard our children? The one on procuring, whereby he established the greatest penalties if someone procures a free boy or woman. [15] And what else? The one on outrage (*hybris*), which covers all together in one clause all such actions.[13] In this law it is written explicitly that if someone subjects a boy to outrage (and the man who hires him certainly commits outrage), or a man or woman, free or slave, or commits an illegal act against their person, a prosecution for outrage is to be commenced and the punishment can be whatever is deemed necessary for him to suffer or pay. Read the law.

---

12. Aeschines contradicts himself by applying retrospectively the disabilities of the law for male prostitutes to teenage boys procured by their father or guardian, and by almost in the same breath stating that no legal action is taken against the boys themselves. Since the law is clear in this case, his interpretation is mistaken. Boys who had been procured before reaching adulthood but stopped as adults had nothing to fear from the law, as they could not be considered legally responsible for actions arranged by their guardians before they were independent.

13. For the meaning of *hybris,* see the introduction to **Demosthenes 21**.

LAW

[16] {*If any Athenian subjects a free boy to outrage, the legal guardian
of the boy is to submit an indictment to the thesmothetai with a penalty
proposed. The man found guilty by the court is to be handed over to the
Eleven and put to death on the same day. If he is sentenced to a fine, he
must pay within eleven days from the trial, if he cannot pay immediately.
In this case, he is to be imprisoned until he pays. Even persons who have
treated abusively the bodies of slaves are to be liable under the same rules.*}[14]

[17] Someone might wonder, if he heard it suddenly, why on earth this
wording concerning slaves has been written into the law of outrage. If you
look into it, men of Athens, you will find that this particular provision is
the most sound of all.[15] The lawgiver was not concerned with the slaves,
but because he wanted you to become accustomed to abstaining entirely
from outrage against free persons, he wrote down that one is not to exhibit
such behavior even towards slaves.[16] He considered the man who subjects
anyone to outrage unsuitable to be a citizen in a democracy.

[18] Remember also, men of Athens, that until that point the lawgiver does not even address the boy directly but those around him—the
father, the brother, the guardian, the teachers, and those responsible for
him. However, once he is inscribed into the register of the citizens, comes
to know the laws of the city, and is in the position to know the difference
between what is good and what is not, the lawgiver is no longer addressing others but Timarchus himself.[17] [19] And what does he say? If any

---

14. This is not an authentic quote. First, it differs from the description of the law
provided in section **15** and the case against Meidias (see **Dem. 21.47**). Second,
there are several glaring oddities regarding procedure, which could not belong to
a legal document of the classical period, such as the requirement that the fine be
paid within eleven days (an obvious error influenced by the previous reference to
the Eleven, that is, the magistrates in charge of the prisons). Fines needed to be
paid before the ninth prytany or else they were doubled (see Dem. 24.98, 169;
[Dem.] 59.8). Third, the language of the final condition of this law concerning
slaves is linguistically odd, and this becomes more evident when we compare it
with the concise summation of the law in **15**. Undoubtedly this document was
composed much later by someone who poorly understood the finer points of
Athenian legal procedure.

15. Here we depart from the text of Dilts, who obelizes *touto* although transmitted
by all manuscripts.

16. Cf. **Dem. 21.46**.

17. When a boy of Athenian descent reached the age of eighteen, he was then
considered an adult and was registered in the deme of his father, thus permitting him to

Athenian, he says, works as a prostitute, he cannot be appointed as one of
the nine archons (I believe because this is a crowned office), nor assume
any priesthood (because his body is not clean), nor become a public advocate, nor serve as a magistrate, either at home or abroad, appointed by lot or
elected; [20] he is not to serve as a herald or an ambassador (and he is not to
prosecute those who have served as ambassadors or engage in sykophantic
activities for money), nor can he voice his opinion either in the Council
or in the Assembly (not even if he is a highly accomplished speaker).[18] If
someone disobeys these laws, the lawgiver has established an indictment for
prostitution and the most severe penalties. Read for them this law too so
that you may recognize that although such laws have been established, so
good and wise, Timarchus, a man of such character as you already know,
has the temerity to give public speeches.

LAW

[21] {*If an Athenian man prostitutes himself, he is not to be allowed to
become one of the nine archons nor assume any priesthood nor become a
public advocate nor serve as a magistrate, either at home or abroad,
appointed by lot or elected, nor is he to be sent as a herald or make a
proposal or enter the public temple or wear a crown during ceremonies in
which everyone else is wearing a crown or step inside the boundaries of the
market place. If someone acts contrary to these provisions, once he is
convicted for prostitution he is to be punished by death.[19]*}

[22] He established this law to deal with the young men who recklessly
abuse their own bodies. The laws read awhile ago concern the boys, while
the ones that I will mention now concern the rest of the Athenians. When
he was finished with these laws, he considered the manner in which you
should debate the most important matters, coming together in the Assembly.

---

exercise the rights of citizenship after completing two years of military service as an
ephebe (see the introduction to **Isaeus 12**). Until then he was legally represented
by his guardian (*kyrios*).

18. From **19** through the beginning of **20**, Aeschines intersperses quotations of the
law with his inferences. Since the text of the law has not survived independently,
it is not easy to separate the sections of the legal document from his comments.
Even where he appears to be quoting the law, his citation may not be exact. So,
following Dilts, we use parentheses to indicate where Aeschines has inserted his
inferences.

19. The repetition in wording with the previous sections has led scholars to reject
this document universally as spurious.

And where does he begin? "Laws," he says, "on Orderly Conduct."[20] He started with decency because he believed that the city that exhibits the best behavior is the one that is going to be the most prosperous. [23] And how does he order the presiding officers (*proedroi*) to conduct business? After the sacrificial victim is carried around and the herald says the traditional prayers, he orders the presiding officers to offer the preliminary vote on matters related to ancestral rituals, heralds, embassies, and religious matters, and after this the herald asks, "Who wishes to speak among those who are over fifty years of age?"[21] When all men from this group have spoken, he then invites any Athenian who is entitled and wishes to speak.

[24] Consider, men of Athens, how beneficial this is. The lawgiver, I believe, was aware of the fact that the elders are at their peak in wisdom, but their boldness has started to abandon them because of their experience in matters. So since the lawgiver wants to accustom the wisest men to speak about public affairs, but could not call each one of them by name, he invites the entire age group to the roster and admonishes them to speak. At the same time, he teaches the younger men to have respect for their elders, always defer, and honor old age, which is where we will all go, if we live long enough. [25] So wise were all those ancient orators, Pericles and Themistocles and Aristeides, (the one who has a very different nickname from Timarchus {being called "the Just"}), that what we do habitually— that is, speak with the hand outside the cloak—they considered to be some- what inappropriate and refrained from doing it. And I think I can show you some very good proof of this. I know for a fact that all of you have sailed to Salamis and seen the statue of Solon, and you yourselves can testify that in the market place of Salamis Solon stands with his hand inside his cloak. This, men of Athens, is an imitation and a representation of the stance of Solon and the manner in which he addressed the Athenian people.[22]

[26] Consider, men of Athens, how great is the difference between Timarchus and Solon and those other men, whom I mentioned a short while ago in my speech. These men were ashamed to speak with the hand outside the cloak, while this one here not long ago but only recently cast off his cloak and got into an all-out brawl in the Assembly, naked, even though his body was in such a bad state from the drunkenness and the filthy

---

20. Following Dilts, quotation marks are used here and in the following sections (i.e., **22–23, 27–32)** to indicate where Aeschines appears to be quoting the law.

21. Kapparis (1998: 255–59) has argued that this law was obsolete.

22. Although this statue depicted in idealized form what the Athenians considered to be the appropriate manners and pose for an Athenian statesman, obviously for most of the classical period Athenians had to use their hands when speaking before the Assembly in order to maximize the impact of their words.

lifestyle that men with good sense covered their eyes, ashamed on behalf of the city that we use such advisors. [27] The lawgiver was well aware of all this when he explicitly stated who should and who should not speak in the Assembly. He bars from the roster neither a man who is not the descendant of generals nor someone who practices some lowly craft in order to earn a living; on the contrary, he honors such men, and for that reason he asks many times the question, "Who wishes to speak?"[23]

[28] Who did he consider unsuitable for speaking? Those who have lived inappropriately; he does not allow these men to address the Assembly. Where does he say so? "Scrutiny of the speakers," he says, "If someone addresses the Assembly who beats his father or mother or does not support them or provide them a home," he does not allow this man to speak, rightly so, by Zeus, in my opinion. Why? Because if someone is vile towards those whom he should honor equally with the gods, what are strangers and the city as a whole going to suffer at his hands? [29] Whom did he bar next from speaking? "The man," he says, "who has not taken part in the military campaigns assigned to him or has dropped his shield," correctly so. Why? Because, my man, if you do not take up arms for the city or cannot defend it because of cowardice, you do not deserve to offer advice to it. Then, whom does he discuss? "A man who has been a male prostitute," he says, "or has sold his body," because he believed that a man who has sold his own body to be abused would easily sell the public interests of the city. [30] Then, whom does he mention? "If he has squandered his parental estate," he says, "or his inheritance," because he believed that a man who has mismanaged his own estate would dispose of the goods of the state in a similar fashion. The lawgiver did not believe that it was possible for the same man to be bad in his private life and good in public. Moreover, the lawgiver did not think that a man should step on the roster having taken care of his speech but not his own life. [31] He believed that a good man's speech, even very badly or plainly presented, is always useful for the listeners; however, the words of a vile man who has treated his own body with contempt and has shamefully squandered his inheritance, even if they are very elegant, are not going to be of any benefit {to the listeners}. [32] So, he keeps such men away from the roster; he bars them from speaking.

---

23. I.e., poor citizens or persons of undistinguished ancestry would presumably need a great deal of encouragement before they could sum up the courage to address the Assembly. As Fisher (2001: 157) puts it, "The language here is apparently designed to celebrate the absence of prejudice against the poor as potential speakers; it also clearly reveals the obstacles the poor might face, and hence the limitations to Athenian egalitarianism." This prejudice is famously echoed in the *Knights* of Aristophanes.

If anyone, despite all this, not only speaks but also lodges malicious accusations and acts viciously, and the city cannot put up with such a man, "any fully enfranchised Athenian who wishes," he says, "can initiate a scrutiny." Then he instructs you to pronounce judgment on this matter in court; and I brought this lawsuit before you in accordance with this law.

[33] These laws were established a long time ago; however, you added a new law after that majestic all-out brawl[24] that he waged in the Assembly, since you were appalled by this action: in each Assembly you choose by lot one tribe to preside over the roster. What did the lawgiver order? He asks the members of the tribe to sit in support of the laws and the democracy because, unless we send in help from somewhere against men who have lived like this, we will not be able to hold debates over the most important matters. [34] It is to no avail, men of Athens, to attempt the removal of such men with jeers, since they have no shame, but it is necessary to dissuade them with punishment, because this is the only way that they can become bearable.

So he will read to you the laws on the orderly conduct of the orators. Timarchus here and a few other politicians of his sort have banded together and brought an indictment against the law on the presidency of the tribes, arguing that it is unsuitable, because they want to speak and live as permissively as they like.

LAWS

[35] {*If one of the orators speaks either in the Council or in the Assembly on some other matter and not the proposed motion, or not on each of the issues separately or twice on the same matter, the same man in the same day, or uses ridicule or badmouths someone or interrupts, or stands up and starts talking in the middle of a discussion without asking for permission to speak from the roster or cheers or assaults the chairman after the Assembly or Council has adjourned, the presiding officers have the authority to record a fine for the collectors in the amount of fifty drachmas for each offense. If he deserves a greater penalty, they can impose a fine of fifty drachmas and refer him to the Council or the next Assembly. When the summons go out, he should be judged, and if he is found guilty by a secret ballot, the presiding officers are to record a fine for the collectors.}*[25]

---

24. The *pankration* (literally translated as an "all-out fight") was a rather savage athletic competition that included elements of boxing and wrestling.

25. Since so many of the details of this document appear to be made up, it is probably not authentic.

[36] You heard the laws, men of Athens, and I know that you find them fair, but whether these laws are to be useful or useless is up to you. If you punish the offenders, your laws will remain good and valid; if you let them go, they will remain good but no longer valid.

[37] As I promised at the beginning of my speech, since I have spoken about the laws, I now wish to examine the ways of Timarchus so that you can see how far apart they are from your laws. I apologize in advance, men of Athens, if, in the process of speaking about actions that are inherently shameful but nonetheless performed by him, I am forced to say something similar to the actions of Timarchus. [38] It would not be fair to chastise me if I should say something explicit while I am trying to inform you; rather you should blame him all the more. His lifestyle has been so filthy that anyone trying to explain his actions cannot speak as he wishes but inevitably will utter some words of this sort. I will refrain from using such language as much as I can.

[39] Consider, men of Athens, how leniently I am going to treat Timarchus: the abuses that he inflicted upon his own body while he was still underage I will disregard; let them go unpunished just like that which happened during the Thirty or before Eucleides or whenever else there was such a statue of limitations.[26] However, what he did when he knew better, was a young man, and understood the laws of the city—this will be the basis of my prosecution, and I ask you to pay serious attention to it.

[40] First of all, when he was a grown-up and no longer a child, he was established in the Piraeus at the practice of Euthydicus the physician, pretending to be a doctor's apprentice while in reality he had already chosen to sell his body, as the actions themselves proved. The men who used the body of Timarchus at that time, whether merchants or other foreigners or citizens, I will voluntarily pass over so that no one can accuse me of being too engrossed in detail. However, the men in whose houses he went to disgrace his own body and the city, receiving money for the act that the law prohibits him from doing, or else he cannot speak in the Assembly, those I will mention.

[41] Misgolas, the son of Naucrates, men of Athens, from the deme of Collytus, is a good man in every other respect, and no one could find blame with him, but when it comes to this act, he has studied it in great detail and has always been accustomed to have around him some singers and cithara

---

26. Aeschines compares his generosity to Timarchus with the amnesty granted to the supporters of the Thirty following the restoration of the Athenian democracy in 403 (see the introduction to **Lysias 12**). However, in reality, it would not have helped his case to discuss offenses that Timarchus allegedly committed when he was a minor, since he could not have been prosecuted for them (see **13**).

players. I do not mean to sound boorish; I am only saying this so that you get to know who the man is. When he sensed the reason why Timarchus was frequenting the doctor's practice, he spent some money and took him away into his house. He was beautifully built and young and depraved and suited for the act that Misgolas preferred to do and he preferred to have done. [42] And Timarchus did not hesitate, but endured it even though he was in need of nothing. His father had left him a great deal of property that he squandered, as I will demonstrate to you later in my speech. But he did this because he was a slave to the most depraved pleasures, expensive seafood and fancy dinners, flute players, courtesans, gambling and other such things to which no well-bred, free person should be subservient. He was not ashamed, this filthy man here, to leave his father's home and go and live with Misgolas, although the latter was neither a friend of his father nor a man of his own age nor his guardian but a stranger, older than himself, a man who could not quench his desires, while he was in his prime.

[43] Many other ridiculous feats were performed by Timarchus here those days, but there is one in particular that I would like to share with you. It was at the procession of the City Dionysia, and Misgolas, who had taken in Timarchus here, and Phaedrus, son of Callias of Sphettus, were planning to participate in the procession. Although Timarchus here had agreed to participate in the procession with them, he did not turn up while the other two were busy with the preparations. Misgolas was irritated and went out to search for him along with Phaedrus, and they were directed to find him in some apartment dining with a group of foreigners. Misgolas and Phaedrus threatened the foreigners and commanded them to follow them to the prison house because they had allegedly corrupted a free youth. The foreigners ran away, scared, leaving behind everything they had prepared for lunch. [44] That I am telling the truth, everyone who knew Misgolas and Timarchus those days knows it. I am very glad that this legal dispute of mine is with a man notorious among you not for anything else but for the same profession about which you will be voting. It is perhaps the duty of the prosecutor to present clear evidence on unknown matters, but on agreed issues I do not believe that prosecuting is difficult; all that is needed is to refresh the memory of the audience. [45] Even though the act itself is common knowledge, since we are in court, I have prepared testimony for Misgolas, true but not improper, I am convinced of that. I am not writing the name of the act he did to this man here, nor have I included anything else that might be incriminating for someone who has spoken the truth. I have only written down what is familiar to the listeners but neither incriminating for the witness nor shameful.

[46] If Misgolas voluntarily comes forward to testify to the truth, he will be doing the right thing; however, if he chooses rather to be summoned

than to testify to the truth, you will know the entire affair.[27] If the man who actually had the active role is ashamed and would rather choose to pay a fine of one thousand drachmas rather than show his face, while the one who took the passive role is giving speeches in the Assembly, then the lawgiver was wise when he excluded those disgusting men from the roster. [47] If, on the other hand, he obeys but shamelessly ends up denying the truth under oath, saying that he was doing favors for Timarchus or he was showing off to his friends, since he is an expert in this kind of cover up, he will be doing himself no favors and will gain no advantage. I have prepared further testimonies for the people who know that Timarchus, this man here, abandoned his father's home and went to stay with Misgolas. I think this is a hard task to accomplish, since I feel that it is my duty to call to the stand not my own friends or their enemies or those who do not know any of them, but their friends. [48] Now, if they dissuade these men too from testifying (I do not think they will, not all of them anyway), one thing they will not be able to do is to expunge the truth or the reputation of Timarchus around the city, which I did not generate; he did with his own actions. For the lifestyle of a prudent man should be so clean that there is not even a shadow of negative criticism.[28] [49] I would also like to tell you in advance, just in case Misgolas decides to obey you and the laws, that physical appearance at a certain age differs quite a lot from person to person. Some people, although still young, appear to be run-down and older, while others, although advanced in years, look very young. Misgolas is one of those men. He happens to be the same age as I, and we reached our adolescence at the same time. We are forty-five years old, but while I have so much grey hair, as you can see, he has none. Why am I telling you all this in advance? I am telling you so that you won't be amazed when you see him, and have this sort of thought in your mind: "By Heracles, he doesn't

---

27. The reference is to the legal procedure known as *kleteuein*. A reluctant witness could be formally required to testify. If he was summoned and did not testify, he was then fined one thousand drachmas. Aeschines believes that Misgolas would rather pay the fine than testify because he was ashamed to talk about his affair with Timarchus in public.

28. This view is frequently expressed in moralizing passages. Perhaps the most famous incident was the one surrounding the second marriage of Julius Caesar: *Caesar divorced Pompeia at once, but when he was summoned to testify at the trial, he said he knew nothing about the matters with which Clodius was charged. His statement appeared strange, and the prosecutor therefore asked, "Why, then, didst thou divorce thy wife?" "Because," said Caesar, "I thought my wife ought not even to be under suspicion"* (Plu. *Caes.* 10).

look much older than the other one." This is the natural appearance of the man; he was sleeping with Timarchus when he was already a young man.[29]

[50] So that I not waste more time, please call first the witnesses who know that Timarchus was staying in the house of Misgolas. Then read the testimony of Phaedrus. Finally, bring me the testimony of Misgolas himself. If by any chance he has any fear of the gods and has a sense of shame before those who know—the rest of the citizens, and you the jurors—he will be willing to testify to the truth.

TESTIMONY

{*Misgolas son of Nicias from the Piraeus testifies. I became acquainted with Timarchus, who once stayed at the house of the doctor Euthydicus, and I held him in high regard before and still do now.*}[30]

[51] If Timarchus here, men of Athens, had stayed with Misgolas and had not taken another lover, he would have done better, if "better" is the right term for an arrangement of this sort. I would not have been able to accuse him of anything except the one thing explicitly mentioned by the lawgiver—that he has been a companion. A man who does it with one man, and does it for money, seems to me to be guilty of this. [52] However, leaving aside savage men like Cedonides and Autocleides and Thersandrus, in whose houses he was received, if I can jolt your memory and demonstrate that he did not hire out his body only at Misgolas' house but also at another's house and then another's, and from there he moved

---

29. Aeschines is concerned that Misgolas' appearance might cause the jurors to doubt his allegation because they would have taken it for granted that a male prostitute had to be younger than his clients. So he attempts to convince them that Misgolas is older than he looks while Timarchus is younger. But as is indicated in this section, Misgolas was forty-five years old at the time of the trial. Since Timarchus had been a member of the Council in 361, and councilors had to be at least thirty years old, he had to have been born before 391, which would have made him forty-five years old in 346 (see Fisher 2001: 20), if he joined the Council when he first became eligible. What probably was a short-lived fling between two young lovers is misrepresented by Aeschines as an imbalanced relationship between a wealthy older gentleman and a young prostitute.

30. Undoubtedly a spurious document; the forger could not easily extrapolate what kind of information would be appropriate to be included in accordance with the restrictions announced by Aeschines in **45–46**, and so he composed some vague generalities, which could not have been the testimony presented in court, since they did not help Aeschines' case. Moreover, the context suggests that there was testimony from more than one witness.

to someone else's house, he will no longer appear to have worked as a paid companion but—by Dionysus, I cannot keep dancing around it all day—as a prostitute. For the man who for a fee does it with many different men indiscriminately seems to me to be guilty of this charge.[31]

[53] When Misgolas was no longer prepared to bear the expense and dismissed him from his house, Anticles, son of Callias from Euonymon, took him in. Since this man is away in Samos with the cleruchs,[32] I will move on to what happened afterwards. When Timarchus left Anticles and Misgolas, he did not wise up nor was he leading a more respectable lifestyle but spent his days in the gambling house where the dice boards are set up and cockfights are held. I believe some of you may have seen what I am talking about or at least heard about it. [54] One of the men involved in this kind of business is Pittalacus, a public slave, a servant of the city. He had plenty of money, and when he saw Timarchus in that place, he took him in to live in his house. And this filthy scum did not feel at all embarrassed if he was going to disgrace himself with a public slave, a servant of the city. His only concern was whether he would have a provider for his shamelessness; he could not care less about the difference between propriety and impropriety. [55] I hear that the body of Timarchus was subjected by this man to such indignities and such violations, that, by the Olympian Zeus, I would not dare to relate them to you. What he was not ashamed to do in deed, I would prefer not to live than tell you explicitly in words.[33] Around the same time when he was still with Pittalacus, Hegesandrus arrived from the Hellespont, and I know that you have been wondering for some time now why I have not mentioned him; what I am going to say is so apparent.

[56] Hegesandrus arrived, this man whom you know better than I do. He had sailed to the Hellespont as a treasurer with Timomachus of Acharnae, and it is said that he enjoyed the unsuspecting trust of that man and came back with no less than eighty minas of silver, and in some way he was not less responsible for Timomachus' downfall. [57] With all this money on him, he was spending time in the house of Pittalacus, since he was his gambling partner, and there he saw Timarchus for the first time. He liked what

---

31. This difference in the terminology between a paid companion, or escort (*hetairekos*), and a common prostitute (*peporneumenos*), as described by Aeschines, would be broadly acceptable, although may not be universally applicable (see Kapparis 1999: 408–9).

32. That is, he moved to the island of Samos because he was offered property there.

33. This is a classic and effective use of innuendo. Hiding behind decorum, Aeschines avoids having to substantiate his allegations and invites the jury to imagine the worst.

he saw and desired him, and he wanted to take him under his wing, since he realized, I suppose, that Timarchus was of the same nature as he.[34] First he talked to Pittalacus, pleading with him to hand over this man; when he failed in his request, he approached Timarchus in person and did not need to use too many words but immediately persuaded him. In this sordid affair, his wickedness and infidelity were terrible, and one would be justified to despise him on account of this alone.

[58] When he left the house of Pittalacus and was taken into the house of Hegesandrus, Pittalacus was very upset because, I believe, he had spent all this money for nothing and was jealous at what was happening, and he frequently paid them visits. When he became annoying, listen to what those high and mighty men here did. [59] Timarchus and Hegesandrus and some others, whose names I do not want to mention, got drunk one night and broke into the house where Pittalacus was living. First they broke his equipment and threw it into the street—some shaking knucklebones, dice boards and other dicing pieces—and the quails and roosters, of whom that wretched man was very fond, they killed. In the end, they tied Pittalacus himself to a pillar and whipped him as a slave for so long that the neighbors heard the screams. [60] The next day Pittalacus with great indignation over the whole matter walked naked into the agora and sat by the altar of the Mother of the Gods. When a crowd gathered, as usually happens, Hegesandrus and Timarchus, afraid that their disgusting behavior would be revealed to the entire city (for an Assembly was coming up), ran to the altar themselves with some of their fellow gamblers, [61] and standing around, they were pleading with Pittalacus to leave, saying that the whole thing happened in a drunken stupor, and this one here, who at the time was not as disgusting in appearance as he is now, but, on the contrary, still quite charming, was touching the man affectionately and promising to do anything he wanted. Finally they persuaded him to leave the altar because he thought he would obtain justice. When he left the agora, they ignored him. [62] The man, gravely insulted by their act of outrage, brought a lawsuit against each one of them.

When he sued, consider what the mighty Hegesandrus did; a man who had done him no wrong but who, on the contrary, had been wronged by him, although not owned by Hegesandrus but a public slave of the city, Hegesandrus seized him as slave, claiming that he belonged to him. Since Pittalacus was in grave danger, he threw himself at the mercy of a decent man, someone called Glaucon from Cholargus. This man secured his freedom.[35]

---

34. Namely, that they were extravagant, indulgent, and unable to curb their desires.

35. Glaucon literally "removed Pittalacus to freedom," that is, he secured the release of Pittalacus by declaring that he was free and providing sureties to insure

[63] After this incident they went ahead with the hearings for the lawsuits, but later on they deferred the matter to Diopeithes of Sunium for private arbitration. He was from the same deme as Hegesandrus and had even been his lover for a while when he was young. When Diopeithes took over the case as a favor to these two, he came up with one postponement after another. [64] Hegesandrus was speaking in the Assembly at the time when he was also engaged in a prolonged fight with Aristophon of Azenia until Aristophon threatened to go before the Assembly and lodge the same action against him that I brought against Timarchus.[36] His brother Crobylus was also a politician, and the two of them had the audacity to offer advice to you on Greek affairs. At this point Pittalacus blamed himself, considered what kind of men he was fighting against, and came to his senses (one must tell the truth); he kept quiet and was content not to have some new evil inflicted upon him. Hegesandrus then, once he won this great victory without a fight, kept Timarchus here at his house. [65] You all know that I am telling the truth, for who among you has ever gone to the fish-sellers and not witnessed their lavish expenditure? Is there a man who came across their revelries and street fights and did not feel embarrassed on behalf of the city? But since we are in court, call for me as a witness Glaucon of Cholargus, the one who secured Pittalacus' freedom, and read the rest of the testimonies:

TESTIMONIES

[66] {*Glaucon, son of Timaeus, from Cholargus testifies: When Hegesandrus seized Pittalacus as a slave, I secured his freedom. Some time later Pittalacus came to me and said that he wanted to resolve his dispute with Hegesandrus and proposed to him to have both lawsuits dropped, the one he*

---

that he would not flee before the trial to determine his status (see **Lys. 23.9** n.). Many of the details in the narrative make sense only if Pittalacus was in fact a free man at the time when he met Timarchus: he was the owner of a gambling business, quite well off, and capable of personally taking legal action against his abusers. Thus Aeschines' assertion that Pittalacus was a public slave (**54**, twice), is probably elliptical, omitting the fact that, although perhaps previously a public slave, he had been set free well before he met Timarchus and long enough to amass significant property. This would suit the argument of Aeschines at that point where he wanted to suggest how shameless it was of Timarchus to allow himself to become the lover of a lowly slave. See also Fisher 2001: 190–91.

36. Aristophon was a prominent political figure in the first half of the fourth century, frequently, it seems, engaged in litigation over his various proposals. At a time when politics was a rather dangerous business, he seems to have enjoyed widespread respect.

had brought against Hegesandrus and Timarchus, and the one Hegesandrus
had brought against him with the charge of slavery; and they were dropped.

TESTIMONY

<Likewise>, Amphisthenes testifies that, when Pittalacus was seized as a
slave by Hegesandrus, I secured his freedom, and so on.}[37]

[67] Finally, I call Hegesandrus himself. I have written for him a testimony
more decent than he, but a little more explicit than that for Misgolas. I am
sure that he will deny everything and lie under oath. So, why am I calling
him? In order to show you what kind of men this lifestyle generates—
men who despise the gods, have contempt for the laws, and give so little
thought to all forms of shameful behavior. Please call Hegesandrus.

TESTIMONY

[68] {*Hegesandrus, son of Diphilus, from Steiria, testifies: When I arrived*
from the Hellespont, I encountered Timarchus, the son of Arizelus, living
with Pittalacus the gambler, and from that acquaintance I had a relationship
with Timarchus and was intimate with him in the same way as I had been
before with Leodamas.}[38]

[69] I knew that he was going to show contempt for the oath, men of
Athens, and I told you so in advance. Moreover, it is apparently clear that
while he does not want to testify now, he will come running when the

---

37. The first document is unlikely to be authentic. Besides the fact that it adds
nothing that we do not already know from the narrative, the legal language is
inaccurate and inappropriate for a fourth-century trial. The second document
is even more odd. Only the first name of a man not named elsewhere in the speech
is provided, and he testifies that he lodged the action that in the narrative above
Glaucon is said to have initiated. The only plausible explanation would be that
Amphisthenes was the second guarantor for the freedom of Pittalacus, but if this
were the case, the authentic document would have explained more precisely, even
if briefly, his involvement in the matter for the benefit of the jury.

38. This testimony is not authentic, as is obvious from the content (e.g., the
erroneous patronymic and demotic of Hegesandrus, who, in reality, was the son
of Hegesias from Sunium, and the unexpected reference to the relationship of
Hegesandrus with another man, which is obviously derived from the narrative
of **69**) and from the language (e.g., the post-classical use of the noun *gnosis* to
indicate "acquaintance").

defense calls him. There is no surprise there, by Zeus; he will stand up here with every confidence in his way of life, as a virtuous man, who hates wickedness and does not know Leodamas, whose name alone caused quite a stir among you when the testimony was read. [70] Am I going to be compelled to use more explicit language than what comes natural to me? Tell me, by Zeus and the other gods, men of Athens: he who shamed himself with Hegesandrus—does he not appear to you to have been the prostitute of a prostitute? In what kind of filthy excesses do we think that they would not engage when they are drunk and left to their own devices? Don't you think that Hegesandrus, in his attempt to clean up his reputation over the notorious acts with Leodamas, which all of you know well, would have made outrageous demands upon him in order to make his own behavior appear modest by comparison to the excesses of this man here?[39]

[71] You will see, however, that he himself and his brother Crobylus will jump up here and argue with great rhetorical skill and turn of phrase that all that I am saying is nonsense, and they will demand witnesses offering unequivocal testimonies of where he did it, speaking without shame. [72] I really do not think that you are so absent minded that you have already forgotten what you heard only a short while ago when the laws were recited, in which it is written that if someone hires an Athenian citizen for this act or if someone hires out himself, he is guilty of the greatest offenses and deserves an equivalent penalty. What man is so foolish that he would willingly offer a detailed testimony when, by simply telling the truth, he would prove himself to be guilty of the most serious offenses? [73] The only other possibility would be for the passive partner to confess. But he is on trial for this, because he was participating in politics although he had done such acts contrary to the laws. So would you prefer that we drop the entire case and stop inquiring? We are going to run the city really well if we are prepared to forget acts that we know are happening, unless someone comes forward and without shame testifies about them![40] [74] Now consider some examples; and it is necessary for these examples to be similar to the manners of Timarchus here. You see those who are established in brothels, men who are openly performing this act, when they find themselves in the grip of necessity, still they somehow cover themselves and keep the

---

39. Aeschines makes an interesting observation regarding the psychology of the abused when he becomes the abuser. He argues that Hegesandrus will subject Timarchus to worse indignities than those to which he was subjected by Leodamas so that his previous indiscretions appear to be less extreme. The traditional Greek pederastic pattern is described here, with the older, active partner being more assertive in the relationship.

40. The orator is sarcastic at this point.

doors half closed. So if you happened to be passing by and someone asked you what this man was doing, you would be able to name the act right away even though you could not see the person inside, because you know the purpose of the man's work and the act itself. [75] In the same manner you should deliberate about Timarchus, not questioning whether anyone saw him, but whether he did it. By the gods, Timarchus, what would you yourself say if someone else was on trial on this charge? Or what should someone say when a young boy has left his father's home and spends the night in the houses of others, especially if he is exceptionally good looking, participates for free in luxurious dinners surrounded by the most expensive courtesans, gambles, and never has to put down a penny because someone else is paying on his behalf?[41] [76] Does this need an oracle? Is it not obvious that the man who makes such demands upon others will inevitably need to pay back those financing his habits with some sort of sexual favors? By Zeus, I cannot think of a more euphemistic way of mentioning the ridiculous acts that you have performed.

[77] Consider, if you wish, the entire case in the light of some examples from the political arena, especially those matters you now have in hand. The demes have been holding ballots and each one of you has had a vote cast concerning his own person, as to whether he is truly an Athenian or not. When I am present in court and listen to the speeches of the litigants, I can see that with you the same rule always applies. [78] When the prosecutor says, "Men of the jury, the demesmen voted under oath against this man on the basis of their own personal knowledge, even though no one ever accused him or testified against him," immediately you create a ruckus, since you believe that the defendant is not a citizen. You think, as I understand, that there is not any need for additional speeches or testimonies for matters one knows personally. [79] By Zeus, if in the same way that Timarchus had to submit to a vote regarding his birth, so he also had to regarding his lifestyle, whether he was guilty or not, and the case was tried in court, and it came before you in the same manner as it has come now, but in accordance with some law or decree that did not allow me to speak against him or him to defend himself, but nevertheless the herald here

---

41. The theme of young men enjoying a luxurious lifestyle in exchange for sexual favors abounds in the parasitic literature of later antiquity (see, for example, the collection of letters in Alciphron, Book 3). Aeschines is suggesting that since nothing is free, Timarchus paid for these pleasures with his body. Apollodorus makes a similar remark when he refers to the extravagance of Neaera (**[Dem.] 59.42**). The exceedingly good looks of Timarchus could work to the advantage of Aeschines, as the jury might be more readily prepared to believe these stories. The link between the beauty of Timarchus and the charges of prostitution is acknowledged by both Aeschines and Demosthenes (cf. **126** and Dem. 19.233).

{the one standing next to me} put to you the question necessitated by law, "the punched ballot is for those who believe that Timarchus has been a prostitute, while the whole one is for those who believe that he hasn't, what would you vote? I know for sure that you would have voted against him.[42] [80] If one of you asked me, "How do you know that we would have voted against him?" I would say, "Because you have openly expressed your opinion and told me," and I will remind you when and where each of you did. Every time he stepped on the roster in the Assembly, especially last year when he was a councilor, if he ever happened to mention repairs of the walls or some tower, or that someone was taken somewhere, right away you were shouting and laughing, and you yourselves revealed the name of the acts that you knew that he had committed. [81] I will pass over many of the incidents from long ago, but I would like to refresh your memory on what took place in the same Assembly when I initiated proceedings against Timarchus here with this denunciation.

When the council of the Areopagus was presenting a report to the people, in accordance with the decree that he had proposed regarding the buildings of the Pnyx, Autolycus was the member of the Areopagus who spoke, a man who, by the Olympian Zeus, has truly lived in a good and respectable manner befitting that council.[43] [82] When at some point in his speech he mentioned that the council does not approve the proposal of Timarchus, and he said, "You should not be surprised if Timarchus is

---

42. This convoluted argument refers to the procedure of *diapsephisis,* as set forth by the decree of Demophilus (346). The purpose of this procedure was to purge the registers of Athenian citizens from ineligible persons. The *diapsephisis* of 346 was an exceptional but obligatory procedure. Aeschines has telescoped the proceedings before the deme with the appeal proceedings before the court into one and the same process. In his attempt to compensate for the lack of witnesses, he wants to present testimonies as unnecessary. However, in reality the Athenian legal system did not work as Aeschines suggests here. It is true that in a *diapsephisis,* especially an uncontroversial one, there were no speeches for or against a candidate. There was simply a ballot to confirm that this person should stay registered as a citizen or should be deleted from the registers and considered to be a non-citizen, and, indeed, the personal knowledge of a candidate was the most important factor in this vote. However, if someone was rejected and he then appealed this decision before a court, then a normal trial would follow where witnesses and testimony would be presented (see introduction to **Isaeus 12**).

43. The Areopagus had always retained within its powers the procedure of *apophasis,* that is, the ability to conduct an investigation into a matter either at the invitation of the Assembly or on its own initiative. In this case the council was obviously following a request of the Assembly to prepare a report about the planned expansion of the Assembly area, around the Pnyx.

more familiar with this deserted location and the area around the Pnyx than the Areopagus council," you shouted at this point and said that Autolycus was telling the truth; Timarchus is indeed familiar with these places. [83] Autolycus ignored the noise, put on a very serious expression, and went on to say, "We, the members of the Areopagus, men of Athens, neither assign blame nor defend any individual, for this is not our custom, but we understand the point of view of Timarchus." "Perhaps he thought," he said, "that in this deserted area each one of you will have to spend a very small amount of money." Again when he mentioned the deserted area and the small amount of money, you responded with more noise and laughter. [84] And when he mentioned building sites and holes, you could no longer hold yourselves back. At this point, Pyrrandrus came forward to chastise you and asked the people if they were not ashamed to be laughing in the presence of the council of the Areopagus. You drove him away, replying, "We know, Pyrrandrus, that we should not be laughing in front of them, but the truth is so strong that it prevails over all other human considerations."[44] [85] This I take to be the testimony provided by the people of Athens, whom it is not right to convict for false testimony. It would be illogical, men of Athens, if you were the ones shouting the name of the acts that you know he committed without me saying anything, and yet now, when I am telling you, you are prepared to forget, and if there were no trial over this matter, he would have been convicted, but now that there is one, he escapes conviction.

[86] Since I mentioned the citizenship scrutiny and the measures of Demophilus, I would like to give you another example on these matters. The same man had introduced a similar measure before. He alleged that there were some men attempting to bribe the Assembly and the courts, just as Nicostratus is now alleging. There have been some trials on these charges, but others are still pending. [87] Now, in the name of Zeus and the gods, if they had resorted to the same tactics as Timarchus and his cospeakers and demanded that either someone should openly testify about this accusation or the jury should give no credence, it would have been necessary, following this logic, for someone to testify that he offered bribes and someone else to admit that he accepted them, even though death is the penalty

---

44. As Fisher (2001: 217–22) points out, Aeschines does not go into detail about Timarchus' proposal or the possible objections of the Areopagus, which may have been concerned that his proposal was less ambitious than it had wanted. If so, Autolycus had the uphill task of convincing the Assembly that they should spend much more, and perhaps the uproar from the Assembly had nothing to do with the morals of Timarchus or any unintentional innuendos to the activities of a prostitute in deserted and dark places around the city.

prescribed by the law for both, as in this case if someone hires an Athenian man to subject him to outrage or if an Athenian voluntarily accepts money to subject his own body to shameful acts. [88] Was there any witness to give evidence or a prosecutor who attempted to prove the case in this manner? Of course not! So, did the accused get away? No, by Hercules; they were sentenced to death, even though they had committed a lesser crime than this man here. Those poor men, unable to cope with poverty and old age at the same time—the two greatest evils among people—fell into this misfortune; however, this one here did not want to contain his filth.

[89] If this trial were held in some other city, then, acting as arbitrator,[45] I would invite all of you as my witnesses, since you know that I am telling the truth; but if the trial is in Athens, where you are both my judges and my witnesses, I need to refresh your memory, and you need not disbelieve me. It seems to me that Timarchus here, men of Athens, has worked things out not only for himself but also for all those who are committing the same acts. [90] For if the act will occur in the future as it typically has in the past—in deserted places and in private houses—and the person who knows best and has shamed one of the citizens will be liable to the most severe penalties should he tell the truth, and if the one who is being prosecuted on account of the testimony provided by his own life and the truth asks to be tried not on account of what is known but from the testimony of witnesses, then the law and the truth have been subverted, and the way has been shown by which those who commit the gravest crimes will escape. [91] Who among the robbers, the thieves, the adulterers, the murderers, or those committing the worst offenses, but doing so in secret, will be convicted? Those caught red-handed, if they confess, are instantly put to death, but those who escape detection and deny it, are judged in court, and the truth is discovered from arguments of probability.[46]

[92] Take as an example the council of the Areopagus, the most reliable and fair body in the city. I have seen many who were convicted even though they spoke very well and presented many witnesses before this court, and others win who spoke badly and had no witnesses. This is because they do not judge only on the basis of the speeches and the

45. This is a reference to the use of a neutral city as the place to arbitrate a dispute between two cities.

46. Aeschines is suggesting that the burden of proof demanded by Timarchus would make it impossible for any offender to be convicted unless caught in the act, but he protests too much. For most, if not all cases, the jurors reached their decision by weighing the various arguments, proofs, and evidence that the litigants presented, including the testimony of witnesses. Arguments of probability were always an essential component of the litigant's case.

testimonies but also by what they know and what they have investigated personally.⁴⁷ For that reason this council is held in high esteem in the city. [93] By the same standard, men of Athens, you should judge this case. First you should consider nothing more reliable than what you have known and found out yourselves about Timarchus here. Then consider the case not on the basis of the present but of the past. For what was said about Timarchus and his lifestyle in the past was said truthfully, but what is going to be said today for the trial will be said with the intent to deceive you. So you should vote for the larger span of time and the truth and what you know yourselves.

[94] A certain speechwriter, the one who is in charge of his defense, claims that I am contradicting myself, because it does not seem possible to him for the same person to be a male prostitute and squander his inheritance.⁴⁸ He says that it is for a boy to subject his body to abuse and for a man to squander his inheritance. Moreover, he says that those who shame themselves accept payment for the act. So he walks all over the agora wondering in amazement whether the same man can be a prostitute and squander his inheritance. [95] In case someone does not know how this is, I will try to explain it to you in my speech, with greater clarity. As long as the estate of the heiress whom Hegesandrus had married—the same man who was keeping this one here—and the money that he had brought from the expedition with Timomachus were sufficient, they were living in abundance and much debauchery. When this money ran out and was gambled away and used up for fancy dinners, this man here was past his prime and no one was providing for him anymore, but his filthy and unholy nature still desired the same things and, with excessive greed, demanded and obtained one whimsical wish after another. [96] This was the time when he turned to his inheritance, and in a manner of speaking, he ate and drank it all. And he did not sell each piece of property for the right price nor could he wait for a better price or even a profit but he gave it away to whomever he could find; he was so hasty to have his pleasures. [97] His father

---

47. See **81** n.

48. This is a reference to Demosthenes, a long-standing political friend and ally of Timarchus. Aeschines is trying to minimize the significance of this argument of the defense, but he clearly runs into trouble. It appears that the defense intended to argue that if Timarchus had proceeds from his activities as a prostitute then he would not have needed to sell his property. Aeschines responded by admitting that Timarchus hired out his body only while he was in his prime, which means while he was still a boy and before he was a fully grown man. If this were indeed the case, Timarchus would not have done anything illegal and by law, could not have been charged for acts that he had performed while he was still underage.

left him so much property that another man could have performed liturgies, while he could not even preserve it for himself. There was a house behind the Acropolis, a hillside estate at Sphettus, and another piece of land at Alopece, not to mention the skilled slaves who made shoes, about nine or ten in number, each one of whom paid him two obols a day, while the foreman of the workshop paid him three. On top of that there was a woman who could work with fine linen and took the things she made into the market and a man who could weave complex patterns and some people who owed him money and furniture.

[98] That I am telling the truth, in this instance I will present witnesses, who will provide very clear and explicit testimony. For unlike before, there is no danger or shame for the person who tells the truth. The house in the city he sold to Nausicrates the comic poet, from whom Cleaenetus the chorus instructor bought it afterwards for twenty minas; Mnesitheus of Myrrhinous bought the hillside estate from him, which was a lot of land but was reduced to a state of total wilderness by him. [99] His own mother was begging and pleading with him not to sell the land at Alopece, about eleven or twelve stades away from the city wall, but at least leave this field to her to be buried in it. Still he did not keep his hands off this one too, but sold it for two thousand drachmas, and of the servants and the domestic slaves, he left not one but sold every single one of them. In order to prove that I am not lying, I will present testimonies that his father left this property to him, and if he denies that he sold it, let him present the slaves in person. [100] That his father had also loaned money, which Timarchus recovered and spent, I will call as a witness Metagenes of Sphettus, who had borrowed from his father more than thirty minas and at the death of his father paid back the remaining sum of seven minas to Timarchus. Please call Metagenes of Sphettus. From the testimonies, read first the one by Nausicrates, who bought the house, then take the rest that I mentioned about the same matter.

TESTIMONIES

[101] I will demonstrate to you that his father had acquired a lot of money, which he squandered. Fearing that he might have to pay for liturgies, his father sold many of his possessions, except the ones I just mentioned, that is, a field in Cephisia, another one in Amphitrope, and two workshops by the silver mines, one in Aulon, the other at Thrasyllus. [102] How he did so well, I will tell you. There were three brothers, Eupolemus the trainer, Arizelus the father of Timarchus, and Arignotus, who is still alive but old and blind. Of the three, Eupolemus died first, while the estate was still undivided; Arizelus, the father of Timarchus, died second. While he

was alive, he was managing the entire estate because of the infirmity and eye condition of Arignotus and because Eupolemus had died, and he had even set aside an allowance for the maintenance of Arignotus. [103] When Arizelus, the father of Timarchus here died too at first, while this one was still a child, Arignotus was properly treated by the guardians in all affairs; however, when Timarchus here was registered as an adult and took control of the estate, pushing aside his uncle—an old man who had been struck by misfortune—he squandered the estate and provided nothing for Arignotus, and he watched him receive the disability benefit after all this property.⁴⁹ [104] Finally, worst of all, when the old man failed to attend the scrutiny for disabled persons and placed a suppliant bough in the Council for his benefit, although Timarchus was a member of the Council and moreover one of the presiding officers for that day, he did not deem it worthy to speak in his defense but allowed him to lose his benefit for that prytany.⁵⁰ That I am telling the truth, please call Arignotus of Sphettus, and read the testimony.⁵¹

TESTIMONY

[105] One might say that, after he sold his parental house, he bought another one in the city, and that from the sale of the hillside estate, the land on Alopece, the skilled workers, and the rest, he set up something in the silver mines, like his father had done before. But he has nothing left, no house, no apartment, no land, no servants, no money owed to him, nor anything else from which those who are not perpetrators make a living. Instead of his parental estate he has abundant debauchery, slander, boldness,

---

49. Only poor citizens who were disabled and unable to work were eligible for the disability benefit. Originally the benefit was one obol per day, but later in the fourth century it was increased to two obols per day (see the introduction to **Lysias 24**).

50. All recipients received the benefit once per prytany (i.e., ten times per year) by appearing before the Council. Even if Timarchus wanted to be supportive of his uncle, he might have been unable to convince his fellow presiding officers (*proedroi*) to overlook the absence of Arignotus and belatedly award him his benefit.

51. The testimony of Arignotus against his nephew could be quite devastating for the defense of Timarchus. Obviously Arignotus was upset at his nephew for failing to support his appeal to the Council, and this is why he agreed to testify against Timarchus concerning his disability benefit. This testimony was irrelevant from a legal point of view, but in the eyes of the jurors the presence of a blind uncle testifying against Timarchus probably supported the words of the prosecutor—that the defendant was selfish and heartless and mistreated the members of his family who depended upon him, like his old mother and his disabled uncle.

luxury, cowardice, and shamelessness, and he does not know how to blush in the face of shameful acts. From these qualities one would become the worst and most useless citizen. [106] He squandered not only his parental estate but also your own resources, whenever he was in charge of them. There is no public office that this man has not occupied—although you can see how old he is—and he was not appointed by lot or elected to a single one of them, but he bought his way into all of them contrary to the laws.⁵² I will omit most of them and only mention two or three.

[107] When he was appointed an auditor, he damaged the city greatly by accepting bribes from men who had been dishonest while in office, even though he was very quick to lodge malicious accusations when men were being audited who had done nothing wrong. He was also appointed as chief magistrate on Andros, an office he bought for thirty minas, borrowing at a rate of nine obols per mina, turning your allies to providers for his debauchery. He treated freeborn women with such contempt as no one had ever shown before. I will not invite anyone up here to give evidence in public about his misfortune, which he chose to keep secret, but I will leave this to you to consider. [108] What do you expect? In Athens he has subjected not only others to outrage but even his own body, where there are laws and you are watching and enemies are lurking; so when the same man got the license and the power and the authority, who could hope that he would refrain from any of the most excessive abuses? By Zeus and Apollo, I have already recalled many times the blessings of our city, as far as many things go, and not least for this—that in those years there was no buyer available for the city of Andros.⁵³

[109] But perhaps he was a bad magistrate on his own and he was upstanding in a group with many others. How? When he was a member of the Council during the archonship of Nicophemus,⁵⁴ he committed so

---

52. All Athenian officials, except the assessors (*paredroi*) of the three senior archons, were appointed either by lot or through direct election. This is why the claim of Aeschines that Timarchus had bought every single office he ever occupied is undoubtedly an exaggeration. Corruption of public officials in fourth-century Athens was a *topos* in the literature of the period, but bribery was only possible after someone entered office. Of the offices mentioned as examples, Aeschines admits that Timarchus was appointed by lot to be an auditor and a councilor (**113**). While he may have bought the office of archon at the island of Andros, this office was probably for tax collection, and as such, it went to the highest bidder (see the introduction to this speech).

53. As Fisher (2001: 247) points out, in this "final effective hyperbole," Aeschines suggests that if a buyer could be found for the entire city of Andros, Timarchus would have sold it the way he sold his entire parental estate.

54. Nicophemus was archon in 361/0.

many atrocities that it would take me the whole day to go through all of them. But those that are most relevant for the charge that the present trial concerns, I will briefly relate to you. [110] During the same archonship, when he was on the Council, Hegesandrus the brother of Crobylus was a treasurer of the goddess, and they were in the process of stealing together—like good friends—one thousand drachmas. When a decent man, Pamphilus of Acherdous, who was angry with and irritated by him, learned of the matter, he stood up in the Assembly and said, "Men of Athens, a man and a woman are conspiring to steal one thousand drachmas." [111] When you were wondering what he meant by a man and a woman, and what he was talking about, he said after a short break, "Do you not know what I'm talking about? The man now is Hegesandrus over there," he said, "and he was previously Leodamas' woman, and the woman is Timarchus here. How the money is being embezzled, I will tell you." After that he explained the whole case, in a very knowledgeable and clear manner. Once he explained all this, he said, "So what am I advising you to do, men of Athens? If the Council finds against him and, after an olive-leaf ballot, decides to hand him over to court, give them their award, but if they do not punish him, do not give it to them but hold the memory of this day against them." [112] After all this, when the Council returned to the Council House, they took an olive-leaf ballot, and it went against him, but they exonerated him in the final ballot. They did not hand him over to court and did not expel him, and it pains me to say it, but I must tell you that this Council did not receive its award.[55] Do not appear, men of Athens, to be angry at the Council and leave five hundred men among your citizens without a wreath because it failed to punish this man here but then you yourselves let him go and preserve for the Assembly the speaker who did not prove useful to the Council.

[113] But perhaps this was his conduct in offices appointed by lot and he was better in elected offices. Who among you does not know how famously he was caught stealing when he was sent as an inspector of the foreigners in Eretria? He alone among the inspectors admitted that he accepted money, and he did not even try to defend himself but admitted

---

55. The Council of the Five Hundred, according to a very old, traditional procedure, took the initial vote using olive leaves to decide whether they would pursue the matter further and have a proper hearing over these charges. They decided to have a hearing, and in the end of the process with a regular ballot, they exonerated Timarchus. At the end of their term the Assembly voted whether the councilors should be awarded wreaths in recognition of their service. That year the Council was denied this honor. Undoubtedly this decision was based upon the conduct of that particular Council during its entire year in office and probably concerned matters of greater importance than this rather minor and unsubstantiated incident.

that he had done wrong and pleaded about the penalty.[56] You imposed a penalty of one talent upon those who denied it, but thirty minas upon him. The laws, however, dictate that the thieves who confess are to be punished by death, while those who deny it are to stand trial.

[114] Ultimately, he has demonstrated such contempt for you that he accepted two thousand drachmas during the citizens' scrutiny to claim that Philotades of Cydathenaeum, one of the citizens, was a manumitted slave of his. He persuaded his demesmen to vote against him, turned up in court, took in his hands the sacred offerings, and took an oath that he had not received nor was going to receive any bribes, invoking the gods of oaths and destruction upon himself if he lied. [115] However, it was revealed that he had received twenty minas from Leuconides, the brother-in-law of Philotades, through Philemon the actor. This money he spent on Philoxene the courtesan in a very short period of time, and thus he abandoned the case and lied under oath. That I am telling the truth, please call Philemon, who gave Timarchus the money, and Leuconides the brother-in-law of Philotades, and read the copy of the agreement, according to which he sold the case.[57]

TESTIMONIES, AGREEMENTS

[116] How he has conducted himself towards the citizens and his relatives and how shamefully he squandered his parental estate and how he tolerated the abuse against his own body, you knew even before I said it, but my speech also has served as a good reminder. There are only two items in this prosecution speech that I need to go through—and I pray to all the gods and goddesses that I speak on behalf of the city, as I have prepared to

---

56. The inspectors were in charge of the assessment and payment of mercenary troops the Athenians maintained on the island of Euboea. Fisher (2001: 251–52) suggests that the lack of witnesses confirming such a public and recent event is suspicious.

57. This is another puzzling instance where Aeschines is probably making excessive use of circumstantial evidence. It is very unlikely that a written contract detailing such illegal and immoral activities existed between Timarchus and the men who wanted Philotades removed from the citizen register of the deme of Cydathenaeum. We cannot extrapolate from the narrative of Aeschines what the contract said, if it was a genuine document at all, and we cannot fully understand the details of this affair. What is clear is that Timarchus spoke against the registration of Philotades during the latter's scrutiny and won the vote in the deme. Then Timarchus had to go to court when Philotades appealed the decision of the deme, and he lost that case, since Philotades was obviously a full citizen. Aeschines alleges that Timarchus spoke against Philotades because he had been bribed by the latter's brother-in-law.

do—and I would like you to pay attention and follow closely what I am going to say.[58]

[117] The first item in my speech is a refutation of the defense, which I hear that they intend to make, in order to prevent an omission of mine from allowing the man who promises to teach the young the art of speaking to trick you with some deceit and deprive the city of what is beneficial. The second part of my speech is an exhortation of citizens to exercise virtue. I can see many of the younger people present in court, many of the elders, and not a few from the rest of Greece gathered for the hearing. [118] You should not think that they came to see me, but rather to find out whether you not only know how to enact good laws but also can judge what is good and what is not good and whether you know how to honor good men and punish those who inflict shame upon the city with their lifestyle. But first I will talk to you about the defense.

[119] Demosthenes, that long-winded speaker, says that you need to either abolish the laws or pay no attention to my words. He wonders in amazement whether you all remember that every year the Council auctions the prostitution tax, and those who buy this tax do not guess but know exactly who practices this trade. So when I dare to accuse Timarchus of not being permitted to address the Assembly, since he is a prostitute, he says that he wants not accusations from a prosecutor but the testimony from a tax collector who collected this tax from Timarchus.[59] [120] In response to that, men of Athens, consider whether I will appear to you to be saying something straightforward and fitting for a free man. For I am ashamed on behalf of the city if Timarchus, the advisor of the people, who was boldly serving as ambassador throughout Greece, will not attempt to expunge this accusation in its entirety, but he will ask me to indicate the places where he was established and whether the tax collectors ever took from him the prostitute tax. [121] For your sake, he ought to forego this kind of defense. I will suggest to you another speech, a good and just one, which you will

---

58. This transitional section concludes the narrative and serves as a proemium for the refutation of the anticipated arguments of the defense and as a section which Aeschines calls a *paraklesis,* an exhortation of citizens to follow virtue. This means that no new material will be presented regarding the case; what follows will be a further analysis of the material already presented.

59. Aeschines uses a dramatic present tense at this point, hoping to bring the alleged defense of Timarchus by Demosthenes to life, as if it were happening right now in front of the eyes of the judges. If indeed Demosthenes were to use this argument, it would have been for rhetorical effect, since only those involved in organized prostitution were taxed. Freelance prostitutes at the higher end of the market, maintained by rich lovers in luxurious surroundings, were beyond the reach of tax collectors.

deliver if you know in your conscience that you have done nothing wrong. Dare to look the judges in the eye and say what it is appropriate for a man who has conducted himself properly in his prime: "Men of Athens, I have been brought up among you since my childhood and adolescence; I do not engage in secretive activities, but I am seen among you in the Assembly. [122] I think that if I had to defend myself before another body against the charges for which I am now on trial, I would have been able to dispel the prosecutor's accusations very easily with your testimonies. Not only if I have actually done anything of the sort but even if I only appear to have lived in a manner that resembles their accusations, I would consider the rest of my life to be unlivable, and I submit my own punishment as an apology on behalf of the city to the rest of the Greek world. I did not come here to plead with you; do whatever you want with me if I appear to you to be this kind of man."

This is, Timarchus, the defense of a good and decent man, who trusts in his own lifestyle and rightly treats any insult with contempt. [123] What Demosthenes is advising you to say are not the words of a free man but those of a prostitute fussing about places. But since you want to know the names of the places, demanding that the case be based on the buildings where you were established, listen to what I am going to say, and you will not use such an argument again, if you have any decency. It is not the buildings or the dwellings that give the name to their inhabitants, but the inhabitants with their practices that give the names to the places. [124] Where many renters hold one residence divided up between them, we call this an apartment complex, but where one person lives, we call it a house. If a doctor moves into one of these workshops on the streets, it is called a doctor's practice; if he moves out and a blacksmith moves into the same workshop, it is called a blacksmith shop; if a fuller, a laundry; if a carpenter, a carpenter's shop; if a pimp and prostitute, then from the work itself it is called a brothel. So you have turned many places into brothels by your skill in the trade. So do not ask where you practiced this trade; your defense should be that you did not practice this trade.

[125] It seems that another argument will follow, assembled by the same sophist. He says that there is nothing more unjust than rumor, providing evidence from the market place, which follows closely his own lifestyle. First he says that the apartment complex in Colonus, the one that is called the House of Demon, is falsely named because it does not belong to Demon. Then the so-called Herm of Andocides is not from Andocides but a dedication of the Aegeis tribe. [126] Then, in some kind of joke, he puts himself forward as a likeable man and funny in his private life. "If I were to listen to the crowds," he says, "then I should not be called Demosthenes but Batalus, because this is the affectionate nickname that I have from my

nurse." And he says that if Timarchus was handsome and is ridiculed with slander for that reason and not for his own actions, he does not deserve to suffer misfortune because of this.

[127] I hear, Demosthenes, many names of all sorts that are used and never the same ones for dedications, houses, possessions, and in general all mute objects. Good and bad actions do not apply to them, but whoever happens to be associated with the objects gives them his name depending on the greatness of his own reputation. But when it comes to the lives of people and their actions, a true rumor spontaneously roams through the city, reveals private acts to the people, and foretells much about the future. [128] What I am saying is so obvious and so free from fabrication that you will find even our city and ancestors have erected an altar for Rumor, as a great goddess, and Homer says many times in the *Iliad* before something is about to happen, "Rumor came into the army,"[60] and again Euripides declares that this goddess reveals what kind of persons not only the living people are but also the dead, when he says:

Rumor reveals the glorious man even in the recesses of the earth.[61]

[129] Hesiod expressly shows her to be a goddess, talking very clearly to those who want to understand; he says:

Rumor never dissipates completely, spoken by many peoples; for she is a goddess herself.[62]

You will find that men who have lived appropriately praise these poems, because those who seek public honor expect to find glory in their good reputation. However, those whose lifestyle has been indecent do not honor this goddess, because they think that she is their eternal accuser. [130] Now recall, men of Athens, what kind of rumor you circulate in the case of Timarchus. As soon as his name is mentioned, you ask this question, "Which Timarchus? The whore?" If I presented witnesses over something you would believe me; however, if I present the goddess herself as a witness, are you not going to believe me? It is not appropriate even to accuse her of false testimony. [131] Likewise, in the case of the nickname of Demosthenes, he is fittingly called Batalus not by his nurse but by rumor, because of his lack of manhood and effeminacy. If someone removed from you those elegant cloaks and the soft tunics that you wear when you write speeches against your friends and, carrying them around, gave them to the

---

60. Since this line does not appear in the *Iliad*, Aeschines probably remembered incorrectly.

61. Eur. fr. 865.

62. Hes. *Op.* 763–64.

jurors, I think that unless one told them in advance they would wonder whether they are holding a man's or a woman's outfit.

[132] One of the generals will stand up for the defense, as I hear, with an air of superiority, giving the impression that he has spent much time in gymnasia and leisurely discussions. He will attempt to ridicule the whole basis of this trial, arguing that I have not come up with a court case but the beginning of a terrible lack of education, giving as an example your benefactors, Harmodius and Aristogeiton, and the trust they had in each other and how this proved advantageous for the city. [133] He will not keep away, as they say, not even from the poems of Homer or the names of heroes; he will also praise the friendship that was born from the love of Patroclus and Achilles, and he will sing praises to beauty, as if it had not long been celebrated as a fortunate gift when combined with wisdom. He will argue that if some people through slander turn good looks into a curse for those who have them, what you vote in public will not be the same with what you wish in private. [134] He will say that he finds it illogical if when you are going to have children you pray for your unborn sons to be handsome and noble in their appearance and worthy of the city, but those already born—of whom the city should be very proud if they amaze some with their exceptional beauty and youth and have people fight for their love—you will disfranchise should you be persuaded to do as Aeschines recommends. [135] Then, as I hear, he is planning to go after me, asking if I am not ashamed, since I am such a nuisance in the gymnasia and I have been the lover of many, to bring this act into disrepute and into the courts. Finally, as some people tell me, in order to reduce you to laughter and tomfoolery, he will say that he will show all the erotic poems that I composed for lovers, and he will produces witnesses to some of the ridicule and blows that I received in this pursuit.

[136] I do not fault fair love, nor do I say that exceptionally good-looking persons are prostitutes. I do not deny that I have been in love affairs and still am even now, and I do not deny that the arguments and fights that occur with other men from this matter happened to me. Regarding the poems they claim that I have composed: I will acknowledge some, but others, which they mangle, I deny that they are of the tenor that they will give them. [137] I define the desire for those who are beautiful and prudent as the passion of a generous and sensible soul, while I believe that performing shameless acts for money is the work of an insolent and uneducated man. I say that love free of corruption is a beautiful thing, but to become a prostitute out of a desire for money is a shameful thing. How far apart these two stand from each other and how much they differ, I will try to explain subsequently in my speech. [138] Our fathers, when they were introducing laws on ways of living and what is necessary by nature, whatever

they considered suitable for free people they forbade slaves. "A slave," says the law, "is not to be training or anointing himself in the wrestling arena." When the lawgivers forbade the slaves from participating, because they could see the benefits of wrestling, in the same law they deemed it appropriate to encourage free persons to take up what they had forbidden for the slaves. [139] Again, the same lawgiver said, "A slave is not to desire or pursue a free-born child, or else he is to receive fifty lashes with the public whip." However, he did not prevent the desire and association and pursuit by free persons, and he did not consider this to be harmful for the boy but a testimony of good character. Since the boy is still underage and incapable of judging for himself who is a true friend and who is not, the lawgiver expects good conduct from the lover and postpones the words of friendship until he reaches an older and wiser age. However, to follow the boy and watch over him he considered the most effective guard and protection of his good conduct.[63] [140] This is why the benefactors of the city, Harmodius and Aristogeiton, who have excelled in virtue, were educated to become this kind of men by this prudent and lawful love, or whatever else it is appropriate to call it, so that those who praise their actions appear to fall short in their praise of the achievements of those men.

[141] Since you mentioned Achilles and Patroclus, and Homer and the other poets, as if the jurors were uneducated while you pretend to be sophisticated, and with your learning you look down on the people, we will say something about this, too, to show you that we also have heard and learned a few things. Since they are attempting to make references to philosophers, and resort to words said in verse, take a look at the poets who are recognized by all as good and wise, men of Athens, and consider to what extent they deemed it appropriate to separate prudent men who love those like themselves from men who cannot curb their unlawful desires and commit outrage. [142] First I will talk about Homer, whom we count among the oldest and wisest poets. Although he has mentioned Achilles and Patroclus many times, he hides their love and the name of their relationship because he believes that the abundance of their affection will make this clear to the educated members of the audience. [143] Achilles says somewhere, mourning

---

63. Passages such as this have been widely interpreted as an indication that the *erastes* (the pursuer) should not have sexual contact with the *eromenos* (the pursued), and that the relationship was essentially platonic. This interpretation was undoubtedly generated under the influence of modern sexual norms and does not make any sense. It defies logic to suggest that one would go through considerable trouble and expense without the expectation of sexual rewards in the end, and is explicitly contradicted by a vast number of references in Greek literature and art. Aeschines does not wish to speak about such matters more explicitly before a jury and may be cautious, trying not to offend anyone.

the death of Patroclus, as he remembers one of the saddest things—that unintentionally he did not keep the promise he made to the father of Patroclus,
Menoetius. He promised to bring Patroclus safely back to Opus if Menoetius
sent him to Troy with Achilles and entrusted him to his care. At this point it
becomes apparent that Achilles took charge of him because of love.

[144] These are the verses that I am now going to recite for you:

> Alas, the words in vain I uttered on that day,
> encouraging Menoetius the hero in his halls.
> I promised him to bring back to Opus his glorious son
> once he had conquered Ilion and acquired his share of the booty.
> But Zeus does not fulfill all the designs of men;
> for it is destined for both of us to dye red the same earth.[64]

[145] Now, this is not the only place where he expresses his grief, but he
mourned him so intensely that—although he had heard from his mother,
Thetis, that if he did not go after his enemies but left the death of Patroclus
unavenged, he would return home and die an old man in his homeland,
but if he avenged him, very soon his own life would end—still he chose to
honor his pledge to the dead above his own salvation. With such magna-
nimity he rushed to punish the killer of Patroclus that although everyone
was consoling him and begging him to bathe himself and take some food,
he swore not to do any of these before he brought the head of Hector onto
the grave of Patroclus. [146] When he was sleeping next to the funeral pyre,
as the poet says, the ghost of Patroclus appeared and reminded Achilles of
such things that it is worthy to weep and envy their virtue and friendship.
When he prophesized that Achilles, too, was not far away from the end of
his own life, he instructed him that if there was a way to arrange it, in the
same manner as they were brought up and lived together, so also when dead
their bones would be placed in the same coffin. [147] Crying and going
through the pursuits they shared in their lives, Patroclus says, "we will no
longer discuss the most important matters as before, sitting with each other
alone away from our other friends." He means, I believe, that trust and
affection are most desirable. The secretary will read the verses that Homer
has composed about this so that you can hear in meter the opinions of the
poet. [148] First read the passages that relate to the punishment of Hector:

> But since, beloved friend, I am following you under the earth,
> I promise not to bury you before I bring here
> the weapons and the head of Hector, the magnanimous killer.[65]

---

64. Hom. *Il.* 18.324–29.
65. Hom. *Il.* 17.333–35.

[149] Now read what Patroclus says in the dream about them being buried together and the kind of pursuits that they shared with each other.

> No longer alive, apart from our beloved friends
> we will sit and take decisions, but I was swallowed
> by dire fate, which was allotted to me from birth
> and the same fate awaits you, Achilles, like to the gods,
> to die under the wall of the noble Trojans,
> fighting for the divine Helen, with the beautiful hair.
> But I will tell you one more thing, and keep it in your mind.
> Do not place my bones far away from yours, Achilles,
> but so that the same earth covers both you and myself
> in a golden amphora, which your mother has supplied,
> as we were brought up together in your house,
> when Menoetius brought me from Opus to your house,
> still a little boy after the terrible manslaughter,
> on the day when I killed the son of Amphidamas,
> while still very young, unwillingly, angered over a game of
>   knucklebones.
> Then Peleus the knight accepted me in his house
> and brought me up with kindness, and named me your follower;
> so let the same coffin also engulf our bones.[66]

[150] To show that he could have saved himself by not avenging the death of Patroclus, read what Thetis says:

> "You will die soon, my child, by what you say;
> for after Hector, your death will be ready and waiting."
> But the swift-footed, divine Achilles said to her,
> "I'd rather die right now, if I'm not going to avenge
> the death of my friend, whom I love most dearly." [67]

[151] Euripides, not less wise than any other poet, considers love with decorum to be one of the worthiest things and includes love in a prayer when he says somewhere:

> Love leading to temperance and virtue
> is to be envied among people, of whom I may be one.[68]

---

66. Hom. *Il.* 23.77–91.

67. Hom. *Il.* 18.95–99.

68. Eur. *Sthen.* fr. 762 Nauck.

[152] The same poet declares in the *Phoenix,* responding to the charges of his father and admonishing people not to pass judgments on the basis of suspicion or slander but on evidence from one's lifestyle:

> I have already been appointed to judge many disputes
> and I have often heard opposing views on the same misfortune
> presented with equal persuasiveness by witnesses.
> And I, like any man who is wise, in this manner
> I reach the truth: I observe a man's nature
> and the kind of lifestyle he leads every day.
> The man who takes pleasure in the company of wicked people,
> I have never questioned, knowing that
> he is of the same character as those men whose company he enjoys.[69]

[153] Consider, men of Athens, the ideas expressed by the poet: he declares that he has already served as a judge in many disputes, like you, men of the jury, and admits that he has passed judgment on the basis not of testimonies but of lifestyles and associations, by looking into the way a defendant lives his day-to-day life and how he administers his own household—on the grounds that he would administer the affairs of the city in the same manner—and who his associates are. In conclusion, he did not hesitate to declare that a man is the same as those whose company he enjoys. It is fair for you to apply the same reasoning as Euripides also to the case of Timarchus. [154] How did he administer his own estate? He squandered his paternal inheritance, and then having sold his own body and taken bribes from the state he has wasted everything so that he is left with nothing else except shame. And whose company does he enjoy? Hegesandrus'. And what kind of lifestyle does Hegesandrus live? The one that by law bars him from speaking in the Assembly. And what am I saying about Timarchus, and what am I accusing him of? That Timarchus should not speak in the Assembly because he has been a prostitute, and he has squandered his parental estate. And what oath did you swear? To cast your vote only in relation to the offense for which this trial is being held.

[155] So as not to speak for too long about the poets, now I will mention to you the names of men more senior and well known, and also young men and boys, who became the lovers of many because of their good looks, and some in their prime still even now have lovers; none of them has ever been accused of the same thing as Timarchus. Then I will contrast them with the men who have prostituted themselves shamefully and openly so that you can recall them and then assign Timarchus to the appropriate group. [156] First I will remind you of the names of those who have lived

---

69. Eur. *Phoen.* fr. 812 Nauck.

well and in a manner befitting free men. You know, men of Athens, Crito the son of Astyochus and Pericleides of Perithoedae and Polemagenes and Pantaleon the son of Cleagoras and Timesitheus the runner. They were the most beautiful men not only among the citizens but among all Greeks, and they were the lovers of many very discreet men yet no one ever found fault with them. [157] From the young men and those who are still among the boys, I will mention the nephew of Iphicrates, the son of Teisias of Rhamnus, who has the same name as Timarchus, who is now on trial.[70] Although he is very good looking, he abstains from inappropriate behavior to such an extent that recently, when comedies were performed in Collytus during the rural Dionysia, and Parmenon the comic actor addressed an anapest to the chorus, in which it was said that there are some really great Timarchian whores, no one thought of the boy but everyone thought of you; so obviously you are the heir of this trade. Then I will mention Anticles the stadium runner and Pheidias, the brother of Melesias. I could still mention many more, but I will stop so as not to arouse suspicion that I use their praise as a form of flattery.

[158] When it comes to those who share the ways of Timarchus, so as not to incur animosity, I will mention those who concern me the least.[71] Who among you does not know Diophantus, the so-called orphan, who arrested a foreigner and brought him to the archon, whose assessor was Aristophon of Azenia?[72] He accused him of nonpayment of four drachmas, which he was owed for this act, and invoked the laws that command the archon to look after the orphans, while he himself had violated the laws on good conduct. Who among the citizens was not upset at Cephisodorus, known as the son of Molon, for infamously wasting his splendid youthful looks, or Mnesitheus, known as the son of the cook, or many others whom I want to forget? [159] I do not wish to bitterly go through the names of

---

70. The identification of this particular boy is unusual; hence it is done with deference to the boy and his powerful family. His uncle Iphicrates was one of the most prominent Athenian generals in the first quarter of the fourth century, and his was certainly a household name at the time of Aeschines.

71. The Greek is not very clear. Most previous translators have understood *apechtheia* (here translated "animosity") to mean "enmity," and thus this sentence as a rhetorical explanation. Aeschines is saying that he will avoid mentioning distasteful details and limit himself only to people whose mention does not bother him too much.

72. Each of the three senior archons, the *basileus,* the polemarch, and the archon (or eponymous archon), had two assessors (*paredroi*) of his own choosing, and these could be family members or trusted friends of the archon or experienced politicians, like Aristophon of Azenia in this case, capable of providing assistance to the archon with the demands and challenges of his office.

each one of them, but I would rather pray to find it difficult to mention such names in my speech for the sake of the city. Since we chose a few from each group and went through their names, separating those who are loved with propriety from those who shame themselves, answer me now the question that I have already asked you: in which class would you assign Timarchus—among those who are loved or those who have been prostituted? So do not abandon the group that you have chosen and flee to the pursuits befitting free men.⁷³

[160] If they attempt to say that he has not been a prostitute because he was not hired on a contract and ask me to present the document and the witnesses for those acts, first remember the laws on male prostitution, in which the lawgiver nowhere mentions a written contract. He did not consider whether someone shamed himself in accordance with the terms of a written contract but ordered the man who had engaged in such activities, no matter how the act was done, to refrain from the affairs of the city. Naturally the lawgiver did not believe that a man who in his youth and because of base lust lacked the drive towards good things deserved the full honors of a citizen when he was older. [161] Then it is easy to see also the naïveté of such a statement. We would all confess that we enter into contracts because of our mistrust towards each other, so that the person who did not breach the contract can obtain justice in court from the person who breached it. So if the case needs to go to trial for those who have prostituted themselves in accordance with a written contract if they suffer injustice, the assistance of the laws, as they claim, is their only refuge. And what would the speech of each one look like? Think that you do not see the whole thing told by me, but actually happening. [162] Let the customer have justice on his side while the hired man is unjust and not trustworthy, or perhaps the other way around—the hired man is fair and doing what was agreed while the one who took his youth and hired him has been lying. And imagine that you are sitting as jurors. So the older man, when he gets the water and the time to speak, he will hurry to the roster, look at you, and say, [163] "I hired Timarchus, men of Athens, to be my prostitute according to the terms of the tablet that lies next to Demosthenes" (for there

---

73. The direct address to Timarchus in the last sentence is unexpected. The orator urges him to stay within the group of his choice (namely, the prostitutes). It is difficult to find in English a more accurate term than "group" or something similar, for Greek *symmoria,* which refers to the groups to which wealthy citizens were assigned for paying a levied tax (*eisphora*) and sharing the costs for maintaining and repairing Athenian triremes (see **Dem. 21.153** n.). Ironically, its Modern Greek meaning, translated as "gang," would be well suited here, but the word does not seem to have this meaning in fourth-century Greek.

is nothing preventing such a statement), "but he does not do for me what we agreed." He goes in great detail in front of the jurors about everything that such a man ought to do. Is he not going to be stoned, the man who hired an Athenian citizen against the laws, and is he not going to leave the court not only with a large fine but also with a lot of scorn? [164] Now suppose he is not standing trial but the one who was hired. Let him come up here and speak, or maybe the wise Batalus will speak on his behalf so that we can see what he is going to say.[74] "Men of the jury, he hired me to be his prostitute for whatever sum of money" (it does not really make any difference); "and I have done everything, and I still do what the prostitute needs to do, as stated in the contract, but he is breaking the agreement." Is he not going to encounter a lot of shouting from the jurors in response? For who is not going to say, "Then do you make your way into the agora, wear crowns, and perform the same duties as us?" So the contract was no use to him.

[165] I will tell you how it prevailed and became custom to say that some have prostituted themselves "under contract." One of your fellow citizens (I won't mention his name, in order to avoid hostility), not foreseeing what I just mentioned to you, is said to have prostituted himself according to the terms of a contract deposited with Anticles. Since he was not a private citizen but involved in politics and incurring a lot of ridicule, he made this saying customary in the city, and for that reason some people ask if the act has been happening "under contract." However, the lawgiver did not care how the act happened; if there was any form of hiring, he attached shame to the wrongdoer.

[166] Even though these matters are so clearly defined, many irrelevant arguments will be invented by Demosthenes. One might be less indignant about all the nasty words that are relevant to the case, but the irrelevant arguments that he is going to bring up, polluting what is fair for the city, deserve to invoke your wrath. There is going to be much talk about Philip, and even the name of his son, Alexander, is going to be thrown in. On top of his many flaws, this man, Demosthenes, is uncultured and uneducated. [167] To offend Philip in his speech is boorish and untimely, but a lesser

---

74. The text of Dilts, which this translation follows, has adopted an emendation of Blass; the text of the manuscripts would be translated as "let the wise Batalus come up here and speak on this behalf." Blass changed the transmitted text because of the first person which follows immediately afterwards suggesting that the prostitute himself is speaking, not Batalus (i.e., Demosthenes; cf. **127**) as his advocate. However, there is a good possibility that the transmitted text is correct. The meaning would be that these are the words of Demosthenes, pulling the strings from the background, even though they are delivered by the prostitute himself.

error than the one I am going to expose. Admittedly he will throw insults against a man even though he is not a man himself. However, when he casts shameful suspicions upon the boy with crafty verbal shifts, he makes the city the subject of ridicule. [168] In order to undermine my forthcoming audit regarding the embassy, he says that when he was talking about the boy Alexander in a prior meeting of the Council, how he was playing the cithara in a drinking party and exchanging lines and responses with another boy, and when he was revealing to the Council whatever he happened to know about these matters, I was upset over the jibes directed at the boy, as if I were a relative, not a fellow ambassador. [169] Of course I have not spoken directly to Alexander because of his young age, but I praise Philip for the good words that he has spoken. If his actions towards us match his promises, he will earn safe and easy praise. I rebuked Demosthenes in the Council House, not in order to earn favor with the boy but because I thought that if you put up with this, the city will appear to have the same sort of indecency as the speaker.[75]

[170] Altogether, men of Athens, do not accept arguments for the defense that do not concern this case—first, on account of the oaths that you have sworn and second, in order to avoid being distracted by a man skilled with words. I will begin to instruct you, going back a little. Demosthenes, after squandering his paternal estate, went around the city on the hunt for rich orphaned young men, whose fathers had passed away and the mothers were in charge of the estate. Skipping many, I will mention one of those who suffered terribly. [171] He saw a rich but not well-run house, and the head of it was an arrogant but stupid woman while a young half-crazy man was the manager of the estate, Aristarchus the son of Moschus. He pretended to be his lover and invited the youngster to experience his kind of generosity, filling his head with empty promises to make him the best orator in town, showing him a list. [172] He introduced him and taught him such acts for which he is living in exile while Demosthenes has deprived him of the three talents, which he received in advance, intended for the maintenance of Aristarchus while in exile. Nicodemus of Aphidna died a violent death at the hands of Aristarchus. The poor man had both his eyes

---

75. Aeschines at this point is subject to the same fault for which he is accusing the defense of Timarchus: the reference to the episode in the Council House where Aeschines protested over the jibes of Demosthenes at the young Alexander has nothing to do with the case against Timarchus. It is a personal attack on Demosthenes and an opportunity for Aeschines to demonstrate his own sense of propriety, by mentioning that he never directly conversed with the still underage Alexander, lest such a conversation be misconstrued for inappropriate courtship.

pulled out and his tongue cut off, with which he was speaking freely, trusting in the laws and you yourselves.

[173] You put to death, men of Athens, Socrates the sophist, because it was shown that he had educated Critias, one of the thirty tyrants who overthrew the democracy.[76] Demosthenes, however, is going to steal away from you his friends, the same man who has inflicted such punishment upon private citizens with solid democratic credentials for exercising their freedom of speech. Several of his pupils have been invited here to listen to the trial; he promises to them, as I hear, that he will surreptitiously subvert the course of this trial and your hearing [174] and that he will inspire confidence in the defendant when he comes up here to speak. He will also scare off the prosecutor and make him fear for himself, and he will raise such great outcry among the jurors, by making references to my own public speeches and blaming the peace, which was concluded through me and Philocrates, so that I will not even dare to respond to him in court but I will be content if I am fined with a moderate fine and not condemned to death. [175] Do not, under any circumstances, allow this sophist to laugh and have fun at your expense, but imagine that you can see him coming home from court and boasting in the company of young men and telling them how much he stole the case from the jurors: "Leading them away from the charges against Timarchus, I made them focus upon the prosecutor and Philip and the Phocians, and I inspired fear in the audience. As a result, the defendant was the prosecutor, and the prosecutor was on trial, and the jurors forgot the matter for which they were sitting in judgment, and listened to matters that they were not to judge." [176] It is your task to object to this, and keeping an eye on him constantly, do not allow him to deviate or use one of those arguments that do not concern the case. But like horse races, keep him running inside the prescribed route of the case. If you do this, you will not be scorned and you will have the same opinion when you pass the laws as when you judge cases. Otherwise, you will appear to be angry when you sense in advance crimes to be committed in the future, but when they have already happened you no longer care.

[177] In order to summarize, if you punish those who have committed crimes, your laws will be good and valid, but if you let them get away, they will still be good, but no longer valid. Why I am saying this, I will

---

76. Until the Hellenistic period, the term "'sophist" did not always carry negative connotations; see for example [Dem.] 59.17, but here and in section 175, (cf. 125) there are negative undertones, since Aeschines criticizes Socrates and Demosthenes for engaging in those practices that Athenians regarded as morally reprehensible and were commonly attributed to sophists, i.e., the ability to mislead a mass audience through deceptive rhetoric and corrupt young men by teaching them this skill.

not hesitate to explain to you openly. I'll tell you with an example. Why do you think, men of Athens, that the established laws are sound but the decrees of the city are inferior and sometimes the judgments of the courts attract criticism? I will explain to you the reasons for this. [178] You establish the laws, aiming at all things that are just, and not with an eye on unjust profit or favor or enmity but only upon what is just and expedient. And since, I think, you are by nature more ingenious than others, expectedly you set the best laws. However, many a time in the assemblies and the courts, because you have a relaxed attitude towards speeches that are outside the case itself, you are led astray by deceit and arrogance and admit into the trial the most unjust custom of all: you allow the defendants to turn around and prosecute the prosecutors. [179] Once you are distracted by the defense and turn your minds elsewhere, you forget the prosecution, and you leave the court without punishing either of them, neither the prosecutor (because you do not get to vote on him), nor the defendant (because he brushed aside the charges against him with accusations against others and walked free from court). The laws are rendered invalid, and democracy is becoming corrupt and the custom goes too far; for sometimes you easily accept words without a moral lifestyle.

[180] The Lacedaemonians, however, do not; and it is good to adopt the virtues of foreigners, too. A man was speaking in the Spartan Assembly who had lived improperly, but he was a particularly effective speaker. As the story goes, the Lacedaemonians were just about to vote for his proposal, but one of the Elders came forward—those men whom they respect and fear and which particular age group has given its name to an office they regard as the highest. They appoint them from among men who have lived properly from childhood to their old age. One of them, it is said, came forward and vehemently chastised the Lacedaemonians, and he even insulted them in this manner—saying that they would not keep Sparta impregnable for much longer if they rely on such advisors in the Assembly. [181] Then he invited another man from among the Lacedaemonians, not naturally good at speaking but a splendid warrior and distinguished for his sense of justice and discipline. He told him to express the same opinions, as best as he could, that the previous orator had said, "so that," he said, "the Lacedaemonians will vote for the words of a good man while the voices of cowardly and wicked men will not even reach their ears." This is what the old man who had lived his life with decency since childhood advised his fellow citizens. He would certainly allow Timarchus or the deviant Demosthenes to participate in politics.[77]

---

77. This is a sarcastic statement; he means that such men would never participate in politics in Sparta. Aeschines here transfers Athenian political procedures to Sparta. In

[182] In order not to appear to be lavishing praise on the Lacedaemonians, I will also mention our own ancestors. They were so strict about shameful behavior and prized so highly the virtuous behavior of their children that one man among the citizens, when he found that his daughter had been corrupted and she had not saved her virginity until her wedding, he fenced her inside a deserted house together with a horse, which was certainly going to kill her, since they were imprisoned together. The site of this house is still in the city, and the area is called "the place of the horse and the girl." [183] Moreover, Solon, the most glorious lawgiver, introduced ancient and solemn laws on the orderly conduct of women. He forbids a woman with whom an adulterer has been caught to adorn herself or enter into the public temples, so that she will not contaminate the chaste women by associating with them. If she enters or adorns herself, he commands any citizen to tear her clothes and remove her jewelry and hit her but not kill or injure her permanently, thus disenfranchising this kind of woman and making her life unlivable.[78] [184] He also orders public prosecutions against procuresses and procurers, and if they are convicted he orders the death penalty, because those who have a desire to engage in shameful acts may be hesitant and ashamed to have encounters with each other, but the procurers, by hiring out their own shamelessness, allow the affair to reach the stage of trial and negotiation.[79]

[185] Then, our ancestors had made such wise decisions regarding good and shameful conduct, but you are going to acquit Timarchus although he is guilty of the most shameful conduct? This man who has a male body, but has committed female sins? Who of you will punish a woman if he catches her? Or who will not appear stupid if he is upset at the woman who has sinned according to her nature but uses as an advisor the man who has abused himself against his own nature? [186] What opinion will each

---

the Spartan Assembly speakers were not given equal access to the political process. From the little we know about it, it does seem that the procedure normally was hierarchical, as Aeschines suggests, and the Elders and more influential citizens were leading the political proceedings while the rest of the Assembly simply rubber-stamped their decisions.

78. The original text of this law is quoted in [Dem.] 59.87. There it becomes clear that the law only allowed the humiliation of an adulteress who had entered a temple, and it did not specify the forms of punishment. Aeschines may be reflecting social practice here or, at least, circulating tales of morality about such incidents.

79. The law probably was intended to protect the exploitation of free children, not stop the activities in the brothels of Attica, which, according to a certain tradition, Solon himself established. Aeschines is probably exaggerating the penalty, as there is no reference to executions of pimps despite the fact that prostitution of slaves and free persons in the classical period was undoubtedly widespread.

one of you have when you return home from the court? The defendant is not obscure but well known, and the law concerning the scrutiny of the speakers is not bad but a very fine law. It will be expected that each one of you face questions from your own relatives—boys and young men—about how this case went. [187] What are you going to say, you who have been in charge of this verdict, when your boys will ask you whether you condemned or acquitted Timarchus? Are you not turning upside down their entire educational system if you confess that you acquitted Timarchus? What is the benefit of keeping attendants and putting trainers and teachers in charge of the children when those who are entrusted with the enforcement of the laws are turning soft towards shameful acts?[80]

[188] I wonder, men of Athens, how you can hate pimps but you are prepared to absolve those who willingly have prostituted themselves. It appears that the same man, who cannot be appointed by lot to the priesthood of any god because according to the laws he is not clean in his body, will be writing in decrees prayers to the Solemn Goddesses on behalf of the city. Then why do we find strange the common indifference towards politics when such are the speakers who put their name to the decisions of the people? And are we going to send as an ambassador to other cities entrusted with the most serious matters the man who has lived improperly at home? What won't he sell who has sold the shame of his own body? Whom would he pity who has not pitied himself?

[189] Who among you is not well aware of the shamelessness of Timarchus? As we recognize those who work out, even if we do not frequent the gymnasia, by looking at their good physique, in the same manner we recognize the whores, even if we have not observed their acts, by their shamelessness, their boldness, and their lifestyle. The man who has been contemptuous of the laws and decency concerning the greatest matters, he has a certain character of the soul, which becomes transparent by the disorder in his demeanor.

[190] You will find that most of these men have overturned entire cities and they themselves have fallen into the greatest misfortunes. Do not believe, men of Athens, that the beginnings of misfortunes stem from the gods and not from the deplorable behavior of men, or that those who have committed impieties are, like in the tragedies, "driven away and punished with blazing torches by the Furies."[81] [191] But the propensity towards the

---

80. In the closing sections of his speech "Against Neaera," Apollodorus, in a similar tone, invites the jurors to consider the answers they will give to their wives and daughters when they are asked how they had voted in the trial against Neaera (**[Dem.] 59.111**).

81. Cf. Aes. *Eum.* 94–376.

pleasures of the body and the feeling that nothing is ever enough, these are the vices that fill the gangs with robbers and the pirate ships with sailors; these are the Fury for each man, they admonish him to slaughter citizens, serve tyrants, and dissolve the democracy. They do not consider shame or possible penalties, but they are delighted by pleasures that they are going to reap if they succeed. Uproot such natures, men of Athens, and turn the goals of young men towards virtue.

[192] Be well aware of it, and do remember what I am about to say: if Timarchus is punished for his lifestyle, you will begin to establish good order in the city; but if he escapes, it would have been better if this trial never took place. Before Timarchus went to trial, at least some were afraid of the law and the courts; however, if the leader of indecency and the most notorious of all is brought to court and acquitted, he will encourage many others, and in the end it won't be words but dire straits that will excite your anger.[82] [193] So do not wait to knock them down when they are assembled, but one at a time, and watch out for their preparation and their advocates. I will not mention any of them by name so that they cannot make this the opening of their speech, that they would not have come up here if someone had not mentioned them by name. But I will do this: By omitting their names and mentioning only their actions I shall make their persons identifiable. Let everyone be responsible for himself if he comes up here and disgraces himself. [194] This man has advocates from three categories: First there are those who have squandered their parental estate with daily extravagance. Then there are those who have improperly used their youth and their own bodies and are now afraid not for Timarchus but for themselves and their own lifestyle, in case they come to trial. Finally there are those indecent men who have made liberal use of such people in order that some might trust their assistance and be more ready to commit offenses. [195] Before you listen to the defense, recall their lifestyles, and those who have abused their bodies, tell them not to bother you but to stop talking. The law does not examine private citizens but political figures; you tell people who have squandered their parental inheritance to work and make their living from other resources. Tell those hunters of young men who are easily caught to turn their attentions to foreigners and metics so that they are not deprived of their preference but you are not harmed either.[83]

---

82. Apollodorus uses a very similar argument to suggest that it would be better if Neaera's trial had never taken place than for the jury to acquit her (**[Dem.] 59.113–15**).

83. The tone of these sections is characteristic of the general arguments in this speech. This technique, by which specific references to facts are replaced by

[196] You have received from me everything that is just; I explained to you the laws, and I examined the life of the defendant. Now you are the judges of my words, and at the same time I become your spectator; the case rests upon your judgment. If you wish to do what is just and beneficial, we will be more eager to investigate those who commit crimes.

vague allusions to acts of indecency by unspecified individuals, successfully creates the impression that he has already proven the immorality of Timarchus and his associates and he does not need to say anything more about it.

Glossary

Amphictyony: An alliance typically of neighboring cities that oversaw a local sanctuary and had primarily religious functions, but some, such as the Amphictyony of Delphi, had members from throughout the Greek world and acquired significant political importance.

antidosis: Wealthy Athenians were required to perform public services for the city, such as the *choregia, proeisphora,* and the trierarchy. These public services were called liturgies. If an Athenian assigned to perform a liturgy identified another citizen who was wealthier and was not exempt from the liturgy, he could challenge that individual to either perform the liturgy or exchange property (*antidosis*).

aphairesis eis eleutherian: Literally, "removal to freedom." This is a legal action to demand the release of a free individual who has been wrongfully seized as a slave.

apographe: A process used for the recovery of debts to the state. Athens relied on private individuals to initiate proceedings and present a list of property that was in the possession of a debtor to the public treasury and that could be used to pay off the full amount or a part of the debt. The person who initiated the proceedings was rewarded with one-third of the property the state recovered.

architheoros: The leader of the city's sacred embassy to a Panhellenic festival.

archons: The chief officials of Athens. Nine were selected by lot annually to hold office for a period of one year: the *basileus* (king archon), polemarch (war archon), archon (also known as the eponymous archon because the year was named after him), and the six *thesmothetai.*

Areopagus, council of the: Ex-archons served on the council of the Areopagus for life. After Ephialtes stripped the Areopagus of most of its political powers in 462, it functioned primarily as a homicide court. (NB: When "the Council" is mentioned in the translations, it always refers to "the Council of Five Hundred" [*boule*] and should not be confused with "the Areopagus" or "the council of the Areopagus.")

Assembly: See *ekklesia.*

atimia: Disfranchisement, namely the loss of civic rights, in particular the right to participate in politics, Athenian religious festivals and cult activities, and recourse to the Athenian legal system. *Atimia* could be imposed as a penalty for certain offenses or as a result of an unpaid debt to the state.

basanos: Testimony of a slave was only admissible in court if submitted under torture (*basanos*). A party could offer to submit his own slave to torture or challenge the opposing party to submit his. *Basanos* only occurred if the other party accepted the terms of the challenge, which included the questions the slave was to be asked.

basileus: King archon. One of the nine archons selected by lot each year. The *basileus* oversaw the homicide courts.

blabe: damage. An individual could bring a private suit against another for damage to property (*dike blabes*). It covered both physical and financial loss as well as the failure to repay a debt.

boule: The Council, that is, the Council of Five Hundred, which consisted of fifty councilors from each of the ten Athenian tribes. The Council prepared the agenda of the Assembly.

choregia: A type of liturgy performed by a chorus producer (*choregos*), who was responsible for paying the expenses to perform either a dramatic or lyric chorus at one of the religious festivals sponsored by Athens, such as the Dionysia.

deme: Village. The smallest political unit in Athens. Athenian citizenship was based on enrollment in a deme. Athens had 139 demes distributed into the ten tribes so that each tribe had demes from the city, country, and costal regions of Attica.

demarch: The highest official of the deme. He presided over the assembly meetings of the deme.

diapsephisis: A vote in the deme to determine the citizenship status of the members which it had enrolled. In 346, the decree of Demophilus required all demes to review their registers and expunge any individual who was not a citizen. A person who had his name removed from a deme register could appeal the decision before the popular law courts.

dikasteria: The popular law courts of Athens, in contrast to the Areopagus and other homicide courts, were manned by panels of regular jurors (*dikastai*), consisting either of 201 or 401 jurors for private suits, depending on the size of the fine, and 501 and even more for public suits. The jurors were selected by lot each day the courts convened, from those 6,000 Athenians who were picked in the annual sortition to serve on the juries for that year.

dike: Private lawsuit. Only the injured party was permitted to lodge a *dike*. The prosecutor of a *dike* was permitted to drop the suit and settle out of court at any point up to the trial. If the prosecutor won, he received the penalty imposed on the defendant.

dokimasia: Scrutiny. Before holding any office, a candidate—whether elected or selected by lot—had to undergo a scrutiny to verify his eligibility. The primary purpose of the scrutiny was to ensure that the candidate was an Athenian citizen who had not been convicted of a legal offense that barred him from holding public office. Any Athenian could come forward with accusations against the candidate. There was also a scrutiny for newly enrolled ephebes, recipients of the disability benefit, and public speakers.

drachma: A unit of Athenian money. One hundred drachmas equal one mina and six thousand drachmas equal one talent. In the fourth century, daily wages for workers ranged from 1½ to 2½ drachmas.

eisangelia: Literally, "announcement," *eisangelia* was a public denouncement that could be brought either (1) before the Council against an Athenian official in order to impeach him or (2) before the Assembly against a citizen accused of treason.

eisphora: A tax on only wealthy Athenians and metics, first introduced to support military campaigns but later extended for other purposes as well.

ekklesia: The Assembly met forty times per year, four times per prytany. It had a quorum of six thousand. Every citizen had the right to attend, vote, and speak at meetings of the Assembly. Pay for attendance was introduced in the beginning of the fourth century.

Eleven, the: Officials in charge of the Athenian prisons. As their number indicates they formed a board consisting of eleven citizens, assisted by a number of Scythian archers.

ephebe: Once a young man of Athenian birth had reached the age of eighteen, he was introduced by his father or guardian to his deme. If the deme determined that the ephebe was eighteen years old and his parents were Athenian, he was registered in the deme and then underwent a scrutiny (*dokimasia*) before the Council to verify that he had reached the requisite age to be registered as a citizen. All new citizens had to swear the ephebic oath and undergo two years of military training before exercising their civic rights.

ephetai: A panel of fifty-one *ephetai,* probably selected from the members of the Areopagus, heard homicide cases that came before the Palladium and the Delphinium.

eranos: A loan whereby the borrower raised the full amount of the loan by collecting separate contributions from individual friends and usually repaid them in installments without interest or with a very favorable interest rate.

ethopoeia: Characterization. The art of conveying to the audience the character of the speaker.

euthyna: Audit. Every official had to submit to an *euthyna* at the end of his term. Any Athenian could come forward with accusations against the official for misconduct.

exoule: Ejectment. When one party refused to surrender property, which another party had the legal authority to take (e.g., by a court ruling), a suit of ejectment (*dike exoules*) could be lodged to recover the property in question. If found guilty, the defendant was required to return the property to the rightful owner and pay a fine to the city equivalent to the value of the property in question. If he refused to surrender the property, the rightful owner had the right to use force to recover it.

genos: A subdivision of the phratry, probably a privileged clan within it. In the classical period several prominent *gene* retained their role in religion, such as the Eteobutadae, who always supplied the priestess of Athena, and the sacred *gene* of the Ceryces and Eumolpidae, who continued to perform their traditional rights and duties for the cult of Demeter at Eleusis.

graphe: A public suit. Any citizen was permitted to lodge a *graphe* against the alleged offender. The prosecutor could not withdraw the suit once it was lodged, and he was fined one thousand drachmas if he dropped the suit or if he failed to receive at least one-fifth of the jurors' votes.

graphe paranomon: An action lodged against an Athenian who proposed a decree in the Assembly that was unconstitutional.

Herm: A bust of Hermes on a column or rectangular pillar with genitals sculpted in the base. Herms were placed at crossroads and at boundaries of property and buildings. In 415, shortly before the Athenians launched the Sicilian expedition, the Herms of Athens were destroyed one night, leading the Athenians to fear that *hetaireiai* were plotting against the mission.

hetaira: Initially the term meant "female companion," but it became synonymous with a high-class prostitute in the classical period.

hetaireia: A group of (male) companions (*hetairoi*) which met together at private dinner parties and supported each other in politics. Athenians regarded them with suspicion because several *hetaireiai* had plotted to overthrow the democracy during the Peloponnesian War.

hybris: An offense, punishable by Athenian law, that brought shame and disgrace on another, typically committed by a man who thought too much of his own worth and too little of his victim and who committed the offense simply for his own pleasure. The offense was often violent and even sexual.

kyrios: Literally, "master," *kyrios* refers to the owner of property or the master of a slave. It was also used to refer to the guardian of a woman or a minor. Typically, the father was the *kyrios* for the unmarried girl, the husband for the wife, and the brother or son for the widow.

liturgy: A public service, such as the *choregia* and the trierarchy, that wealthy Athenians were required to perform on behalf of the community.

logographer: Speechwriter who was paid to write a speech for a client to deliver in court.

metic: Resident alien living in Athens.

mina: A unit of Athenian currency. One hundred drachmas equal one mina. Sixty minas equal one talent.

moicheia: Seduction. In Athens, it was illegal for a man to have a sexual relationship with a respectable Athenian woman without the permission of her guardian (*kyrios*). Thus in some ways *moicheia* was broader than "adultery," since it applied to unmarried women, and in other ways it was narrower, since Athenian men were not legally required to remain faithful to their wives. *Moicheia* was a much more serious offense than the English translation, "seduction," implies.

obol: A unit of Athenian currency. Six obols equal one drachma. Jurors received three obols per day for their service on the courts. In the fourth century, daily wages for workers ranged from 1½ to 2½ drachmas (i.e., nine to fifteen obols).

paidagogoi: Slaves responsible for walking children to and from school.

paredros: Assessor. Each of the three senior archons (the *basileus,* the polemarch, and the eponymous archon) appointed two *paredroi* to assist him in his duties.

paragraphe: A defendant could stop a suit lodged against him on the grounds that it was unlawful by using the procedure of *paragraphe.* A court then decided whether the suit was lawful. If the jurors sided with the defendant, the suit was dismissed. If the jurors ruled in favor of the prosecutor, he was then permitted to pursue the original suit.

phratry: Brotherhood. A hereditary organization that was thought to be based on kinship. Before Cleisthenes, membership in a phratry probably determined citizenship. After the Cleisthenic reforms, phratries served primarily religious functions.

phylarch: Commander of the unit of cavalry for one of the ten tribes.

Pnyx: Location where the Assembly convened.

polemarch: War archon. One of the nine archons selected by lot each year, the polemarch oversaw suits concerning metics.

porne: A female prostitute.

probole: A type of suit heard in the Assembly before it appeared in an Athenian court. The vote of the Assembly was merely prejudicial and did not necessarily affect the outcome in the court.

proedroi: Presiding officers. These nine councilors were selected by lot for one day from those councilors who were not serving as *prytaneis; proedroi* chaired the meetings of the Council of Five Hundred and the Assembly.

proeisphora: Advancement of the occasional tax (*eisphora*). In order for the city to expedite collection of the *eisphora,* the wealthiest Athenians were required to pay in advance the full amount that their symmory owed. They would then be reimbursed by the members of their symmory for their share.

prytaneis: Presidents. This is the title of those fifty councilors who acted as the steering committee for the Council of Five Hundred. Every councilor served for one-tenth of the year as one of the *prytaneis* with the other councilors from his tribe.

Prytaneum: This building served as the town hall and housed the public hearth. Foreign dignitaries were entertained here. Olympic victors and the descendants of Harmodius and Aristogeiton were also granted the privilege of dining in the Prytaneum.

prytany: The period of time during which the fifty councilors from a tribe served as *prytaneis.* There were ten prytanies per year, one for each tribe.

rhetor: Orator. *Rhetor* refers both to those Athenians who spoke regularly in the Assembly, Council, and courts and to those who taught rhetoric.

sykophancy: Malicious prosecution, often for pecuniary motives.

sykophant: One who engaged in sykophancy.

symmory: A group of Athenians of the liturgical class who shared the burdens of performing a trierarchy or paying the *eisphora*. In the fourth century, members of the liturgical class were organized into symmories to reduce the financial burden associated with the more costly liturgies.

synegoros: Supporting speaker. Athenians had to speak on their own behalf in court, but they could either hire a logographer to write a speech for them or share their time with a supporting speaker. The *synegoros* could not be paid.

talent: A unit of Athenian money. Six thousand drachmas (or sixty minas) equal one talent. The liturgical class had property worth at least three or four talents. It cost one talent to man an Athenian trireme for one month.

taxiarch: Each of the ten tribes provided a regiment of heavily-armed soldiers (hoplites) commanded by a taxiarch.

techne: A model speech. *Techne* refers both to a speech that a student wrote as an exercise and to an example provided by a *rhetor* to illustrate how to write and present a public speech.

thesmothetes **(pl. *thesmothetai*):** The *thesmothetai* were the six junior archons. Their main responsibility was to oversee the *dikasteria*.

topos: Commonplace. *Topos* is used to refer to a type of statement, appeal, or conceit that appears frequently in Attic oratory. For example, litigants often tell the jury that they are inexperienced speakers.

trireme: An Athenian warship with three banks of oars.

trierarchy: One of the costliest liturgies, the trierarchy was performed by the trierarch who was responsible for the maintenance and command of an Athenian trireme.

Bibliography

Adams, Charles D. 1905. *Lysias: Selected Speeches*. New York: American Book Company.

Albini, Umberto. 1952. "L'orazione lisiana per l'invalido." *Rheinisches Museum für Philologie* 95: 328–38.

Arnaoutoglou, Ilias. 1993. "Pollution in the Athenian Homicide Law." *Revue internationale des droits de l'antiquité* 40: 109–37.

Avery, H. C. 1991. "Was Eratosthenes the Oligarch Eratosthenes the Adulterer?" *Hermes* 119: 380–84.

Bers, Victor, tr. 2003. *Demosthenes, Speeches 50–59*. Austin: The University of Texas Press.

Blass, Friedrich. 1887–98. *Die attische Beredsamkeit*. 2nd ed., 3 vols. Leipzig: Teubner.

Boegehold, Alan L. 1995. *The Lawcourts at Athens: Sites, Buildings, Equipment, Procedure, and Testimonia*. Princeton: Princeton University Press.

Bugh, Glenn. 1988. *The Horsemen of Athens*. Princeton: Princeton University Press.

Burkert, Walter. 1985. *Greek Religion: Archaic and Classical*. Cambridge, MA: Harvard University Press.

Cairns, Douglas, L. 1996. "*Hybris*, Dishonour, and Thinking Big." *Journal of Hellenic Studies* 116: 1–32.

Carawan, Edwin. 1991. "*Ephetai* and Athenian Courts for Homicide in the Age of the Orators." *Classical Philology* 86: 1–16.

———. 1998. *Rhetoric and the Law of Draco*. Oxford: Oxford University Press.

———. 2006. "Amnesty and Accountings for the Thirty." *Classical Quarterly* 56: 57–76.

———, ed. 2007. *Oxford Readings in the Attic Orators*. Oxford: Oxford University Press.

Carey, Christopher, ed. 1989. *Lysias: Selected Speeches*. Cambridge: Cambridge University Press.

———. 1990. "Structure and Strategy in Lysias XXIV." *Greece and Rome* 37: 44–51.

———. 1995a. "Rape and Adultery in Athenian Law." *Classical Quarterly* 45: 407–17.

———. 1995b. "The Witness's *Exomosia* in the Athenian Courts." *Classical Quarterly* 45: 114–19.

———, tr. 1997. *Trials from Classical Athens*. London: Routledge.

Carey, Christopher, and R. A. Reid, eds. 1985. *Demosthenes: Selected Private Speeches*. Cambridge: Cambridge University Press.

Cartledge, Paul Millett, and Stephen Todd, eds. In *Nomos: Essays in Athenian Law, Politics and Society*. Cambridge: Cambridge University Press.

Christ, Matthew R. 1998. *The Litigious Athenian*. Baltimore: Johns Hopkins University Press.

Cohen, David. 1989. "Seclusion, Separation, and the Status of Women in Classical Athens." *Greece and Rome* 36: 3–15.

———. 1991. *Law, Sexuality, and Society: The Enforcement of Morals in Classical Athens*. Cambridge: Cambridge University Press.

———. 1995. *Law, Violence, and Community in Classical Athens*. Cambridge: Cambridge University Press.

———. 1998. "Women, Property, and Status in Demosthenes 41 and 57." *Dike* 1: 53–61.

Cohen, Edward E. 1973. *Ancient Athenian Maritime Courts*. Princeton: Princeton University Press.

———. 2002. "An Unprofitable Masculinity." In *Money, Labour and Land: Approaches to the Economies of Ancient Greece*, ed. Paul Cartledge, Edward E. Cohen, and Lin Foxhall, 100–12. London: Routledge.

Darkow, Angela C. 1917. "The Spurious Speeches in the Lysianic Corpus." Ph.D. diss., Bryn Mawr College.

Davidson, James. 1998. *Courtesans and Fishcakes: The Consuming Passions of Classical Athens*. New York: St. Martin's Press.

———. 2007. *The Greeks and Greek Love: A Radical Reappraisal of Homosexuality in Ancient Greece*. London: Weidenfeld and Nicolson.

Dillon, Matthew P. J. 1995. "Payments for the Disabled at Athens: Social Justice or Fear of Aristocratic Patronage?" *Ancient Society* 26: 27–57.

Dorjahn, Alfred. P. 1935. "Anticipation of Arguments in Athenian Courts." *Transactions of the American Philological Association* 66: 274–95.

Dover, Kenneth J. 1950. "The Chronology of Antiphon's Speeches." *Classical Quarterly* 44: 44–60.

———. 1968. *Lysias and the Corpus Lysiacum*. Berkeley: University of California Press.

———. 1974. *Greek Popular Morality in the Time of Plato and Aristotle*. Berkeley: University of California Press.

———. 1978. *Greek Homosexuality*. Cambridge, MA: Harvard University Press.

Edwards, Michael, and Stephen Usher, trs. 1985. *Greek Orators I: Antiphon and Lysias*. Warminster, UK: Aris and Phillips.

Finley. M. I. 1952 [reprinted 1985]. *Studies in Land and Credit in Ancient Athens, 500–200 B.C.: The Horos Inscriptions*. New Brunswick: Rutgers University Press.

Fisher, N. R. E. 1992. *Hybris: A Study in the Values of Honour and Shame in Ancient Greece*. Warminster, UK: Aris and Phillips.

———, tr. 2001. *Aeschines: Against Timarchos*. Oxford: Oxford University Press.

Foxhall, Lin. 1989. "Household, Gender and Property in Classical Athens." *Classical Quarterly* 39: 22–44.

Foxhall, Lin, and John Salmon, eds. 1998. *When Men Were Men: Masculinity, Power and Identity in Classical Antiquity.* London: Routledge.

Gagarin, Michael. 1979. "The Prosecution of Homicide in Athens." *Greek, Roman and Byzantine Studies* 20: 301–23.

———. 1981. *Drakon and Early Athenian Homicide Law.* New Haven: Yale University Press.

———. 1990. "*Bouleusis* in Athenian Homicide Law." In *Symposium 1988: Vorträge zur griechischen und hellenistischen Rechtsgeschichte,* ed. Giuseppe Nenci and Gerhard Thür, 81–99. Cologne: Böhlau.

———. 1996. "The Torture of Slaves in Athenian Law." *Classical Philology* 91: 1–18.

———. 1997. *Antiphon: The Speeches.* Cambridge: Cambridge University Press.

———. 2002. *Antiphon the Athenian: Oratory, Law, and Justice in the Age of the Sophists.* Austin: University of Texas Press.

———. 2008. *Writing Greek Law.* Cambridge: Cambridge University Press.

Gallant, Thomas W. 1991. *Risk and Survival in Ancient Greece: Reconstructing the Rural Domestic Economy.* Stanford: Stanford University Press.

Garland, Robert. 1995. *The Eye of the Beholder: Deformity and Disability in the Graeco-Roman World.* Ithaca: Cornell University Press.

Garnsey, Peter. 1988. *Famine and Food Supply in the Greco-Roman World: Responses to Risk and Crisis.* Cambridge: Cambridge University Press.

Gernet, Louis. 1955. *Droit et société dans la Grèce ancienne.* Paris: Sirey.

Haj, Fareed. 1970. *Disability in Antiquity.* New York: Philosophical Library.

Halperin, David M. 1990. *One Hundred Years of Homosexuality: And Other Essays on Greek Love.* London: Routledge.

Hamilton, Richard. 1992. *Choes and Anthesteria: Athenian Iconography and Ritual.* Ann Arbor: University of Michigan Press.

Hansen, Mogens Herman. 1976a. *Apagoge, Endeixis and Ephegesis against Kakourgoi, Atimoi and Pheugontes: A Study in the Athenian Administration of Justice in the Fourth Century B.C.* Odense: Odense University Press.

———. 1976b. "The Theoric Fund and the *Graphe Paranomon* against Apollodorus." *Greek, Roman and Byzantine Studies* 17: 235–46.

———. 1990. "The Political Powers of the People's Court in Fourth-Century Athens." In *The Greek City from Homer to Alexander,* ed. Oswyn Murray and Simon Price, 215–43. Oxford: Oxford University Press.

———. 1991. *The Athenian Democracy in the Age of Demosthenes: Structure, Principles, and Ideology.* Oxford: Blackwell.

Harris, Edward M. 1985. "The Date of the Trial of Timarchus." *Hermes* 113: 376–80.

———. 1989. "Demosthenes' Speech against Meidias." *Harvard Studies in Classical Philology* 92: 117–36.

———. 1990. "Did the Athenians Regard Seduction as a Worse Crime Than Rape?" *Classical Quarterly* 40: 370–77.

————. 1992. "Women and Lending in Athenian Society: A Horos Re-examined." *Phoenix* 46: 309–21.

————, tr. 2008. *Demosthenes, Speeches 20–22*. Austin: University of Texas Press.

Harrison, A. R. W. 1968–71. *The Law of Athens*. 2 vols. Oxford: Oxford University Press.

Harvey, David. 1990. "The Sykophant and Sykophancy: Vexatious Redefinition?" In Cartledge, Millett, and Todd, 103–21.

Herman, Gabriel. 2006. *Morality and Behaviour in Democratic Athens: A Social History*. Cambridge: Cambridge University Press.

Hirayama, Koji. 1998. "Pollution of Homicide in Ancient Greece." *Classical Studies* 15: 37–71.

Humphreys, S. C. 1985. "Social Relations on Stage: Witnesses in Classical Athens." *History and Anthropology* 1: 313–69.

Hunter, Virginia J. 1994. *Policing Athens: Social Control in the Attic Lawsuits, 420–320 B.C.* Princeton: Princeton University Press.

Hutton, William. 2005. *Describing Greece: Landscape and Literature in the Periegesis of Pausanias*. Cambridge: Cambridge University Press.

Isager, Signe, and Mogens Herman Hansen. 1975. *Aspects of Athenian Society in the Fourth Century B.C.* Odense: Odense University Press.

Jebb, Richard. C. 1893. *The Attic Orators: From Antiphon to Isaeus*. 2nd ed. London: Macmillan.

Johnstone, Steven. 1998. "Cracking the Code of Silence: Athenian Legal Oratory and the Histories of Slaves and Women." In *Women and Slaves in Greco-Roman Culture: Differential Equations*, ed. Sandra R. Joshel and Sheila Murnaghan, 221–35. London: Routledge.

Just, Roger. 1989. *Women in Athenian Law and Life*. London: Routledge.

Kapparis, Konstantinos. 1995. "The Athenian Decree for the Naturalisation of the Plataeans." *Greek, Roman and Byzantine Studies* 36: 359–78.

————. 1996. "Humiliating the Adulterer: The Law and the Practice in Classical Athens." *Revue internationale des droits de l'antiquité* 43: 63–77.

————. 1998. "The Law on the Age of the Speakers in the Athenian Assembly." *Rheinisches Museum für Philologie* 141: 255–59.

————. 1999. *Apollodoros "Against Neaira" [D. 59]: Edited with Introduction, Translation and Commentary*. Berlin: de Gruyter.

————. 2000. "Has Chariton Read Lysias 1 'On the Murder of Eratosthenes'?" *Hermes* 128: 380–83.

————. 2005. "Immigration and Citizenship Procedures in Athenian Law." *Revue internationale des droits de l'antiquité* 52: 71–113.

Katz, Marilyn A. 1995. "Ideology and 'the Status of Women' in Ancient Greece." In *Women in Antiquity: New Assessments*, ed. Richard Hawley and Barbara Levick, 21–43. London: Routledge.

Konstan, David. 2001. *Pity Transformed*. London: Duckworth.

Krentz, Peter. 1982. *The Thirty at Athens*. Ithaca: Cornell University Press.

Lacey, Walter K. 1968. *The Family in Classical Greece*. London: Thames and Hudson.

Lanni, Adriaan M. 1997. "Spectator Sport or Serious Politics? *Hoi Periestekotes* and the Athenian Lawcourts." *Journal of Hellenic Studies* 117: 183–89.

———. 2004. "Arguing from 'Precedent': Modern Perspectives on Athenian Practice." In *The Law and the Courts in Ancient Greece,* ed. Edward M. Harris and Lene Rubinstein, 159–71. London: Duckworth.

———. 2006. *Law and Justice in the Courts of Classical Athens*. Cambridge: Cambridge University Press.

Lear, Andrew, and Eva Cantarella, eds. 2008. *Images of Ancient Greek Pederasty: Boys Were Their Gods*. London: Routledge.

Loomis, William T. 1972. "The Nature of Premeditation in Athenian Homicide Law." *Journal of Hellenic Studies* 92: 86–95.

Loraux, Nicole. 1993: *The Children of Athena: Athenian Ideas about Citizenship and the Division between the Sexes*, tr. Caroline Levine. Princeton: Princeton University Press.

———. 2002. *The Divided City: On Memory and Forgetting in Ancient Athens,* tr. Corinne Pache with Jeff Fort. New York: Zone Books.

MacDowell, Douglas M. 1963. *Athenian Homicide Law in the Age of the Orators*. Manchester, UK: Manchester University Press.

———. 1976. "*Hybris* in Athens." *Greece and Rome* 23: 14–31.

———. 1978. *The Law in Classical Athens*. London: Thames and Hudson.

———, ed. 1990. *Demosthenes, Against Meidias (Orations 21)*. Oxford: Clarendon Press.

———. 2000. "Athenian Laws about Homosexuality." *Revue internationale des droits de l'antiquité* 47: 13–27.

———, tr. 2004. *Demosthenes, Speeches 27–38*. Austin: University of Texas Press.

Mirhady, David C. 1996. "Torture and Rhetoric in Athens." *JHS* 116: 119–34.

——— . 2002. "Athens' Democratic Witnesses." *Phoenix* 56: 255–74.

Munn, Mark. 2000. *The School of History: Athens in the Age of Socrates*. Berkeley: University of California Press.

Murray, A. T. 1939. *Demosthenes: Orations (50-59)*. Vol. 5. Cambridge, MA: Harvard University Press.

Nevett, Lisa C. 1999. *House and Society in the Ancient Greek World*. Cambridge: Cambridge University Press.

North, Helen. 1966. *Sophrosyne: Self-Knowledge and Self-Restraint in Greek Literature*. Ithaca: Cornell University Press.

Ober, Josiah. 1989. *Mass and Elite in Democratic Athens: Rhetoric, Ideology, and the Power of the People*. Princeton: Princeton University Press.

———. 1996. *The Athenian Revolution: Essays on Ancient Greek Democracy and Political Theory*. Princeton: Princeton University Press.

Omitowoju, Rosanna. 2002. *Rape and the Politics of Consent in Classical Athens.* Cambridge: Cambridge University Press.

Osborne, Robin. 1985. "Law in Action in Classical Athens." *Journal of Hellenic Studies* 105: 40–58.

———. 1990. "Vexatious Litigation in Classical Athens: Sykophancy and the Sykophant." In Cartledge, Millett, and Todd, 83–102.

Ostwald, Martin. 1986. *From Popular Sovereignty to the Sovereignty of Law: Law, Society, and Politics in Fifth-Century Athens.* Berkeley: University of California Press.

Parke, H. W. 1977. *Festivals of the Athenians.* London: Thames and Hudson.

Parker, Robert. 1983. *Miasma: Pollution and Purification in Early Greek Religion.* Oxford: Clarendon Press.

———. 1996. *Athenian Religion: A History.* Oxford: Clarendon Press.

Patterson, Cynthia. 1981. *Pericles' Citizenship Law of 451–50 B.C.* New York: Arno Press.

———. 1998. *The Family in Greek History.* Cambridge, MA: Harvard University Press.

Pearson, Lionel. 1972. *Demosthenes: Six Private Speeches.* Norman: University of Oklahoma Press.

———.1983. *Selected Papers of Lionel Pearson.* Chico, CA: Scholars Press.

Phillips, David D. 2004. *Athenian Political Oratory: 16 Key Speeches.* New York: Routledge.

———. 2007. "*Trauma ek Pronoias* in Athenian Law." *Journal of Hellenic Studies* 127: 74–105.

———. 2008. *Avengers of Blood: Homicide in Athenian Law and Custom from Draco to Demosthenes.* Stuttgart: Franz Steiner.

Porter, John R. 1997. "Adultery by the Book: Lysias 1 (*On the Murder of Eratosthenes*) and Comic *Diegesis.*" *Echos du monde classique / Classical Views* 16: 421–53.

Rhodes, P. J. 1981. *A Commentary on the Aristotelian Athenaion Politeia.* Oxford: Clarendon Press.

Roisman, Joseph. 2006. *The Rhetoric of Conspiracy in Ancient Athens.* Berkeley: University of California Press.

Rosivach, Vincent J. 1987. "Autochthony and the Athenians." *Classical Quarterly* 37: 294–306.

Roussel, Louis. 1966. *Pseudo-Lysias: L'invalide.* Paris: Presses universitaires de France.

Rowe, Galen O. 1994. "The Charge against Meidias." *Hermes* 122: 55–63.

Rubinstein, Lene. 1993. *Adoption in IV. Century Athens.* Copenhagen: Museum Tusculanum Press.

———. 2000. *Litigation and Cooperation: Supporting Speakers in the Courts of Classical Athens.* Stuttgart: Franz Steiner.

Ruschenbusch, Eberhard. 1966. *Solonos Nomoi: Die Fragmente des solonischen Gesetzeswerkes mit einer Text und Uberlieferungsgeschichte*. Wiesbaden: Franz Steiner.

Sallares, Robert. 1991. *Ecology of the Ancient Greek World*. London: Duckworth.

Schaefer, Arnold. 1885–87. *Demosthenes und seine Zeit*. 2nd ed., 3 vols. Leipzig: Teubner.

Schaps, David M. 1977. "The Women Least Mentioned: Etiquette and Women's Names." *Classical Quarterly* 27: 323–30.

———. 1979. *Economic Rights of Women in Ancient Greece*. Edinburgh: Edinburgh University Press.

Shapiro, Harvey Alan. 1998. "Autochthony and the Visual Arts in Fifth-Century Athens." In *Democracy, Empire, and the Arts in Fifth-Century Athens*, ed. Deborah Boedeker and Kurt A. Raaflaub, 127–51. Cambridge, MA: Harvard University Press.

Sickinger, James. P. 1995. "A Security *Horos* in the Collection of the American School." *Hesperia* 64: 333–36.

Thomas, Rosalind. 1989. *Oral Tradition and Written Record in Classical Athens*. Cambridge: Cambridge University Press.

Thompson, W. E. 1981. "Apollodoros v. Phormion: The Computation of Damages." *Revue internationale des droits de l'antiquité* 28: 83–94.

Thür, Gerhard. 1977. *Beweisführung vor den Schwurgerichtshöfen Athens: Die Proklesis zur Basanos*. Vienna: Österreichische Akademie der Wissenschaften.

———. 2005. "The Role of the Witness in Athenian Law." In *The Cambridge Companion to Ancient Greek Law,* ed. Michael Gagarin and David Cohen, 146–69. Cambridge: Cambridge University Press.

Todd, Stephen C. 1990a. "The Purpose of Evidence in Athenian Courts." In Cartledge, Millett, and Todd, 19–39.

———. 1990b. "The Use and Abuse of the Attic Orators." *Greece and Rome* 37: 159–77.

———. 1993. *The Shape of Athenian Law*. Oxford: Clarendon Press.

———, tr. 2000. *Lysias*. Austin: University of Texas Press.

———, ed. 2007. *A Commentary on Lysias, Speeches 1–11*. Oxford: Oxford University Press.

Trevett, Jeremy C. 1992. *Apollodoros, the Son of Pasion*. Oxford: Oxford University Press.

Tulin, Alexander. 1996. *Dike Phonou: The Right of Prosecution and Attic Homicide Procedure*. Stuttgart: Teubner.

Usher, Stephen. 1965. "Individual Characterisation in Lysias." *Eranos* 63: 99–119.

———. 1966. "The Speech against Pancleon." *Classical Review* 16: 10–12.

Wallace, Robert W. 1985. *The Areopagos Council, to 507 B.C.* Baltimore: Johns Hopkins University Press.

Walters, K. R. 1983. "Perikles' Citizenship Law." *Classical Antiquity* 2: 314–36.

Whitby, Michael. 1998. "The Grain Trade of Athens in the Fourth Century B.C." In *Trade, Traders and the Ancient City,* ed. Helen Parkins and Christopher Smith, 102–26. London: Routledge.

Wilson, Peter J. 1991. "Demosthenes 21 (*Against Meidias*): Democratic Abuse." *Proceedings of the Cambridge Philological Society* 37: 164–95.

Winkler, John J. 1990. *The Constraints of Desire: The Anthropology of Sex and Gender in Ancient Greece.* London: Routledge.

Wolff, Hans J. 1966. *Die attische Paragraphe: Ein Beitrag zum Problem der Auflockerung archaischer Prozessformen.* Weimar: Böhlau.

Wolpert, Andrew. 2001. "Lysias 1 and the Politics of the Oikos." *Classical Journal* 96: 416–24.

———. 2002. *Remembering Defeat: Civil War and Civic Memory in Ancient Athens.* Baltimore: Johns Hopkins University Press.

———. 2003. "Addresses to the Jury in the Attic Orators." *American Journal of Philology* 124: 537–55.

———. 2006. "The Violence of the Thirty." In *Ancient Tyranny,* ed. Sian Lewis, 213–23. Edinburgh: Edinburgh University Press.

Wyse, William. 1904. *The Speeches of Isaeus.* Cambridge: Cambridge University Press.

Index